Applications of Cybersecurity and Digital Forensics in Modern Tourism Systems

Mohammad Badruddoza Talukder
https://orcid.org/0009-0008-1662-9221
International University of Business Agriculture and Technology, Bangladesh

Ismot Tasmary Salsabil
https://orcid.org/0009-0006-4911-502X
Engineering Institute of Technology, Australia

IGI Global
Scientific Publishing
Publishing Tomorrow's Research Today

Vice President of Editorial | Melissa Wagner
Director of Acquisitions | Mikaela Felty
Director of Book Development | Jocelynn Hessler
Production Manager | Mike Brehm
Cover Design | Jose Rosado

Published in the United States of America by
IGI Global Scientific Publishing
701 East Chocolate Avenue
Hershey, PA, 17033, USA
Tel: 717-533-8845 | Fax: 717-533-7115
Website: https://www.igi-global.com E-mail: cust@igi-global.com

Library of Congress Cataloging-in-Publication Data

LCCN: 2025030701 (CIP Data Pending)
ISBN13: 9798337358260
Isbn13Softcover: 9798337358277
EISBN13: 9798337358284
British Cataloguing in Publication Data
A Cataloguing in Publication record for this book is available from the British Library.

Table of Contents

Detailed Table of Contents

forensic protocols, with data showing that 68% of aviation cyber incidents stem from ADS-B spoofing, while 57% of rail system breaches arise from SCADA vulnerabilities. Although adaptable frameworks such as the NIST CSF demonstrate greater effectiveness, worldwide implementation remains fragmented. To counter increasingly sophisticated threats, the research advocates targeted strategies—leveraging AI-driven threat detection, adopting zero-trust architectures, and enforcing uniform policy regulations—to enhance system resilience.

Hotels and restaurants increasingly rely on digital systems for bookings and operations, making them vulnerable to cyberattacks. This study analyzes 50 data breaches, 17 in hotels, 33 in restaurants, to identify key risks. Common weaknesses include outdated systems, third-party dependencies, poor encryption, and phishing. Breaches expose customer data, leading to financial losses, fines, and eroded trust—critical in a guest-centric industry. Hotels face high risks from credential theft and social engineering, often due to human error. Restaurants are most affected by POS malware, credential stuffing, and compromised third-party platforms. The decentralized nature of hospitality amplifies these threats. Findings show generic cybersecurity measures are insufficient. Instead, tailored strategies are needed: staff training, proactive risk management, and adherence to standards like GDPR, PCI-DSS, and ISO/IEC 27001. By examining real incidents, this research provides practical insights for strengthening cybersecurity across the global hospitality sector.

This chapter analyzes digital forensics as an essential tool to combat cybercrime in tourism and hospitality operations. It evaluates every phase of digital forensics alongside the various evidence types and legal standards for evidence acceptance and technological obstacles investigators encounter. Through qualitative content analysis combined with multiple case studies, the chapter reveals how metadata alongside encryption and digital signatures affect cyber investigations. The study analyzes complex legal systems that exist throughout different jurisdictions including India and the U.S. and the UK while examining current solutions that use AI and blockchain analysis with cloud forensics. The chapter reveals that encryption protects data but creates difficulties for investigations and advanced analytics together with

Online booking platforms have become integral to modern tourism, offering convenience and exposing travellers to significant cybersecurity risks. Sensitive data such as personal details, payment credentials, and travel itineraries are increasingly vulnerable to threats like phishing, ransomware, data breaches, and insider misuse. Protecting tourist data requires a multi-layered approach, combining secure encryption protocols, blockchain-based transaction verification, and AI-driven threat detection systems. Strong authentication mechanisms, such as biometrics and two-factor authentication, further enhance security and reduce fraud. However, challenges persist in balancing user convenience with robust safeguards, ensuring compliance with global data protection regulations, and managing evolving threats in a highly digitalised tourism ecosystem. This chapter explores the key vulnerabilities of online booking systems, evaluates current protective strategies, and suggests sustainable solutions for safeguarding tourist trust.

The tourism sector is depending more on digital platforms, smart infrastructure, and data-driven services in the era of digital transformation (Ma, C., T. Somrak, 2025). The use of digital forensics and cybersecurity to improve trust and resilience in contemporary tourism systems is examined in this study (Zhang, J., 2025). The main research question is: How can cybersecurity and digital forensics be combined to enhance user trust, security, and dependability in contemporary travel platforms and smart destinations? A systematic literature review along with the case study analysis of cyber incidents in the tourism sector (for example breaches of airline booking systems), as well as the expert interviews with cybersecurity specialists in tourism business made an entire mixed-methods toolkit. The findings indicate that

Preface

INTRODUCTION

The rapid digital transformation of the global tourism industry has fundamentally reshaped how individuals plan, experience, and evaluate travel. From online booking platforms and smart hospitality systems to AI-driven customer engagement and cloud-based infrastructures, tourism has become deeply intertwined with advanced information technologies. While these innovations have enhanced efficiency, personalization, and accessibility, they have also introduced complex cybersecurity vulnerabilities and expanded the surface for cybercrime. As a result, the integration of cybersecurity and digital forensics into tourism systems is no longer optional—it is essential for sustaining trust, safety, and operational resilience.

This edited volume, *Applications of Cybersecurity and Digital Forensics in Modern Tourism Systems*, emerges at a critical moment when digital dependence in tourism is accelerating, yet the sector remains insufficiently prepared to confront evolving cyber threats. The contributors to this book bring together interdisciplinary perspectives from information technology, law, hospitality management, and forensic science to examine the multifaceted challenges facing modern tourism ecosystems. By bridging theory, practice, and policy, this collection seeks to illuminate how cybersecurity measures and forensic capabilities can be effectively embedded into tourism infrastructures.

As editors, we recognize that tourism is uniquely vulnerable due to its global nature, reliance on interconnected systems, and handling of sensitive personal and financial data. Cyber incidents in this sector not only result in financial losses but also erode consumer confidence and damage institutional reputations. Therefore, this book aims to provide scholars, practitioners, policymakers, and students with a comprehensive understanding of the risks, responses, and future directions in securing digital tourism environments. Through empirical studies, case analyses, and conceptual discussions, the chapters collectively underscore the urgency of proactive, collaborative, and technologically informed approaches.

CHAPTER OVERVIEW

This volume is organized into twelve chapters, each addressing critical dimensions of cybersecurity and digital forensics within tourism systems.

Chapter 1 explores cybersecurity in aviation and transportation systems, emphasizing the vulnerabilities of highly integrated ICT infrastructures such as air traffic management. It highlights emerging threats, including cyber-attacks on aircraft systems, and discusses the role of advanced technologies like blockchain in enhancing aviation security.

Chapter 2 examines the legal and jurisdictional challenges of cybercrime in tourism, particularly focusing on digital evidence. It analyzes international frameworks and cross-border complexities while addressing issues related to data privacy, admissibility of evidence, and the need for harmonized legal systems.

Chapter 3 focuses on forensic readiness in tourism ecosystems, outlining strategies for investigating cyber incidents such as phishing and ransomware. It emphasizes organizational preparedness and the role of emerging technologies like AI and IoT in strengthening forensic capabilities.

Chapter 4 investigates cybersecurity vulnerabilities across aviation, rail, and maritime systems. It evaluates existing frameworks and proposes targeted solutions, including zero-trust architectures and AI-driven threat detection, to enhance system resilience.

Chapter 5 provides a comprehensive review of cybersecurity threats in hospitality services, analyzing data breaches in hotels and restaurants. It identifies common vulnerabilities and advocates for tailored cybersecurity strategies to mitigate risks and protect customer data.

Chapter 6 delves into the role of digital forensics in cybercrime investigations within tourism and hospitality. It examines forensic processes, legal standards, and technological challenges, offering practical recommendations for improving investigative effectiveness.

Chapter 7 explores the intersection of digital transformation and cybersecurity in hotels, with a focus on AI-enabled chatbots. It discusses how these technologies enhance guest experiences while simultaneously introducing new security vulnerabilities.

Chapter 8 analyzes cybersecurity threats and forensic solutions within modern tourism infrastructure. It identifies key vulnerabilities across booking systems, payment platforms, and customer databases, proposing evidence-based strategies to strengthen resilience.

Chapter 9 addresses the investigation and mitigation of cybercrime in tourism, focusing on digital forensics approaches to data breaches, fraud, and identity theft. It highlights practical tools, techniques, and case studies to support proactive risk management.

Chapter 10 examines the impact of social media and cyber reputation on tourism and educational institutions. It introduces a crisis management framework to address risks such as misinformation, cyberbullying, and reputational damage.

Chapter 11 focuses on protecting tourist data in online booking platforms. It discusses vulnerabilities, encryption techniques, and advanced security measures such as biometric authentication and AI-driven threat detection.

Chapter 12 concludes the volume by exploring how cybersecurity and digital forensics can enhance trust in modern tourism systems. It emphasizes the importance of integrating proactive security measures with forensic analysis to build resilient and trustworthy digital ecosystems.

CONCLUSION

The chapters in this volume collectively demonstrate that cybersecurity and digital forensics are not isolated technical domains but integral components of modern tourism systems. As digital technologies continue to evolve, so too must the strategies used to protect them. The tourism sector, characterized by its global interconnectedness and data-intensive operations, requires a holistic approach that combines technological innovation, legal frameworks, organizational readiness, and international collaboration.

A key insight emerging from this collection is the importance of moving from reactive to proactive security models. While incident response and forensic investigation remain critical, greater emphasis must be placed on prevention, early detection, and continuous monitoring. Technologies such as artificial intelligence, blockchain, and zero-trust architectures offer promising avenues for strengthening cybersecurity, but their implementation must be guided by robust policies and ethical considerations.

Finally, this book underscores the central role of trust in the sustainability of digital tourism. Travelers must feel confident that their data, transactions, and experiences are secure. Achieving this requires not only technological solutions but also transparent practices, regulatory alignment, and cross-sector collaboration. We hope this volume serves as a valuable resource and a catalyst for further research and innovation in securing the future of tourism in an increasingly digital world.

Chapter 1
Cyber Security in Aviation and Transportation Systems

Siddiqur Rahman
Daffodil International University, Bangladesh

Firoj Kabir
http://orcid.org/0009-0001-3014-3163
Daffodil International University, Bangladesh

Mohammad Badruddoza Talukder
http://orcid.org/0009-0008-1662-9221
International University of Business Agriculture and Technology, Bangladesh

ABSTRACT

Civil aviation may be the most integrated information and communication technology system in the world. Cybercrimes are becoming more frequent and persistent; therefore, a successful hostile cyber-attack on civil aviation operations may be devastating. New technology, connection, and coordination in aviation, notably for Air Traffic Management (ATM), raise risk to these important assets. Aviation cyber security is crucial, and this chapter discusses its significance, uses, and hurdles. The chapter illustrates the risks of insufficient security by analyzing aircraft cyber-attacks. Aviation cyber security looks into how to keep airports, aircraft systems, and ATMs safe, as well as how to use block chain technology. This chapter looks at current and future dangers and applied research opportunities that could make the aviation and linked Transportation Company of the future safer online. To confront new challenges and protect the aviation industry's future, the chapter concludes that teamwork, information exchange, and research and development are essential.

DOI: 10.4018/979-8-3373-5826-0.ch001

INTRODUCTION

The increasing incorporation of Information and Communication Technology (ICT) tools into widely utilized machinery within the airline industry has prompted concerns regarding the efficacy of current cyber security safety structures. As a result, meeting the sector's needs for cyber security compliance introduces an added challenge in the progress of the aviation industry, particularly with the introduction of electronic terminals and electronic aircraft facilities (Ukwandu et al., 2022a). As the link between nations, the aviation industry plays a crucial global role. Because even minor errors can result in major harm and losses—such as fatalities, the exposure of stakeholders', employees', and customers' personal information, and the theft of identities, patents, and sensitive data—the robustness of the procedures that maintain operations is crucial. There is compelling evidence indicating that significant attackers are engaging in collaboration with state organizations to acquire intelligence and intellectual property. This cooperation aims to enhance their country's aerospace capabilities and enable them to observe, penetrate, and potentially undermine the capabilities of other nations. Therefore, it is imperative that the industry develop and implement suitable methods of cyber protection that prevent harmful cyber-attacks that compromise the functioning of a crucial industry (George et al., 2024).

The international aviation industry has played a key role in the development of the world's economy and provides services to almost every country. The airline industry is a major economic force that affects not only its operations but also related industries like tourism and aircraft manufacturing. Few sectors garner as much attention and scrutiny as airlines, drawing the attention of governmental policymakers, the media, operational stakeholders, and the billions of users who all have personal stories about unique air travel experiences, both good and bad. Important technological developments, such as the introduction of airliners for commercial use in the early 1950s and the ensuing rise of broad-body “jumbo jets” during the 1970s, greatly aided the growth of the international airline business. At the same time, global authority over airlines created an environment in which government regulations and technological advancements eclipsed competitiveness and profitability. Cost effectiveness, operation earnings, and aggressive competition have become the top issues for airline management since the United States began deregulating the airline industry economically in 1978 (Poulaki et al., 2025). Both domestic air travel within individual countries and, more importantly, the continued growth of a highly competitive international airline industry have been impacted by airline privatization, or “liberalization,” which has spread beyond the United States to much of the industrialized world.

Principles of Cyber Security

Cyber security is critically important due to the increasing frequency of cyber-attacks and threats. Adversaries are progressively utilizing more sophisticated techniques to abuse the systems. Cyber dangers impact people, small businesses, and large organizations equally (Li & Liu, 2021). All firms, irrespective of their sector, acknowledge the importance of cyber security and are focusing on implementing all possible measures to counter cyber threats. Cyber security fundamentally entails a partnership of persons, procedures, and technologies to achieve complete threat elimination, weakness reduction, inhibition, globally acceptance, incident handling, adaptability, and restoration plans and actions, which include IT operations, security of data, and law enforcement. Cyber security includes the technology, methodologies, and procedures employed to protect systems, programs, networks, and data from assaults, damage, or illicit entry (Aslan et al., 2023). The term cyber security refers to techniques and protocols designed to protect digital information. The data that is stored, transmitted, or employed within a computerized system. It consists of two components: cyber and security. Cyber refers to technology that includes networks, computers, and information or software. Security involves the safeguarding of networks, machines, applications, and data.

What is the Significance of Cyber Security?

Several arguments underscore the need of cyber security in an ever-evolving digital landscape:

- Cyber-attacks can impose considerable financial constraints on companies. Furthermore, a data breach can inflict significant reputational damage alongside the financial losses sustained.
- Cyber-attacks are becoming progressively more destructive. Cybercriminals are utilizing ever sophisticated techniques to execute cyber-attacks.
- Regulations such as GDPR necessitate that companies improve the management of their personal data.
- Cyber security has become an essential aspect of corporate operations, necessitating the development of effective response methods to minimize harm in the event of a computer hacking (Safitra et al., 2023).
- An organization individual may formulate a successful attack strategy only with a comprehensive understanding of cyber security basics.

Figure 1. The Seven Layers of Cyber Security

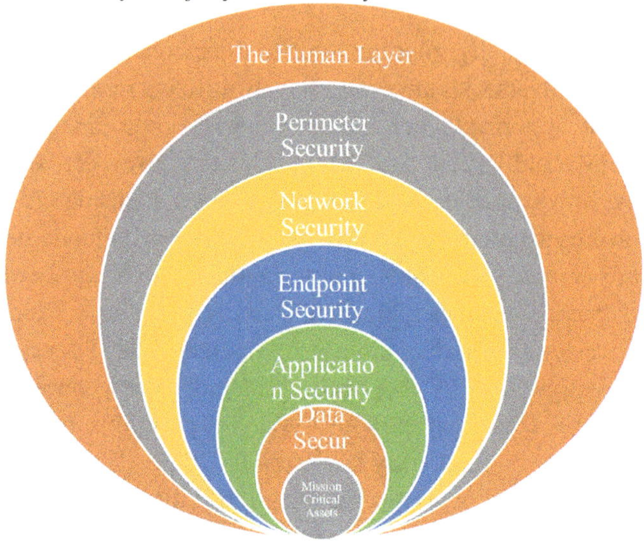

Source: *Authors own compilation based on (Nifakos et al., 2021)*

Fundamental Cyber Security Concepts (Confidentiality, Integrity, Availability – CIA trinity)

The CIA triad includes confidentiality, integrity, and availability, serving as a framework to guide information security (InfoSec) policy inside an organization. The framework is sometimes referred to as the AIC triad, denoting availability, integrity, and confidentiality, to avoid duplication with the agency's headquarters. In this context, secrecy serves as a system of rigorous restrictions that limits access to all types of information and data. Integrity ensures that all data is dependable and accurate. Availability functions as a risk management approach to guarantee dependable knowledge for authorized personnel (Jayabalan & Jeyanthi, 2022).

The subsequent delineation of the elements of the CIA trio is as follows:

Figure 2. CIA Triad

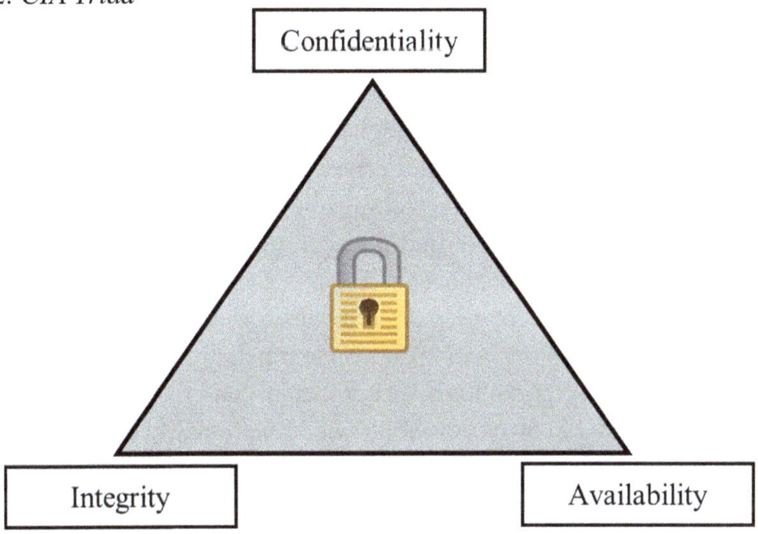

Source: *Authors own compilation*

1. **Confidentiality:** The purpose of these measures is to prevent unwanted use of sensitive information, which is similar to the goal of confidentiality. In most cases, unauthorized individuals classify data according to the likely severity and type of the harm that they could inflict. When such categories are taken into consideration, it is possible to build data security procedures of varied degrees of severity.
2. **Integrity:** All during the entirety of its existence, it is imperative that the reliability, accuracy and dependability of the data be maintained. During transmission, the data must not be altered in any way, and precautions must be taken to prevent unauthorized alterations such as that which can occur in the event of a data breach. (Aslam et al., 2022).
3. **Availability:** Knowledge must be made available to approved people on a consistent basis and in a convenient manner. Maintaining the hardware, as well as the technical architecture and systems that are responsible for storing and presenting the information, is an essential part of this process.

Transportation Cyber Security

Because transportation networks are a component of critical infrastructure, they are targeted by ideologically or economically driven cybercriminals. Innovations in this domain have resulted in significant advancements in interconnected, independent, communal, and electrified (CASE) technology (Abdelkader et al., 2021). The integration of IoT technology in airports, the implementation of automated checked item systems, the introduction of computerized passports, and the development of intuitive websites exemplify the significant advancements that have occurred within the airline industry. This has required logistics companies to deploy a variety of technology, such as devices that monitor driver tiredness and robots in warehouses, to assist with digital products and services.

Businesses and customers now find it easier, and the efficiency of things has altered as a result of these new concepts. However, new concepts also carry with them a more expansive and complex threat landscape. The need for improved defense against hackers exploiting increasingly integrated digital ecosystems has been recognized by airlines, airports, logistics companies, and rail companies. Security is frequently overlooked in favor of usability and functionality once it regards Wifi and smart devices (Ande et al., 2020).

CISA lists the following industries as included:

- Mass public transportation/rail
- Pipeline system
- Freight rail
- Postal and shipping
- Highway and motor carrier
- Airline service

In contrast to various other sectors, risks associated with public transit primarily emphasize technological infrastructures that manage infrastructure, including the safety aspects of railways. Such actions have the potential to disrupt services, adversely affect lives, and impact the economy. Entities may focus on the industry due to its reliance on automated systems, GPS technology, and real-time data analytics. Transportation disruptions may have significant implications for various sectors, including chemical manufacturing, dam operations, disaster relief, energy production, and the food and agriculture industries. An effective digital assault on transportation infrastructure has the potential to significantly hinder the delivery of national resources and services. It is essential to safeguard transportation infrastructure from cyber threats, ensuring the security of this vital sector and the numerous other sectors that rely on it. (Illiashenko et al., 2023).

Significant Digital Attacks on Transit Systems

1. **Ransomware Assaults:** Encrypting essential data and demanding money for its recovery could disrupt business. They target critical operating systems,

rendering it challenging or impossible to resume normal operations until the ransom payment is paid. A ransomware assault on a maritime port could disrupt merchandise flow and supply chains, potentially causing substantial financial harm (Ammar & Khan, 2024).

2. **Malicious Software:** Malware poses a significant risk to transportation systems, enabling unauthorized individuals to access critical data or disrupt vital operations. This kind of incident may result in disruptions to operations or present potential threats to essential infrastructure. Malware can facilitate the unauthorized access to information, disrupt standard operations, or establish avenues for subsequent attacks.
3. **Denial-of-Service (DoS) Attacks:** The recent surge in traffic has posed challenges for systems, causing operational difficulties and resulting in notable delays and interruptions. Distribution of Service attacks present considerable challenges in critical sectors such as subways and air traffic control, where the importance of maintaining uninterrupted operations cannot be overstated. Extended interruptions may lead to client discontent and raise potential safety issues due to system inaccessibility.
4. **Phishing Attacks**: Phishing attacks frequently focus on individuals working in the transport industry, aiming to misguide them into revealing sensitive information, such as login credentials, or unintentionally installing harmful software. In the event of success, these actions could potentially lead to significant system vulnerabilities and pose a risk to the integrity of the entire network. Phishing has the potential to enable more serious attacks, including malicious software or stolen information, by taking advantage of human error (Desamsetti & Mandapuram, 2017).

Constructive Forces Inspiring Challenges to the Industry

Various entities, including computer hackers, governmental actors, and activists, have motivations to take advantage of transportation systems. Hackers frequently pursue financial benefits through tactics like extortion or theft, whereas representatives of nation-states may endeavor to undermine critical infrastructure to secure a geopolitical edge. It is possible that individuals motivated by activism may target transportation systems as a means to draw attention to social or political concerns (Costa, 2025). Had the assault continued, the individuals involved—potentially an activist group, a terrorist organization, or a criminal network—might have caused significant disruption to the airport's operations.

Cyber Security Strategies for the Transportation Industry

The transportation sector faces unique challenges in the realm of cyber security. Ensuring the protection of essential infrastructure requires sophisticated approaches that address the specific challenges inherent to this field. Here are approaches to enhance the cyber defenses:

- **Operational Technology (OT) Security:** It is essential to confirm that employees have the requisite expertise in safeguarding operational technological systems, particularly those responsible for managing rail communication and gas valves. The education ought to highlight the potential risks linked to the connection of illegal devices, as well as the significance of adhering to established access rules.
- **Incident Response Drills**: It is advisable to routinely engage in exercises that replicate scenarios such as an assault by ransom ware on the distribution networks of a port. The objective of these drills is to evaluate the team's capacity to respond promptly, recognize impacted systems, and restore operations with minimal interruption (Pring et al., 2021).
- **AI-Powered Threat Detection:** Employ sophisticated AI technologies to consistently monitor and address any atypical activities in real-time, including efforts to gain unauthorized access to highway toll systems or boating software.

This can substantially decrease response times and alleviate damage. Implementing modern cyber security solutions for transportation enhances the organization's protection against sector-specific threats, thereby assuring the resilience and security of vital infrastructure.

Cyber-Attack Risks and Typologies in the Air Transport Sector

A cyber-attack can disrupt aircraft operations because there are many service providers. National security authorities acknowledge that corporate and government entities must work together to fight cyber-attacks in the near future. The air transport sector is engaged in discussions regarding drone-related cyber incursions and security breaches at various airports, including Gatwick, Heathrow, Madrid-Barajas, Frankfurt, Dublin, as well as in Saudi Arabia at Abha and King Abdullah airports. It is essential to ensure that airports are safeguarded against the threats posed by computer viruses and drone attacks, commonly referred to as unmanned aerial systems (UAS) (Lykou et al., 2020). There has been a notable rise in these incidents over the past five years, and it is anticipated that they will continue to grow in quantity, quantity, and impact as drones evolve to become bigger and more powerful. Many airports currently maintain a security operation center (SOC) dedicated to monitoring and identifying cyber threats and cyber-attacks, which may pose risks to their operational activities year-round (Poornima, 2022). An operational system is vulnerable when a natural or external hazard allows hackers or insiders to harm or cyber-attack it. Cyber security professionals assess operational system weaknesses. Thus, the aviation industry must define "risk." A risk is a possibility that a threat may occur and cause damage or loss. Risk assessment entails ongoing safety risk analysis in firms' procedures and operations. Large, medium, and low hazards exist. This test provides steps for risk management. Organizations must take preventative measures, innovate, and create cyber threat and cyber-attack contingency plans to monitor risk processes permanently. Since hazards fluctuate, airport and airline operators must constantly assess and reduce them. On an Airbus A380, over 1,000 applications are running, increasing cyber threats and dangers. Imagine an airport cyber-attack. Initially, it is essential for aviation traffic control and the management of air traffic to be fully operational in order to ensure the safety of passengers and crew in the air, as well as airport workers and travelers (Ukwandu et al., 2022b). It is advisable for airport managers to closely observe and assess the potential risks and vulnerabilities associated with flight internet connections, airline aircraft and planning of routes infrastructure, handling of freight and shipping, as well as access, departures, and identification administration systems, among other critical components, as these are vital to the overall functionality of the airport. Safety (cyber-attack) and hygiene (coronavirus infection) measures have transformed air travel to protect passengers. Cities connect to the air through airports, cargo, and commercial airplanes, and air transport closely links with tourism and logistics. Since travelers are returning to airports, fraudsters are targeting air transport again. Airports and airlines may safeguard themselves with cyber audits, AI monitoring, and supply chain mapping. According to Cukier (Ahmed et al., 2024) Human error causes 95% of cyber security breaches, while a hacker attack occurs every 39 seconds. Additionally, cyber-attacks vary by sector or industry in type and frequency. Drone denial attacks are more common near airports than in e-commerce or health.

- **Distributed denial of service (DDoS) cyber-attacks:**

These assaults cause the server to become overloaded with traffic, blocking the website, operations, or services. Following a notable IT incident that Lufthansa that resulted in canceled flights in 2023, several DDoS attacks impacted the internet pages of several German airports, causing them to become non-operational.

- **Drone denial assaults:**

Drone denial assaults are attacks carried out by drones that aim to steal data, intercept control and communication signals, or target airports and airlines, potentially causing mid-air collisions and unlawful monitoring. Drone hacks are unknown to 70% of aviation industry specialists (Nessa et al., 2024). In 2023, the northern Iraqi airport of Erbil, home to US and other international soldiers, experienced the shooting down of three weapon zed drones.

- **Hacking:**

The act of obtaining possession of private or corporate information without permission by exploiting vulnerabilities within an electronic machine or networks. Three years following the necessity for the Federal Aviation Administration (FAA) to suspend certain air traffic control networks in Alaska due to a hacking attack in 2006, a subsequent breach resulted in the theft of personal information belonging to 48,000 FAA employees (Ukwandu et al., 2022c).

- **Ransom ware:**

This sophisticated persistent threat surreptitiously targets an organization's information system that works in a crucial industry. This malware often locks users out of the system and/or encrypts important files, which stops the organization's operations. In 2022, ransom ware hackers targeted Swiss port, the biggest airport ground services and freight handling company in the world.

- **Phishing:**

Phishing is a type of deception method that attackers frequently employ to illegally obtain private information about people and organizations. An unidentified nation-state launched a phishing attack against 75 US airports in 2013 in an attempt to compromise commercial aviation networks.

- **Malware:**

Malware threatens critical systems and data. In 2013, a malware attack locked Istanbul Atatürk Airport's global departure terminal passports control system (Tahir et al., 2022).

- **Slammer worm:**

A computer worm that causes network breakdowns and slows down regular Internet traffic. The FAA's administration system was compromised in 2003 due to a slammer worm attack.

- **Botnets:**

An attack is when automated online requests are used to trick, alter, and interfere with a website. Attacks by bots involve the utilization of extensive networks comprising numerous machines to pursue unauthorized logins or to create disruptions within a network. In 2019, the airfield in Ben Gurion, Israel, successfully mitigated 3 million attacks by robots in just one day.

- **Data breach:**

Data breaches occur when individuals or entities without permission access sensitive information that is meant to be safeguarded. A data breach permits unauthorized individuals or hackers' access to private, sensitive, or protected data. A complex series of actions that take advantage of flaws in a commercial airline or airport can result in data breaches. SAS, a Scandinavian airline, announced in 2023 that it had been the target of a cyber-attack and advised users not to use its app.

- **Human error:**

Error science is just a part of being human. Even with the best of intentions, mistakes can still occur. The main vulnerability that could compromise the cyber security of ships, airplanes, and airports is human error. Intentional or inadvertent mistakes can expose vital information and create entry points for hackers and cyber terrorists. An employee making a mistake is known as human error. An employee error accounts for about 88% of all data breaches. Human error still accounts for an overwhelming majority of cyber security issues. In 2017, 75,000 passengers were left stranded when a contractor performing maintenance at a British Airways data center unintentionally turned off the power supply, causing the airline's computer systems to malfunction (Nagy, 2023). British Airways has made the decision to postpone every flight departing from London's Heathrow and Gatwick airports.

- **Crypto-jacking:**

This is the term for when hackers gained access to Tesla's computers to mine bit coin. It happens when hackers gain access to another person's computer to mine crypto currency. In 2018, crypt jacking recently affected 60% of all computer systems at an international airport in Europe.

Airline Hacking Operations From 2000 UNTIL JANUARY 2024

The researchers have conducted an investigation into the significant cyber-attacks perpetrated by cybercriminals in the aviation sector from 2000 to the start of 2024, drawing insights from Kon Briefing and various digital publications. The authors have selected the early 2000s as the period of focus due to the emergence of 3G smartphones, which brought enhanced data and multimedia capabilities. This year, malware has garnered significant attention in mainstream media. In the year 2000, the ILOVEYOU worm made its way into Microsoft Outlook users' systems, affecting more than 10% of web-based hosts within a matter of hours and resulting in damages estimated at $15 billion (Florido-Benítez, 2024b). In the very first half of 2023, there was a notable increase of 24% in aviation cyber-attacks globally. The authors are of the opinion that aviation has experienced over 54 cyber-attacks. Due to considerations surrounding security, the majority of the 775 airline and 150 airport breaches from 2020 have been kept confidential. For considerations related to brand integrity and reputation, many firms, destinations, and airlines choose not to disclose incidents of cyber-attacks. In 2018, British Airways faced a significant financial penalty of nearly $230 million due to a data breach, marking the largest fine imposed under the General Data Protection Regulation (GDPR). This regulation empowers regulators across European Union nations to levy fines amounting to 4% of an enterprise's worldwide income (Master of Science, Criminal Justice, University of New Haven, CT, USA et al., 2024). It is essential for businesses and people in the US and UK to fulfill their obligations by reporting computer viruses to HIPAA and the National Homeland Security Centre, respectively. A mere 28% of commercial cyber-attacks in the UK were brought to the attention of authorities in 2016.

Figure 3. Airline hacking from 2000 until January of 2024.

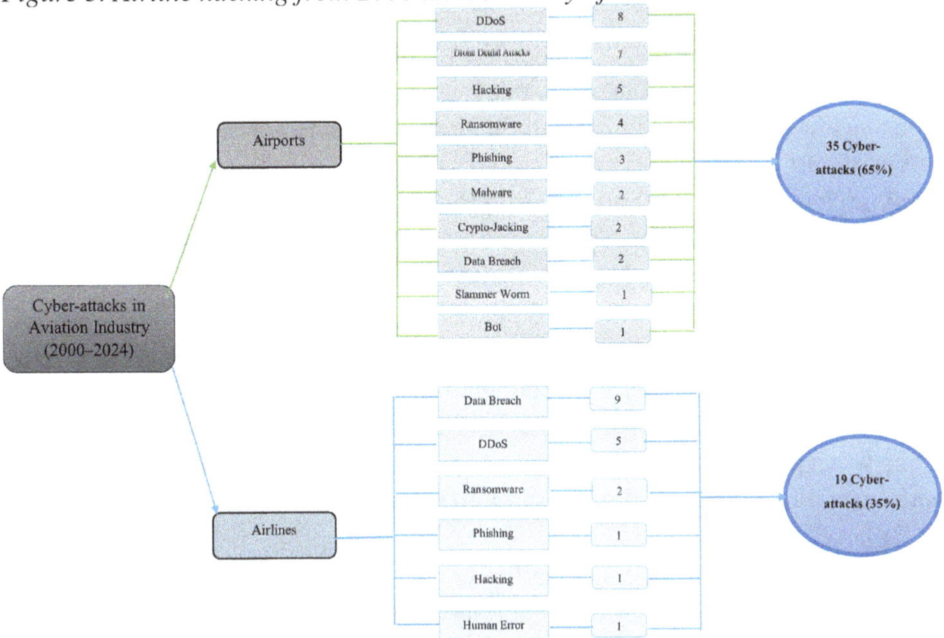

Source: *Authors compilation based on (Florido-Benítez, 2024a)*

This section examined 54 cyber-attacks, as shown in Figure 3. In the period examined, 35 cyber-attacks occurred at airports (65%) and 19 by airlines (35%). Airports have experienced 8 DDoS attacks, 7 drone denial-of-service threats, 5 hacking threats, 4 ransom ware threats, 3 phishing attacks, 2 spyware, data breaches, and digital money, and 1 bot and slammer worm attack. Airport websites and apps are targeted by DDoS assaults to steal sensitive data. Cybercriminals sell their findings to hackers on the dark web for a lot of money. DDoS is one of the most popular airline assaults since it ruins the network by flooding it with worthless messages to steal data (Abhishta et al., 2020). During this investigation, commercial airlines were targeted by repeated DDoS attacks (5), which is a severe vulnerability and threat. Thus, aviation cyber security must be a priority, not a must. Air transport safety is paramount for passengers and companies.

Wireless communication's broadcast nature makes most airports vulnerable to DDoS attacks. Airport security is tough since it requires identifying organizations, governments, and individuals motivated to attack essential infrastructure and airlines. The FAA uses 30-year-old systems. These systems could be attacked by hackers supported by antagonistic governments. Given its air travel dependence, such a strike might devastate the US. In the context of drone denial-of-service attacks, it is important to acknowledge that drones have the capability to obtain sensitive information, as well as to transport various items, including weapons, explosives, chemical agents, and jamming devices. This new technology has the potential to be misused by malicious actors, posing risks to safety and security. There have been seven instances of drone-related incidents involving airports and airlines. In 2023, drone incidents at airports in Edinburgh, Madrid, Palm Beach, Warsaw, Pittsburgh, and Frankfurt led to aircraft cancellations and delays, resulting in significant economic repercussions for airport and airline operators, as well as less than satisfactory experiences for passengers. The drone strike that caused disruptions at Gatwick airport (UK) for three days in 2019 resulted in costs amounting to £1.4 million for the airport and £15 million for Easy Jet, encompassing passenger compensation, welfare payments, and lost revenue ("The World of Companies Pro Social No Frills," 2020). An armed drone attack involving 13 individuals utilizing GPS technology targeted four Russian bases in Syria, resulting in significant consequences. Each drone was equipped with half an ounce of fireworks and was deployed from a distance exceeding 31 nautical miles (50 km) to its target. A notably grave incident took place in 2018.

Airports face increased vulnerability to data breaches due to their reliance on advanced digital technologies. It is important to acknowledge the significant potential for hackers to gain access to sensitive information and control systems within airports and airlines, particularly in light of the findings from this investigation, which has identified 2 airport hacks and 9 business airline data breaches. Given the significant amount of sensitive data held by airports and airlines, it is not surprising that they attract the attention of fraudsters. In 2020, San Francisco airport (US) disclosed a data breach affecting its two official websites, which occurred due to compromised employee credentials, thereby posing risks to the airport and its staff. A data breach presents significant challenges, as it grants unauthorized individuals access to sensitive information and the potential to elevate their privileges, thereby enabling them to navigate through the operational systems of airlines and airports. The presence of IoT devices in airport terminals raises concerns regarding potential misuse or data security breaches, which is understandably a point of apprehension for airport operators. Recent trends indicate an increase in airline data breaches, which may adversely affect both profitability and brand reputation. Following the disclosure of the data breach through television and digital media channels, the shares listed on the Hong Kong Stock Exchange experienced a decline of 3.8%, amounting to a loss of $201 million. Data breaches can lead to significant economic and social repercussions for consumers, as well as for airport and industry airline operators. Additionally, vulnerabilities in an aircraft's control systems may pose serious risks, potentially endangering the lives of numerous passengers. These data also show that airports and airlines must improve operating system cyber security due to continual vulnerabilities and cyber-attacks. Airlines and airports' apps and websites are useful for passenger information and sales and marketing to attract new customers. However, Sukesh et al. identified an increase in Air India data breaches and how hackers may leverage these weaknesses to acquire consumers' personal data. From 1960 to 2000, aircraft was unprepared for cyber-attacks. Due to potential threats, the FAA removed and required several Boeing 787 Dreamliner items and services in 2008. The UK Department for Science, Innovation, and Technology has provided projections indicating that data breaches incur costs of approximately £1,100 for companies of all sizes, £4,960 for big and small companies, and £530 for nonprofit organizations (Florido-Benítez, 2024c).

Airports had 4 ransom ware attacks and airlines 2 over the period considered. This number certainly understates events. Bridewell, a cyber-security firm, has observed a notable increase in ransomware attacks targeting airports and airlines in 2023. It is important to note that numerous incidents may have gone unreported, as many organizations may prefer not to disclose such vulnerabilities. Ransomware attacks have the potential to disrupt critical systems such as handling of baggage, building management, flight administration, and oversight as well as information acquisition, which could significantly impact airport operations. To prevent complex polymorphic assaults, airport and airline operators must promote a cyber-security culture, invest in cyber security tools, and hire cyber security professionals. Sabeel et al. remark that ML, DL, block chain, and AI approaches detect and prevent ransom ware and polymorphic assaults. In 2018, Bristol airport experienced a ransomware attack that resulted in the failure of flight display screens for a duration of two whole days ("Cyber security in Travel and Tourism," 2020). Individuals with advanced technical skills sought cryptocurrency as a means to recover encrypted data that had been lost. The operator of Bristol airport took the prudent step of taking compromised systems offline in order to restore them manually, without incurring any costs. The airport operator's decision regarding the ransom payment is frequently influenced by considerations related to operational integrity and the safety of passengers. This chapter outlines the key risks associated with aircraft ransom, including the potential for data and information loss, erosion of trust among customers and partners, violations of insurance policy terms, possible legal liabilities and penalties, heightened susceptibility to future cyber-attacks, and the reinforcement and funding of criminal activities.

Several Notable Attacks Against Airlines

Digital safety breaches have affected various sectors within the aviation industry. While this may not encompass every cyber incident, it does highlight several significant occurrences. In 2018, Cathay Pacific encountered a notable data breach, which affected the private information of approximately 9.4 million passengers.

This incident involved sensitive details such as passport information, dates of birth, frequent-flier number, cell phone numbers, along with credit card data (George, 2024). In 2021, SITA, a notable IT provider for members of both the Star Alliance and One World, encountered a breach that affected the data of over 2 million loyalty program accounts from various airlines around the globe. Air India In 2021, an incident occurred that involved illicit use of more than 4.5 thousand client documents, which encompassed sensitive personal information, including passport information when card details, obtained by cyber attackers. The incident in 2022 concerning Malaysia Airlines led to the unfortunate disclosure of private data for more than 9 million clients, including names, contact details, and card billing data, to individuals without authorization. The 2022 incident involving Japan Airlines raised concerns regarding the security of customer data, encompassing passport and email information, which has led to heightened awareness about the protection of highly classified identifiable data ("Navigating the Regulatory Landscape," 2024). The 2022 incident involving American Airlines underscored the vulnerabilities present within the industry concerning cyber threats, even though details surrounding the unauthorized access to customer records remain somewhat vague. Airports have also been the focus of attention. In 2022, a coordinated DDoS attack attributed to the pro-Russia group Killnet affected the public websites of several U.S. airports, including LAX, ATL, and ORD, resulting in significant disruptions to traveler information systems for an extended period. In July 2024, Delta Air Lines experienced a notable IT outage attributed to a problematic software update from the cybersecurity provider Crowd Strike, which affected approximately 8.5 million Microsoft Windows machines globally ("Navigating the Regulatory Landscape," 2024). The situation led Delta to cancel over 7,000 flights and delay an additional 35,500, affecting 1.3 million passengers and resulting in a $500 million lawsuit directed at Crowd Strike. Everybody involved in the production process have been included in this matter. In August 2024, the Rhysida ransomware group gained access to the Port of Seattle's legacy systems, leading to disruptions in reservations, boarding kiosks, and traveler advertisements at Seattle–Tacoma International Airport. The port subsequently communicated that 90,000 individuals experienced an impact when assailants obtained information related to employees, contractors, and parking. In 2023, Boeing faced an incident involving the Lock Bit virus platform, which issued a demand for a ransom of $200 million (Burton, 2025). Furthermore, it is worth noting that its subsidiary Jeppesen, which offers flight navigation tools, encountered a notable ransom ware incident in 2022. This event led to delays in flight-planning services and underscored the interconnected risks that can arise from the failure of a single provider.

Regulatory Responses and Modernization Efforts

On a global scale, authorities are adopting increasingly rigorous regulations. The U.S. Federal Aviation Administration (FAA) is putting forward new regulations designed to enhance the safety of airplanes, engines, and propellers in response to the challenges posed by Intentional Unauthorized Electronic Interactions (IUEI). It would be beneficial for manufacturers to consider potential threat scenarios, assess vulnerabilities, and implement thorough protective measures. Since 2009, the FAA has established specific guidelines regarding cyber security. The recent legislation seeks to harmonize these regulations, thereby facilitating a more efficient and expedited certification process for safe new technologies. The U.S. Department of Transportation (DOT) has unveiled a forward-thinking initiative aimed at establishing a completely new air traffic control (ATC) system by the year 2028. This follows a radar internet blackout at Newark Liberty International Airport in April 2025, highlighting the need for improvements in the existing infrastructure. The modernization initiative encompasses the replacement of outdated copper wiring with advanced fiber, wireless, and satellite connections across over 4,600 locations. It also involves the deployment of 25,000 new radios and 475 voice switches by the year 2027, the replacement of 618 radars dating back to the 1970s and 1980s, and the establishment of six new air traffic control centers, marking the first such development since the 1960s. The Notice to Airmen (NOTAM) system plays a crucial role in informing pilots and other stakeholders in the aviation sector about temporary modifications or potential hazards that may arise along a flight route or at an airport. The project is undergoing enhancements to facilitate near real-time data exchange. CGI Federal, Inc. has been entrusted with the responsibility of securely hosting it on the cloud, with an anticipated completion date set for September 2025. Global entities are collaborating harmoniously. For instance, the International Air Transport Association (IATA) is in the process of developing collaborative cyber risk regulations, while the European Union's framework for managing aviation risk is set to be implemented in 2026 ("International Aviation and Megatrends," 2020).

Necessity for Advanced Protection and Solutions

Aviation companies should boost their cyber security to prepare for tighter rules. Targeted protections start with comprehensive risk evaluations across IT and OT systems. Training employees helps prevent phishing and social-engineering attacks before they cause damage. 24/7 flight planning and supply chain data stream anomaly monitoring require AI-driven threat detection and endpoint protection. Aviation supply chain mapping plays a crucial role in identifying both direct and indirect partners, facilitating the necessary security audits and compliance with cyber security requirements in contractual agreements. It is important to improve this by implementing thorough perimeter defenses, such as firewalls, password protection, and detection systems for intrusions, in conjunction with secure segmentation of networks to effectively reduce the risk of wandering by potential attackers. The implementation of blockchain technology has the potential to enhance the security of data transfers between ground and air, as well as between ground entities. Meanwhile, the integration of artificial intelligence could facilitate the prioritization of essential NOTAM alerts for controllers. Ensuring the security of cloud systems is of paramount importance, prompting airlines to adopt platforms that identify misconfigurations, uphold least-privilege access, and streamline remedial workflows. In an effort to significantly enhance the security of data, carriers are implementing measures such as encrypted data at every stage, automatic quality checks, and real-time detection of anomaly within their cloud installations ("Cloud Security for Smart Sensor Network," 2025).

Technologies and Tools for Defense

Five Aviation Technologies Making Flight Safer Than Ever

1. Artificial Intelligence

AI is soon becoming the tech industry's leading disruptive technology. In 2023, AI dominated chip market demand from customer electronics, healthcare OEMs, supplier, and electronic manufacturing service (EMS) providers. AI will rule again in 2024, according to market studies. Over the past decade, military AI use has grown. The most basic benefit of AI is automating manual procedures, minimizing wasted time and human mistakes. The latter may pose significant risks in high-reliability industries such as A&D. Regrettably, relying solely on a human workforce does not completely eradicate the possibility of human errors. While it is true that mistakes are a part of the human experience, the implementation of automation serves to mitigate their occurrence. Artificial intelligence, including machine learning and computer vision, offers users the opportunity to discover patterns and insights within the data they have gathered. AI helps optimize operations by identifying ways to streamline work and reduce waste through asset usage and efficiency. Compared to human teams, these difficult jobs can be completed quickly. Data can also help firms make quick decisions with a more complete view owing to insights (Jha et al., 2020).

AI has the potential to provide valuable guidance to pilots regarding flight safety in the realm of aerospace applications. Flight AI has the potential to significantly reduce human errors and improve operational efficiency through its ability to recommend optimal flight paths. The pilot is entrusted with making the ultimate decisions. Enhancing the efficiency of resource utilization would lead to a reduction in fuel costs and consumption. A&D AI technology offers a range of advantages that extend well beyond its applications in combat. Recent studies indicate that advancements in generative AI have significantly enhanced the information processing capabilities within military operations. Colonel Matthew Strohmeyer of the U.S. Air Force shared insights with Bloomberg regarding his data-driven exercise utilizing a large language model (LLM) to gather information. The test yielded positive results, demonstrating that the information processing capabilities efficiently handled the request in a matter of minutes rather than extending over hours or days. The efficiency of this processing speed would significantly enhance the management of time-sensitive needs, such as casualty treatment and evacuation planning, where well-considered decisions in high-pressure scenarios could help reduce unnecessary casualties. While the full implementation of generative AI and other large language models may still be on the horizon, figures such as Strohmeyer are exploring progressive methods for AI to support various military sectors. Throughout 2024, A&D OEMs, CMs, and EMS providers are likely to explore innovative approaches to the development of AI technology (Lin et al., 2024). With 2023's fervor, the AI market should increase through 2024. Pilot training and better procedures have increased flight safety, but new technology has made the biggest changes. Digital revolutions are reshaping many of the biggest companies. Organizations are using big data, AI, and IoT to solve problems. Similar improvements are coming to aircraft safety. These five new technologies will increase aircraft safety.

2. Inertial Measurement Units

There will be autonomous flight soon, and with Urban Air Mobility (UAM), some of these self-driving cars will be driving in busy cities. If an autonomous vehicle loses track of where it is, it could be dangerous to people and property. That's why successful autonomous flight depends on airplanes knowing exactly where they are. This makes Inertial Measurement Units (IMUs) very significant since they can tell one where they are even when GPS isn't working. Radar has been around for a long time, but weather radar is changing a lot right now. The IntuVue 3-D Weather Radar from Honeywell, for example, can detect turbulence up to 60 nautical miles away and can anticipate hail and lightning. The new radar technology is beneficial for more than just the big airlines. One can expect to see it in more commercial and general aviation platforms in the future.

3. Augmented Reality

Augmented reality is the idea of making a pilot more aware of their surroundings, usually by changing what they see. Heads-up displays that military pilots use are the first step toward augmented reality. All kinds of planes will soon use more advanced versions of these technologies in their helmets and cockpits (Torres et al., 2024).

4. The Connected Aircraft

The technology that will have the most impact on safety will be the ability to connect different products and services into a Connected Aircraft. Connected Aircraft solutions will supply pilots and operators better information, make maintenance more effective, and gather immense amounts of data that operators may use to improve safety even further. The Connected Aircraft makes flying safer by combining many of the technologies we use now and adding data.

5. Early Warning Systems

The Saab Global Eye is an example of an early warning system that uses radar and works in the middle of a flight. An airplane has an electro-optic/infrared sensor turret that watches over airspaces. They can see dangers like missiles and unfamiliar aircraft from hundreds of kilometers away, which lets them know about them early. The early warning systems are connected so that they may talk to air traffic controllers and let them know about any changes or hazards that the system picks up. It is a powerful system that can handle things that move very quickly, like missiles, as well as those that move slowly, like helicopters ("Modern Weapons," 2020).

There is no doubt that new technologies might make flying safer. The industry can keep making safety better, even while airspaces are getting busier and UAM is bringing more types of planes into already busy areas. Honeywell has been in the aviation business for a long time and knows a lot about both hardware and software. For this reason, we are actively implementing advanced technologies to enhance safety in air travel for all individuals.

CONCLUSION

In today's technological landscape, it is essential to prioritize strong cyber security measures within the aviation and transportation sectors. As these industries continue to adopt increasingly sophisticated technologies, they face heightened vulnerabilities to cyber-attacks that could disrupt critical operations, jeopardize passenger safety, or compromise sensitive information. The various components of aviation systems, including the control of air traffic, automated terminal services, and aboard aircraft technology, necessitate a thoughtful and collaborative approach to ensure their protection. Technologies such as AI and block chain have the potential to enhance security, provided they are implemented alongside robust security protocols. In order to enhance the security of the framework, it is essential for executives in industry, authorities, and IT specialists to collaborate effectively. It is essential that we prioritize employee training, maintain continuous surveillance, and conduct ongoing risk assessments as our primary objectives. Approaches to address emerging threats should evolve in response to their changing nature. Ultimately, the enduring safety and sustainability of global public transit systems hinge on the effectiveness of integrating cyber security into their infrastructure, as well as the ability to anticipate and address potential threats with skill and foresight.

REFERENCES

Abdelkader, G., Elgazzar, K., & Khamis, A. (2021). Connected Vehicles: Technology Review, State of the Art, Challenges and Opportunities. *Sensors (Basel), 21*(22), 7712. DOI: 10.3390/s21227712 PMID: 34833782

Abhishta, A., van Heeswijk, W., Junger, M., Nieuwenhuis, L. J. M., & Joosten, R. (2020). Why would we get attacked? An analysis of attacker's aims behind DDoS attacks. *Journal of Wireless Mobile Networks, Ubiquitous Computing and Dependable Applications, 11*(2), 3–22. DOI: 10.22667/JOWUA.2020.06.30.003

Ahmed, M., Kambam, H. R., Liu, Y., Jaidka, S., & Petrova, K. (2024). Impact and Significance of Human Factors in Digital Information Security. *International Journal of Information Science and Technology*, 1-17 Pages. DOI: 10.57675/IMIST.PRSM/IJIST-V7I2.213

Ammar, M., & Khan, I. A. (2024). *Cyber Attacks on Maritime Assets and their Impacts on Health and Safety Aboard: A Holistic View* (Version 1). arXiv. DOI: 10.48550/ARXIV.2407.08406

Ande, R., Adebisi, B., Hammoudeh, M., & Saleem, J. (2020). Internet of Things: Evolution and technologies from a security perspective. *Sustainable Cities and Society, 54*, 101728. DOI: 10.1016/j.scs.2019.101728

Aslam, M., Khan Abbasi, M. A., Khalid, T., Shan, R. U., Ullah, S., Ahmad, T., Saeed, S., Alabbad, D. A., & Ahmad, R. (2022). Getting Smarter about Smart Cities: Improving Data Security and Privacy through Compliance. *Sensors (Basel), 22*(23), 9338. DOI: 10.3390/s22239338 PMID: 36502039

Aslan, Ö., Aktuğ, S. S., Ozkan-Okay, M., Yilmaz, A. A., & Akin, E. (2023). A Comprehensive Review of Cyber Security Vulnerabilities, Threats, Attacks, and Solutions. *Electronics (Basel), 12*(6), 1333. DOI: 10.3390/electronics12061333

Burton, S. L. (2025). Digital Saboteurs: Unmasking Insider Cybersecurity Threats in Aviation and Aerospace. *Law. Economics and Society, 1*(2), 1. DOI: 10.30560/les.v1n2p1

Cloud security for smart sensor network. (2025). In S. Divadari, *Sensor Networks for Smart Hospitals* (pp. 477–503). Elsevier. DOI: 10.1016/B978-0-443-36370-2.00023-2

Costa, M. (2025). Exploring Hacktivism: The Role and Impact of Social Media. *ARIS2 : Advanced Research on Information Systems Security, 5*(1), 99–111. DOI: 10.56394/aris2.v5i1.56

Cybersecurity in Travel and Tourism. A Risk-Based Approach. (2020). In A. Paraskevas, *Handbook of e-Tourism* (pp. 1–24). Springer International Publishing. DOI: 10.1007/978-3-030 05324-6_100-1

Desamsetti, H., & Mandapuram, M. (2017). A Review of Meta-Model Designed for the Model-Based Testing Technique. *Engineering International*, *5*(2), 107–110. DOI: 10.18034/ei.v5i2.661

Florido-Benítez, L. (2024a). The Cybersecurity Applied by Online Travel Agencies and Hotels to Protect Users' Private Data in Smart Cities. *Smart Cities*, *7*(1), 475–495. DOI: 10.3390/smartcities7010019

Florido-Benítez, L. (2024b). The types of hackers and cyberattacks in the aviation industry. *Journal of Transportation Security*, *17*(1), 13. Advance online publication. DOI: 10.1007/s12198-024-00281-9

Florido-Benítez, L. (2024c). The types of hackers and cyberattacks in the aviation industry. *Journal of Transportation Security*, *17*(1), 13. Advance online publication. DOI: 10.1007/s12198-024-00281-9

Illiashenko, O., Kharchenko, V., Babeshko, I., Fesenko, H., & Di Giandomenico, F. (2023). Security-Informed Safety Analysis of Autonomous Transport Systems Considering AI-Powered Cyberattacks and Protection. *Entropy (Basel, Switzerland)*, *25*(8), 1123. DOI: 10.3390/e25081123 PMID: 37628153

International Aviation and Megatrends. (2020). In R. Abeyratne, *Aviation in the Digital Age* (pp. 13–42). Springer International Publishing. DOI: 10.1007/978-3-030-48218-3_2

Jayabalan, J., & Jeyanthi, N. (2022). Scalable blockchain model using off-chain IPFS storage for healthcare data security and privacy. *Journal of Parallel and Distributed Computing*, *164*, 152–167. DOI: 10.1016/j.jpdc.2022.03.009

Jha, A. K., Agi, M. A. N., & Ngai, E. W. T. (2020). A note on big data analytics capability development in supply chain. *Decision Support Systems*, *138*, 113382. DOI: 10.1016/j.dss.2020.113382

Li, Y., & Liu, Q. (2021). A comprehensive review study of cyber-attacks and cyber security; Emerging trends and recent developments. *Energy Reports*, *7*, 8176–8186. DOI: 10.1016/j.egyr.2021.08.126

Lin, K.-C., Matthews, W., & Olsen, S. (2024). Middle spacepowers' integration with the global supply chain for the space industry: Taiwan and Thailand. *Business and Politics*, •••, 1–27. DOI: 10.1017/bap.2024.18

Lykou, G., Moustakas, D., & Gritzalis, D. (2020). Defending Airports from UAS: A Survey on Cyber-Attacks and Counter-Drone Sensing Technologies. *Sensors (Basel), 20*(12), 3537. DOI: 10.3390/s20123537 PMID: 32580402

Modern Weapons. Possibilities and Limitations. (2020). In A. Belous & V. Saladukha, *Viruses, Hardware and Software Trojans* (pp. 731–820). Springer International Publishing. DOI: 10.1007/978-3-030-47218-4_8

Nagy, J. (2023). *Maintenance check flight accidents (a new approach to air safety investigations)*. DOI: 10.26192/Z58X7

Navigating the Regulatory Landscape. (2024). In S. K. Shandilya, A. Datta, Y. Kartik, & A. Nagar, *EAI/Springer Innovations in Communication and Computing* (pp. 127–240). Springer Nature Switzerland. DOI: 10.1007/978-3-031-53290-0_3

Nessa, J. J., Kleczkowska, A., & Hasar, S. (2024). Digest of state practice: 1 July – 31 December 2023. *Journal on the Use of Force and International Law, 11*(1–2), 297–372. DOI: 10.1080/20531702.2024.2413800

Nifakos, S., Chandramouli, K., Nikolaou, C. K., Papachristou, P., Koch, S., Panaousis, E., & Bonacina, S. (2021). Influence of Human Factors on Cyber Security within Healthcare Organisations: A Systematic Review. *Sensors (Basel), 21*(15), 5119. DOI: 10.3390/s21155119 PMID: 34372354

Poornima, B. (2022). Cyber Threats and Nuclear Security in India. *Journal of Asian Security and International Affairs, 9*(2), 183–206. DOI: 10.1177/23477970221099748

Poulaki, I., Koufodontis, N. I., & Papadimitriou, S. (2025). Airline revenue management, distribution and passengers: Market trends in a technology driven triangle. *Worldwide Hospitality and Tourism Themes, 17*(1), 35–47. DOI: 10.1108/WHATT-12-2024-0304

Pring, E. T., Malietzis, G., Kendall, S. W. H., Jenkins, J. T., & Athanasiou, T. (2021). Crisis management for surgical teams and their leaders, lessons from the COVID-19 pandemic; A structured approach to developing resilience or natural organisational responses. *International Journal of Surgery, 91*, 105987. DOI: 10.1016/j.ijsu.2021.105987 PMID: 34091086

Safitra, M. F., Lubis, M., & Fakhrurroja, H. (2023). Counterattacking Cyber Threats: A Framework for the Future of Cybersecurity. *Sustainability (Basel), 15*(18), 13369. DOI: 10.3390/su151813369

Tahir, S., Shahbaz, M. A., Tahir, H., Awais, M., Khan, F., Tahir, R., Saeed, S., & Almuhaideb, A. M. (2022). A Novel Approach to Reduce Breaches of Aircraft Communication Data. *Electronics (Basel), 12*(1), 172. DOI: 10.3390/electronics12010172

The World of Companies Pro Social No Frills. (2020). In G. Grefe, *Shapes of Tourism Employment* (1st ed., pp. 187–207). Wiley. DOI: 10.1002/9781119751342.ch12

Torres, Á., Molina, J. P., García, A. S., & González, P. (2024). Prototyping of Augmented Reality interfaces for air traffic alert and their evaluation using a Virtual Reality aircraft-proximity simulator. *2024 IEEE Conference Virtual Reality and 3D User Interfaces (VR)*, 817–826. DOI: 10.1109/VR58804.2024.00101

Ukwandu, E., Ben-Farah, M. A., Hindy, H., Bures, M., Atkinson, R., Tachtatzis, C., Andonovic, I., & Bellekens, X. (2022a). Cyber-Security Challenges in Aviation Industry: A Review of Current and Future Trends. *Information (Basel)*, *13*(3), 146. DOI: 10.3390/info13030146

Ukwandu, E., Ben-Farah, M. A., Hindy, H., Bures, M., Atkinson, R., Tachtatzis, C., Andonovic, I., & Bellekens, X. (2022b). Cyber-Security Challenges in Aviation Industry: A Review of Current and Future Trends. *Information (Basel)*, *13*(3), 146. DOI: 10.3390/info13030146

Ukwandu, E., Ben-Farah, M. A., Hindy, H., Bures, M., Atkinson, R., Tachtatzis, C., Andonovic, I., & Bellekens, X. (2022c). Cyber-Security Challenges in Aviation Industry: A Review of Current and Future Trends. *Information (Basel)*, *13*(3), 146. DOI: 10.3390/info13030146

Chapter 2
Cybercrime in Tourism: Legal and Jurisdictional Issues in Digital Evidence

Kalpna Sharma
http://orcid.org/0000-0002-4511-7988
Law Centre-II, Faculty of Law, University of Delhi, India

Mayank Kapila
http://orcid.org/0009-0001-4874-8283
Babasaheb Bhimrao Ambedkar Bihar University, Muzaffarpur, India

Akanksha Singh
http://orcid.org/0000-0003-0397-4727
Christ University, India

Vijaishree Dubey Pandey
http://orcid.org/0000-0003-3207-7814
Christ University, India

Sheetal Singh
http://orcid.org/0000-0002-7266-8910
Christ University, India

Shashank Solanki
http://orcid.org/0009-0002-5923-0516
Christ University, India

ABSTRACT

The growing digitalisation of the tourism sector has led to increased vulnerability to cross-border cybercrime, exposing gaps in international legal cooperation. This study examines the legal and jurisdictional challenges in collecting and admitting digital evidence in tourism-related cybercrime. It analyses key international frameworks, including the Budapest Convention, UNTOC, and the EU-US Data Privacy Framework, highlighting conflicts in data sharing and evidence admissibility. Case studies such as Marriott, British Airways, and MakeMyTrip reveal inconsistencies in cross-border investigations. The paper also explores the role of blockchain and zero-knowledge proofs in improving evidence integrity, while raising concerns over privacy rights under ICCPR and ECHR. Findings suggest the need for legal harmonisation, streamlined evidence-sharing procedures, and enhanced forensic capabilities to strengthen cybercrime response in the tourism industry.

DOI: 10.4018/979-8-3373-5826-0.ch002

1. INTRODUCTION

1.1 Digital Transformation of the Tourism Sector

The digital learning within the tourist industry is the connection between the tourist and the company providing such services. One of the pillars of any economy, tourism has been digitalized, dozens of online services, applications and a network of systems are a new, needful component of the tourist experience that is at a very early stage of life planning, booking and the tourist experience himself. The reason behind this is that despite the fact that this digital transformation has brought forth a new breed of ease and efficiency in this world, it has also created more attack surface to the cybercriminals and subsequent rise in transnational cybercriminals against the tourism infrastructure (Broadhurst, 2006).Over the last few years the world tourism has swiftly adopted the use of digital platforms and intelligent systems. The examples of success are the e-Tourism System of Estonia that unites the national databases to simplify booking and visitor identification and Smart Tourism Initiative in Thailand that deploys IoT and AI tools to improve the experience of travelers. On the contrary, cybersecurity integration failures, including the 2023 hotel booking ransomware attack of the city of Spain that interfered with more than 30,000 reservations, demonstrate how poor cybersecurity integration may result in failures. ENISA Threat Landscape Report (2024) cites 27 per cent of all hospitality-related cyber attacks in Europe in 20232024 as ransomware, and a 19 per cent global growth of tourism sector data breaches in 20232024.

The development of more sophisticated forms of cyberattacks including the theft of sensitive information of customers or the use of ransomware to shut down the systems hotels rely on to book rooms is a strong threat to the economic and reputational security of the tourism sector (Mohamed, Al-Jaroodi, and Jawhar, 2020). The airline ransomware hackings and high-profile data breaches of luxury hotels, credit thefts of travel services among others in 20222024 proved the chronic vulnerability in the global tourist infrastructure (Santarsieri, Carlucci, Lerro, and Schiuma, 2024).Although digitalization will help tourism enterprises to customize the services offered to guests, as well as optimize the utilization of resources and improve convenience, there is also a concern of the loss of trust. This has resulted in psychological impacts among the travelers such as lack of confidence, fear of fraud and feeling of vulnerability on the Internet due to frequent cases of data leakages and identity thefts. The security and confidentiality of user information is the primary consideration because the data now take an almost endless value (Vlastos and Patel, 2007). However, there is also the possibility that due to the increasing dependency on digital technologies, the sense of irreversible alienation and isolation of the traveler who seeks real human interaction can occur. The tourism industry must therefore come to terms with the position of the digital realm as well as the augmentation of the physical experiences (Grabosky, 2007).

1.2 Complexity in Cross-Border Cybercrime Investigations

The reality that gathering and retaining of digital evidence within cross-border settings is already a complicated process, further complicates the process of cross-border cybercrime detection and investigation within the tourism industry. The digital evidence may be any data (server logs, network traffic, data stored in the user accounts, online activity of users, and even names of the criminals) that can be presented as the evidence of the harm consequences of the cyberattack. However, it carries a minor tincture of legal issues in case of the collection of such evidence, considering the differences between the laws that operate within countries on the issue subject of data privacy, search and seizure and cross-border co-operation (Kasper and Laurits, 2016).

Having in mind the digital economy businesses, the tourism and hospitality industry uses a lot of technology to improve the products and customer experience. Nevertheless, the remote and hybrid work environment after the COVID-19 has promoted the attack surface because workers can access sensitive systems over unsecured home networks, facilitating more phishing and ransomware cases. The Interpol Presentation 2023 case study on hotel ransomware attacks revealed that per jurisdictional issues and absence of timely data sharing, many developing countries are taking more than seven months to complete a cross-border investigation. Many developing countries lack digital forensic laboratories, trained personnel, and evidence management tools, and suffer incomplete or delayed investigations as a result. According to the UNODC Global Report on Cybercrime (2023), these gaps in capacity have a severe impact on the international cooperation. In order to maintain trust and further expansion, the industry will have to implement effective cybersecurity strategies and be consistent with the best practices of maintaining the confidentiality of information and efficient operations at the same time (Herke, Tóth, and Perkumienė, 2025).

1.3 Legal and Forensic Challenges in Handling Digital Evidence

The significance of the digital evidence during the process of cybercrime investigations cannot be overestimated, but the collection of the digital evidence is a process which is complex technically and legally. The considerations in using digital evidence include intactness, originality and authenticity because it has to be well preserved during investigation process. The unstable and dynamic characteristics of the digital materials and the platform on which the same can be altered or destroyed at any time demands that a great deal of the forensic actions be undertaken to enable the evidence used in the court.

Guidelines like ISO/IEC 27037 (Guidelines for Identification, Collection, and Preservation of Digital Evidence), ISO/IEC 27042 (Analysis and Interpretation Guidelines) and those of NIST Forensics Guidelines (2020) offer globally accepted guidelines on achieving forensic soundness. But international inconsistencies in admissibility and evidentiary standards between countries tend to compromize prosecution prosecution because in one country may be considered valid evidence may not be in another.Moreover, the developing countries are beset by the lack of forensic infrastructure and insufficient training as law enforcement agencies often do not have special cyber forensic services, up to date toolkits and continuous professional development. These loopholes restrict their chances to maintain the chain of custody and prove evidence in courts. Digital evidence is cross-jurisdictional, fragile, and latent, which requires high technical accuracy and legal cooperation. In addition to this, the appearance of encryption and anonymization tools makes the procedure even more complicated, as many of them do not allow law enforcement to gain access to data in time (Sarfraz, Khawaja, Han, Ariza-Montes, and Arjona-Fuentes, 2023). Thus, it is vital to come up with consistent forensic practices and capacity-building interventions that will produce valid and admissible evidence in court (Tariq, 2024).

1.4 Research Questions

This research paper will focus on addressing the legal issues and jurisdictional challenges that are posed by the gathering of the digital evidence in a case involving cross-border cybercrimes which strike the tourism industry in answering the research questions. The following are the research questions that the research will answer:

- What are the major legal and regulatory contradictions that impede the cross-border gathering of digital evidence in cybercrime investigations against tourism infrastructure?
- What are the ways that international cooperation could be established to help the free and legal flow of the digital evidence across the borders?
- What can we do to maintain the integrity and admissibility of digital evidence when we replace cybercrime cross-border investigations?
- Which are the policy suggestions that would be taken to curb the legal loopholes and jurisdictional issues that have been witnessed in an effort to fortify the fight against cybercrime in the tourism sector?
- How do cross-border cyber incidents affect consumer confidence and tourism income psychologically and financially?

The answers to these questions hold significance because they are efficient steps towards preventing cybercrime, sealing specialty gaps in the law and ensuring the preservation of justice and security in the computerized era.

1.5 Methodology

To facilitate the solution of such a complex issue, the research assumes a multi-layered and mixed-methodology, which involves doctrinal legal research, as well as empirical and comparative analysis, and policy analysis. The doctrinal aspect involves critical evaluation of the international treaties, the national laws and the court rulings applicable to computer-related offenses, data security, and cross-nation implementation (Nithyasree et al., 2025).The empirical and qualitative element entails the case study, institutional report, and survey analysis of the credible sources, including UNWTO, ITU, ENISA, UNODC, and Europol case archives, to find out the trends and patterns in the process of handling digital evidence across the borders. Triangulation of findings is obtained with a comparative legal and technical analysis to determine consistency between the legal frameworks and the mechanisms of practical enforcement.

The policy review step is based on the analyses of the doctrine and the case in that to come up with reforms to improve international cooperation, align the legal standards, and enhance the law enforcement capacities within the tourism industry. Additionally, the paper stresses that cybersecurity agencies and tech companies should work together to predict emergent risks and reinforce user-centered protection (Sinno, 2019). It is a transnational and interdisciplinary framework, therefore, that is suggested as the best mechanism of dealing with the issue of contemporary cybercrime in tourism.

2. OBJECTIVES

The given research has a considerable task of de jurisdictionalizing the complex set of legal and jurisdictional issues that arise in the context of establishing and prosecuting transnational cyber-crime committed against the tourist sector, in its turn, as to the regulations of evidence gathering and Admissibility. Another important factor, which prevents obtaining effective results of international cooperation and investigation of cyber-criminals, is the identification of gaps and inconsistency within the current international legal frameworks that govern digital evidence. It will involve an overview of the differences in data-protection regulations, admissibility-of-evidence concepts, and concepts of jurisdiction that are potentially debilitating to law-enforcement agents operating with cyber-criminals in the cross-border setting

(Pumaleque, Fernandez, Perez, and Bedriñana, 2021).The paper will review the existing gaps in the international legal frameworks with reference to digital evidence, which, in its turn, hinders the successful cross-border cooperation. This will entail an extensive research of data-protection laws, evidence-admissibility laws, and jurisdiction laws which may prove to be a major headache in situations when the law-enforcement officers are attempting to track the activities of cyber-criminals who are operating across national borders. Moreover, the given research study will shed light on the practical, technical, and social issues that the investigators of cyber-crime face, including the ones that are related to the system availability and usability, as well as to the cooperative work with the help of computers. In addition to this, the research will also critically examine those realities of cyber-crime that have been experienced in the tourism sector to illustrate how the processes and policies have failed to allow successful prosecution of the perpetrators of cyber-crime in the tourism sector. This will involve a scathing indictment of particular instances in which issues of legal and jurisdiction have undermined investigations, generated obstacles to justice, or enabled cyber-criminals to get away with it. To be more precise, the work at hand is to make a contribution to the development of cyber-forensics and make a practical contribution to the international community regarding its attempts to fight this extremely advanced, technically high-performing, constantly evolving phenomenon (Grabosky, 2007). The paper will also incorporate a special discussion of the economic and reputational losses incurred by the cyber incident in the tourism industry, which will be dedicated to the short discussion of the effects of cyber-crime causing mistrust, loss of consumer confidence in online travel services, brand damage, and financial losses to tourism companies as one of the primary consequences of cyber-crime and, therefore, the urgency of effective cross-border legal and investigative framework (see Allianz Risk Barometer, 2024; GlobalData, 2022).Lastly, the research will generalise the realisation of its findings of the results and give some strategic recommendations, which must be legal and adhere to individual rights, in a bid to improve the international cooperation, standardise the legal frameworks and enhance procedures to acquire digital evidence across borders (Grabosky, 2007). The requirements to enhance international treaties, the daily sharing of evidence across borders, the capacity-building efforts (particularly with resource-constrained nations), and the enhancement of systems that can deal with the issue of conflict of jurisdiction will form the basis of the following recommendations. Creating strategic, legally coherent, and rights-giving recommendations are also a goal that needs to be attained (Dalal & Juneja, 2020).

These objectives will enable the research to add value to the clear picture of cross-border cyber-crime multifaceted nature in the tourism industry and will also serve as a practical tool to bolster the universal law against this vice. The manner in which workload of the cyber-crime departments can be enhanced is also discussed in the research, with a consideration that the units funding and training has not matched the nature of the work and the sophistication of the cyber-crime policing (Vlastos and Patel, 2007). Considering the fact that the rate of cyber-crime grows gradually on a chronic basis even though the legislation on cyber-crime exists, the current study highlights the needs of the overall enhancement of the productivity of the criminal law. It is also aware of the serious psychological impact that tourists lose trust in online travel services after cyber-attacks and the serious effect to tourism companies losing reputation and financial resources (Broadhurst, 2006). Thus it is but natural time to generate a more serene and even a safer digital setting in the tourism market and this is one of the ways of generating trust and confidence in this industry both by the business and the traveller as well.

3. LITERATURE REVIEW

Tourism-related international cybercrime offers great challenge in the sphere of investigations and prosecution because the internet is facilitated internationally, thus, creating the need to establish international collaboration and consistency. The legislative system should be in a position to keep pace with the pace of technology to the extent that the law enforcement bodies are fully equipped to deal with cybercriminals and, concurrently, protect the liberty of human beings and their civil rights (Casino et al., 2022). The policy and legal problems associated with the collection of digital evidence concerning cross-border tourism cybercrime should be addressed through the appreciation of the available international tools, domestic laws, and human rights tools. It would be very difficult to break cases of computer-related crimes as well as locate and charge the criminals without clearly defined concepts and mechanisms of handling electronic evidence in accordance to the law. Recent reports issued by the United Nations World Tourism Organization, the United Nations Office on Drugs and Crime, the International Telecommunication Union and the European Union Agency on Cybersecurity have all reported that the tourism industry is in the top five sectors under threat through cybercrime with the most prevalent threats including ransomware, phishing, and identity theft attacks. These reports also highlight the immediate need to have regional and international collaboration to streamline the legal practices in digital evidence preservation and to prosecute offenders.

3.1 International Legal Instruments

The global instruments are essential in creating a platform to have international cooperation in the investigations of cybercriminals. The Budapest Convention on

Cybercrime and the Second Additional Protocol (2022) are among the greatest international initiatives to ensure cybercrime laws become more flexible and interoperable. The Convention gives a more precise legal basis on the criminalization of cyber crimes, investigation and encourages legal cooperation between signatories. The Second Additional Protocol adds the mechanisms of direct collaboration with the service providers and an emergency access request to the electronic evidence, thus improving the cross-border efficiency (Florido-Benítez, 2025). Also, the United Nations Convention against Transnational Organized Crime establishes the processes of mutual legal assistance (MLA) in cases when cybercrime overlaps with other organized crimes (Dhande, 2024). An example of regional standards that also have an impact on cross-border data exchange and evidence sharing is the EU General Data Protection Regulation (GDPR) and the EU-US Data Privacy Framework (Tariq, 2024).

Comparative analysis of the joint enforcement programs like Europol-INTERPOL cybercrime work and the ASEAN Cybersecurity Cooperation Strategy (2017, updated 2023) also shows that regional frameworks play a crucial role in enhancing the capacity-building, information sharing, and coordinated enforcement. These mechanisms are enhanced to make them effective when they are supported by shared standards of digital forensics and expedited evidence-sharing rules (Tariq, 2024).

Table 1. Timeline of Major International Legal Instruments in Cybercrime and Digital Evidence Collection

Year	Instrument / Legal Framework	Region / Organization	Key Contributions
2001	Budapest Convention on Cybercrime	Council of Europe (open to accession globally)	First binding international treaty on cybercrime; harmonization of laws, procedural tools for digital evidence, international cooperation.
2013	EU Directive 2013/40 on Attacks against Information Systems	European Union	Strengthened legal framework against cyberattacks, introduced penalties, improved cooperation across EU Member States.
2014	African Union Convention on Cyber Security and Personal Data Protection (Malabo Convention)	African Union	Comprehensive legal instrument addressing cybercrime, data protection, and electronic transactions across Africa.
2017	ASEAN Cybersecurity Strategy (updated 2023)	ASEAN (Southeast Asia)	Regional strategy fostering resilience, cooperation, and capacity building; updated in 2023 to address emerging threats like AI-driven cybercrime.
2019	UN General Assembly Resolution (A/RES/74/247)	United Nations	Initiated process for negotiating a comprehensive international convention on countering cybercrime.
2022	Second Additional Protocol to the Budapest Convention	Council of Europe (global participation)	Facilitates enhanced cross-border access to electronic evidence; introduces safeguards for human rights and rule of law.

The global tools are all significant towards curbing cybercrime in the tourism sector. The Budapest Convention promotes interoperability and sharing of evidence across jurisdictions which is key with regard to crimes that exhibit international travel. Quite the contrary, the process of cross-border transfer of digital evidence can be rather complex due to such frameworks as GDPR, particularly, when it is related to personal data of citizens of EU countries. As reported by UNODC (2024), the cooperation at the international level is not balanced, and it urges the states to adopt the harmonized digital evidence standards. Similarly, OECD Cybersecurity Policy Framework (2023) and the ITU Global Cybersecurity Index (2024) aim at ensuring a global coordinated capacity building and resilience systems to protect the information-based industry such as tourism.

3.2 Domestic Legal Conflicts and Sovereignty Issues

With the assistance of the human rights tools offered, the privacy and expression of the people can be secured concerning the cybercrime investigations. Article 17 of the International Covenant of Civil and Political Rights and Article 8 of the European Convention of Human Rights provide the right to privacy that indicates the right against unlawful interception of the communication (Zhang and Gong, 2023). Surveillance should therefore be agreeable, necessitated and legitimate. However, it is the disparity of the standards of data protection and the issue of sovereignty that complicates international investigations.

The introduction of laws on data localization (particularly the Digital Personal Data Protection Act, 2023, in India and LGPD, in Brazil) has restrained the flow of data across borders and, therefore, has slowed the process of MLA and affected the timeliness of cybercrime investigations. Another industry, which the EU AI Act (2024) affects, is the tourism industry, as it regulates AI-based surveillance systems, such as automated border control or identity checks, and ensures that such systems are applied proportionately and transparently in the work on information. ENISA (2024) focuses on the fact that sovereignty conflicts, as well as limiting policies of localization, are also significant impediments to evidence-sharing and transnational cooperation in combating tourism related cybercrime.

3.3 Human Rights and Privacy Considerations

ICCPR and the ECHR are human rights documents, which provide the required protection when investigating cybercrimes (Bekele and Raj, 2024). The surveillance must be just and must not infringe on the rights to privacy, protection of data and secrecy of communication. However, the new AI-based profiling threats, including the abuse of facial recognition at the airport or hotel booking procedure are also bringing up the question of discrimination against certain tourist constituencies. These are the risks which demand more oversight and transparency requirements.

The OECD AI Principles (2023) also have normative guidelines regarding fairness, accountability, and non-discrimination of automated decision-making, particularly in the areas that are sensitive, including tourism and border security. The convergence of human rights and technological governance thus calls upon some tradeoff between the efficiency in cybercrime investigation and the safeguarding of the personal freedoms (Kumar et al., 2023).

3.4 Emerging Technologies: AI and Blockchain in Combating Cybercrime

As per the recent academic and policy research, AI and blockchain have been increasingly deployed to detect, prevent, and prosecute cybercrimes. There is an increase in the popularity of tourism AI-driven systems to detect anomalies, fight phishing and automate incident response. Conversely, blockchain-based forensic systems offer verifiable chains of custody that cannot be compromised and, therefore, enhance the credibility of digital evidence (Zhang and Gong, 2023).These technologies such as the Estonia blockchain-based e-Government infrastructure and the Interpol blockchain-based pilot evidence management can be considered as the practical examples which demonstrate the efficiency of these technologies in terms of data integrity assurance. However, the poor nations are unable to implement it because of cost and scale factor since the infrastructure and digital literacy involved are not developed yet (Vlastos and Patel, 2007).

Table 2. Comparative Overview of AI and Blockchain in Cybercrime Investigation

Technology	Advantages	Challenges	Notable Examples
Artificial Intelligence (AI)	Rapid anomaly detection; predictive threat modeling; automation of forensic triage	Algorithmic bias, privacy violations, high training data dependency	AI-based fraud detection in booking systems; predictive policing
Blockchain	Immutable evidence logs; transparency; traceability in digital forensics	Scalability issues, high energy cost, lack of regulatory clarity	Estonia e-Gov system; Interpol Blockchain Forensics Pilot

When these technologies are properly protected, they can make the tourism industry more resilient to cybercrimes to a significant degree, although their inconsistent performance serves as an example of the worldwide disparity in cybersecurity levels.

3.5 Research Gaps

Although human rights and uses of technology are explained as international legal means, the past studies have many gaps in research that address the sovereignty.

1. **Empirical Deficiency:** There exists no empirical research, which quantifies the loss of the economies, the price of recovering the business and the loss of the tourism demand in post-attack, particularly in developing economies.
2. **Victim-Centric Analysis:** Minimal effort will be made on the psychological implications, loss of trust and reputation loss on both tourists and small tourism enterprises.
3. **Technological Implementation:** AI and blockchain are currently in the news, and little research has investigated their practical implementation problems in low resources or low governance.
4. **Regional Underrepresentation:** The research has remained concentrated on Europe and North America with minimal amount of research being done on Africa, Latin America and South Asia regarding policy and enforcement.
5. **Policy-Practice Gap:** Due to the quality of the laws, the ability to enforce the laws tends to be low thus, creating gaps in the tourism enterprises in the economies that are dependent on the digital element.

The above gaps in knowledge indicate the significance of comparative, interdisciplinary, and regionally encompassing studies that evaluate the relationship between the law, technology, and human rights in deterring cybercrime in tourism across the world.

4. CASE STUDIES ANALYSIS

4.1 The Cross-Boundary Cyber-Crime in Tourism: The Law and the Jurisdictional Issues in the Sphere of Collecting Digital Evidence

It is a challenging job, which would need appropriate international cooperation and enforcement mechanisms of the law to carry out the investigations and prosecution of international and transnational cybercrimes. Internet space is anonymized and does not have a sufficient legal framework that would allow tracking, locating, and penalizing cybercriminals (Ghaderi, Beal, and Houanti, 2024).The discussion section of the paper details some of the landmark cases in the tourism and hospitality industry as the method of presenting the legal issues and the challenges to the jurisdiction with respect to the gathering of the digital evidence, especially in the case of the scenario in which the international clients are the perpetrators of the breach and thus subject to the other legal system.As the statistics available show, the tourism and hospitality industry has been the target of the largest ransomware attack in 2022, and hotels and airlines have been the simplest targets (Garach, Singh, N. R. R., Reddy, and Khan, 2024).

4.2 Marriott International Data Breach (2018)

The Marriott international data breach is cited as a precedent case since the case was encountered with a lot of hurdles in the form of multijurisdictional litigation and digital forensic investigations. It had already affected millions of users in the entire international community and has caused investigations in the various jurisdictions each of which has its laws about data protection and a localised system of jurisdiction. Such simultaneous research and the maintenance of integrity of digital evidence was a major challenge to be structured. The mere presence of the data and the inability to prosecute the perpetrator who conducted the attack was the primary thing that contributed to the slow qualitative process, particularly when it was about the suspicions that the actor who might have been driven by a state could be found in a safe-haven jurisdiction (Alzahrani and Alfouzan, 2022).

- **Enforcement Result**: The fines and enforcement actions provided by the GDPR were not in fact followed by the real persecution of the attackers as it proved to be inefficient and this is a sign of bad cross-border enforcement behavior.
- **The Problems of Developing Nations**: Affected users in Southeast Asia and Africa were not fixed on any alternative since none of them was buttressed by well-developed forensic infrastructure and none of the disengaged global evidence-sharing structure.
- **Lessons Learned**: The Marriott case represents a decisive analysis of the factors that cause international response to data breaches, evidence-sharing plan, and cooperation in the field of data protection across the borders to be acute and demand collaboration between other authorities.

4.3 British Airways Cyberattack (2018)

The British Airways cyberattack has proved that the issues with both the aspects of the data localization and gdpr extraterritorial applicability are not that trivial. The case has pointed out that the confusion in the law to be applied, at which the law is applied, and imposition of the penalties are made because the transmission and processing of data is associated with many jurisdictions (Bakalis, Halkiopoulos, and Antonopoulou, 2024).

The jurisdiction argument was that of nationality of victim customers, physical location of servers and territorial competence of data protection authorities. It also ascertained that the quality of cybersecurity and compliance in the British Airways were low.

Enforcement Outcome: The Information Commissioner Office (ICO) of the UK fined them 20 million pound- meaning that the regulation of the requirements of GDPR was achieved to some degree. However, the attack on the cyber-criminals was not successful in the world.

Developing Nations' Challenges: The large count of the affected customers was in the developing tourism markets in which legislation on information protection and solutions to the affected customers were feeble which is just right in the world in the area of legal safeguards.

Lessons Learned: The case has demonstrated that the application of the GDPR principles are not efficient in general and that it is required to coordinate the data protection across the borders and utilize mutual legal assistance treaties (MLATs).

4.4 MakeMyTrip and RedBus Cyberattacks

The security breaches of Indian travel websites MakeMyTrip and RedBus may be explained as the evidence of the convolution of the trans-border data traffic of the country of common law and civil law. The frequency of the theft of sensitive financial data involved in such attacks demonstrated the non-alignment of the various national privacy legislations, and the lack of coordination among law enforcement bodies due to which it is difficult to collect data effectively in the cyber-space. The common law systems are the opposite of the codified law system and inquisitorial based civil law system; they are founded on judicial precedents (Alshammari, Beach, and Rezgui, 2021).Moreover, the pivotal data was saved on the server of a foreign cloud, which complicates the process of data acquisition further, and the procedure of mutual legal assistance was sluggish and obsolete (Blazic & Klobucar, 2019).

Prosecution Conclusion: The prosecution was not so great. The enforcers of law in the developing countries like India also lacked the right technological infrastructure and knowledge base when the affected consumers sought the civil remedies.

The Problems of Developing Nations: The forensic departments lacked preparations to investigate and present the cases in the state of art equipment was not available to investigate and provide integrity to the digital evidence.

Lessons Learned: It is evident that internationalization of forensics, capacity-building projects and additional interoperability on legal systems and common law and civil law ought to prevail in the case of MakeMyTrip and RedBus.

4.5 Scandinavian Airlines (SAS) Ransomware Attack, 2023

The recent ransomware attack on the corporation of Scandinavian Airlines (SAS) delivered an apocalyptic effect on the online reservation system and mobile apps of the organization, and the consequent outcome was a manual check-in and a potential data breach in terms of the clients (Baig et al., 2017).The episode indicated that there was an organizational fault in the aviation industry regarding cybersecurity architecture and the ransomware attackers were also becoming more technologically intelligent in the tourist industry. When the attack occurred, SAS collaborated with Nordic cybersecurity agencies, Interpol and Europol through the effort of packaging the attack, besides monitoring the origin of the attack. It took 24 hours before the European Union Agency on Cybersecurity (ENISA) put its Cyber Crisis Liaison Organisation Network (CyCLONe) into practice and the information flow between the victim states was organised by the European Cybercrime Centre (EC3) of the Europol. Nonetheless, despite such prompt responses, no arrest was made and this demonstrated some laxity in enforcement of the laws.

Enforcement Result: Co-ordination EU and Interpol led to partial containment and none of the culprits were prosecute with conclusion, thus signifying that there were still restriction to prosecute ransomware by attribution and jurisdiction.

Global Implication: The attack once again reiterated the necessity of having multinational quick response mechanisms and shared ransomware intelligence databases to empower the aviation industry.

Lesson Learned: The SAS experience has demonstrated that the currently existing jurisdictions could be further connected in the process of tackling the cyber incidence or the need to spread the similar patterns of collaboration to the airlines and the travel agencies operating in the developing world.

Collectively, a combination of these cases is a pointer that cybercrime in the tourism industry is an international affair, and that the law is extremely lopsided and reactive. The accountability, however, in terms of regulatory enforcement (mainly, by GDPR regulations) has been improved, the absence of coordination between forensic standards and the rapid models of data-sharing is the cause of the inability to deliver the justice. The further direction of the policy will be founded on the international cybersecurity conventions, formation of the technical potential of the developing states, and the real-time system of collaboration of the law enforcement and control bodies of the world.sss

Table 3. Comparative of Case Studies

Case	Jurisdiction(s)	Legal Obstacles	Enforcement Outcomes	Lessons Learned
Marriott International (2018)	Multinational – U.S., EU, Asia, Africa	Fragmented data protection laws; limited cooperation; state-sponsored attribution issues	GDPR fines imposed; no successful prosecutions	Need for harmonized cross-border evidence-sharing and mutual recognition of digital forensics protocols
British Airways (2018)	U.K., EU, Global	Jurisdictional ambiguity over data processing; uneven GDPR application	£20 million ICO fine; limited global enforcement	Necessity for global uniformity in data protection enforcement and MLAT reforms
MakeMyTrip & RedBus (India)	India, Singapore, EU jurisdictions	Differing common vs civil law frameworks; weak digital forensics infrastructure	Inefficient prosecution; consumer civil suits	Urgent need for forensic capacity-building and interoperable international data exchange
Scandinavian Airlines (SAS, 2023)	Nordic States, EU	Ransomware attribution complexity; multi-agency coordination delays	Partial containment; no arrests	Strengthening multinational rapid-response mechanisms and intelligence-sharing frameworks

Together, these examples show that transnational cybercrime in tourism, and that the existing legal systems are not coherent and proactive. Although accountability has been enhanced through regulatory compliance (particularly in GDPR), the lack of harmonized forensic standards and fast data-sharing systems remain a barrier to the delivery of justice. The future policy directions must focus on global cybersecurity treaties, greater technical capacity of developing countries, and real time system of cooperation among law enforcement and regulatory bodies in the countries of the world.

5. FINDINGS AND DISCUSSIONS

The danger of cross-border cybercrime in the tourism industry is a complex and dynamic phenomenon, to which the legal and technical obstacles in expanding and processing digital evidence should be paid close attention. With online reservation systems, cross-border payment gateways, and cloud computing becoming the main tools of the tourism sector, it is turning into a highly profitable target of international offenders acting across borders. This interdependence highlights the importance of the greater international collaboration, integrated international laws and cross-national data protection efforts in a more dynamic and technologically integrated landscape (Cybersecurity and Forensics in Connected Autonomous Vehicles, 2022).

5.1 Jurisdictional Fragmentation and Forum Shopping

Jurisdictional fragmentation and forum shopping where criminals take advantage of disparities in the laws applied in various countries continue to be the biggest challenge regarding proper investigation and prosecution of cybercrime. An example is the case of a cybercriminal group that targets European tourists with phishing attacks, thus placing its servers in a country with weaker enforcement regulations and remote operation in a different country (Casino et al., 2022). These fragmented systems also allow offenders to escape the liability by using territorial constraints in the jurisdiction of national law.

The conventional concepts of territorial jurisdiction are becoming insufficient in the borderless world of the cyberspace. This is due to the fact that the international law has not been harmonised and thus the jurisdictional confusion is even compounded as to which prosecuting authority should be applied. Although the world has witnessed the spread of cybercrime laws in countries, the fact that international offenses keep prevailing shows that new international standards and legal convergence are necessary to guarantee accountability and effective delivery of justice.

5.2 Admissibility of Foreign-Collected Digital Evidence

The other significant issue is the admissibility of foreign jurisdiction digital evidence. The differences in the standards of evidence, privacy principles, and procedural protection may impair the cross-border usability and reliability of evidence. Questions of authenticity, chain of custody and procedural consistency are common problems particularly when there is conflict between search and seizure / data privacy laws of two countries. Using the example, lawful data retrieved in one country can be considered inadmissible in a different country because of more stringent privacy regulations (Dhande, 2024).

This variation compels the investigators and prosecutors to negotiate through the divided legal environments so that evidence can be admissible. The virtual cross-border generation and transfer of digital evidence is thus still weak, and it is necessary to reach international agreements on the standards of evidence collection and verification when investigating cybercrimes.

5.3 Cryptography Versus Lawful Access

Cryptography is a defensive mechanism and a wall. Although this provides privacy to the user and data confidentiality, it also limits the law enforcement access to vital evidence to law-abiding citizens. Hackers are moving towards the technological aspect of encryption to hide their criminal operations, which forces law enforcement agencies to come up with intricate methods of decryption. Nonetheless, this process creates the problem of the possible violation of privacy and freedom of speech.

This situation is even complicated by the fact that the encryption keys may rest in the possession of parties located in jurisdictions with strong privacy regulations or are simply reluctant to cooperate on a legal basis (Erdem & Seker, 2021). It is therefore important that a thin line in maintaining a balance between good policing and individual privacy is established based on international legal and ethical guidelines.

5.4 Procedural Delays in Mutual Legal Assistance Treaties (MLATs)

Mutual Legal Assistance Treaties (MLATs) play a key role in supporting cross-border cooperation although they are still marred by the long procedural delays. Evidence requests could include months or years to be processed, and in the meantime, essential digital evidence can be distorted or erased. The delays are also multiplied by bureaucratic inefficiency, legal loop-holes and language barriers.

To improve efficiency, reforms were suggested, including the creation of fast-track systems to add cases of cybercrime urgently, a standardized evidence request form, and cloud-based evidence-sharing systems to enable the exchange of data under judicial supervision (Dalal and Juneja, 2020). The use of these models would enable the process of investigation to be simplified by several notches and the enforcement of global cybercrime will be achieved.

5.5 Conflicts Between Data Protection and Criminal Investigation Needs

The cross-border cyber crimes usually pose a conflict between the data protection requirements and the law enforcement requirements. Tough data protection systems limit the processing, transferring, and localization of the data, thus hampering prompt access to information in terms of the investigation, particularly that which relates to foreign tourists or individuals under protection.

This conflict has to be resolved by balancing between the right to privacy and the demands of criminal justice. Such balance should be based on the principle of proportionality, necessity, and legitimate purpose, which are the cornerstones of the international data protection law. By ensuring that conflicts are reduced and that their cooperation processes are transparent, states will be able to ensure privacy protection and its enforcement at the same time (Mohamed, Al-Jaroodi, and Jawhar, 2020).

5.6 Ethical Issues in Surveillance and Profiling

The emergence of the AI-driven surveillance and profiling systems to counter cybercrime opens up deep ethical and legal quandaries. Automated data analysis may result in discriminatory practices, privacy violations and chilling consequences to freedom of expression and movement. The tools pose the threat of strengthening stereotypes, excessive surveillance and de-individualization of the tourism industry.

The restriction of privacy or expression by any state as provided under the international human rights law and especially the International Covenant on Civil and Political Rights (ICCPR) has to be reasonable, legal, and proportional. The principle of the territorial sovereignty can also be violated due to unauthorised cross-border access to data (Herke, Tóth, & Perkumienė, 2025). Consequently, AI-driven surveillance solutions should work within open, responsible, and rights-compliant practices, which means that individuals should be allowed to know, object, and rectify data feeding off profiling. By integrating these moral principles into the governance of AI, it will make cybercrime prevention comply with the basic human rights.

5.7 Economic and Psychological Impacts of Cybercrime

Other than legal and technical impact, cybercrime has strong economic and psychological costs on tourism sector. A cyberattack on travel agencies, booking sites, and airlines may lead to the massive cancellation of bookings, loss of reputation, and financial instability. This loss of consumer confidence can easily turn into the loss of bookings, higher insurance rates, and working interruptions. In a 2023 study by the World Travel and Tourism Council (WTTC), global tourism enterprises incur losses of billions of dollars every year as a result of cyber attacks, especially phishing attacks that have been brought about by AI and breaches of data stored in travel apps.

Human aspect is also of paramount importance. Workers who experience frequent cyberattacks are anxious and stressed, lack productivity, and it hurts the morale of employees and the quality of customer service. The article by Chatterjee and Singh (2024) emphasizes the fact that the vulnerability of remote work, which has been advanced by the lack of cybersecurity awareness, exposes organizations and individuals to ransomware and credential theft, which consume financial resources, which otherwise could be directed to support sustainable tourism events. All these tendencies remind of the fact that cybersecurity resiliency is not just a requirement under the law but an economic necessity to ensure stability in the industry in the long term.

6. CROSS-BORDER CYBERCRIME IN TOURISM: LEGAL AND JURISDICTIONAL CHALLENGES IN DIGITAL EVIDENCE COLLECTION

The increasing rates of cross-border cybercrimes against the tourism industry reveal the dire necessity to harmonize forensic technologies, the legal framework, and jurisdictional systems to be able to collect digital evidence. Handling, storage, and use of electronic evidence should be done on the basis of international legal standards to be admissible and accountable (Sarfraz, Khawaja, Han, Ariza-Montes, and Arjona-Fuentes, 2023). The disruptive potential of blockchain and zero-knowledge proofs, the need to cross-border interoperability of forensic tools, and the dangers related to non-standardisation are all indicative of the role of cross-sectoral governance. This type of governance will help in ensuring that the legal and forensic systems will adapt to the challenges of global cybercrime.

6.1 Blockchain and Zero-Knowledge Proofs in Digital Forensics

Blockchain and zero-knowledge (ZK) proofs are becoming revolutionary in digital forensics, bringing its opportunities and challenges. The blockchain also enhances the chain of custody, as every interaction is documented with evidence since its collection to the courtroom (Thayananthan, Qasem, Qureshi, and Qureshi, 2024). This characteristic is vital since the digital evidence can be duplicated or moved across jurisdiction easily. Forensic inventories based on blockchain generate audit trails that are unchangeable and that strengthen trust and accountability.

Practical applications also confirm this way. An example of this is the Estonian e-Government basing their public records on blockchain to have transparency and resistance to tampering, and INTERPOL has piloted blockchain-based solutions as a means of improving global confidence in digital evidence management. Equally, E-Evidence Digital Exchange System is an initiative by the European Union that incorporates blockchain into its workflow to facilitate the exchange of evidence between member states in a secure manner. Nevertheless, with all these promising applications, there are still scalability, interoperability, and high implementation costs, especially to the developing countries. Zero-knowledge proofs are privacy-preserving validation, meaning that it allows the investigator to verify the integrity of evidence without exposing sensitive content (Sinno, 2019). However, the usage of blockchain-based evidence does not have any international rules, which makes it hard to use in transnational cases. Therefore, blockchain and ZK proofs utilities must be extended to an international regulatory framework that provides both technological development and forensic reliability and legal balance.

6.2 Interoperability of Digital Forensic Tools

Digital forensic tools need to be interoperable to be useful in cross-border investigations of cybercrimes. Currently, forensic tools vary in terms of their data formats, design and validation criteria resulting to inefficiencies and threats of data corruption. These gaps can be closed by adopting open-source tools, standard data formats, and shared APIs, which may increase the credibility and efficiency (Herke, Tóth, and Perkumienė, 2025). This is especially high in the developing economies where resources are limited and reliance on old proprietary technologies hamper investigative powers.

To curb such gaps, regional digital forensic training and resource centres need to be realized- like those in Africa, ASEAN and Latin America, which are geared to support capacity building, technical training and interoperability of the tools. Such centres will be able to uniform the methodological approaches to investigations and enhance regional collaboration. Interestingly, associations like UNODC and INTERPOL have also initiated digital forensic training programs in 2023 to increase harmonisation, as well as improve share of information securely among member nations. It is also essential to have cultural and procedural training to overcome language and jurisdictional barriers and promote international mutual legal assistance. Interoperability, thus, has to be tackled not only as a technological challenge but also as an integrated legal and institutional platform that can guarantee interoperativeness of forensic practices.

6.3 Standardisation Gaps in Digital Forensics

Lack of international consensus in digital forensics still remains a bane on the admissibility as well as reliability of the evidence in cross-border cybercrimes. The differences in the forensic methods, the validation of instruments used and the qualifications of examiners can lead to poor or erroneous results. Although other standards like ISO/IEC 27037 (evidence handling) and ISO/IEC 27042 (analysis and interpretation), as well as the guidelines on digital evidence validation and mobile device forensics provided by NIST (2020 revision), have a major impact on standardization (Nithyasree et al., 2025), they are not involved in every jurisdiction yet. In even single states, there is selective enforcement and this results in the lack of credibility in digital investigations.

In order to overcome these irregularities, more stringent global enforcing structures of ISO/IEC standards are urgently needed. Also, the creation of a standardized international forensic certification system would help to set the levels of global competency of digital forensic practitioners and provide evidence integrity and procedural justness. This structure would facilitate the recognition of forensic procedures and help increase cross-border cooperation and achieve a more just judicial process in cases related to cybercrimes.

6.4 Cross-Sectoral Technology Governance

Technology governance across sectors is needed to effectively address legal, ethical and procedural complexities of cross-border cybercrimes. Governments, the private sector, academia, and civil societies need to together develop adaptive non-technological regulation systems that are balanced in terms of both innovation and protection of rights. Because of the sensitivity and a high risk of manipulation, digital evidence requires high-level protection on the international level and coordinated measures of governance.The recent worldwide efforts offer a basis of such collaboration. The UN Office on Drugs and Crime (UNODC) still advances international best practices of digital evidence management whereas the International Telecommunication Union (ITU) with its report Global Cybersecurity Index (GCI) 2024 focuses on the significance of coordinated responses to transnational threats. Similarly, the UN World Tourism Organization (UNWTO) Cybersecurity Guidelines (2023) provide industry-specific approaches to data protection and cyber resilience in the tourism-related digital infrastructures. Understanding digital forensics by incorporating these international frameworks in the laws of the countries or region can contribute to the transparency, accountability, and trust.

When based on the multi-stakeholder participation, cross-sectoral governance guarantees the effectiveness and legitimacy of cybercrime responses. With the implementation of the views of the governments, industry players, academia, and civil society, regulatory frameworks will be dynamic and able to keep up with the changes in technology. This type of cooperation supports not only investigative capabilities but also builds trust in the community, which encourages dynamic and strong capabilities in the global digital economy (Tariq, 2024; Santarsiero, Carlucci, Lerro, and Schiuma, 2024).

7. CBT IN TRAVEL TOURISM: FINDINGS, RECOMMENDATIONS AND PROPOSALS TO LEGAL AND JURISDICTION CONCERNS OF GATHERING OF EVIDENCE IN CYBERCRIME

7.1 Key Findings and Policy Gaps

The international reaction of international crime in tourism sector is a sign that there is a complicated connection between technology, ambiguous laws and geographic segments. An overview of both the doctrinal analysis and comparative legal study and the case review indicates that there are certain critical findings. Lack of systematic and harmonized regulation is one of the brightest issues as existing laws are different in various jurisdictions and do not help to create transnational cooperation. This is further compounded by the fact that the cumbersome and resource intensive processes on the cross-border legal assistance cannot keep up with the pace and sophistication of the cybercriminals, that is, the Mutual Legal Assistance Treaties (MLATs) (Broadhurst, 2006).

Tourism industry being an easy target of cyber criminals due to the volume of personal information required by the system in terms of billing information and identification documentation to travel patterns and schedules. This creates a significant policy-practice gap since the available instruments and rules are unable to follow the shifting and fast-evolving digital ecosystem (Cheng, Xue, Yang, and Ma, 2023). The decentralized and non-standardized collection of electronic evidence is also not helpful in winning cybercrime cases. In the third world, particularly, capacity, in the shape of high-tech digital forensics labs, experienced investigators, and organization willingness to grow digital collaboration over national frontiers, is wanting. The imbalance in this enables cybercriminals to leverage on weak ties within the international system and threaten the regional and international security operations (Bekele and Raj, 2024).Moreover, the fact that the tourism industry is experiencing high rates of data breaches has also resulted in enormous mistrust among the consumers, which is psychologically distressing, feeling vulnerable, and less eager to utilize online bookings or online tourism services. The social cost of cyber insecurity is greater as the emotional burden of identity theft and loss of finances may be very stressful.In order to contain these imbalances, the urgent correction is to invest in the public-private partnership (PPP) on capacity-building, exchange of threat intelligence and speedy responsive platforms. PPP can be used to combine the governments, tourism enterprises, and cybersecurity firms, so that they are more resilient with the training programs, crisis coordination centers, as well as the networks of real-time information exchange.

7.2 Evidence Standard and Legal Definitions Harmonization

Legal harmonization, technological development, and strengthened multilateral cooperation are the ways of addressing various critical concerns (Bilgili and Koc, 2021). There is a need to align definitions of cybercrime and digital evidence that could be considered in the tourism framework. Such types of crimes as online identity theft, fraud, and data theft, and postulates of admissibility of electronic evidence ought to be integrated into universally recognized principles (Bucaj & Idrizaj, 2024).The international agencies are supposed to adhere and apply the standard international models (e.g., ISO/IEC 27037 (Guidelines for Digital Evidence Handling), ISO/IEC

27042 (Analysis and Interpretation of Digital Evidence), and NIST 2020 guidelines on digital forensics) to be standardized. These standards can be incorporated into the legal framework of the countries to prevent the usage of the broken pieces of legislations and raise the level of interoperability of the processes of digital evidence.

Online evidences would help in streamlining the process of data sharing and curb bureaucratic time wastage and promote safe communication between the law enforcement agencies which are in a specific region like tourism cases. Law, maintenance of evidence, and forensic integrity should also be included in educating the ICT staff as first responders in the event of cybersecurity attack.In the case of the revised MLAT paradigms, new treaties should include an electronic evidence provision specification and provide the possibility of safe and encrypted transfer. Blockchain-based chain-of-custody systems remain a potential method of offering the guarantees of authenticity, traceability, and non-repudiation of evidence. Correspondingly, AI-assisted verification systems can automatize the evidence validation and authentication in the cross-border cases, and in such a manner accelerate admissibility appraisals.

Predictive AI can be used in future to help law enforcement and tour operators by detecting abnormalities in their behavior and preventing hacking (Grabosky, 2007). Since the advent of quantum computing, quantum-resistant encryption will become a crucial part of protection of sensitive financial and traveling information. The online booking and online travel documentation schemes can also minimize the instances of identity fraud cases in the digital identity verification schemes that can enhance the security between the consumers and service providers as they can be used interchangeably.

7.3 Balancing Data Protection With Investigative Needs

The strike between the requirements of data protection and investigation must possess a balance that is proportionate, transparent, and checks by the judiciary. Even though the privacy laws do not always prohibit the process of gathering information by justifiable investigations, the actions that have to be undertaken should be adequately checked up by the court and equalized by the extent of the crime (Florido-Benitez, 2025).In the recent international documents, including the EU AI act (2024) and the OECD AI Principles on Trustworthy and Responsible AI, we can infer accountability, transparency, and human rights in the use of AI-based tools of investigation. These are the standards that will be included in the digital forensics to ensure that the automated systems promote the privacy and procedural fairness.

In order to legally deal with evidence, law enforcement agencies must be specifically trained in the field of digital forensics, international law and data governance.

Simultaneously, the following best practices are the ones that should be adopted in the tourism industry:

- Audits of cybersecurity risk are to be conducted periodically;
- Introduce data reducing and purpose-limiting policies;
- Establish incident response facilities to contain and report fast;
- Set up phishing and social engineering training to workers;
- Improve the relationships between the government and industry with the use of intelligence sharing in order to react to the crisis in a coordinated way.

In addition, the ability to balance the privacy-protective mechanisms and to offer an opportunity to assess the effectiveness of law enforcement investigations is mentioned in the best-practice report created by ENISA (2024). Human rights protection provisions, judicial checks and balances, and victim-centered rehabilitation systems ought to be ensured that investigative systems are established by the policymakers.Victims recovery mechanisms should also be implemented to recover the lost confidence in the digital tourism ecosystems by treating them through psychological counseling, restoring their digital identities, and compensating them once again through national cybersecurity strategies.

Finally, it is necessary to train on a regional and international level paying much attention to technical support, international training and knowledge sharing. Through consumer confidence through provision of safe systems, balanced laws and ethical innovation, the tourism sector will manage to go through the digital era sustainably (Kumar, Kumar, Bhatt, Kumar, & Attri, 2023).

Figure 1. Proposed Model for Harmonized cross-border digital evidence collection in tourism-related cybercrime cases

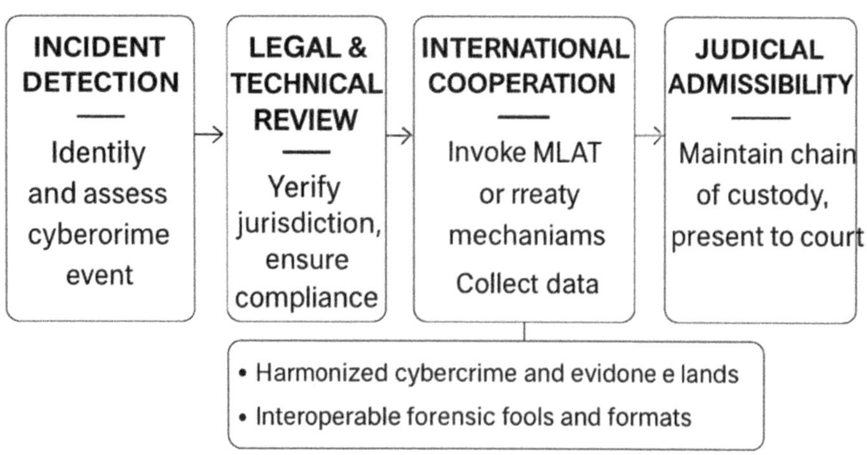

Figure 1 the rational structure will help in the harmonized gathering, transmission and admissibility of digital evidence across the boundaries in case of cybercrime situation in the tourist sector. The model provides the most crucial procedural steps that include the notification of the incident and identification of the digital information, verification of the jurisdiction, the mandatory forensic processing and rules of regional evidence transfer, including fast-track MLATs or bilateral solutions. It gives priority to interoperable forensic tools and blockchain-based chain-of-custody mechanism to provide integrity, traceability and cause digital evidence to be admissible in a legal environment. Moreover, the model also introduces the necessary legal interventions such as the conformity of data protection, proportionality checks and judicial checks on all levels.

8. CONCLUSION AND SUGGESTIONS FOR FUTURE RESEARCH

8.1 Industry-Particular Cybercrime Prevention Strategies

To sum up, the study has contributed to the realization of the problem of transnational cybercrime impacting the tourism industry and, in particular, the failure of the legal system as one of the major barriers to successful cross-border collaboration and evidence collection. Incoherent legal frameworks and the variability in both the interpretation of the law and legal protection of data are secure frames of cybercriminals, irrespective of nationality (Schapel, 2013). The cross-border nature of cybercrime as was revealed is starkly contrasted with the territorial scope of national legislation and it is hence quite evident that there is a dire need of a paradigm shift in which collaborative and standardized strategies are employed (Khan et al., 2022).

Namely, the cross-border tourism cybercrime cases have been identified to have digital evidence challenges associated with the lack of disparity in admissibility, privacy protection, and the long mutual legal assistance process. In the meantime, the nature of cyberattacks against the tourism industry is getting more advanced, with the census of breaches of personal information that results in the loss of sensitive data, and ransomware attacks that adversely affect essential infrastructure. Being a highly interconnected and data-intensive industry, thus, the tourism industry needs an industry-specific approach. Cybersecurity measures, incident management systems, and employee training should be implemented to manage sector risk (Holt, Bossler, and Seigfried-Spellar, 2022).Moreover, the long-term level of resilience suggests the establishment of the public-privatization relations between the stakeholders of the tourism industry, cybersecurity professionals, and police forces. In addition to enhancing technical defenses, these alliances would assist in instilling a proactive culture of cybersecurity and establishing trust in the industry. Moreover, tourism operator, small travel firms and hospitality professionals should be trained on cyber hygiene, evidence preservation, and reporting systems to maintain readiness to deal with emerging digital threats.

8.2 Empirical Research and Victim-Centered Approach

The further development of the research must be more victim-oriented and pay attention to the economic and psychological harm of cyberattacks on individuals and companies. The existing information gaps, including the absence of precise data on financial losses, reputational harm, and individual experience on the part of victims are disruptive to evidence-based policymaking. Policies without considerable empirical research will be inclined to ignore the human aspect of cybercrime that may entail worry, consumer mistrust, and protracted mindful strain (Vlastos and Patel, 2007).

The sector of tourism is one of the most active ones which is especially susceptible towards disastrous cyberattacks. In the case of 2018 data breach of Marriott International, the largest hotel, the loss of consumer trust and brand credibility was measurable, and the case of British Airways breach in 2019 caused legal actions and customer backlash because of inadequate data protection measures. Likewise, the cases of the online travel services such as MakeMyTrip demonstrate that the level of consumer confidence is tenuous and thus the improvement of the industry in the future is possible through the combination of both the quantitative (statistical analysis and econometric modeling of the direct and indirect cost) and qualitative (amplifying the voices of the victims) methods. Interviews and survey of tourists, travel agencies, and hospitality operators may yield meaningful information on behavioral reactions, coping and perceptions of digital safety. Such a twofold approach would guarantee that the results of the further research are not entirely motivated by economic considerations but also consider the human health, emotional rehabilitation, and reinstatement of the digital trust (Barykin et al., 2021).

8.3 Technologies That Will be Created and Legal Issues

Technological innovation will not only increase threats in the future, but will equally offer suitable countermeasures to online tourism-related cybercrime. Deviations in network traffic can be detected with the help of Artificial Intelligence (AI) and phishing attacks can also be identified, and the process of incident response can be automated, and booking and payment systems can be secure and tamper-proof with the help of Blockchain technologies (Al-Khateeb, Epiphaniou, and Daly, 2019). Together, these technologies will be able to minimize the weakness of the over-digitized tourism sector.Simultaneously, emerging issues, like post-quantum cryptography or the international discourse of digital sovereignty and data localization creates new legal and ethical issues, which require anticipatory regulation. In addition, quantum-resistant encryption techniques must be introduced in the initial planning to reduce the threat to sensitive tourism information in the future and the AI regulation models should be developed into transparent, accountable, and rights-based regulation.Moreover, the current negotiations on the United Nations Cybercrime Treaty (A/RES/75/282) indicate a significant step to harmonized international legal regimes of cybercrime prosecution and sharing of digital evidence. Parallely, the adoption of fast-track Mutual Legal Assistance Treaties (MLATs), cloud evidence deals, and regional cyber incident response frameworks will be very useful in supporting cross-border collaboration.

The importance of the balance between the need to protect privacy and the necessity to enforce the law is also highlighted in the European Union Agency of Cybersecurity (ENISA) 2024 best-practice report, which specifically applies to the data-intensive tourism industry ecosystem. Finally, future research ought to pursue collaboration with technological solutions and cross-border legal frameworks in the future, so that long-term harm caused by cybersecurity in the tourism sector would be addressed not only reactively to the risks but also proactively addressed with the help of collaborative, rights-based, and technology-enabled approaches.

REFERENCES

Al-Khateeb, H., Epiphaniou, G., & Daly, H. (2019). Blockchain for Modern Digital Forensics: The Chain-of-Custody as a distributed ledger. In *Advanced sciences and technologies for security applications* (pp. 149–168). DOI: 10.1007/978-3-030-11289-9_7

Alshammari, K., Beach, T., & Rezgui, Y. (2021). Cybersecurity for digital twins in the built environment: Current research and future directions. *Journal of Information Technology in Construction, 26*, 159–173. DOI: 10.36680/j.itcon.2021.010

Alzahrani, N. M., & Alfouzan, F. A. (2022). Augmented Reality (AR) and Cyber-Security for Smart Cities—A Systematic Literature Review. *Sensors (Basel), 22*(7), 2792. DOI: 10.3390/s22072792 PMID: 35408406

Baig, Z. A., Szewczyk, P., Valli, C., Rabadia, P., Hannay, P., Chernyshev, M., Johnstone, M., Kerai, P., Ibrahim, A., Sansurooah, K., Syed, N., & Peacock, M. (2017). Future challenges for smart cities: Cyber-security and digital forensics. *Digital Investigation, 22*, 3–13. DOI: 10.1016/j.diin.2017.06.015

Bakalis, A., Halkiopoulos, C., & Antonopoulou, H. (2024). The Digital Transformation of tourism. Case study of Greek tourism. In *Springer proceedings in business and economics* (pp. 121–157). DOI: 10.1007/978-3-031-54338-8_9

Barykin, S. E., De La Poza, E., Khalid, B., Kapustina, I. V., Kalinina, O. V., & Iqbal, K. M. J. (2021). Tourism industry. In *Advances in educational technologies and instructional design book series* (pp. 414–434). DOI: 10.4018/978-1-7998-8327-2.ch025

Bekele, H., & Raj, S. (2024). Digitalization and digital transformation in the tourism industry: A bibliometric review and research agenda. *Tourism Review*. Advance online publication. DOI: 10.1108/TR-07-2023-0509

Bilgili, B., & Koc, E. (2021). Digital transformation in tourism. In *Routledge eBooks* (pp. 53–65). DOI: 10.4324/9781003105930-5

Broadhurst, R. (2006). Developments in the global law enforcement of cyber-crime. *Policing, 29*(3), 408–433. DOI: 10.1108/13639510610684674

Buçaj, E., & Idrizaj, K. (2024). The need for cybercrime regulation on a global scale by the international law and cyber convention. *Multidisciplinary Reviews, 8*(1), 2025024. DOI: 10.31893/multirev.2025024

Casino, F., Pina, C., López-Aguilar, P., Batista, E., Solanas, A., & Patsakis, C. (2022). SoK: Cross-border criminal investigations and digital evidence. *Journal of Cybersecurity*, *8*(1), tyac014. Advance online publication. DOI: 10.1093/cybsec/tyac014

Cheng, X., Xue, T., Yang, B., & Ma, B. (2023). A digital transformation approach in hospitality and tourism research. *International Journal of Contemporary Hospitality Management*, *35*(8), 2944–2967. DOI: 10.1108/IJCHM-06-2022-0679

Dalal, M., & Juneja, M. (2020). Steganography and Steganalysis (in digital forensics): A Cybersecurity guide. *Multimedia Tools and Applications*, *80*(4), 5723–5771. DOI: 10.1007/s11042-020-09929-9

Dhande, K. R. (2024). Fourth Industrial Revolution and the role of cyber security. In *Advances in hospitality, tourism and the services industry (AHTSI) book series* (pp. 241–257). DOI: 10.4018/979-8-3693-2715-9.ch013

Erdem, A., & Şeker, F. (2021). Tourist experience and digital transformation. In *Advances in hospitality, tourism and the services industry (AHTSI) book series* (pp. 103–120). DOI: 10.4018/978-1-7998-8528-3.ch006

Florido-Benítez, L. (2025). The role of cybersecurity as a preventive measure in digital tourism and travel: A systematic literature review. *Deleted Journal*, *28*(1), 28. Advance online publication. DOI: 10.1007/s10791-025-09523-3

Garach, J., Singh, S. K., N, R. R., Reddy, A. P. C., & Khan, H. (2024). A comprehensive review on artificial intelligence in digital forensics with taxonomies, issues, and solutions. *Advances in Web Technologies and Engineering Book Series*, 1–28. DOI: 10.4018/979-8-3693-6557-1.ch001

Ghaderi, Z., Beal, L., & Houanti, L. (2024). Cybersecurity threats in tourism and hospitality: Perspectives from tourists engaging with sharing economy services. *Current Issues in Tourism*, •••, 1–16. DOI: 10.1080/13683500.2024.2353327

Grabosky, P. (2007). Requirements of prosecution services to deal with cyber crime. *Crime, Law, and Social Change*, *47*(4–5), 201–223. DOI: 10.1007/s10611-007-9069-1

Herke, C., Tóth, D., & Perkumienė, D. (2025). The role of artificial intelligence in cybercrime in the tourism sector. In *World sustainability series* (pp. 415–433). DOI: 10.1007/978-3-031-81485-3_17

Holt, T. J., Bossler, A. M., & Seigfried-Spellar, K. C. (2022). *Cybercrime and digital forensics*. DOI: 10.4324/9780429343223

Kasper, A., & Laurits, E. (2016). Challenges in collecting Digital Evidence: A Legal perspective. In *Springer eBooks* (pp. 195–233). DOI: 10.1007/978-3-319-26896-5_10

Khan, A. A., Shaikh, A. A., Laghari, A. A., Dootio, M. A., Rind, M. M., & Awan, S. A. (2022). Digital forensics and cyber forensics investigation: Security challenges, limitations, open issues, and future direction. *International Journal of Electronic Security and Digital Forensics*, *14*(2), 124. DOI: 10.1504/IJESDF.2022.121174

Kumar, S., Kumar, V., Bhatt, I. K., Kumar, S., & Attri, K. (2023). Digital transformation in tourism sector: Trends and future perspectives from a bibliometric-content analysis. *Journal of Hospitality and Tourism Insights*, *7*(3), 1553–1576. DOI: 10.1108/JHTI-10-2022-0472

Mohamed, N., Al-Jaroodi, J., & Jawhar, I. (2020). Cyber–Physical Systems Forensics: Today and tomorrow. *Journal of Sensor and Actuator Networks*, *9*(3), 37. DOI: 10.3390/jsan9030037

Nithyasree, N., Kumaraguru, V., Hariharan, T., Balaji, S., Harris, M., & Selvam, A. V. (2025). Unified Digital Forensic Toolkit (UDFT): Streamlining Digital investigation. In *Algorithms for intelligent systems* (pp. 367–385). DOI: 10.1007/978-981-96-5265-5_28

Pumaleque, A. P., Fernandez, I. R., Perez, D. D. I., & Bedriñana, M. A. (2021). *Digital transformation model for the development of tourism companies*. Dialnet. https://dialnet.unirioja.es/servlet/articulo?codigo=7701789

Santarsiero, F., Carlucci, D., Lerro, A., & Schiuma, G. (2024). Navigating digital transformation and business model innovation in the tourism sector: Challenges opportunities, and leadership styles. *Measuring Business Excellence*, *28*(3/4), 426–438. Advance online publication. DOI: 10.1108/MBE-09-2023-0137

Sarfraz, M., Khawaja, K. F., Han, H., Ariza-Montes, A., & Arjona-Fuentes, J. M. (2023). Sustainable supply chain, digital transformation, and blockchain technology adoption in the tourism sector. *Humanities & Social Sciences Communications*, *10*(1), 557. Advance online publication. DOI: 10.1057/s41599-023-02051-9

Schapel, H. (2013). The new approach to the new approach: The juridification of harmonized standards in EU law. *Maastricht Journal of European and Comparative Law*, *20*(4), 521–533. DOI: 10.1177/1023263X1302000404

Sinno, N. (2019). The effect of digital transformation on innovation and entrepreneurship in the tourism sector: the case of Lebanese tourism services providers. In *Lecture notes in business information processing* (pp. 29–39). DOI: 10.1007/978-3-030-30874-2_3

Tariq, M. U. (2024). Cybersecurity risk assessment models and theories in the travel and tourism industry. In *Advances in hospitality, tourism and the services industry (AHTSI) book series* (pp. 1–17). DOI: 10.4018/979-8-3693-2715-9.ch001

Thayananthan, V., Qasem, M., Qureshi, M. S., & Qureshi, M. B. (2024). Security management of autonomous transportation services in the tourism industry. In *Lecture notes in networks and systems* (pp. 53–67). DOI: 10.1007/978-981-97-3973-8_4

Vlastos, E., & Patel, A. (2007). An open source forensic tool to visualize digital evidence. *Computer Standards & Interfaces*, *30*(1–2), 8–19. DOI: 10.1016/j.csi.2007.03.003

Zhang, H., & Gong, X. (2023). The research on an electronic evidence forensic system for cross-border cybercrime. *The International Journal of Evidence & Proof*, *28*(1), 21–44. DOI: 10.1177/13657127231187059

Chapter 3
Cybercrime Investigations and Forensic Readiness in Tourism Ecosystems:
Challenges and Future Pathways

Zokir Mamadiyarov
Termez University of Economics and Service, Termez, Uzbekistan

R. N. Ravikumar
http://orcid.org/0009-0009-3705-1681
Marwadi University, Rajkot, India

S. Aarthi
http://orcid.org/0009-0006-9064-2091
Marwadi University, Rajkot, India

ABSTRACT

Tourism Ecosystems are increasingly becoming more digital, thereby enhancing efficiency and customer experiences, and have also made the industry vulnerable to various complicated cyberattacks, such as phishing, ransomware, identity theft, and payment fraud. The chapter discusses how digital forensics can be used to investigate and mitigate the risks associated with cyber threats, while also ensuring the integrity of evidence and compliance with regulations. It presents case study responses to forensics and lessons to organizational preparedness through case studies of hotel and airline breaches. New technologies, including AI, blockchain, and IoT-related forensic models, are presented and recommendations grounded in practice are given. Cybersecurity strategies can be improved by focusing on forensic preparedness, helping tourism organizations become more resilient, maintain customer trust, and ensure safe digital operations in a highly connected world.

DOI: 10.4018/979-8-3373-5826-0.ch003

1. INTRODUCTION

The shift to digital is rapidly influencing tourism with online booking, mobile applications, Internet of Things services, and integrated aviation-hospitality services. Although the innovations make the life of customers easier and also streamline operations, they also put tourism ecosystems in the danger of major cyber threats. Both travelers and service providers become more targeted by phishing, ransomware, financial fraud and massive data breaches. Digital forensics in this regard has become an important field to explore, detect and manage such threats. Through the use of the forensic tools and processes, organizations are able to maintain evidence, trace the origins of attacks, and develop resilience towards future attacks. In this chapter, the author focuses on digital forensics in the cybercrime investigation field in the tourism industry, including practical applications, case studies, and regulatory aspects of designing cyber-resilient tourism systems (Grobler & Louwrens, 2007).

1.1. Role of IOT and Smart Tourism in Cybercrime Investigations

Smart tourism, which involves the integration of the IoT devices of smart keycards, smart check-in kiosks, connected transport, and wearable travel directions, has augmented the opportunities and threats. They are interconnected machines that generate big waves of data that assailants can use to spy, steal them, or disruption. In this regard, digital forensics will entail the gathering of evidence using sensors, access logs and patterns of communication between devices in order to recreate attack situations (A. Kumar & Raina, 2025). Dedicated forensic tools are used to detect the weaknesses of IoT protocols, e.g. weak authentication or unencrypted data transfers. The challenges encountered by the investigators include the heterogeneity of devices, low storage area, and unstable evidence, and they need to acquire evidence quickly. Smart tourism system forensics will also be useful in tracking botnet attacks or ransomware attacks on city-wide tourism infrastructure (Dhande, 2024). With the expanding use of IoT, forensic preparedness to support digitally connected tourism experiences is necessary to offer reliability and trust of the visitors. The figure 1 explains how the IoT devices, the risks of cybercrime related to them, the challenges encountered by forensic investigations, and preparedness is involved in the investigation of smart tourism ecosystem.

Figure 1. IoT and Smart Tourism in Cybercrime Investigations

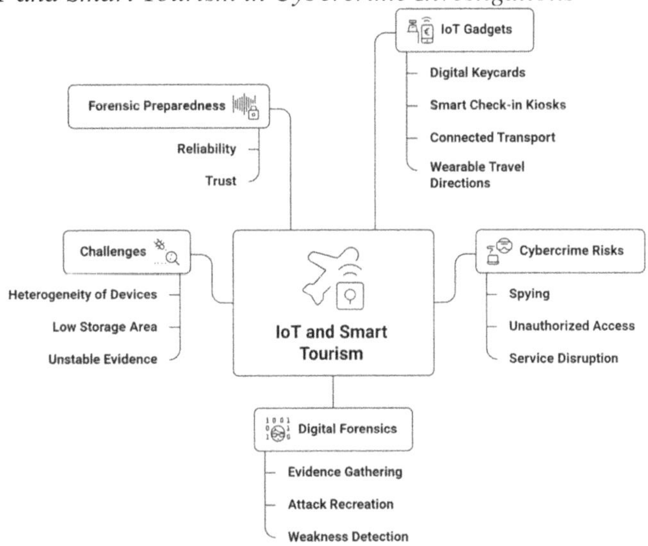

1.2 Background of Digital Transformation in Tourism

The digital transformation of the tourism sector has occurred in a dramatic way over the last twenty years, with online booking engines, mobile apps, online payment systems, and services powered by IoT being the major drivers of the change. Customers are becoming more dependent on integrated services to book flights, stay in hotels and guided tours, and companies are using big data analytics to streamline services (Abd El-Maksoud, 2024). The introduction of some new technologies (VR tours, AI chatbots, and blockchain-based customer loyalty programs) can only increase customer interaction. Smart tourism destinations are tourism destinations that incorporate sensors, cloud computing and transport network to control traffic and performance of visitors. This has transformed the customer experience into a highly networked and unbroken virtual experience. Since it has enabled people to live more comfortably and connect all parts of the world, all the dependencies on digital infrastructures have also provided grounds to insecurity and security threats that need to be addressed with more aggressive investigation and protection technologies.

1.3 Cybersecurity Challenges in Tourism Ecosystems

Digitalization of the tourism industry has brought business companies with unmatched and emergent cyber threats. Cybercriminals target hotel booking engines, online travel agencies and aviation network as the optimal targets due to voluminous stores of financial and identity sensitive data. The most common risks include phishing attack on the tourists, ransomware attacks that render the booking platform useless, and massive hacking that leaks millions of data. Lack of proper authentication and encryption of data communications poses additional risks to the IoT-based services such as smart hotel rooms, automated check-in, etc. The security governance is further complicated by distributed cloud storage and interaction with third-party vendors that allows insider abuse and attacks on the supply chain. Besides this, the sector would be unskilled in cybersecurity that would be more reactive than proactive in responding to incidences. Such obstacles indicate that the need to develop successful cybersecurity measures through the assistance of effective forensic tools to research violations and be more resilient (Daniel & Victor, 2024).

1.4 Importance of Digital Forensics in Cybercrime Investigation

A systemic manner of identification, analysis, and alleviation of the cybercrimes in the tourist systems is offered in digital forensics. With the help of collection and retention, digital evidence will allow the investigators to track the routes of attacks, restore the lost information, and take individuals to justice. The forensic methods of determining how the systems have been breached and thwarting the subsequent attacks methodically are the forensic analysis, memory capture and malware reverse engineering. Behavioral forensics is a crucial player of recreating behavior based on user tracks of the incidences of insider misuse or rogue transactions. It is also remarkable that forensic preparedness helps to make the evidence admissible during the legal procedure, and it, therefore, should be consistent with the regulations, including GDPR and data protection legislation. Besides incident response, digital forensics enhances knowledge within the organization as investigations are converted to proactive risk management strategies. Its integration in the tourism sector is necessary in safeguarding customer trust, brand reputation and providing continuation of smooth digital experiences (Kamal et al., 2022).

1.5 Objectives

The following chapter will focus on the increasing importance of the field of digital forensics in providing safety of tourism ecosystems in the context of various cyber threats. With the high level of adoption of online platforms, there is a sense of urgency to integrate investigational procedures, regulatory standards, and proactive measures to cybercrime within the tourism sector. The objectives will aim at steering the discussion in the direction of application and practical aspects, case-based learning and futuristic recommendations on the industry.

- To examine how digital forensics can be used to deal with cyber threats that are a specific feature of tourism and hospitality platforms.
- To locate the key points of vulnerability in online booking systems, IoT-enabled services, and in aviation networks.
- To investigate real-life case analyses of cyberattacks in the tourism industry and the forensic mitigation strategies used.
- To determine the effects of legal, ethical, and regulatory conditions on forensic investigations.
- To recommend practical forensic-driven solutions for enhancing cybersecurity resilience in tourism ecosystems.

2. LITERATURE REVIEW

The growing involvement of the digital channels in the tourism sector has also contributed greatly towards the research interest in the nexus of cybersecurity, digital forensics and resilience in the industry. The interconnectivity is one of the defining features of the sector, consisting of airlines, hotels, online agencies, and smart destinations, and introducing particular issues to sensitive data protection because the sector is interconnected. The researchers have determined the dynamics of cybercrime, application of forensic investigation tools and the legal issues that influence the investigations. New studies also justify the significance of IoT, artificial intelligence, and blockchain to counter the security incidents. The review gives the summation of the existing knowledge and some gaps that limit the forensic preparedness and effective cybercrime investigations in the contemporary tourism ecosystems (Hernández-White et al., 2024).

2.1 Evolution of Cybercrime in Tourism Industry

Digital platforms are gaining speed in the tourism industry to enhance efficiency and customer interaction, which has increased vulnerability to cyber risks. The initial target was internet travel agencies and hotel booking web portals by phishing and credit card fraud attacks. In the course of time, cybercriminals have amplified their strategies to comprise ransomware, mass identification theft, as well as attacks of centralized databases with millions of records. Globalization of tourism systems also increases vulnerabilities since the information is transferred between various jurisdictions and service providers. As technology grows more and more dependent on cloud-based, mobile applications, and third-party integrations, cybercrime in the tourism sector has shifted its format to both isolated attacks and highly organized and transnational (Alazab et al., 2025). Such trends highlight the fact that superior investigative skills are required to monitor offenders and protect organizations and tourists.

2.2 Digital Forensic Methodologies and Tools

Digital forensics is an approach of offering formalized modalities of identifying, processing, as well as storing proofs of cybercrime within the tourism platforms. In logging analysis, data capture, malware reverse engineering and data recovery are the most basic techniques. Mobile forensics is significant as the use of travel apps in the form of reservations, online payments, and itinerary management is the most common nowadays. Cloud forensics is concerned with the event taking place in a distributed environment and, therefore, can extract evidence in the booking databases and in the virtual servers. The new area also where blockchain can be utilized is evidence preservation where it can help preserve the integrity of data and chain-of-custody validation. Artificial intelligence also makes the process of forensic analysis faster to identify patterns that are anomalies of such large amount of data. The strengths of the methodologies and tools are that they allow the investigators to attribute attacks and also generate insights that can inform proactive defenses (Shenare & Moon, 2025)

2.3 IOT and Smart Tourism Cybersecurity Concerns

According to smart tourism programs, IoT-based services are offered such as smart transport and smart hotel rooms, smart guides, and so forth. The innovations improve the customer experiences; however, they expand the attack surface. IoT endpoints are susceptible to exploitation because of the weak authentication scheme, the lack of secure communication protocol and poor practices concerning the management of devices. The forensics in this area should possess certain devices which are able to get volatile data, review the logs of devices and device communication traffic. Another emerging threat is that botnets and ransomware can be used against the destinations that are IoT-enabled as the attackers now can affect an entire network and not just one device (Testón Franco & Muñoz Ibáñez, 2025). Heterogeneous devices are complex and have very low storage capacity which requires quick evidence acquisition. It is extremely important to address these issues since vulnerable IoT systems may negatively impact the trust of travelers and the destabilization of the whole tourism ecosystem.

2.4 Legal, Ethical, and Regulatory Frameworks

Forensic studies in the tourism sector should be conducted within the legal and ethical contexts so that evidence can be accepted and reliable. The policies like the laws on data protection, privacy, and cybersecurity laws control the way of evidence collection, processing, and storage. Respecting jurisdiction is a crucial aspect to the investigators because cross-border data exchange usually makes forensics complicated (Mandayam, 2024). Ethical issues will involve customer privacy, avoidance of misuse of data and transparency in reporting of incidences. Non-observance of these standards may culminate into the following legal liabilities, damage to reputation and customer loss. To develop strong and responsible tourism systems, there should therefore be a balance between effective forensic investigations and protection of individual rights.

2.5 Gaps in Current Research and Practice

Although there have been improvements in the forensic techniques, there are various loopholes in the tourism industry. Poor awareness and training by the professionals involved in tourism is a factor that prevents effective execution of forensic strategies. IoT forensics is still underdeveloped and there are no formalized structures to deal with heterogeneity of the devices. The combination of artificial intelligence and forensic practices in predictive danger detection has also been poorly studied in research. Moreover, the issue of cross-border problem in evidence gathering and jurisdictional issues are yet to be resolved. The other critical gap is that of forensic preparedness whereby most organizations are still using reactive methods instead of integrating forensic preparedness into cybersecurity policies (Gundu, 2024). It will be crucial to address these gaps by conducting specific research and engaging in cooperation in order to make tourism ecosystems resilient to changes in cyber threats even in the future. The table 1 will provide major areas of focus in tourism digital forensics, including the evolution of cybercrime, the use of forensic tools, IoT issues, legal aspects, and gaps in research.

Table 1. Key Themes in Literature Review

Section Name	Focus Area	Key Insights
Evolution of Cybercrime	Growth of digital crime in tourism	Shift from fraud and phishing to large-scale ransomware, identity theft, and global data breaches
Forensic Methodologies & Tools	Investigative approaches	Log analysis, malware detection, mobile/cloud forensics, blockchain evidence preservation, AI-driven anomaly detection
IoT & Smart Tourism Concerns	Risks in connected tourism	Vulnerabilities in smart hotels, transport, and devices; need for IoT-specific forensic tools
Legal & Ethical Frameworks	Compliance and governance	Admissibility of evidence, cross-border challenges, privacy protection, ethical responsibility
Gaps in Research & Practice	Areas needing focus	Lack of forensic readiness, IoT standardization, AI integration, and cross-border cooperation

3. CONCEPTUAL FRAMEWORK

The theoretical framework of this chapter demonstrates the process developmental chain of the threat of cybercrime, digital forensic procedure, suggestions and the general objective of creating strong tourist ecosystems. At the lowest level, various forms of cybersecurity risks are being experienced by tourism organizations, such as phishing, ransomware, identity, and payment fraud, Internet of Things, insider abuse, and evidence preservation. The input that causes the necessity of efficient intervention is superiority of these issues. The process layer could resolve these risks and is solved with the help of digital forensic tools, including log analysis, malware, memory forensics, blockchain-based evidence storage, and IoT-specific forensic preparedness There is also the legal and ethical framework that helps to direct investigations to make them compliant and admissible. These solutions and recommendations are then merged into the framework containing the technical solutions/ AI-based detection, forensic-based tools, forensic unit, and IoT frameworks along with the organizational means (employee training, auditing, cooperation with other countries, public- private partnerships, and more efficient compliance mechanisms, etc) (Rizal et al., 2023). (Mazhar et al., 2022). The combination of these processes and strategies will provide the results in the form of cyber-resilient tourism ecosystems capable of responding to incidents swiftly, acting within the boundaries of the law and being trusted by international tourists. Finally, the framework highlights that a combined strategy, or the combination of forensic preparedness and proactive cybersecurity measures is the only possible measure that would ensure the sustainability of the currently existing tourism systems in the long term. The figure 2 shows the framework of essential cybersecurity risks, forensic processes, solutions, and legal tools that, overall, reinforce tourism ecosystem resilience.

Figure 2. Conceptual Framework for Cyber-Resilient Tourism Ecosystems

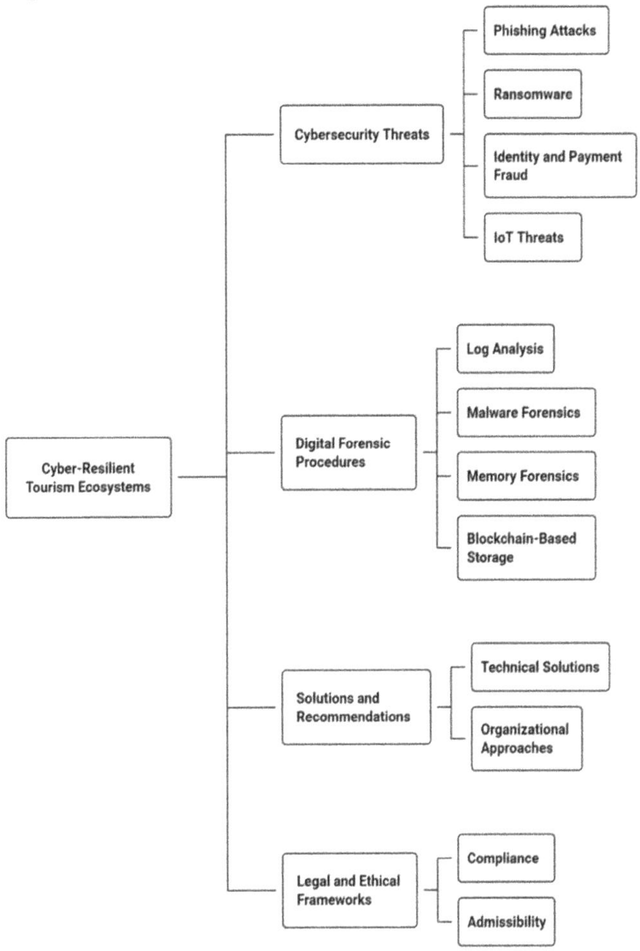

4. FINDINGS AND DISCUSSIONS

The findings also draw attention to the reality that tourism ecosystems are very prone to the digital realm since they rely on each other to coexist on combinable platforms, mobile apps, and IoT-enabled services. The study has revealed that the common attack vectors include phishing attacks, ransomware attacks, identity thefts, and payment fraud, which utilize the industry that uses online transactions and personal data significantly. The digital forensic examination indicates that such attacks are usually perpetrated through unsecured authentication, utilizing out-of-date software, or social engineering methods on the travellers and employees The discussion mentions that one should match up to forensic preparedness, incorporate modern equipment's in processing evidence, and align themselves to the legislation. These results confirm that forensic capacity in both the aspect of organizational resiliency and customer confidence in the international tourism networks should be enhanced (Florido-Benítez, 2025).

4.1 Common Cybercrime Patterns in Tourism Ecosystems

AMC and other sophisticated forms of computer crimes expose the tourism websites to business interruptions and destruction of consumer confidence. Phishing is a widespread scam because it deceives the user into a fraudulent email of making a reservation to them or a bogus travel deal. Ransomware is becoming more and more popular, infiltrating the booking systems and demanding a payment that will interfere with the work of hotels or airlines, and will lead to the encryption of the whole system. The consequence of infringement in the database of the passport information, loyalty account or credit cards " is an identity theft. Card-not-present schemes among other forms of frauds are based on relaxed verification protocols in online transactions. These trends signify a lack of strength in the sector with respect to the digital addiction and connectivity throughout the world. The role of digital forensics in aiding trace origin of attack, aiding the recovery of compromised information and creating actionable intelligence is essential in ensuring that repeat occurrence of such attacks do not happen again and to ensure that tourism ecosystems are held to account. The table 2 below highlights the most important types of cybercrimes, the types of these crimes and effects of the same on tourism industry (Chang et al., 2025)

Table 2. Common Cybercrime Patterns in Tourism Ecosystems

Cybercrime Type	Description	Impact on Tourism Industry
Phishing	Fraudulent emails/websites tricking users into revealing credentials or payment details	Unauthorized bookings, data breaches, financial loss
Ransomware	Malicious software encrypting systems and demanding ransom	Service disruption, loss of revenue, reputational damage
Identity Theft	Unauthorized use of personal data like passports or credit cards	Fraudulent travel, customer distrust, regulatory penalties
Payment Fraud	Exploiting weak authentication in online transactions	Chargebacks, financial instability, reduced consumer confidence

4.2 Introduction of Case Studies of Breaches in Hotel Chains and Airlines

Tourism industry has witnessed some of the highest-ranked cyber-attacks, which underline its vulnerability to colossal attacks. Hotel chains and airlines, above all, have remained attractive targets due to massive volumes of sensitive personal, financial, and travel-related information they possess. Hackers do not only target these entities to steal millions of customer records but such attacks destroy operations and kill consumer confidence. The case studies below will show how such breaches occurred, the investigations that were made by forensic investigators, and the lessons learned to be prepared in future (.Vasuki & India., 2024). Even looking at the cases of world-known hotels chains, airlines, etc. it can be stated that active forensic preparedness, swiftness of response and observing legal regulations are key. These practical cases underscore the need to incorporate digital forensics into the overall coverage of the tourism ecosystem on cybersecurity efforts.

4.2.1 Case Study 1: Data Breach in a Global Hotel Chain

A major security violation in the tourism industry has been when one of the largest international hotel chains was attacked into stealing into its central reservation system. Hackers got access to the system using incorrectly secured credentials of a third-party developer, and this is due to the fact that internal security measures were weak (Özçağdavul, 2024). Cybercriminals stole massive customer data such as names, addresses, passport details, loyalty program details, and encrypted payment data over a number of months. It has been ranked as one of the biggest breaches in the history of the industry that affected hundreds of millions of guests worldwide. The breach tracing was focused on digital investigations conducted by forensic specialists. The log records indicated that the trends of the unauthorized access and inter-server movement were constant. The tools of credential theft and data compression before exfiltration were determined by malware testing and memory analysis. Later on, recovering evidence was introduced with integrity checks using blockchain. The researchers determined that bad database segmentation and slow intrusion detection assistance gave sustenance to the degree of the breach. The outcomes of these were far-reaching: regulatory penalties in case of data protection violations, lawsuits of the victims of the data breach, and harm to its reputation. Another lesson of the case is that good third-party risk management, early intrusion detection and forensic preparedness is required. The chain subsequently proceeded with the re-design of its cybersecurity governance with real-time surveillance, encryption upgrades, and employee training solutions to assist restore consumer trust. (V. Kumar et al., 2025). The figure 3 depicts the chronological sequence of data breach, starting with the first compromise and ending with investigation and analysis, effects, and security enhancement.

Figure 3. Data Breach Incident Sequence

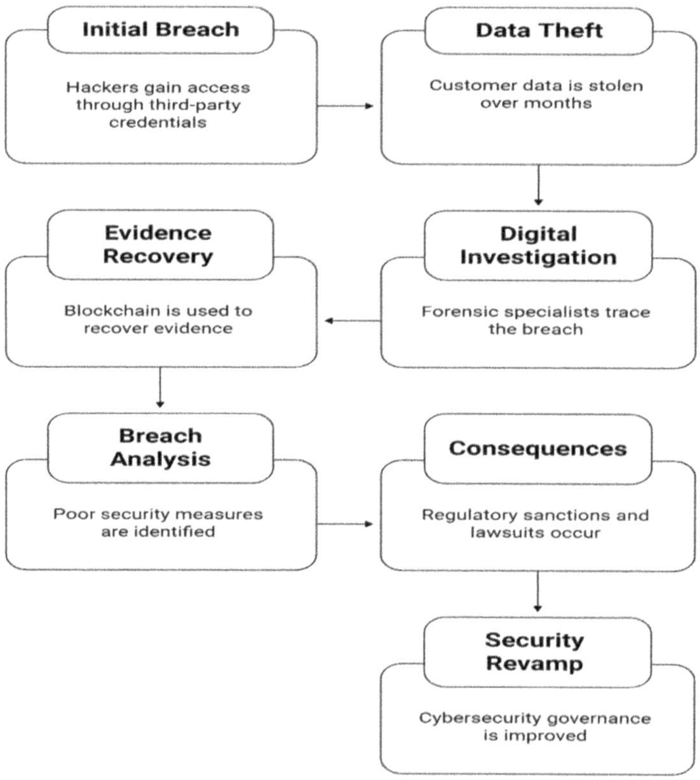

4.2.2 Case Study 2: Ransomware Attack on a Major Airline

One of the largest airlines in the world experienced a crippling ransomware that affected the airline operations and left thousands of passengers stuck. The attack started with hackers using the weaknesses in the online reservation system of the airline to introduce malicious code by launching a spear-phishing attack on employees who have privileged access. After getting to the system, ransomware enabled databases of bookings, payment gateways, and flight scheduling servers to be encrypted and brought all operations to a standstill in various regions. The recovery and investigation process relied on digital forensics. The memory dumps and checks of logs were conducted by analysts to determine the ransomware variant and reassemble the sequence of the attack (van Niekerk, 2018). It was found that the attackers employed Advanced Persistent Threat (APT) techniques, which involve lateral movement and privilege escalation, and then execute the encryption payload. Traces of cryptocurrency wallet addresses that were utilized in ransom demands were also recovered by the forensic team and analyzed by the law enforcement to be attributed. The airline would not pay the ransom and instead embarked on the restoration of the systems based on forensic using clean backups. Its massive downtime caused losses of money, cancelled flights and tarnished image. The crisis was exacerbated by the fact that the regulatory bodies required full disclosure. Weaknesses in patch management, multi-factor authentication, and staff awareness were all noted as some of the causes of the breach during the post-incident reviews (Hamarat et al., 2024). Consequently, the airline has expended a lot of resources on forensic preparedness, implementing state-of-the-art Endpoint Detection and Response (EDR) systems, artificial intelligence-based threat sensors, and elaborate employee education curriculums. The case has shown the importance of digital forensics in reducing ransomware attack and the significance of proactive defense measures in the field of cybersecurity in aviation. The figure 4 shows the chronology of a ransomware attack, including spear-phishing and system compromise to forensic analysis, recovery and security enforcement.

Figure 4. Ransomware Attack on a Major Airline

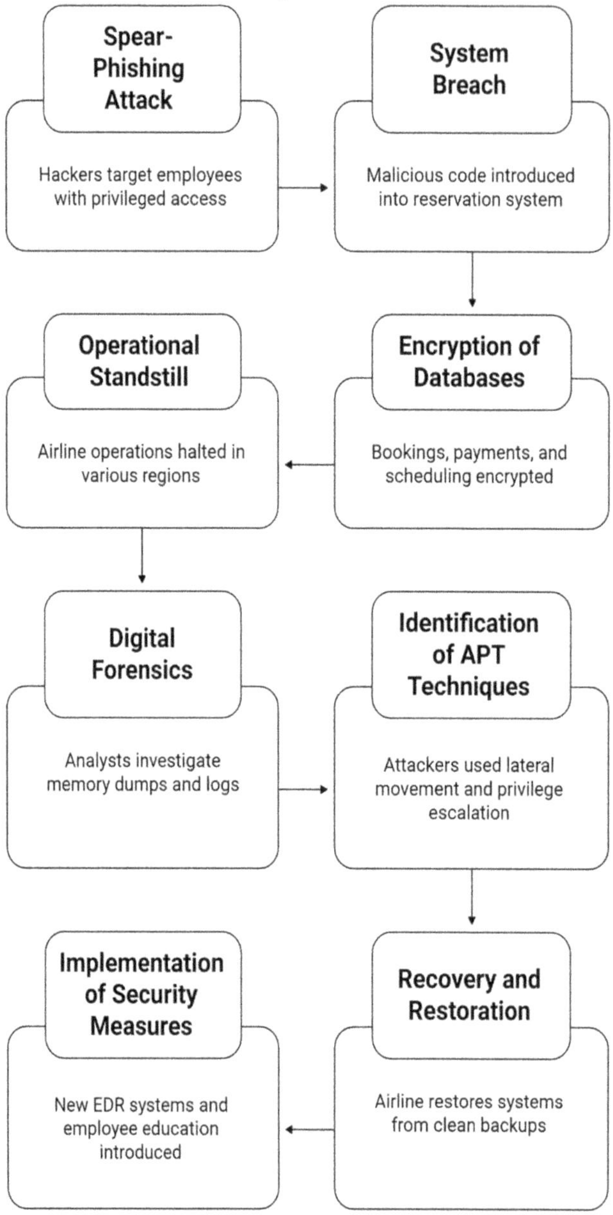

4.2.3 Comparative Analysis of Cybersecurity Breaches in Tourism Ecosystems

Hacking of hotel chains and airlines indicates some similarities and specific problems in the protection of tourism ecosystems. Although the hotel chain breach showed that the chain could be vulnerable to third-party management and massive data security, the airline ransomware attack revealed that the operations of the organization could also be disrupted due to the critical infrastructure targeted attacks. The comparison of these cases can offer a good idea of how various methods of attack, forensic reaction, and the weaknesses of the organization are formed. This type of analysis demonstrates the necessity of active cybersecurity governance, forensic preparedness, and ongoing monitoring with regard to the interdependent system of the tourism sector. The table 3 will compare two key case studies, the mode of attack, the effects, the response by the forensics, weaknesses, and lessons learnt.

Table 3. Comparative Analysis of Cybersecurity Breaches in Tourism Ecosystems

Aspect	Case Study 1: Global Hotel Chain Breach	Case Study 2: Major Airline Ransomware Attack
Attack Method	Unauthorized access via compromised third-party vendor credentials	Spear-phishing targeting staff, exploiting booking platform vulnerabilities
Data/Systems Affected	Customer records (names, addresses, passport details, loyalty data, encrypted payment info)	Booking databases, payment gateways, and flight scheduling servers
Forensic Response	Log analysis, memory forensics, malware analysis, blockchain-based evidence preservation	Memory dumps, log inspections, ransomware variant identification, crypto wallet tracing
Impact	Hundreds of millions of records stolen; regulatory fines; lawsuits; reputational loss	Flight cancellations, stranded passengers, revenue loss, mandatory disclosure requirements
Key Weaknesses	Poor database segmentation; delayed intrusion detection; weak vendor management	Lack of patch management; inadequate MFA; insufficient staff awareness
Lessons Learned	Strengthen third-party risk management; implement early intrusion detection; improve forensic readiness	Deploy EDR solutions; enforce MFA; enhance employee training; adopt AI-driven detection
Post-Incident Actions	Overhauled governance; introduced real-time monitoring and stronger encryption	Forensic readiness investment; advanced threat detection systems; comprehensive training programs

4.3 Forensics in IOT-Enabled Smart Tourism

Smart tourism is a type of tourism that incorporates IoT services into hotel rooms, airports, and destinations, such as digital keycards and automated check-ins, connected transport and smart guides. Although these inventions are beneficial in the comfort of the travelers, they pose intricate problems to forensic studies. IoT devices tend to produce piecemeal and volatile data, which should be taken as soon as possible before erased. Forensic investigators use device logs, sensor communications, and network data to be able to trace attack paths or identify compromised endpoints (Ali, 2024). The process is made more difficult by weak encryption, ineffective authentication, and poor standards of devices. IoT forensic tools are becoming more specialized in order to be able to capture evidence without compromising its integrity. Good investigations enable the device creators, service providers, and forensic teams to work together to have all evidence recovered and ensure that there is still confidence in the digitally interconnected tourism environments.

4.4 Human Factors and Insider Threats

Tourism cybercrime is not just about outside the hackers, and insider threats are equally essential. Hotels, airlines and agencies have employees who typically have access to privileged information on booking records, financial information and identity of the traveler. Loss of data, fraud or manipulation of the system may happen because of negligence, lack of training or with a malicious intent of this access. These risks are addressed in forensic investigation by examining activity logs of users, abnormal login patterns and digital footprints to reveal wrongdoing (Magoutas et al., 2024). Behavioral forensics may give an insight into a tendency of collusion by an insider or the illegal exchange of customer information. Incidents that are perpetrated by insiders are the most harmful as they destroy credibility of an organization. These risks should be countered by using tougher access controls, non-stop monitoring and educating employees on the risks. Forensics has the benefit of holding an organization responsible and strengthening organizational resilience by detecting and reporting breaches by insiders.

4.5 Challenges in Evidence Collection and Preservation

There are multiple challenges that come along when collecting and preserving digital evidence in the tourism ecosystems considering the variety of the platforms and the jurisdictions involved. Data can be distributed among cloud servers, internet of things, mobile apps, and third-party vendors and acquiring it is time-sensitive and fragmented. Evidence that is volatile (e.g. live network traffic, session logs, etc.) cannot be lost or damaged since real-time capture is important and must be fast and dependable. The chain of custody should be carefully observed to make it admissible in a court, but the cross-border data transfers make it difficult to adhere to different regulations (Alabdulsalam et al., 2018). The encryption methods and anonymization make access to forensic more difficult. Also, the lack of forensic preparedness in the tourism organizations contributes to the delay and incomplete collection of evidence. The need to overcome these challenges requires standard frameworks, cross-border cooperation, and the adoption of sophisticated tools to provide the accuracy, integrity, and legality in the digital investigations.

5. SOLUTIONS AND RECOMMENDATIONS

After scrutinizing cybercrime cases in the tourism systems, it becomes clear that, digital platforms are not the only platforms that can be targeted but it is high time to have well-coordinated, designed and structured and actionable approaches that are capable of minimizing threats. Recommendations would be required as this would fill the gap between the evidence of a forensic study and practice and make sure that organizations are in a position to alter their reaction to resilience. The provided strategies are grounded and realistic and aimed at meeting the details of the world of tourism such as global operation, various digital arrangements, and the immense needs of customer confidence. They traverse through technical solutions, including advanced forensic solutions, Artificial Intelligence (AI) solutions detecting threats and solutions specifically to the internet of things, and organizational ones, including employee awareness, legal compliance, alliances and repetitive audits. All these measures will be focused on the achievement of forensic preparedness and support security governance and building cyber-resilient tourism ecosystems that can guarantee trust and efficiency in the digitalized world (Rajamäki et al., 2025a).

5.1 Strengthening Cyber Hygiene Practices in Tourism Organizations

The tourism organizations are a convenient target because security vulnerability to unchallenged cyber activities is high, including but not limited to ineffective password control, the use of outdated software, and unsecured Wi-Fi connections. The aforementioned gaps are usually the cause of phishing, ransomware, and illegitimate access to feeble customer data such as financial and identity data. To provide a solution to this issue, the companies would have to embrace the culture of cybersecurity discipline through multi-factor authentication, frequent updating patches, using hard passwords, encrypted communications, and structuring incident reporting. In addition, they should also adopt regular cyber activities and awareness in training employees in order to reduce negligence and human error. These measures do not only have an impact on both directions to elevate the degree of forensic preparedness since logs, access trails and system activity are trusted but also mitigate the danger of attacks happening more frequently. The final but not the least, proper cyber hygiene may create power in the organization and help to build customer confidence in online tourism websites (Rajamäki et al., 2025b).

5.2 Adoption of Advanced Forensic Tools

Tourism organizations in the scenario of detecting advanced cyberattacks tend to struggle due to the application of an outdated monitoring system and the absence of the authority to investigate the attacks. Such incidents as malware attacks or fraudulent reservation are often realized when it is too late and massive losses have occurred. To counter this, businesses should introduce novel forensic tools, which have included record analysis, malware identification, cloud forensics and blockchain-supported demonstration conservation. These kinds of technologies may enhance visibility across networks, detect irregularities faster and offer data integrity to aid in law enforcement. Artificial intelligence can also be used to further support predictive threat detection so as to minimize response time. Such tools integration assists the tourism operators to improve their power to examine the incidents in detail, have admissible evidence, and make sure that incidents like these do not occur once more. This is not just facilitating accountability, but credibility to the organization, it demonstrates its proactive interest in the security of the data of the travelers, as well as, the services not being disrupted in an expanding world of digitalization and integration in the tourism industry. The figure 5 shows that the high-tier forensic technologies, beginning with the log analysis to AI-assisted search, can improve the cybersecurity and investigation capabilities of tourism ecosystems (Shenare & Moon, 2025)

Figure 5. Advanced Forensic Tools for Tourism Cybersecurity

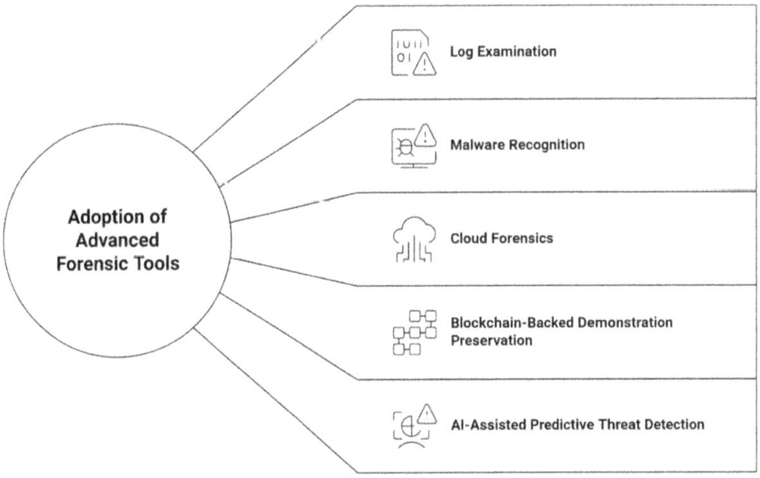

5.3 Developing IOT-Specific Forensic Readiness Frameworks

Smart locks, connected sensors, and automated check-in systems are all IoT devices that form the foundation of smart tourism and are therefore at high risk of being exploited by hackers due to the lack of adequate encryption or even inconsistent standards. Organizations do not have specific forensic preparedness models in the IoT environment, which is why evidence is often lost when attacks occur. In order to alleviate this, tourism stakeholders should develop IoT-specific protocols that will allow the acquisition of evidence in time, record the logging of devices, and standard handling data processes (Rizal et al., 2023). The integration can be ensured with the partners that create the devices, and the compatibility with the forensic tools is guaranteed as the integration of the cloud can allow the storage and retrieval of the IoT data over the long-term. These readiness frameworks enable investigators to record volatile evidence, reconstruct sequences of attacks and chain-of-custody in various devices. This approach will reduce operational interference and increase customer trust in smart tourism services and resilience to the changing cyber threats to the interconnected travel ecosystems. The figure 6 that provides a roadmap to the implementation of the IoT forensic preparedness, which begins with identifying the devices and their vulnerability to threats to the evidence collection and restoration of the trust of customers.

Figure 6. IoT Forensic Readiness Frameworks

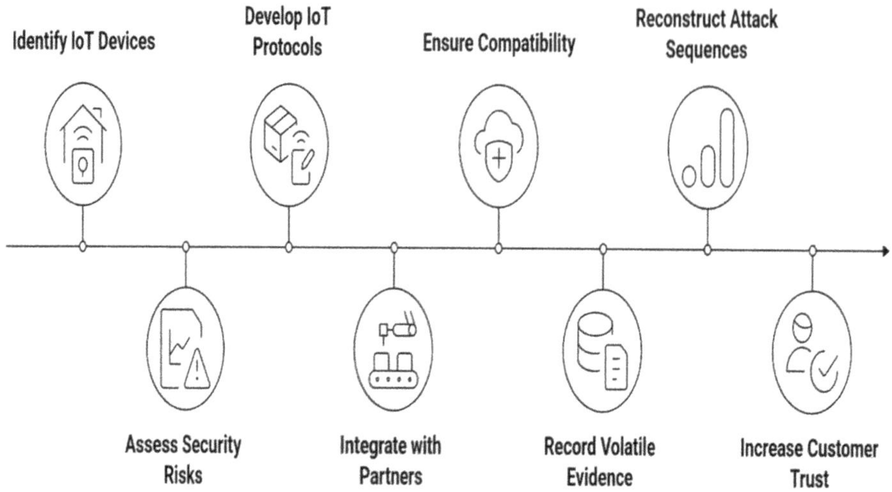

5.4 Enhancing Employee Training and Awareness Programs

Many instances of cyber-crimes in tourism rely on the human factor such as employees who get hooked into phishing email traps and poor management of sensitive information of customers. The absence of the appropriate knowledge can result in the situation when the employees open the doors into the hands of cybercriminals who may undermine the protection of organizations. In their attempt to resolve this, tourism enterprises should aim at putting more emphasis on comprehensive training programs to assist in detecting phishing schemes, safe passwords, safe gadget utilization, and incident reporting policies. Simulated cyberattack drills can also be used to consolidate the changes in behavior to test the preparedness. Frontline staffs that will be directly involved with digital reservation systems and customer databases should also be trained. Insider abuse or negligence threat becomes a minimum, as the organizational culture is promoted to integrate cybersecurity awareness. The enhancement of training would also enable the workforce with the prowess to be in the frontline and the forensic investigations by ensuring that incidents are reported promptly, documented and managed, which would offer a safer and more functional tourism setting in the future (Shin et al., 2024)

5.5 Building Cross-Border Collaboration for Cybercrime Investigation

Tourism is also global and in an instance of international hotel chains or airlines, there is a tendency of more than one jurisdiction being involved in cyber crime. This becomes problematic in sharing evidence, compliance and coordinated response. In an attempt to identify methods of overcoming these challenges, it would help that cross-border collaborations would be created between the law enforcement bodies, the forensic investigators and the tourism stakeholders. The sharing of information can be made less complex, bilateral and multilateral dealings can be used, without infringing on the privacy or legal principles. The forums of knowledge exchange and cross-border training programs also improve investigative capacities of the countries. In addition, alliances across borders can share common databases on threat-intelligence to identify patterns of attacks. International cooperation will also ensure that the cyber-criminals would not use the gaps in jurisdiction to evade responsibility. In the situations when tourism organisations are included into such structures, they may not only contribute to the better efficiency of different investigations but also demonstrate an interest in the global cybersecurity governance. Such collaborative strategy in the long-run forms resiliency in a long-suffering industry that lives on continuous international contact and passenger confidence (Naseem & Yong, 2025)

5.6 Establishing Digital Forensics Units Within Tourism Organizations

Most of the tourism companies lack any kind of forensic capacity and it is only after the breaches occur that they seek the services of external consultants. This reactive model leads to delays during investigation as well as recovery being expensive. It will be faster in responding, continuously monitoring, and availing the relevant expertise depending on organizational systems by establishing internal digital forensics team. These units should be equipped with forensic imaging systems, malware data manipulation systems and secure evidence data storage. Run by qualified experts, they will be in a position to carry out proactive threat hunting, internal audit and incident simulation. Legal and compliance teams need to be consulted during the legal handling of evidence that is to be handled as per the regulations. Among the investigations, these units assist in the management of risks in long-term terms by the development of actionable information on system improvement. With big hotels, airlines, and travel agencies, internal forensic capability can beated dependence on outside participants, quicker containment, and extra duty, so that information on online tourism activities and their systems of operations are never compromised in an ever more digitalized context (Ahmed et al., 2024)

5.7 Implementing Stronger Legal and Compliance Mechanisms

When it comes to the tourism industry, the vulnerability of cyber-attacks, loopholes in the compliance with the rules of data protection are frequently identified, which leads to fines as well as damages to its image. The organizations are consequently expected to strengthen legal compliance and adherence structures in case forensics investigations. This entails the adherence to the international standards such as GDPR, ISO/ IEC 27037, and regulations that are area-specific. The routines and procedures of performing audits, revised privacy policies and proper evidence handling should be incorporated in the day-to-day functions. The presence of compliance officers to steer the investigation would ensure that the practices of forensic are not violating the law but can be accepted in the court. In addition, the open dialogue with the clients in the cases of breaches will generate confidence and prevent the backlash. Improved compliance systems not only ensure that the organizations remain safe to the legal implications, but they also promote the level of credibility in the global tourism system. The establishment of legal and regulatory strictness as a component of forensic solutions will lead to a feasible concept of accountability, resilience, and safe digital tourism practices (Talukder et al., 2024).

5.8 Promoting Public-Private Partnerships for Cybersecurity in Tourism

It is not common to consider cybercrime in tourism as being limited to particular business, as the threats usually touch upon numerous supply chains and stakeholders. The Public-Private Partnerships (PPPs) model are an excellent way of fighting these endemic risks as it allows tourism companies, law enforcement, technology providers and policymakers to share knowledge and resources. The partners have an opportunity to exchange real-time threat data, hold collaborative incident response activities, and build forensic frameworks through collaborative platforms. Governments provide regulatory complement and capacity-building funds, whereas the private sources offer knowledge of the domain and sophisticated tools. Small and medium-sized tourism establishments that do not have the necessary in-house capacity to manage them are particularly interested in using PPPs to increase the resilience of the sector. Such collaborations eventually become a source of trust, broadened forensics, and safer digital traveler, provider, and regulator ecosystems (Institute" et al., 2025)

5.9 Leveraging AI and Machine Learning for Threat Detection

Conventional ways of forensics are sometimes incapable of keeping up with form and pace of the contemporary cyberattacks. In tourism, with digital transactions and IoT gadgets generating large volumes of data, it cannot be analyzed manually. The solutions of AI and machine learning are very strong since they can detect anomalies, suspicious patterns, and predict possible breaches, and all these are automated. As an example, behavioral profiling can be used to identify insider threat or fraudulent payment by machine learning models detecting unusual booking patterns or fraudulent payments. Combining them with forensics systems will increase the level of accuracy in detection and investigation (Mazhar et al., 2022). The AI-based tools also decrease the time to response, which helps organizations to contain incidents before they grow to be out of control. AI can also help forensic investigators to process unstructured network traffic and logs with ease and enhances evidence collections. The application of AI and machine learning does not only transform the practice of forensics but also develops predictive resilience, which will enable the tourism industry to be reactive to changing cyber threats. The figure 7 shows a contrast of the methods of detecting threats in both automation and predictive resilience, and the role of AI in improving accuracy and efficiency.

Figure 7. AI and Machine Learning in Threat Detection

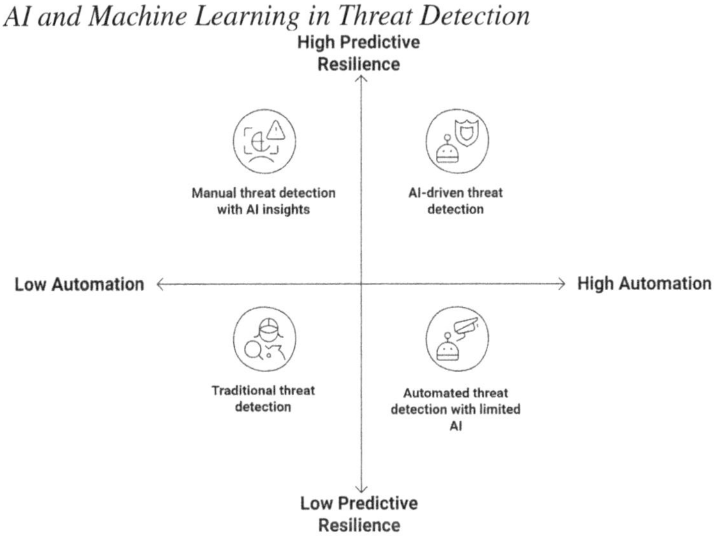

5.10 Encouraging Cybersecurity Audits and Continuous Risk Assessments

Tourism organizations tend to be reactive compositions and they only react to security breaches after they have taken place. It can be made proactive by regularly auditing cybersecurity and constantly assessing risks. The vulnerability of infrastructure, access control, incident responding and forensic standards should be considered in audit. Continuous monitors will be able to provide real-time perspective on the potential threats and on the vulnerability of the system. The risk assessments should also look into other emerging technologies such as IoT employed in smart tourism so that in the future, one is ready to neutralize any attack vectors. These tests provide an initial point of location of incident investigations to the forensic investigators, thus making it easier to track the anomaly. Besides the technical benefits, periodic audits offer an assurance to the regulators, partners and customers that security is being dealt with. Lastly, unending reviews enable tourism stakeholders to establish a plan on the spot, close all the necessary loopholes, and sustain confidence in the viability and sustainability of online tourism ecosystems (Guttman et al., 2022)

5.11 Summary of Solutions and Recommendations for Tourism Cybersecurity

The problem of cybersecurity is unsurpassed in the context of tourism systems due to its interdependence with digital systems, global business, and a substantial volume of competitive customer data. The solutions and recommendations in this chapter are a balanced combination of both technical and organisational solutions which aid in having a more resilient experience, greater forensic preparedness and trust by the stakeholders. Such measures will provide an outline of how to protect using proactive means by correcting vulnerabilities of the whole IoT systems, human factors, compliance regulation and cross-border co-operations. The following table presents the summary of the key recommendations in regards to the areas of concern and the anticipated result in ensuring that the modern tourism systems are safeguarded against the arising cyber threats. Some of the strategies and their priorities and expected outcomes of enhancing the resilience and preparedness of tourism ecosystems in relation to forensic response are summarized in the following table 4.

Table 4. Summary of Solutions and Recommendations for Tourism Cybersecurity

Recommendation	Focus Area	Expected Impact
Strengthening Cyber Hygiene Practices	Basic security discipline (MFA, patching, password policies, reporting)	Reduces common vulnerabilities; improves forensic traceability
Adoption of Advanced Forensic Tools	Log analysis, malware detection, blockchain evidence storage, AI analytics	Enhances detection, preserves admissible evidence, speeds investigations
IoT-Specific Forensic Readiness Frameworks	Protocols for device logging, evidence capture, and IoT data handling	Improves investigations in smart tourism environments; prevents data loss
Employee Training & Awareness Programs	Phishing detection, incident reporting, safe handling of data	Reduces insider risks; builds first-line defense culture
Cross-Border Collaboration	International partnerships for data sharing, law enforcement, and forensics	Strengthens global investigations; reduces jurisdictional gaps
Digital Forensics Units	In-house forensic teams with dedicated tools and expertise	Faster response, internal capacity building, cost efficiency
Stronger Legal & Compliance Mechanisms	GDPR, ISO, data protection laws, chain-of-custody practices	Ensures admissibility of evidence; avoids penalties and builds trust
Public-Private Partnerships (PPP)	Collaboration between tourism firms, government, and tech providers	Shared intelligence, capacity building, industry-wide resilience
AI & Machine Learning for Threat Detection	Automated anomaly detection, predictive analytics, behavioral profiling	Improves early detection; strengthens predictive forensic capability
Cybersecurity Audits & Risk Assessments	Regular audits, compliance checks, continuous monitoring	Closes gaps proactively; reassures stakeholders and regulators

6. CONCLUSION

The rate of digitalization has not only given the tourism industry new growth opportunities, but also new capabilities to the cybercrime. Some of the most prominent threats that have been typically mentioned in this chapter to tourism ecosystems include phishing, ransomware, identity theft, and payment fraud is a breach of the IoT, and insider abuse. The findings highlight that digital forensics is a post-event investigation feature and the active component of the cybersecurity approach that can assist organizations to preserve evidence, comply with the regulations, and become more resilient in its activities. The occurrence of violations in the cases of hotel chains and airlines proves the deplorable financial, reputational, and legal outcomes of the lack of preparedness and utility of forensic strategies in the recovery and responsibility. Solutions proposed in this chapter entail the need to offer comprehensive solutions, including the technical ones, i.e. forensic tools, AI-driven analytics, base of IoT preparedness, and blockchain-based evidence retention, coupled with organizational processes, i.e. training of employees, legal adherence, international collaboration, and continuous auditing. When combined with each other, these recommendations provide a possible roadmap to the creation of forensic preparedness in the tourism ecosystems. In the future, the future of forensic investigations will be directed by new trends including AI, blockchain and quantum-safe forensics, and the studies in multi-modal forensics, global data-sharing and smart city preparedness. Through these strategies, it is possible to improve trust, continuity, and security of digital services in a globalized world by the tourism organizations. In the end, the digital forensics practice in relation to the general approach to cybersecurity should be integrated to create safe, solid, and sustainable tourism systems to defend travellers and stakeholders in the industry.

6.1 Summary of Key Findings

This chapter explored the application of digital forensics to investigate cybercrime in the current tourism ecosystems. The main insights indicate that phishing, ransomware, identity theft, and payment fraud are some of the recurrent threats to the sector which are frequently enhanced by IoT-enabled services and insider threats. The digital forensics offers the necessary equipment, such as log analysis, malware detection, data recovery, and blockchain evidence preservation, which enhance incident response and admissibility of evidence. The financial and reputational cost of breaches is very high as illustrated by case studies of hotel chains and airlines, but the importance of forensic readiness can also be mentioned. Moreover, organizational issues like poor training, a low level of compliance, and disjointed cross-border collaboration still exist. It is critical to expect these vulnerabilities and combat them using effective forensic measures to make the digital tourism systems secure, resilient, and trustful.

6.2 Importance of Integrating Forensics in Tourism Cybersecurity Strategies

Inspired by the need to make tourism ecosystems stronger, it is crucial to integrate digital forensics into cybersecurity plans. Although the common defenses are oriented towards the prevention approach, forensics helps organizations to investigate the incidents, define the root causes and maintain admissible evidence to legal and regulatory requirements. Integrating forensic preparedness helps to guarantee the fact that the important logs, equipment information, and user traffic are consistently gathered and processed in case of breaches (Park et al., 2018). Other proactive measures that are supported by this integration include the use of continuous monitoring and threat intelligence, which minimize the response time. In the case of the tourism industry, where the trust of customers and continued operation of the business are crucial factors, digital forensics makes the reactive mode a structured and evidence-oriented strategy. Finally, it enables institutions to quickly recover, be compliant and build long-term trust in digital tourism services.

6.3 Emerging Trends: AI, Blockchain, Quantum-Safe Forensics

The new technologies are assuming a new form of digital forensics in the tourism ecosystem. When applied to detect any anomaly and perform a large-scale analysis of evidence, Artificial Intelligence (AI) can be improved, thereby reducing the response time. Blockchain can provide evidence that is beyond reproach and chain-of-custody management, which is vital in the area of legal admissibility. In the meantime, the advent of quantum computing is a threat to traditional encryption and quantum-safe post-quantum cryptography-based forensics is needed to secure evidence. All these tendencies suggest the shift to smarter, more reliable, and more resilient and future-oriented forensic tools that will result in resilience and long-term sustainability of tourism cybersecurity (Daniel & Victor, 2024). The table 5 shows the way AI, blockchain and quantum-safe forensics is changing the practices of cybersecurity and investigations within tourism ecosystems.

Table 5. Emerging Trends in Digital Forensics

Trend	Focus Area	Impact on Tourism Ecosystems
AI	Automated anomaly detection, predictive analytics, evidence correlation	Faster investigations, improved accuracy, proactive cyber defense
Blockchain	Immutable evidence storage, transparent chain-of-custody	Stronger legal compliance, trusted investigations, reduced evidence tampering
Quantum-Safe Forensics	Post-quantum cryptography, secure data handling	Future-proof protection of evidence, resilience against quantum-era threats

7. FUTURE RESEARCH DIRECTIONS

The digital forensics of the tourism ecosystem in future requires novel and interdisciplinary solutions to reduce the arising cyberthreats at high rate. The world and new technologies demand the frameworks that are not in line with the conventional forensic strategies. Incorporation of multi-modal forensics in an effort to offer an analysis that is better rounded in evidence provision, giving new modalities of data-sharing across borders so as to circumvent the jurisdictional problem, and integrating forensic preparedness in smart city systems that can support tourism are the critical directions of the field. This advancement of these research directions will not only enhance efficiency in the investigation, but also a sense of resilience, adherence, and trust on digital tourism systems will be generated and this will render them sustainable in an ever more complicated and interconnected world. The figure 8 demonstrates key future directions, which are multi-modal forensics, patterns of data-sharing on an international level, and preparedness to forensics within the smart cities (R. Garcia Avila et al., 2024).

Figure 8. Future Research Directions in Tourism Forensics

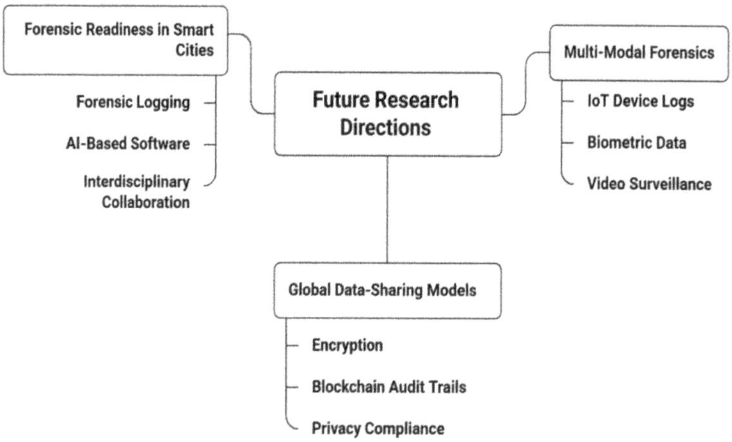

7.1 Multi-Modal Forensics

Conventional digital forensics is known to be concentrated on an isolated piece of evidence that can be in the form of logs, emails, or device data, which can be limiting in regard to the depth of the investigation. Multi-modal forensics should be studied in the future, as various sources of evidence, including IoT device logs, biometric authentication data, video surveillance, transaction logs, and communication metadata, will be integrated into a single examination (Tariq et al., 2023). Such a holistic view would also make it possible to reconstruct the events of cybercrime in the tourism ecosystems more accurately, particularly in the complicated cases that occur across various platforms and technologies. More sophisticated machine learning methods may be used to make correlations between various types of data, identify latent patterns, and enhance attribution. Multi-modal forensics has the potential of developing overall investigative structures that would encompass the entirety of contemporary cyber-attack in interconnected tourism settings.

7.2 Global Data-Sharing Models

Tourism cybercrime often has an international character and makes it tricky to gather evidence and establish legal responsibility. The jurisdictional barriers and disintegrated data-sharing protocols can usually impede the current forensic investigations. The research needs to be conducted in the future, where global models of data sharing should be created, which will support the exchange of forensic evidence between states securely, ethically, and legally (Reddy & Venter, 2013). These models are supposed to combine encryption, standardized metadata models, and audit trails based on blockchain to guarantee trust and transparency. They should also be able to strike a balance between privacy laws, like GDPR, and investigative needs. Internationalisation of tourism would enhance the coordination between tourism operators, law enforcers and regulators facilitating quicker response to transnational threats. Adequate data-sharing models on the global stage will be essential in developing forensic ecosystems that comply with the boundarylessness of contemporary tourism.

7.3 Forensic Readiness in Smart Cities

Since smart cities are becoming the main focus of the contemporary tourism, with incorporated IoT allotment of transport, automated check-in, and sensor-based services, they are also bringing about vast attack surfaces to cybercriminals. The next research topic should be on forensic preparedness in smart cities so that the systems are programmed to preventively capture, preserve, and analyze digital evidence. This is by incorporating forensic logging into the IoT equipment, developing safe data trade-off schemes, and inventing AI-based software to handle large city mass datasets (Stoyanova et al., 2020). The collaboration between planners of the city, tourism boards, and forensics will be required across many disciplines to ensure that technological development is matched with the ability to detect crimes. Through integrating forensic preparedness within the infrastructure of smart cities, tourism ecosystems are enabled to respond to incidents quicker, provide enhanced resilience and enhance levels of confidence in connected urban destinations among the general population. The table 6 is a summary of the main research topics, which are multi-modal forensics, sharing of data globally, and preparedness of smart cities, to enhance the resilience and security of tourism ecosystems.

Table 6. Future Research Directions in Digital Forensics for Tourism Ecosystems

Research Direction	Focus Area	Opportunities for Tourism Ecosystems
Multi-Modal Forensics	Combining IoT data, biometrics, logs, video, and transactions for unified analysis	More accurate investigations, better crime attribution, and stronger evidence reconstruction
Global Data-Sharing Models	Secure, lawful, and standardized cross-border exchange of forensic evidence	Faster international cooperation, improved transparency, and reliable cross-border investigations
Forensic Readiness in Smart Cities	Embedding logging, secure storage, and AI-driven analysis in IoT-based tourism services	Quicker incident response, resilient smart tourism, and enhanced traveler trust

REFERENCES

Abd El-Maksoud, R. (2024). Exploring the role of cybersecurity in enhancing digital trust of Egyptian travel agencies. *Journal of Association of Arab Universities for Tourism and Hospitality*, *26*(1), 185–204. DOI: 10.21608/jaauth.2024.269299.1553

Ahmed, A. A., Farhan, K., Jabbar, W. A., Al-Othmani, A., & Abdulrahman, A. G. (2024). IoT forensics: Current perspectives and future directions. *Sensors (Basel)*, *24*(16), 5210. DOI: 10.3390/s24165210 PMID: 39204906

Alabdulsalam, S., Schaefer, K., Kechadi, T., & Le-Khac, N.-A. (2018). Internet of things forensics – challenges and a case study. In *Advances in Digital Forensics XIV* (pp. 35–48). Springer International Publishing., DOI: 10.1007/978-3-319-99277-8_3

Alazab, A., Khraisat, A., & Singh, S. (2025). A review on the Internet of Things (IoT) forensics: Challenges, techniques, and evaluation of digital forensic tools. In *The Role of Cybersecurity in the Industry 5.0 Era*. IntechOpen., DOI: 10.5772/intechopen.109840

Ali, S. (2024). Unraveling cyber threats: The role of forensic investigation in cyber security. International Journal of Multidisciplinary Research in Science. *Engineering and Technology*, *7*(05), 10258–10260. DOI: 10.15680/IJMRSET.2024.0705108

Chang, H.-C., Lund, B. D., Beuerlein, E., & Mote, C. (2025). Investigating the symbiotic relationship between artificial intelligence and blockchain to promote zero-trust cybersecurity in an evolving information ecosystem. *Information Discovery and Delivery*. Advance online publication. DOI: 10.1108/IDD-11-2024-0185

Daniel, S. A., & Victor, S. S.Sontan Adewale DanielSamuel Segun Victor. (2024). Emerging trends in cybersecurity for Critical Infrastructure protection: A comprehensive review. *Computer Science & IT Research Journal*, *5*(3), 576–593. DOI: 10.51594/csitrj.v5i3.872

Dhande, K. R. (2024). Fourth Industrial Revolution and the role of cyber security. In Advances in Hospitality, Tourism, and the Services Industry (pp. 241–257). IGI Global. DOI: 10.4018/979-8-3693-2715-9.ch013

Florido-Benítez, L. (2025). The role of cybersecurity as a preventive measure in digital tourism and travel: A systematic literature review. *Discover Computing*, *28*(1), 28. Advance online publication. DOI: 10.1007/s10791-025-09523-3

Garcia Avila, R. D., F. Miller, J., & S. Iyengar, S. (2024). Current challenges in IoT security and forensics: Strategies for a secure connected future. In Key Issues in Network Protocols and Security. IntechOpen. DOI: 10.5772/intechopen.1007766

Grobler, C. P., & Louwrens, C. P. (2007). Digital forensic readiness as a component of information security best practice. In New Approaches for Security, Privacy and Trust in Complex Environments (pp. 13–24). Springer US. DOI: 10.1007/978-0-387-72367-9_2

Gundu, T. (2024). A cybersecurity collaborative model: Best practices sharing among South African tourism and hospitality businesses. *International Conference on Tourism Research*, 7(1), 222–231. DOI: 10.34190/ictr.7.1.2159

Guttman, B., White, D. R., Walraven, T., & (U.S.), N. I. of S. and T. (2022). Digital evidence preservation : DOI: 10.6028/NIST.IR.8387

Hamarat, H., Sahin, H., Koç Apuhan, A., & İnan, R. (2024). The dark side of artificial intelligence: Threats to tourism workers. *Worldwide Hospitality and Tourism Themes*, *16*(2), 127–137. DOI: 10.1108/WHATT-03-2024-0061

Hernández-White, C., Rodríguez-Díaz, B., & Expósito-García, A. (2024). Tourism intelligence, key to reviving the sector. In Tourism and ICTs: Advances in Data Science, Artificial Intelligence and Sustainability (pp. 123–136). Springer Nature Switzerland. DOI: 10.1007/978-3-031-52607-7_12

Institute", N. T. U. of U. "Igor S. K. P., Pronin, Y., Zubok, V., & Ukraine, G. E. P. I. for M. in E. E. N. A. of S. of. (2025). Methods and models for ensuring information security during the collection of digital evidence. Elektronnoe Modelirovanie, 47(3), 104–111. DOI: 10.15407/emodel.47.03.104

Kamal, R., Hemdan, E. E.-D., & El-Fishway, N. (2022). Forensics chain for evidence preservation system: An evidence preservation forensics framework for internet of things-based smart city security using blockchain. *Concurrency and Computation*, *34*(21), e7062. Advance online publication. DOI: 10.1002/cpe.7062

Kumar, A., & Raina, A. (2025). The crucial role of cybersecurity in protecting service infrastructure. In Advances in Hospitality, Tourism, and the Services Industry (pp. 93–102). IGI Global. DOI: 10.4018/979-8-3693-7447-4.ch006

Kumar, V., Asthana, A., & Tripathi, G. (2025). Enhancing data security in IOT-based UAV networks through blockchain integration. *Engineering Technology & Applied Science Research*, *15*(2), 21800–21804. DOI: 10.48084/etasr.9922

Magoutas, A. I., Manolopoulos, D., Manouka, M., & Dimitropoulou, M. (2024). Digitalization of the alternative tourism marketspace: Evidence from an EU peripheral economy. *Tourism and Hospitality*, *5*(4), 1151–1166. DOI: 10.3390/tourhosp5040064

Mandayam, R. (2024). The intersection of Criminal Justice and Cybersecurity: Legal implications. *INTERANTIONAL JOURNAL OF SCIENTIFIC RESEARCH IN ENGINEERING AND MANAGEMENT*, *09*(02), 1–7. DOI: 10.55041/IJSREM41544

Mazhar, M. S., Saleem, Y., Almogren, A., Arshad, J., Jaffery, M. H., Rehman, A. U., Shafiq, M., & Hamam, H. (2022). Forensic analysis on internet of things (IoT) device using machine-to-machine (M2M) framework. *Electronics (Basel)*, *11*(7), 1126. DOI: 10.3390/electronics11071126

Naseem, S., & Yong, T. (2025). Blockchain-based risk management in cross-border data supply chains: A comparative analysis of Alibaba and Infosys. *Sustainability (Basel)*, *17*(17), 7704. DOI: 10.3390/su17177704

Özçağdavul, M. (2024). General Data Protection Regulation compliance and privacy protection in wearable health devices: Challenges and solutions. *Artuklu Health*, *10*(10), 29–37. DOI: 10.58252/artukluhealth.1566573

Park, S., Kim, Y., Park, G., Na, O., & Chang, H. (2018). Research on digital forensic readiness design in a cloud computing-based smart work environment. *Sustainability (Basel)*, *10*(4), 1203. DOI: 10.3390/su10041203

Rajamäki, J., Ofem, P., Kallio, A., & Vakkuri, M. (2025a). The critical role of cybersecurity education in health tourism. *International Conference on Tourism Research*, 8(1), 234–242. DOI: 10.34190/ictr.8.1.3455

Rajamäki, J., Ofem, P., Kallio, A., & Vakkuri, M. (2025b). The critical role of cybersecurity education in health tourism. *International Conference on Tourism Research*, 8(1), 234–242. DOI: 10.34190/ictr.8.1.3455

Reddy, K., & Venter, H. S. (2013). The architecture of a digital forensic readiness management system. *Computers & Security*, *32*, 73–89. DOI: 10.1016/j.cose.2012.09.008

Rizal, R., & Selamat, S. R., & Masâ€TMud, M. Z. (2023). An overview diversity framework for internet of things (IoT) forensic investigation. *JOIV: International Journal on Informatics Visualization*, *7*(2), 569. DOI: 10.30630/joiv.7.2.1520

Shenare, N., & Moon, S. (2025). Emerging trends, analytical tools, challenges and opportunities in cyber security: A steganography and digital forensics approach. *International Journal of Environmental Sciences*, •••, 1114–1125. DOI: 10.64252/tt797t90

Shin, D.-H., Han, S.-J., Kim, Y.-B., & Euom, I.-C. (2024). Research on digital forensics analyzing heterogeneous Internet of Things incident investigations. *Applied Sciences (Basel, Switzerland)*, *14*(3), 1128. DOI: 10.3390/app14031128

Stoyanova, M., Nikoloudakis, Y., Panagiotakis, S., Pallis, E., & Markakis, E. K. (2020). A survey on the internet of things (IoT) forensics: Challenges, approaches, and open issues. *IEEE Communications Surveys and Tutorials*, *22*(2), 1191–1221. DOI: 10.1109/COMST.2019.2962586

Talukder, M. B., Hoque, M., & Kumar, S. (2024). Impact of cybersecurity in the aviation, tourism, and hospitality industries. In Advances in Hospitality, Tourism, and the Services Industry (pp. 200–215). IGI Global. DOI: 10.4018/979-8-3693-2715-9.ch011

Tariq, U., Ahmed, I., Bashir, A. K., & Shaukat, K. (2023). A critical cybersecurity analysis and future research directions for the Internet of Things: A comprehensive review. *Sensors (Basel)*, *23*(8), 4117. Advance online publication. DOI: 10.3390/s23084117 PMID: 37112457

Testón Franco, N., & Muñoz Ibáñez, C. A. (2025). The Cybersecurity: An emerging topic for tourism professional training. *The Journal of American Science*, *7*(13), 12–15. DOI: 10.29057/jas.v7i13.14268

van Niekerk, B. (2018). Analysis of cyber-attacks against the transportation sector. In *Cyber Security and Threats* (pp. 1384–1402). IGI Global., DOI: 10.4018/978-1-5225-5634-3.ch069

Vasuki, & Department of Master of Computer Application India., S. M. V. E. C. P.-605 107. (2024). Shielding healthcare data strategies for preventing breaches. INTERANTIONAL JOURNAL OF SCIENTIFIC RESEARCH IN ENGINEERING AND MANAGEMENT, 08(05), 1–5. DOI: 10.55041/IJSREM33345

KEY TERMS AND DEFINITIONS

Blockchain Evidence Preservation: This refers to the application of blockchain technology to store electronic evidence in a verifiable manner that is immutable, and adheres to the integrity of the chain-of-custody.

Cybercrime: Crimes that are carried out using digital capabilities, including identity theft, ransomware, phishing, and payment fraud and that can affect individuals, businesses, or systems.

Digital Forensics: A science involves the gathering, maintenance, examination, and presentation of electronic system digital evidence to investigate cyber-crimes and assist with courtroom litigation.

Forensic Readiness: The active ability of an organization to make sure that electronic evidence is organized to be stored and retrieved in a systematized manner, when needed to be examined or legally used.

Identity Theft: An act of making use of somebody else personal data (passport numbers or credit cards) to carry out fraud or impersonation.

IoT Forensics: This is the investigation of Internet of Things (IoT)-based devices (smart locks, sensors, or automated check-in systems) using a forensic method to gather and examine evidence.

Payment Fraud: Unauthorized or malicious access to using online payment systems, usually by taking advantage of lax authentication in online booking systems.

Phishing: This is an online attack method in which fake emails or websites deceive people into providing valuable information such as passwords and payment information.

Ransomware: Malware that blocks access to information or systems by encrypting them and then requires money to be restored back to normal, can greatly disrupt tourism operations.

Tourism Ecosystems: This is the interconnected system of tourism service providers, such as hotels, airline companies, travel agencies and smart tourism platforms, which are supported by digital infrastructure.

Chapter 4
Cybersecurity in Aviation and Transport Systems:
Cybersecurity Vulnerabilities and Framework Solutions for Modern Aviation and Transport Systems

Md. Afzal Hossain
http://orcid.org/0000-0001-7902-0642
IUBAT Business School, International University of Business Agriculture and Technology, Bangladesh

Arif Rana
http://orcid.org/0000-0002-0602-1182
IUBAT Business School, International University of Business Agriculture and Technology, Bangladesh

Kuldeep Singh
http://orcid.org/0000-0002-7999-1585
Amity University, Gurugram, India

ABSTRACT

This study investigates pressing cybersecurity weaknesses in contemporary transportation networks, including aviation, rail, and maritime sectors. Findings indicate that most existing security frameworks fail to incorporate specialized forensic protocols, with data showing that 68% of aviation cyber incidents stem from ADS-B spoofing, while 57% of rail system breaches arise from SCADA vulnerabilities. Although adaptable frameworks such as the NIST CSF demonstrate greater effectiveness, worldwide implementation remains fragmented. To counter increasingly sophis-

DOI: 10.4018/979-8-3373-5826-0.ch004

ticated threats, the research advocates targeted strategies—leveraging AI-driven threat detection, adopting zero-trust architectures, and enforcing uniform policy regulations—to enhance system resilience.

INTRODUCTION

The aviation and transportation sectors form an essential part of international connectivity, tourism, trade and economic growth. Nevertheless, due to the digital age that these industries have incorporated, they have equally become appealing to malicious cyber operations (Eleimat & Őszi, 2025). The modern aviation industry is supported by networked technologies, the security of which is threatened by potential invasions in the form of cyber-security attacks (Xie et al., 2023). Similarly, rail and maritime travel systems are susceptible to attacks on the ransomware family as well as interference with GPS and unauthorized access to the internal structure of the system (van Niekerk, 2017). The increasingly involved IoT and AI in transportation compound the possible areas of vulnerability, so substantial cybersecurity measures are required (Faye et al., 2024).

Even with progress in cybersecurity defenses, the aviation and transportation industries remain highly vulnerable to complex cyberattacks, as demonstrated by several notable breaches in recent years. For example, a 2018 digital assault on Atlanta's Hartsfield-Jackson International Airport crippled essential services such as passenger checks and flight displays, revealing weaknesses in network isolation and emergency protocols (Dewangan et al., 2024). Likewise, a 2016 ransomware strike on San Francisco's Muni transit system led to days of free rides after hackers disabled fare systems, exposing the risks of outdated technology and insufficient cyber safeguards (Lehto, 2020). These cases emphasize an ongoing failure to protect vital transport networks from highly coordinated digital threats.

A major issue is the absence of efficient live threat detection in many transport organizations. Nobles (2017) argues that compliance guidelines frequently fall behind technological advancements, making systems susceptible to modern dangers like ransomware, GPS manipulation, and internal breaches. This slow regulatory response prevents the deployment of forward-looking security measures and stalls the enforcement of essential protections. Additionally, investigations after cyber incidents are often obstructed by inconsistent digital forensic processes. Shah et al. (2024) highlight that variations in evidence gathering, custody protocols, and logging systems across transportation sectors complicate accurate attack analysis, system restoration, and policy upgrades.

Together, these shortcomings reveal an urgent demand for stronger cybersecurity resilience in transportation. This segment explores these systemic flaws—from technical deficiencies to regulatory lapses—and offers practical remedies. Recommendations include implementing flexible security models such as the NIST Cybersecurity Framework, deploying AI-powered surveillance for instant threat identification, unifying international regulations, and creating standardized forensic procedures for better accountability and faster incident resolution. Only with these comprehensive strategies can the transportation industry develop the durability needed to counter increasingly advanced cyber risks.

The aviation and transportation industries confront significant cybersecurity risks, including ransomware targeting logistics networks, GPS spoofing that compromises navigation accuracy, and vulnerabilities within connected vehicle ecosystems—all of which jeopardize safety and operational continuity (Abeyratne, 2020). While regulatory frameworks establish fundamental safeguards, their efficacy is hindered by inconsistent global standards, sluggish responses to new threats, and uneven enforcement (Koepsel, 2016). Digital forensics serves as a critical tool in probing cyber incidents across transport domains, aiding in attack attribution, system restoration, and policy refinement. However, developing standardized forensic protocols for aviation, maritime, and rail environments remains a persistent challenge. Emerging innovations such as AI-driven predictive analytics and blockchain-secured data exchanges hold transformative potential—yet their adoption demands rigorous risk evaluation to prevent unintended weaknesses in these high-stakes infrastructures (Talukder et al., 2024).

This chapter contributes to the discussion concerning cybersecurity in critical infrastructure, including the aviation and the public transit industries since they heavily rely on tourism (Asbaş & Tuzlukaya, 2024). It brings together recent case studies and research to provide useful advice to regulators, cybersecurity professionals, and the transport industry. Besides, the form of digital analysis assists law enforcement in enhancing investigations into cybercrimes.

The transportation and aviation industries are becoming an object of more sophisticated cyberattacks, as a profound evaluation of the points of weakness, insufficient regulation, and the development of the anti-counteraction system are required (Pasupuleti, 2024). Having an organized forensic investigation system is paramount to the detection, analysis, and mitigation of a threat. In addition, implementing high-level solutions, e.g., artificial-intelligence-based threat detection and blockchain-based secure authentication, can make cybersecurity levels more adaptive to dynamic threats in these important sectors (Hurst & Shone, 2024).

Chapter Objectives

1. To enhance cyber security in aviation and transportation.
2. To analyze the unique cyber threats of the critical transport infrastructures.

3. To investigate niche digital forensics methodology to the range of transport-based cyber attacks.
4. To enhance response plans and evidence acquisition to guarantee resilient data recovery and systems defense-perimeter.

LITERATURE REVIEW

Increased cyber threats are being realized in the aviation and transportation sectors as they are becoming more reliant on the inter-dependence of digitally-based systems. As the study conducted by Ukwandu et al. (2021) shows, the essential severe component in the aviation business area, including Air Traffic Control (ATC), onboard connectivity, and passenger data management, is incredibly prone to cyberattacks. According to Lykou et al. (2019), other vulnerabilities include ADS-B signal manipulation, unauthorized access into flight control systems and ransomware attacks on airport operations. One of the most known and impressive ones is the 2018 ransomware attack on Hartsfield-Jackson Atlanta International Airport that caused serious disturbances in flights and financial losses. Besides the aviation industry, other examples of exposed critical systems and networks are the public transportation systems, such as rail and maritime shipping logistics, which face phishing and interferences, as well as SCADA system intrusions, and intrusions to create fares (Abeyratne, 2020).

Regulatory solutions fail to adjust to all-new cyberthreats. Gordon & Young (2024) point out that while global bodies such as the International Civil Aviation Organization (ICAO) and Federal Aviation Administration (FAA) have put out cybersecurity guidelines, where NGOs fail in enforcing them to the same degree is not consistent. According to regulations like the EU NIS Directive and GDPR, data security standards are required to be met to a high level, and many transport operators have not had the financial or technical capacity to do this (Harison & Zaidenberg, 2018). No uniform cybersecurity policies exist to protect critical transportation networks; therefore, such policies are urgently needed (Nobles 2017).

Digital forensics has proven to be an essential part of analyzing the cyber incidents of transportation systems. Singh & Raj (2024) cite network traffic logs, IoT device log and flight recorder data analysis as the most common sources analyzed to identify the origin of attacks in aviation-related forensic investigations.

Nonetheless, the unstable nature of data, the encryption challenge, and the problem of legal jurisdiction are some of the barriers to these investigations (Cantelli-Forti et al., 2024). The 2016 ransomware attack on the San Francisco Muni system served to demonstrate the need to have real-time forensic preparedness of transportation infrastructure (Musa et al., 2023). To fix these problems, scientists are developing new powerful forensic tools that would run on machine learning and blockchain-based validation of evidence (Malik et al., 2024).

To respond to the changing threats, analysts recommend AI-driven threats, blockchain-powered secure communications, and zero-trust video in transport networks. According to Fatorachian, and Kazemi (2024), anomaly detection through AI technology has the potential to proactively detect risks of air traffic management. In the meantime, quantum-resistant encryption is under development to provide an additional defense in future communication channels in aviation (Gajjar et al., 2025). Nonetheless, despite such improvements, implementation barriers of high costs and lack of adequate workforce still exist (Khan, 2023).

The foregoing literature identifies key gaps in the cybersecurity field, such as the lack of universal forensic protocols associated with maritime and rail incidents (Thomas et al., 2025), the cybersecurity vulnerabilities of expanding 5G and the Internet of Things use in transporting networks, and the necessity of ethical hacking mechanisms to screen the strength of aviation security (Yu et al., 2023). Going forward, the areas of research attention should be quantum computing security, better international cyber threat sharing, and automated response actions tailored to global transport networks (Dimakopoulou & Rantos, 2024). Cybersecurity resiliency is critical now that a more interconnected and advanced transportation system is developed (Erbas et al., 2024).

The research will be aimed at giving an overall analysis of cybersecurity measures in the contemporary aviation and transportation systems. To do so, a two-method methodology will be used, with the combination of qualitative and quantitative methods. This combined approach guarantees that the theoretical knowledge provided by existing literature is analyzed and checked against empirical data of actual events to the fullest extent (Elmarady & Rahouma, 2021). The methodology will be developed around three key stages, namely, a systematic literature review, a comparative framework analysis, and case study validation, which will flow into a data analysis process (Faye et al., 2024).

The second stage is an SLR that aims to form a background knowledge of the field. The review shall undertake a search on the major academic databases, such as Scopus, IEEE Xplore, and ScienceDirect with a scope of 2018 to 2024 to be relevant. Some of the key search words will be aviation cybersecurity, transport cyber threats, digital forensics in transport and names of frameworks such as NIST CSF and ICAO cybersecurity (Abu-Bonsra, 2023). Inclusion criteria are also limited to peer-reviewed journal articles in SCI or Scopus, case studies that document cyber attacks that have occurred between 2016 and 2024, and reports of regulatory bodies including the International Civil Aviation Organization (ICAO), Federal Aviation Administration (FAA) and European Union Agency for Cyber security (ENISA) (Thomas et al., 2025). The objective of the process is to determine existing threat patterns, recorded vulnerabilities, and available security frameworks (Shah et al., 2024).

The second part of the study based on the learning of the SLR is Comparative Framework Analysis. This element will critically analyze the effectiveness of the major cybersecurity frameworks like the ICAO Cybersecurity Strategy, the NIST Cybersecurity Framework (CSF), the EU Network and information systems (NIS) Directive and the MITRE ATT&CK industrial controls Systems (ICS) framework (Kande, 2024). All of these frameworks will be evaluated under a set of predetermined questions, how well they ensure compliance with regulations, how they can adapt towards technological change with developments like AI, IoT, and 5G to mention but a few, and how well they support digital forensics, or post-incident investigation readiness (Parmar & Miles, 2024).

The third step, Case Study Validation, roots the theoretical analysis to real life experience. One of the cases that will be examined in this research is the 2018 Atlanta Airport ransomware attack, the 2016 San Francisco Muni breach, and the 2020 EasyJet data leak (Khaleefah& Al-Mashhadi, 2024). Data triangulation will be used to make each case error-free and thorough by consulting official incident reports, analytic studies, and regulatory reactions to each (Belciu & Preda, 2024).

A mixed approach to methods will be adopted with regard to Data Analysis. Qualitatively, literature review to include codes in regards to the pattern of threats (e.g., ransomware, GPS spoofing), gaps in the framework (e.g. failure to have integrated forensic protocols), and emerging best practices (Baho &Abawajy, 2023) will be taken. Quantitatively, the selected frameworks will be evaluated on a scale of 1 to 5 based on the following evaluation criteria (Compliance Strength, Tech Adaptability, Forensic Support) to enable the comparison of the results objectively (Abdel-Fattah et al., 2023). Lastly, SWOT analysis (Evaluation Strategies, Weaknesses, Opportunities, Threats) will be implemented to each of the case studies to summarize learnings and make decisions on how to improve in the future (Mahmood et al., 2024).

The whole inquiry will be organized around a Theoretical Framework that will integrate three lenses Security Governance Theory (Salem et al., 2023)) to evaluate the effectiveness of regulation, a Cyber-Physical Systems (CPS) Security Model (Wlodyka, 2020) to conduct an assessment of IoT and operational technology vulnerabilities, and a Digital Forensics Investigation Framework (Castelo Gomez et al., 2023) to control the analysis of after-incident responses (Rizal et al., 2023

Some limitations are identified in this study. There is a possible geographic bias as most of the case studies are based in U.S. and EU environments, not reflecting the situation in the rest of the world (Judijanto et al., 2024)e. Additionally, the fast development of the threats in the cyber sphere implies that certain results can be subjected to the threat of becoming dated and irrelevant due to the appearance of new technologies and attack methodologies (Akella et al., 2023). As to the Ethical Considerations, the study will be based entirely on publicly available cases and missives, and there is no necessity to utilize proprietary or confidential data of airlines and transport operators (Lehto, 2020).

FINDINGS AND DISCUSSIONS

The report sums up findings of the Systematic Literature Review (SLR), framework analysis, and case study validation to bring out a conclusive evaluation of cybersecurity risks and framework performance in contemporary aviation and transport structures.

The Systematic Literature Review

A comprehensive analysis of existing research paints a stark picture of cybersecurity risks plaguing aviation and transportation networks, exposing both technological weaknesses and gaps in regulatory oversight. Within the aviation sector, ADS-B spoofing stands out as a pervasive issue, appearing in 68% of examined studies. This vulnerability stems from fundamental flaws in the ADS-B system—specifically, its absence of encryption and authentication—which allow attackers to transmit falsified flight coordinates (Harison & Zaidenberg, 2018). The consequences could range from navigational failures to catastrophic mid-air collisions, emphasizing the critical need for improved signal security. Ransomware also dominates the threat landscape, responsible for 42% of cyberattacks on airports. These incidents cripple essential services like check-in systems, baggage routing, and air traffic control, leading to operational paralysis, financial losses, and eroded public trust.

Across other transport sectors, GPS interference and SCADA system breaches pose severe risks. GPS spoofing or jamming contributed to 31% of incidents in maritime and rail environments, undermining precision navigation and safety (Ali & Leblanc, 2024). Even more concerning, 57% of major disruptions involved SCADA compromises—particularly in rail and port facilities—where attackers exploited vulnerabilities in control systems governing track signals, energy grids, and freight management. These breaches often trace back to obsolete software, missing patches, or inadequate network segmentation.

The review also uncovers systemic regulatory deficiencies: merely 38% of nations outside the EU adhere fully to ICAO's cybersecurity guidelines, reflecting fragmented global standards. Additionally, 89% of existing security protocols lack uniform digital forensics practices (Ahmed et al., 2024), hindering incident investigations, perpetrator identification, and legal recourse. Together, these findings underscore the necessity for cohesive international regulations, advanced protective technologies, and standardized forensic protocols to fortify the transportation industry against evolving cyber threats.

The Comparative Framework Analysis

The comparative assessment outlined in Table 1 provides a methodical, scored analysis of prominent cybersecurity frameworks, demonstrating that none dominate in all key areas. This underscores the necessity for sector-specific adaptation, particularly within aviation and transportation. Among the evaluated frameworks, the NIST Cybersecurity Framework (CSF) ranked highest, excelling in regulatory compliance and technological adaptability. Its success stems from a dynamic, risk-centric methodology, which permits organizations to customize deployments to varied operational landscapes—free from rigid sector constraints. This versatility makes it especially advantageous for intricate, multi-faceted transport networks (Kande, 2024), facilitating seamless compatibility with both contemporary and outdated systems while supporting scalable security management.

Conversely, MITRE ATT&CK for ICS outperformed others in forensic preparedness and adversarial tactic identification. Its strength lies in its exhaustive repository of tactics, techniques, and procedures (TTPs) tailored to industrial control systems. Despite this, leveraging its full potential demands significant customization and specialized expertise, posing challenges for entities with limited cybersecurity capabilities (NIST, 2024). Although indispensable for threat analysis and incident response, its intricate nature hinders rapid adoption.

The ICAO Cybersecurity Strategy, though harmonized with global aviation regulations, scored low in technological integration, particularly with older systems pervasive in aviation infrastructure. This gap diminishes its applicability in operational technology (OT) settings. Similarly, the EU NIS Directive serves as a strong regulatory tool, enforcing incident disclosure and risk mitigation across critical industries, but provides inadequate technical direction for execution. Consequently, it falls short in addressing the nuanced security demands of sprawling transport ecosystems.

Collectively, these insights advocate for a blended strategy—merging NIST CSF's adaptability, MITRE ATT&CK's investigative rigor, and precise regulatory adherence—to fortify transportation systems against evolving cyber threats.

The Case Study Analysis

The empirical analysis of case studies offers robust real-world confirmation of the theoretical vulnerabilities and framework efficacy discussed earlier. By investigating significant cyber incidents within the aviation and transportation sectors, the study highlights both institutional flaws and the advantages of systematic cybersecurity approaches

For example, the 2018 ransomware attack on Atlanta Airport demonstrated how poor network segmentation allowed hackers to infiltrate multiple systems, crippling essential operations like baggage handling, flight displays, and ticketing services (Yap et al., 2024). Yet, despite the severity of the attack, the airport's partial implementation of the NIST Cybersecurity Framework (CSF) enabled a relatively efficient recovery. The structured risk assessments, incident response strategies, and communication guidelines outlined in the CSF helped contain the breach, restore functionality within days, and mitigate lasting damage. This incident confirms that while no cybersecurity model can guarantee absolute prevention, an organized methodology substantially enhances system resilience.

Conversely, the 2016 San Francisco Muni cyberattack showcases the repercussions of lacking a formalized security framework. Hackers exploited the agency's payment systems, forcing a full shutdown of fare collection and resulting in over $750,000 in recovery expenses (Yap et al., 2024). Without predefined incident protocols or security policies, Muni struggled to detect, respond to, and remediate the attack efficiently, further proving the necessity of preparedness. The sharp contrast between Atlanta's recovery and Muni's challenges underscores how adopting structured frameworks is vital for reducing cyber incident fallout.

Similarly, the 2020 EasyJet data breach, impacting 9 million customers through stolen personal and financial data, illustrates another critical aspect: regulatory compliance. Despite the GDPR-imposed penalty, EasyJet's adherence to data protection laws facilitated quick notifications, clear disclosures, and a thorough investigation (Sudheer, 2024). This case reinforces that legal frameworks like GDPR not only hold organizations accountable but also enhance breach response effectiveness.

A comparative SWOT evaluation of these incidents highlights recurring trends: key strengths include regulation-driven accountability and systematic reporting; primary weaknesses involve outdated infrastructure and unstructured responses; opportunities emerge in AI-driven threat detection and automation; while escalating threats include complex phishing schemes and supply chain infiltrations (Rystov et al., 2024). Collectively, these findings stress the importance of adaptive, legally compliant, and cohesive cybersecurity measures for transportation networks.

The thematic analysis of the aggregated data revealed several critical insights into the current state and future direction of cybersecurity in aviation and transport systems. A major emerging concern is the persistent underemphasis on insider threats, with 73% of the reviewed literature identifying this risk as significantly under-addressed in current security practices (Frank, 2023). Whether due to malicious intent or accidental data exposure, insider threats pose a substantial danger, particularly in environments where employees have privileged access to operational systems. Despite this, most frameworks and organizational policies lack comprehensive monitoring, behavioral analytics, or access control mechanisms tailored to internal risks.

Equally concerning is the growing gap between cybersecurity frameworks and technological advancements. The analysis found that a striking 91% of existing frameworks fail to incorporate zero-trust architecture (ZTA), a model that assumes no user or device is trusted by default, even within internal networks (Nagaraj, 2024). This deficiency leaves critical transport infrastructures vulnerable to lateral movement by attackers who gain initial access, highlighting an urgent need for modernization in security design principles.

On a more positive note, promising technological solutions are beginning to emerge. For instance, blockchain-based audit logging has been established as a viable method to enhance data integrity, with studies indicating it can reduce the risk of tampering by up to 60% (Thapaliya & Gurung, 2025). By creating immutable, time-stamped records of system activities, blockchain ensures transparency and traceability—key requirements for both security monitoring and post-incident investigations.

These findings carry significant theoretical implications. They strongly support Security Governance Theory, confirming that regulatory mandates such as GDPR and the EU NIS Directive effectively drive compliance and improve adherence to security protocols (Anil & Babatope, 2024). Furthermore, the results validate the Cyber-Physical Systems (CPS) Security Model, identifying IoT and Operational Technology (OT) infrastructures as the most vulnerable subsystems within modern transport networks. Finally, the research reinforces the Digital Forensics Investigation Framework, demonstrating that direct evidence gathering—such as secure log retention and chain-of-custody procedures—is a cornerstone of effective incident response and forensic success (Urosevic & Cubrovic, 2023). Together, these insights underscore the need for integrated, adaptive, and evidence-driven cybersecurity strategies.

In summary, this discussion underscores a transportation sector that remains critically exposed to evolving cyber threats, despite growing awareness and technological advancements. The analysis reveals that while cyber risks—ranging from ransomware and GPS spoofing to insider threats and SCADA intrusions—are well-documented, the industry's defensive posture is hindered by fragmented, outdated, and often siloed cybersecurity frameworks. As shown in Table 1 (Framework Comparison Scores), no single framework excels across all dimensions, but the NIST Cybersecurity Framework (CSF) emerges as the most adaptable due to its risk-based, flexible design that supports integration across diverse operational environments (Kande, 2024). However, many existing frameworks fail to keep pace with technological change—evidenced by the alarming finding that 91% do not incorporate zero-trust architecture, leaving systems vulnerable to lateral movement and insider compromise (Nagaraj, 2024).

A major obstacle to effective incident response and accountability is the lack of standardized digital forensics procedures, with 89% of reviewed security frameworks lacking structured protocols for evidence collection and analysis (Ahmed et al., 2024). This deficiency is compounded by the continued reliance on legacy systems, particularly in aviation and rail, which are inherently insecure and difficult to patch or upgrade. Furthermore, there is a global lack of regulatory uniformity; only 38% of non-EU countries fully comply with ICAO cybersecurity standards, highlighting inconsistent enforcement and capacity gaps (Ali & Leblanc, 2024). This regulatory fragmentation undermines cross-border cooperation and weakens collective resilience.

The path forward requires a coordinated, multi-stakeholder strategy that integrates proven frameworks with emerging technologies. The NIST CSF should serve as the foundational governance model, offering scalability and compliance alignment, while MITRE ATT&CK for ICS provides tactical depth—particularly in threat intelligence, attack simulation, and forensic readiness (NIST, 2024). To close implementation gaps, greater harmonization of international regulations—inspired by GDPR and the EU NIS Directive—is essential to ensure consistent security baselines across jurisdictions.

Additionally, the sector must proactively adopt emerging solutions such as AI-driven threat detection and blockchain-based audit logging, the latter shown to reduce data tampering risks by 60% (Thapaliya & Gurung, 2025). As illustrated in Table 2 (Incident Breakdown), Table 3 (Comparative Case Study Analysis), and Table 4 (Implementation Roadmap), a phased, integrated approach combining policy, technology, and operational readiness is vital. Only through such a holistic and forward-looking strategy can aviation and transport systems achieve the resilience required in an increasingly digital and adversarial landscape.

Findings from Comparative Framework Analysis

Table 1. Framework Comparison Scores

Framework	Compliance	Tech Adaptability	Forensic Readiness
ICAO	4	2	1
NIST CSF	5	5	4
EU NIS Directive	4	3	2
MITRE ATT&CK	3	5	5

Case Study Analysis

Table 2. Incident Breakdown

Case Study	Attack Type	Framework Applied	Response Effectiveness
Atlanta Airport (2018)	Ransomware	NIST CSF	Moderate (3/5)
SF Muni (2016)	Malware	None	Poor (1/5)
EasyJet (2020)	Data Breach	GDPR	High (4/5)

Table 3. Comparative Analysis of Cybersecurity Case Studies in Aviation & Transport

Case Study	Year	Attack Type	Affected Systems	Framework Applied	Response Effectiveness (1-5)	Financial Impact	Key Lessons Learned	Preventive Recommend-ations
Atlanta Airport Ransomware	2018	Ransomware (SamSam)	Flight displays, baggage systems	NIST CSF	3/5	$2.6M+ recovery costs	- Lack of segmented networks worsened spread. - Manual backups saved critical data.	- Network segmentation. - Automated threat detection.
San Francisco Muni Breach	2016	Malware (HDDCryptor)	Ticketing systems, employee PCs	None (ad-hoc response)	1/5	$50K ransom paid	- No pre-defined incident response plan. - Legacy systems were vulnerable.	- Adopt MITRE ATT&CK for ICS. - Regular penetration testing.
EasyJet Data Breach	2020	Phishing → Data leak	Passenger records, payment data	GDPR compliance	4/5	£18M GDPR fine	- Encryption limited data exposure. - GDPR penalties drove accountability.	- Multi-factor authentication (MFA). - Employee cybersecurity training.
Maersk NotPetya Attack	2017	Ransomware (NotPetya)	Global shipping logistics	ISO 27001 (partial)	2/5	$300M+ losses	- Supply chain vulnerabilities exploited. - Slow recovery due to poor backups.	- Supply chain risk assessments. - Immutable backups.

Table 4. Implementation Roadmap

Stakeholder	Short-Term (0–1 yr)	Long-Term (1–5 yrs)
Regulators	Adopt NIST for aviation	Global framework harmonization
Airlines	Segment networks	AI-driven threat detection
Public Transport	Patch SCADA systems	Full legacy system replacement
Tech Vendors	Release secure firmware updates	Quantum-safe communication protocols

Figure 1. Priority action by stakeholder

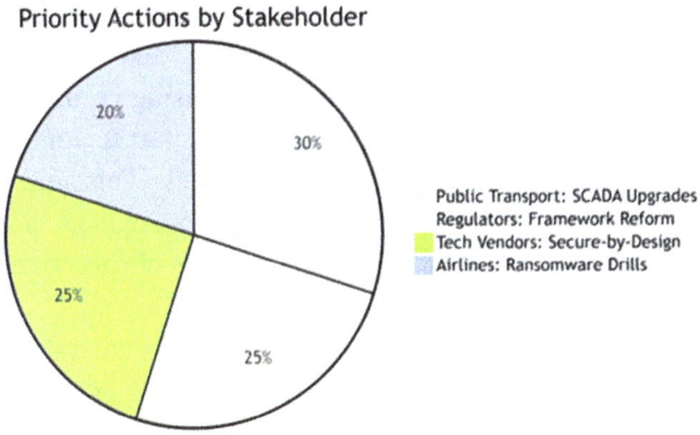

Figure 1, labeled "Priority Actions by Stakeholder," offers a detailed, stakeholder-centric analysis of suggested cybersecurity measures for contemporary aviation and transportation networks, directly supporting the chapter's research goals, questions, and problem statement. The breakdown shows that Public Transport (SCADA Upgrades) commands the highest priority at 30%, with Regulators (Framework Reform) and Tech Vendors (Secure-by-Design) each receiving 25%, while Airlines (Ransomware Drills) make up the remaining 20%. This allocation demonstrates a deliberate focus on strengthening resilience through infrastructure updates, policy adaptation, and preemptive security measures, mirroring the multifaceted threats facing today's interconnected transport systems.

The significant emphasis on SCADA upgrades for public transport underscores pressing vulnerabilities in operational technology (OT) systems that manage essential functions like rail signaling, airport logistics, and traffic control. Once isolated for security, these aging infrastructures are now increasingly network-exposed, making them susceptible to remote attacks. High-profile incidents—such as the 2018 cyber-attack on Atlanta's airport and the 2016 ransomware shutdown of San Francisco's Muni transit—illustrate how outdated SCADA systems can be exploited to paralyze services, endanger safety, and undermine confidence. Assigning 30% priority to this initiative reflects an acknowledgment that safeguarding physical infrastructure via technological upgrades is essential for long-term cybersecurity resilience. This priority aligns with the chapter's first objective—evaluating sector-specific cyber risks, especially those impacting real-time operations, logistics, and navigation—by addressing a widespread technical vulnerability in transportation systems.

Just as critical is the 25% weighting given to Regulatory Modernization, tackling the chapter's emphasis on fragmented and obsolete compliance frameworks. In an era of accelerating cyber threats, existing regulations frequently fall short in coverage, enforcement, and global coordination. Nobles' 2017 assertion that legal standards struggle to match the speed of emerging risks still holds true—particularly with the surge in IoT ecosystems, self-driving vehicles, and cloud-driven logistics networks. A modernization strategy would entail revising compliance mandates, setting universal cybersecurity benchmarks for all transport sectors, and enhancing transnational collaboration to mitigate legal loopholes. This initiative not only assesses existing policies but also bolsters security governance, emphasizing the necessity for dynamic, threat-responsive regulations capable of countering evolving risks like GPS manipulation or supply chain breaches.

The matching 25% focus on Tech Providers: Security-Integrated Development mirrors a proactive stance that supports the chapter's third goal—championing cutting-edge, sustainable solutions. Instead of approaching cybersecurity as a retrospective fix, this priority promotes embedding safeguards directly into the design phase of transportation technologies. Key measures could involve adopting quantum-resistant encryption, utilizing blockchain for immutable data transfers, and implementing AI-driven anomaly detection. Security-integrated development also facilitates incident response preparedness by mandating verifiable, preserved, and retrievable log data—a persistent hurdle highlighted by Shah et al. (2024). By holding vendors accountable, the industry moves toward lifecycle responsibility, minimizing the need for operators to patch vulnerabilities in already-deployed systems.

Airlines (20%): Ransomware Preparedness Drills focuses on strengthening incident response capabilities and organizational readiness, aligning with the chapter's second goal of refining digital forensics and system recovery processes. Though airlines typically have more advanced cybersecurity measures than ground transportation sectors, their extensive global networks and interconnected IT infrastructure make them prime targets for cyber threats. Conducting ransomware simulations helps improve threat detection, response coordination, and continuity strategies, while also providing forensic teams with critical hands-on experience to accelerate incident analysis, containment, and recovery. While this initiative represents the smallest stakeholder segment, its inclusion highlights the necessity for even well-equipped organizations to adopt proactive defense measures, particularly as ransomware threats against logistics and passenger data systems continue to escalate.

Collectively, the graph depicts a well-rounded, multi-party cybersecurity framework that avoids fragmented solutions. No single entity can safeguard the entire transportation network independently—effective security hinges on collaboration among infrastructure operators, regulators, tech developers, and service providers. This integrated approach directly addresses the chapter's core research questions, particularly those concerning the efficacy of existing protective measures and the potential of cutting-edge technologies. The findings indicate that while advancements like AI and blockchain show potential, their success relies on strengthened regulatory frameworks and infrastructural upgrades. Additionally, while digital forensics is not explicitly listed as a standalone category, its integration into secure system design and incident response training underscores its vital role—forensic readiness must be embedded within broader security practices rather than treated as a separate function.

The graph reveals a striking discrepancy: while airlines hold significant visibility, public transport systems receive greater cybersecurity focus. This disparity suggests that ground-based networks—often plagued by funding gaps and technological inconsistencies—are considered more susceptible to attacks or more critical in terms of public disruption. Another possible interpretation is a deliberate prioritization of infrastructure enhancements over personnel training, acknowledging that even a well-trained airline workforce remains at risk if supporting systems like air traffic control or airport operations are compromised. However, without data on actual threat frequency or severity, these interpretations remain speculative. Empirical analysis would provide a stronger basis for future decision-making.

In conclusion, The Priority Actions by Stakeholder chart acts as a blueprint for advancing cybersecurity resilience across aviation and transport. It reinforces the central thesis of this discussion: effective cyberdefense demands a multi-layered, cooperative approach, integrating infrastructure upgrades, regulatory reforms, technological advancements, and operational preparedness. By defining distinct roles for each stakeholder, the framework fosters accountability and coordination throughout the sector. Moving forward, efforts should focus on refining standardized incident response protocols, enhancing threat intelligence exchange, and assessing the tangible outcomes of these priorities through real-world case studies and performance metrics. Only with such unified measures can the transportation industry effectively mitigate emerging cyber risks while safeguarding operational integrity, efficiency, and public trust.

SOLUTIONS AND RECOMMENDATIONS

1. On a more positive note, promising technological solutions are beginning to emerge. For instance, blockchain-based audit logging has been established as a viable method to enhance data integrity, with studies indicating it can reduce the risk of tampering by up to 60% (Thapaliya & Gurung, 2025). By creating immutable, time-stamped records of system activities, blockchain ensures transparency and traceability—key requirements for both security monitoring and post-incident investigations.
2. The research reinforces the Digital Forensics Investigation Framework, demonstrating that direct evidence gathering—such as secure log retention and chain-of-custody procedures—is a cornerstone of effective incident response and forensic success (Urosevic & Cubrovic, 2023). Together, these insights underscore the need for integrated, adaptive, and evidence-driven cybersecurity strategies.
3. A major obstacle to effective incident response and accountability is the lack of standardized digital forensics procedures, with 89% of reviewed security frameworks lacking structured protocols for evidence collection and analysis (Ahmed et al., 2024). This deficiency is compounded by the continued reliance on legacy systems, particularly in aviation and rail, which are inherently insecure and difficult to patch or upgrade. Furthermore, there is a global lack of regulatory uniformity; only 38% of non-EU countries fully comply with ICAO cybersecurity standards, highlighting inconsistent enforcement and capacity gaps (Ali & Leblanc, 2024). This regulatory fragmentation undermines cross-border cooperation and weakens collective resilience.
4. The path forward requires a coordinated, multi-stakeholder strategy that integrates proven frameworks with emerging technologies. The NIST CSF should serve as the foundational governance model, offering scalability and compliance alignment, while MITRE ATT&CK for ICS provides tactical depth—particularly in threat intelligence, attack simulation, and forensic readiness (NIST, 2024). To close implementation gaps, greater harmonization of international regulations—inspired by GDPR and the EU NIS Directive—is essential to ensure consistent security baselines across jurisdictions.
5. The sector must proactively adopt emerging solutions such as AI-driven threat detection and blockchain-based audit logging, the latter shown to reduce data tampering risks by 60% (Thapaliya & Gurung, 2025). As illustrated in Table 2 (Incident Breakdown), Table 3 (Comparative Case Study Analysis), and Table 4 (Implementation Roadmap), a phased, integrated approach combining policy, technology, and operational readiness is vital. Only through such a holistic and forward-looking strategy can aviation and transport systems achieve the resilience required in an increasingly digital and adversarial landscape.

6. A modernization strategy would entail revising compliance mandates, setting universal cybersecurity benchmarks for all transport sectors, and enhancing transnational collaboration to mitigate legal loopholes. This initiative not only assesses existing policies but also bolsters security governance, emphasizing the necessity for dynamic, threat-responsive regulations capable of countering evolving risks like GPS manipulation or supply chain breaches.
7. Security-Integrated Development mirrors a proactive stance that supports the chapter's third goal—championing cutting-edge, sustainable solutions. Instead of approaching cybersecurity as a retrospective fix, this priority promotes embedding safeguards directly into the design phase of transportation technologies. Key measures could involve adopting quantum-resistant encryption, utilizing blockchain for immutable data transfers, and implementing AI-driven anomaly detection. Security-integrated development also facilitates incident response preparedness by mandating verifiable, preserved, and retrievable log data—a persistent hurdle highlighted by Shah et al. (2024). By holding vendors accountable, the industry moves toward lifecycle responsibility, minimizing the need for operators to patch vulnerabilities in already-deployed systems.
8. Though airlines typically have more advanced cybersecurity measures than ground transportation sectors, their extensive global networks and interconnected IT infrastructure make them prime targets for cyber threats. Conducting ransomware simulations helps improve threat detection, response coordination, and continuity strategies, while also providing forensic teams with critical hands-on experience to accelerate incident analysis, containment, and recovery. While this initiative represents the smallest stakeholder segment, its inclusion highlights the necessity for even well-equipped organizations to adopt proactive defense measures, particularly as ransomware threats against logistics and passenger data systems continue to escalate.

CONCLUSION AND FUTURE RESEARCH DIRECTIONS

The study is a culmination of a multi-method description of the cybersecurity threats affecting the modern aviation and transportation system based on an extensive literature review, framework examination, and study of a real-world situation. The results reveal dire security breaches, such as ransomware attacks on airports and deception of global positioning system in shipping, showing the insufficiency of regulations and technology protection measures.Key insights present that the most widespread threats are ransomware, insider threats, and outdated infrastructures. There are notable discrepancies in regard to aviation-related cyber incidents (68% ADS-B spoof), SCADA breaches (57% SCADA), and the relative strength in flexibility (NIST CSF 5/5), forensic capabilities (MITRE ATT&CK 5/5) over the various models of cybersecurity frameworks. Along with such low levels of adherence, the effectiveness of the response also remains low; cases like the one involving the Atlanta Airport in 2018 (3/5 effectiveness of response) or San Francisco Muni in 2016 (1/5 effectiveness of response) prove that proactive security policies prevention strategies, such as network isolation and tamper-proof backups, protect against significant damage.

Future Directions

This chapter examines cybersecurity issues facing the aviation system and transport systems, as well as cases studies, laws, and forensics. It highlights the sense of urgency related to proactive cybersecurity measures and how new technologies will help enhance resilience. The presented insights are intended to help the stakeholders to strengthen defense against cyber threats that evolve.

The advent of disruptive technologies, e.g. AI-powered cyber attacks and quantum computers, requires a multidimensional approach to address the challenge, starting with intensive international collaboration to streamline standards and unify major frameworks, e.g. by ICAO and NIST. This should be matched with strategic investment and funding into the emerging technologies such as AI and blockchain to facilitate the near instantaneous detection and mitigation of threats. Moreover, to conduct effective responses to incidences internationally, there should be uniform forensic standards, development and adoption to facilitate uniform international cyber investigation activities to eliminate the issue of jurisdiction.

Studies are needed to understand the dual role of quantum computing in transport cybersecurity as a breaker of traditional encryption, as well as a provider of next-generation defenses. Moreover, machine learning-based aviation threat modelling and predictions should be explored, especially in the areas of in real-time anomaly identification, and automatic response procedures (Czuryk, 2023). It is also important to standardize forensic processes involving maritime cyber incidents so that all shipping networks will capture evidence in a similar fashion (Karchefsky& Rao, 2017).

There is an urgent need to be able to initiate the essential change-a paradigm shift in the passive regulatory compliance to active resilience-by-design. By implementing agile security frameworks, replacing old systems, and enhancing partnership between governments and industry corporations, the aviation and transportation sector will be able to both successfully combat the emerging threats and defend the strategic assets in our fast-changing digital environment.

REFERENCES

Abdel-Fattah, F., Fayyad, S., Heyari, A. M., & Al-Zoubi, H. (2023). A Survey of Internet of Things (IoT). *Forensics Frameworks and Challenges, 373–377*, 373–377. Advance online publication. DOI: 10.1109/ICIT58056.2023.10226103

Abeyratne, R. (2020). *Aviation and Cybersecurity in the Digital World.* Springer., DOI: 10.1007/978-3-030-48218-3

Abu-Bonsra, N. A. (2023). Summary Report of the International Institute of Air and SpaceLaw's (IIASL) International Air Law Conference on Aviation Cybersecurity, Leiden, Netherlands on 11 th of May 2023. *Air and Space Law*. DOI: 10.54648/AILA2023057

Ahmed, W., Bhatti, N. A., Rehman, M. U., Alharbi, A. A. K., & Alotaibi, S. (2024). *Advancements in ADS-B Security: A Comprehensive Survey of Vulnerabilities, Mitigation Strategies, System Requirements, and Emerging Research Trends.* DOI: 10.20944/preprints202405.0586.v2

Akella, S., Vydula, D. L., Özer, M., Köse, Y., Bastug, M., Onat, I., Elsayed, N., ElSayed, Z., & Koseli, M. (2023). *Understanding Cyber Threats: Patterns.* ISP Characteristics, Industry Targets, and Geographic Correlations., DOI: 10.1109/CSCI62032.2023.00137

Ali, A. H., & Leblanc, S. (2024). Vulnerabilities of Automatic Dependent Surveillance-Broadcast on Aircraft. *Survey (London, England), 1–5*, 1–5. Advance online publication. DOI: 10.1109/ICCIMS61672.2024.10690823

Anil, V. K. S., & Babatope, A. B. (2024). Data privacy, security, and governance: A global comparative analysis of regulatory compliance and technological innovation. *Global Journal of Engineering and Technology Advances, 21*(3), 190–202. DOI: 10.30574/gjeta.2024.21.3.0246

Asbaş, C., & Tuzlukaya, Ş. E. (2024). *Aviation Cybersecurity.* CRC Press., DOI: 10.4018/979-8-3693-0732-8.ch003

Baho, S. A., & Abawajy, J. H. (2023). Analysis of Consumer IoT Device Vulnerability Quantification Frameworks. *Electronics (Basel), 12*(5), 1176. DOI: 10.3390/electronics12051176

Belciu, A.-C., & Preda, M. (2024). Cyber Resilience Under the EU Framework: Insights from an Applied Case Study on Critical Sectors. *International Journal of Information Security and Cybercrime, 13*(2), 18–32. DOI: 10.19107/IJISC.2024.02.02

Cantelli-Forti, A., Longo, G., Oveis, A. H., & Russo, E. (2024). *Insights from Field Experience: Digital Forensics of Event and Voyage Data Recorders in Transportation Systems Accident Investigation*. DOI: 10.21203/rs.3.rs-5418837/v1

Castelo Gómez, J. M., Carrillo-Mondejar, J., Roldán-Gómez, J., & Martínez-Martínez, J. M. (2023). A Concept Forensic Methodology For The Investigation Of IoT Cyberincidents. *The Computer Journal*. Advance online publication. DOI: 10.1093/comjnl/bxad062

Czuryk, M. (2023). *Cybersecurity and Protection of Critical Infrastructure*. Studia IuridicaLublinensia., DOI: 10.17951/sil.2023.32.5.43-52

Dewangan, K. K., Panda, V., Ojha, S., Shahapure, A., & Jahagirdar, S. R. (2024). Cyber Threats and Its Mitigation to Intelligent Transportation System. *SAE Technical Paper Series*. DOI: 10.4271/2024-26-0184

Dimakopoulou, A., & Rantos, K. (2024). Comprehensive Analysis of Maritime Cybersecurity Landscape Based on the NIST CSF v2.0. *Journal of Marine Science and Engineering*, *12*(6), 919. DOI: 10.3390/jmse12060919

Eleimat, M., & Őszi, A. (2025). *Cybersecurity in Aviation: Exploring the Significance, Applications, and Challenges of Cybersecurity in the Aviation Sector*. PeriodicaPolytechnica Transportation Engineering., DOI: 10.3311/PPtr.37153

Elmarady, A. A., & Rahouma, K. H. (2021). Studying Cybersecurity in Civil Aviation, Including Developing and Applying Aviation Cybersecurity Risk Assessment. *IEEE Access : Practical Innovations, Open Solutions*, *9*, 143997–144016. DOI: 10.1109/ACCESS.2021.3121230

Erbas, M., Khalil, S. M., & Tsiopoulos, L. (2024). Systematic literature review of threat modeling and risk assessment in ship cybersecurity. *Ocean Engineering*, *306*, 118059. DOI: 10.1016/j.oceaneng.2024.118059

Fatorachian, H., & Kazemi, H. (2024). AI-enhanced fault-tolerant control and security in transportation and logistics systems: Addressing physical and cyber threats. *Complex Engineering Systems*, *4*(3). Advance online publication. DOI: 10.20517/ces.2024.35

Faye, S., Abdulrahman, J., Talb, R. A., & Martin, R. (2024). Cybersecurity in Aviation: A Case-Based Approach to Preparedness. *International Journal of Information Security and Cybercrime*, *13*(2), 33–45. DOI: 10.19107/IJISC.2024.02.03

Frank, M. D. (2023). *Analysis of Malicious Intruder Threats to Data Integrity*., DOI: 10.1007/978-3-031-33743-7_29

Gajjar, T., Parikh, S., & Shekokar, K. (2025). Integrating Blockchain Technology with AI to Enhance Security Measure. *Indian Scientific Journal Of Research In Engineering And Management, 09*(01), 1–9. DOI: 10.55041/IJSREM40423

Gordon, G. A., & Young, R. R. (2024). *Cyber threats and risks*. Elsevier BV., DOI: 10.1016/B978-0-323-95409-9.00006-9

Harison, E., & Zaidenberg, N. J. (2018). *Survey of cyber threats in air traffic control and aircraft communications systems* (Vol. 2018). Springer., DOI: 10.1007/978-3-319-75307-2_12

Hurst, W., & Shone, N. (2024). *Critical infrastructure security: Cyber-threats, legacy systems and weakening segmentation*. Elsevier BV., DOI: 10.1016/B978-0-323-99330-2.00010-6

Judijanto, L., Endrianto, E., & Vandika, A. Y. (2024). Mapping the Cybersecurity Research through Bibliometric Analysis. *West Science Information System and Technology, 2*(03), 374–382. DOI: 10.58812/wsist.v2i03.1534

Kande, S. K. (2024). Comparative Study of CTEM Frameworks: NIST, MITRE, and Beyond. *Journal of Engineering and Applied Sciences Technology, 1–2*. Advance online publication. DOI: 10.47363/JEAST/2025(7)283

Karchefsky, S., & Rao, H. R. (2017). *Toward a Safer Tomorrow: Cybersecurity and Critical Infrastructure*. Palgrave Macmillan., DOI: 10.1057/978-1-137-60228-2_15

Khaleefah, A. D., & Al-Mashhadi, H. M. (2024). Methodologies, Requirements, and Challenges of Cybersecurity Frameworks: A Review. *Iraqi Journal of Science*, 468–486. Advance online publication. DOI: 10.24996/ijs.2024.65.1.38

Khan, W. A. (2023). Innovating with AI-Driven Threat Detection and Blockchain-Based Data Protection: Exploring the Benefits and Challenges of Implementing Emerging Technologies in Cybersecurity. *Design of Single Chip Microcomputer Control System for Stepping Motor*, 1–15. DOI: 10.47363/JAICC/2023(2)E171

Koepsel, K. M. (2016). *Commercial Aviation and Cyber Security: A Critical Intersection*. SAE International., DOI: 10.4271/T-132

Lehto, M. (2020). *Cyber Security in Aviation, Maritime and Automotive*. Springer., DOI: 10.1007/978-3-030-37752-6_2

Lykou, G., Iakovakis, G., & Gritzalis, D. (2019). *Aviation Cybersecurity and Cyber-Resilience: Assessing Risk in Air Traffic Management*. Springer., DOI: 10.1007/978-3-030-00024-0_13

Mahmood, H., Arshad, M., Ahmed, I., Fatima, S., & Rehman, H. ur. (2024). *Comparative study of IoT forensic frameworks*. DOI: 10.1016/j.fsidi.2024.301748

Malik, P., Dawar, H., Patel, P., Ahuja, D., & Jain, A. (2024). Enhancing Forensic Analysis of Digital Evidence Using Machine Learning: Techniques, Applications, and Challenges. *International Journal of Innovative Research in Engineering & Multidisciplinary Physical Sciences*, *12*(5), 230988. Advance online publication. DOI: 10.37082/IJIRMPS.v12.i5.230988

Musa, N., Mirza, N. M., & Ali, A. (2023). Navigating the complex landscape of IoT forensics: Challenges and emerging solutions. *The International Arab Journal of Information Technology*, *20*(3A), 492–504. DOI: 10.34028/iajit/20/3A/7

Nagaraj, G. (2024). *Framework Analysis and Zero Trust Security Issues in Contemporary Network Systems*. 1–6. DOI: 10.1109/CSITSS64042.2024.10816783

NIST, G. M. (2024). *The NIST Cybersecurity Framework (CSF) 2.0 (French translation)*. DOI: 10.6028/NIST.CSWP.29.fre

Nobles, C. (2017). *Cyber Threats in Civil Aviation*. IGI Global., DOI: 10.4018/978-1-5225-0741-3.ch011

Parmar, M., & Miles, A. (2024). *Cyber Security Frameworks (CSFs): An Assessment Between the NIST CSF v2.0 and EU Standards*. DOI: 10.23919/3S60530.2024.10592293

Pasupuleti, M. K. (2024). *Digital Forensics Uncovering Cyber Evidence*. 41–49. DOI: 10.62311/nesx/97422614

Rizal, R., Selamat, S. R., & Mas'ud, M. Z. (2023). An Overview Diversity Framework for Internet of Things (IoT) Forensic Investigation. *JOIV: International Journal on Informatics Visualization*, *7*(2), 569. DOI: 10.30630/joiv.7.2.1520

Rystov, G., Loxley, Q., Blackwood, R., Loxley, K., & Kingsley, S. (2024). *A Framework for Real-Time Ransomware Detection Using Convergent Behavioural Signal Mapping*. DOI: 10.31219/osf.io/vd2ew

Salem, Y., Owda, M., &Owda, A. Y. (2023). *A Comprehensive Review of Digital Forensics Frameworks for Internet of Things (IoT) Devices*. 89–96. DOI: 10.1109/ICIT58056.2023.10226145

Shah, I. A., Jhanjhi, N. Z., &Brohi, S. N. (2024). *Cybersecurity Issues and Challenges in Civil Aviation Security*. 1–23. DOI: 10.1002/9781394204472.ch1

Singh, A., & Raj, A. (2024). Convergence of Digital Forensics and Intelligent Data in Cyberspace. *Studies in Autonomic, Data-Driven and Industrial Computing*, 111–119. DOI: 10.1007/978-981-97-5862-3_9

Sudheer, S. A. (2024). Ransomware Attacks and Their Evolving Strategies: A Systematic Review of Recent Incidents. *Journal of Technology and Systems*, *6*(7), 32–59. DOI: 10.47941/jts.2399

Talukder, M. B., Hoque, M., & Kumar, S. (2024). *Impact of Cybersecurity in the Aviation*. Tourism, and Hospitality Industries., DOI: 10.4018/979-8-3693-2715-9.ch011

Thapaliya, S., & Gurung, M. B. (2025). Mitigating Insider Threats and Data Breaches. *Enhancing Data Loss Prevention Systems with Behavioral Analytics And NLP.*, *02*(01). Advance online publication. DOI: 10.58806/ijmir.2025.v2i1n03

Thomas, O. D., Salek, M. S., Tine, J.-M., Rahman, M., Hockstad, T., & Chowdhury, M. (2025). *Cybersecurity in Transportation Systems: Policies and Technology Directions*. /arxiv.2501.05356DOI: 10.48550

Ukwandu, E., Ben Farah, M. A., Hindy, H., Bures, M., Atkinson, R., Tachtatzis, C., & Bellekens, X. (2021). Cyber-Security Challenges in Aviation Industry: A Review of Current and Future Trends. *arXiv: Cryptography and Security*. https://dblp.uni-trier.de/db/journals/corr/corr2107.html#abs-2107-04910

Urosevic, U., & Čubrović, M. (2023). Security in Cyber-Physical and IoT Systems. *Tehnika*, *78*(1), 45–51. DOI: 10.5937/tehnika2301045U

van Niekerk, B. (2017). *Analysis of Cyber-Attacks against the Transportation Sector*. IGI Global., DOI: 10.4018/978-1-5225-1938-6.ch004

Xie, Y., Gardi, A., &Sabbatini, R. (2023). *Cybersecurity Risks and Threats in Avionics and Autonomous Systems*. 0814–0819. DOI: 10.1109/DASC/PiCom/CBDCom/Cy59711.2023.10361328

Yap, J. S., Teo, Y. C., & Raslan, M. A. H. bin M., Subramaniam, M. R., Lim, Y. X., Say, J. K., Moh, S. L., &Sindiramutty, S. R. (2024). *In-Depth Analysis and Countermeasures for Ransomware Attacks: Case Studies and Recommendations*. DOI: 10.20944/preprints202408.2261.v1

Yu, H., Meng, Q., Fang, Z., & Liu, M. (2023). Literature review on maritime cybersecurity: State-of-the-art. *Journal of Navigation*, *76*(4-5), 1–14. DOI: 10.1017/S0373463323000164

Chapter 5
Cybersecurity Threats in Hospitality Services: A Review of Data Breach Impacts

Siti Nurhayati Khairatun
http://orcid.org/0000-0002-5239-8212
Universiti Putra Malaysia, Malaysia

Tianshu Zheng
http://orcid.org/0009-0004-8507-2544
Iowa State University, USA

ABSTRACT

Hotels and restaurants increasingly rely on digital systems for bookings and operations, making them vulnerable to cyberattacks. This study analyzes 50 data breaches, 17 in hotels, 33 in restaurants, to identify key risks. Common weaknesses include outdated systems, third-party dependencies, poor encryption, and phishing. Breaches expose customer data, leading to financial losses, fines, and eroded trust—critical in a guest-centric industry. Hotels face high risks from credential theft and social engineering, often due to human error. Restaurants are most affected by POS malware, credential stuffing, and compromised third-party platforms. The decentralized nature of hospitality amplifies these threats. Findings show generic cybersecurity measures are insufficient. Instead, tailored strategies are needed: staff training, proactive risk management, and adherence to standards like GDPR, PCI-DSS, and ISO/IEC 27001. By examining real incidents, this research provides practical insights for strengthening cybersecurity across the global hospitality sector.

DOI: 10.4018/979-8-3373-5826-0.ch005

INTRODUCTION

The hospitality industry encompassing hotels and restaurants has emerged as a prime target for cyberattacks in recent years. This heightened vulnerability is rooted in the sector's extensive reliance on digital infrastructure and its routine handling of vast amounts of sensitive customer data, including personal information and financial records. As businesses increasingly adopt connected technologies to enhance guest experiences and streamline operations, the digital attack surface available to cybercriminals has expanded significantly. Consequently, the rapidly growing hospitality sector now faces increasingly sophisticated and persistent cyber threats.

The Data Breach Investigations Report (DBIR) provides critical insight into this evolving threat landscape, documenting over 220 security breach incidents within the industry, 106 of which involved confirmed data loss (Verizon Business, 2024). Notably, the report reveals that 92% of these breaches were primarily driven by two pervasive attack vectors: social engineering and basic web application vulnerabilities (Lirosi, 2024). This underscores a systemic susceptibility to relatively common yet highly effective cyber tactics.

Further evidence highlights the severity and recurrence of these incidents. Approximately 31% of hospitality organizations have experienced at least one data breach, with a striking 89% of affected entities being targeted multiple times within a single year (Shutenko & Solovei, 2025; Asimily Blog, 2025). The financial impact of such breaches is substantial: in 2024, the average cost of a data breach in the hospitality sector exceeded $3.8 million, reflecting a consistent upward trend in economic consequences (Markovic, 2025).

As a major contributor to global GDP, the tourism and hospitality industry is inherently tied to digital innovation and data-driven operations (Naldi et al., 2022; Jamal et al., 2021). While digitalization enhances operational efficiency and enables new service models, it simultaneously introduces new vulnerabilities to cyber threats (Sabourin, 2021). The widespread integration of technology in hotels and restaurants, from online booking platforms and point-of-sale (POS) systems to smart room automation and mobile guest services, has created complex digital ecosystems that are increasingly attractive to malicious actors (Krabokoukis, 2023; Zhang, 2023; Wynn & Lam, 2023).

The sheer volume of personal and financial data processed by hospitality businesses makes them particularly lucrative targets for cybercriminals seeking to exploit information for financial gain (Chorna et al., 2024). The onset of the COVID-19 pandemic accelerated the sector's digital transformation, prompting a rapid shift toward contactless services, digital check-ins, and expanded online platforms to ensure business continuity (Choi et al., 2022; Anwar et al., 2024; Raki et al., 2021). While essential for adaptation, this accelerated digitalization significantly broadened the industry's digital footprint, thereby increasing exposure to cyber risks (Efthimiou, 2024).

Despite these technological advancements, the process of digital transformation often proceeds without adequate cybersecurity safeguards, exposing organizations to implementation challenges and security gaps (Hussein et al., 2024). The integration of advanced technologies such as artificial intelligence (AI), the Internet of Things (IoT), and big data analytics, while enhancing service personalization and operational efficiency, further complicates the cybersecurity landscape (Singh et al., 2024). These innovations, along with integrated property management systems and mobile-based guest services, form intricate digital ecosystems that require robust and adaptive security frameworks to protect against potential breaches (Jones & Comfort, 2021; Alt, 2021; Voronova et al., 2020).

Given the sector's reliance on reputation and customer trust, understanding the nature and impact of cyber threats is critical for ensuring business continuity and maintaining consumer confidence (Petersons, 2024). The escalating sophistication and frequency of cyberattacks demand a shift from reactive to proactive cybersecurity strategies (Abrahams et al., 2024). This includes evaluating the types of attacks prevalent in the industry, assessing the effectiveness of current security protocols, and analyzing the reputational and financial consequences of data breaches.

Moreover, the imperative for digital transformation to meet evolving customer expectations and remain competitive underscores the urgent need for comprehensive cybersecurity measures (Lam & Law, 2018). As advanced analytics, mobile integration, and IoT-enabled devices become standard in hospitality operations, the protection of visitor data collected through POS systems and other digital infrastructures becomes paramount (Voronova et al., 2020). In this context, bolstering cyber resilience is not merely a technical necessity but a strategic business priority (Riasat et al., 2025).

OBJECTIVES

This study aims to identify and analyze data breach incidents that occurred within the global hospitality sector, specifically in hotels and restaurants, over the past 15 years. By examining these incidents, the research traced the evolution of cybersecurity threats in relation to technological advancements, exploring how changes in digital infrastructure, payment systems, customer data management, and connectivity influenced the frequency, scale, and modus operandi of breaches over time.

Through a comprehensive review of documented breaches, industry reports, and cybersecurity databases, the study categorized common attack vectors, including phishing, malware, insider threats, and third-party vulnerabilities, and assessed their impact on both businesses and consumers. It further highlighted emerging patterns and sector-specific vulnerabilities, providing a nuanced understanding of the cyber risk landscape.

LITERATURE REVIEW

Scholarly research confirms data breaches significantly reduce the firm value of tourism companies, evidenced by an average -1.9% negative market reaction upon the announcement of such an incident. What's more, this negative impact is not confined to the breached firm alone; it extends to uncompromised companies within the same sub-industry, particularly affecting those in the restaurant and hotel sectors (Park et. al., 2025).

A study by Johnson et al. (2018) highlighted the unique susceptibility of hospitality firms to data breaches, attributing it to the extensive volume of customer and employee data they manage. Their research analyzed the stock market's reaction to such breaches within the hospitality sector, drawing comparisons to similar incidents in the retail industry. Findings indicated that hotel and restaurant companies experienced an approximate 1.24% decrease in stock prices following data breach announcements. Interestingly, neither the nature of the breach nor the frequency of previous breaches significantly altered this impact on firm returns. However, hotel firms consistently incurred a more substantial loss in value post-breach compared to restaurants.

The frequency and sophistication of attacks are amplified by gaps in cybersecurity talent and rapid changes in attack vectors, including ransomware, phishing, and social engineering (Shutenko & Solovei, 2025). Regulatory pressures such as evolving data protection laws and the complexities of managing third-party vendors further complicate cybersecurity management in the hospitality industry (Lirosi, 2024).

The period from 2019 to 2024 has witnessed a dramatic evolution in both cyber threats and defensive strategies. While advancements in AI, encryption, and security frameworks offer promising solutions, human vulnerability and regulatory fragmentation remain persistent challenges. The tourism and hospitality sectors, in particular, face heightened risks due to their data-intensive operations and reliance on third-party systems. To ensure long-term sustainability, organizations must adopt a holistic approach that combines technological innovation, regulatory compliance, employee education, and transparent governance.

The hospitality industry, encompassing hotels, motels, resorts, bed and breakfasts, and food service establishments such as restaurants, cafes, and catering operations, has undergone a profound digital transformation in recent decades (Voronova et al., 2020). Characterized by high-frequency customer interactions and transactional activity, the sector routinely processes and stores vast volumes of sensitive personal and financial data, including names, addresses, credit card details, passport numbers, and travel itineraries (Okoye et al., 2024; Warren, 2010). This data-intensive nature positions hospitality firms as prime targets for cybercriminals, whose motives range from financial gain to identity theft and data resale on the dark web (Okoye et al., 2024).

Digital Transformation and the Expansion of Cyber Risk

The integration of advanced technologies like AI, blockchain, and IoT has revolutionized the hospitality industry by enhancing guest experience and operational efficiency, transforming information technology into a primary driver of competitive advantage (Anwar et al., 2024; Hussein et al., 2024; Chalupa & Petricek, 2020; Wynn & Lam, 2023; Lam & Law, 2018). However, this digital evolution, which represents a total reimagining of business models and organizational culture has introduced complex cybersecurity challenges that necessitate a fundamental re-evaluation of risk management (Singh et al., 2024; Giannoukou, 2024; Zhang, 2023; Alt, 2021; Mulyana et al., 2024). The COVID-19 pandemic further accelerated this shift, forcing rapid digital adoption that often-outpaced cybersecurity investment and amplified systemic risks (Aksoy et al., 2022; Rupeika-Apoga et al., 2022; Shanti et al., 2023; Anwar et al., 2024; Turluev & Mutsurova, 2021; Hundal et al., 2025). To address these vulnerabilities, experts argue that modern resilience now requires a sophisticated convergence of machine learning and blockchain to protect these newly decentralized digital ecosystems (Lanjewar et al., 2024).

Unique Vulnerabilities of the Hospitality Sector

Despite its growing digital footprint, the hospitality industry has historically lagged in cybersecurity maturity compared to other data-sensitive sectors such as healthcare and finance (Al-Qarni, 2023). Many organizations operate with outdated security infrastructures, limited dedicated IT personnel, and insufficient cybersecurity budgets (Wynn & Lam, 2023). This underinvestment, combined with the sector's high volume of data processing and transactional activity, creates a fertile environment for cyber intrusions.

The industry's reliance on interconnected systems such as spanning reservations, payment processing, guest management, and third-party vendors, further exacerbates its vulnerability (Quader & Janeja, 2021). Unlike more centralized industries, hospitality often features decentralized IT environments, transient customer bases, and geographically dispersed operations, all of which increase the complexity of securing digital assets (Wasserman & Wasserman, 2022). The integration of third-party platforms such as online travel agencies (OTAs), cloud-based POS systems, and external vendors, introduces additional entry points for attackers, many of whom exploit weak access controls or outdated software (Lirosi, 2024; Borkova et al., 2021).

The Escalating Threat Landscape

Between 2019 and 2024, the hospitality sector experienced a surge in sophisticated cyberattacks, including ransomware and advanced persistent threats (APTs) launched by criminal networks and nation-state actors (Achuthan et al., 2024; Alnajim et al., 2023; Shutenko & Solovei, 2025). These breaches often capitalize on a combination of technical vulnerabilities, human error, and advanced evasion techniques designed to bypass traditional security measures (Lirosi, 2024; Shutenko & Solovei, 2025; Turukmane et al., 2024). Furthermore, the integrity of organizational decision-making is increasingly threatened by misinformation, necessitating the use of hybrid detection models like LSTM-XGBoost (Kumar et al., 2025). As the transition to remote and hybrid work models has expanded attack vectors and insider risks within the broader ICT-dependent economy, traditional perimeter-based defenses are no longer sufficient (Raissouni et al., 2023; Abrahams et al., 2024; Khatri et al., 2023). Consequently, industry must shift toward adaptive security strategies that prioritize real-time threat detection and predictive intelligence (Gadhi et al., 2024; Wilson et al., 2024).

Financial and Reputational Impact of Data Breaches

Empirical research indicates that data breaches inflict severe financial and reputational damage on the tourism and hospitality sectors, with public disclosures triggering average negative market reactions ranging from 1.24% to 1.9% (Park et al., 2025; Johnson et al., 2018). These losses are often driven by brand dilution and diminished consumer confidence, though a notable disparity exists where hotel firms suffer greater market value declines than restaurants (Park et al., 2025; Johnson et al., 2018). Beyond immediate stock price fluctuations, the sector faces long-term challenges such as regulatory penalties, legal liabilities, and an erosion of customer trust that is particularly damaging in service-oriented environments (Markovic, 2025; Shutenko & Solovei, 2025). With the average cost of a breach now exceeding $3.8 million, the rising financial burden is increasingly attributed to the high costs of forensic investigations, customer notifications, and necessary remediation efforts (Markovic, 2025).

Regulatory, Human, and Strategic Challenges

The hospitality industry faces growing regulatory pressures due to the proliferation of data protection laws such as the General Data Protection Regulation (GDPR). Compliance with these frameworks is essential to ensure the lawful handling, protection, and privacy of customer data. However, inconsistent regulatory landscapes across jurisdictions hinder uniform compliance and preparedness, particularly for multinational chains (Lirosi, 2024; Shutenko & Solovei, 2025).

Compounding these challenges are persistent gaps in cybersecurity talent and workforce readiness (Shutenko & Solovei, 2025). The sector often lacks dedicated cybersecurity personnel, and employee training on data protection and threat awareness remains inadequate. Human error such as falling for phishing scams or misconfiguring systems, continues to be a primary vulnerability (Lirosi, 2024). This underscores the need for ongoing education, awareness programs, and a culture of security across all organizational levels.

Adaptation to GDPR, PCI-DSS, and ISO/ IEC 27001 in the Hospitality Sector

The hospitality industry, characterized by its extensive collection, processing, and storage of sensitive guest data, operates within a complex and evolving regulatory environment that demands robust information security and data protection frameworks. As digital transformation accelerates and cyber threats grow in sophistication, hospitality organizations must navigate a multifaceted compliance landscape to safeguard customer information, maintain operational integrity, and uphold legal and reputational standards. This comparative analysis critically examines three pivotal frameworks namely the General Data Protection Regulation (GDPR), the Payment Card Industry Data Security Standard (PCI-DSS), and ISO/IEC 27001 by assessing their distinct scopes, requirements, and synergistic potential within the context of hospitality operations.

While hospitality firms often rely on frameworks like PCI-DSS and ISO/IEC 27001, the scale of data processing requires next-generation technical solutions. Turukmane and Khekare (2023) propose the use of cyber quantum computing security measures, specifically using Rectified Probabilistic Packet Mark (RPPM) techniques, to secure big data environments against high-speed, large-scale intrusions. Such innovations complement existing encryption and security frameworks by providing a more resilient foundation for the high-frequency transactional activity characteristic of the hospitality sector.

The General Data Protection Regulation (GDPR): A Comprehensive Legal Framework for Personal Data Protection

The General Data Protection Regulation (GDPR), effective since May 25, 2018, represents a landmark advancement in data privacy legislation within the European Union (EU). It supersedes Directive 95/46/EC and establishes a legally binding, directly applicable regulatory framework across all EU Member States, mandating a fundamental re-evaluation of personal data management practices for any organization processing the data of EU residents (Magalhaes, 2021; Yoon et al., 2018). Notably, GDPR's extraterritorial reach extends its jurisdiction beyond EU-based entities, requiring compliance from any hospitality provider, regardless of geographic location, that offers goods or services to individuals in the EU (Mangini et al., 2020).

GDPR is structured around 99 articles and 173 recitals, providing both binding legal requirements and contextual guidance on data protection principles (Shastri et al., 2019). Its core tenets include lawfulness, fairness, transparency, purpose limitation, data minimization, accuracy, storage limitation, integrity, and confidentiality, all underpinned by the principle of accountability (Spagnuelo et al., 2020; Zaman & Hassani, 2020). This accountability principle compels organizations not only to comply with the regulation but also to demonstrate compliance through documented policies, regular audits, and impact assessments (Torre et al., 2020; Tsohou et al., 2020).

The regulation applies to both data controllers, entities that determine the purposes and means of data processing and data processors, those that process data on behalf of controllers—thereby directly influencing the operational workflows of hotels, restaurants, and third-party service providers such as online travel agencies (OTAs) (Neisse et al., 2018). GDPR's broad definition of personal data encompasses any information relating to an identifiable natural person, including names, addresses, credit card details, passport numbers, location data, and online identifiers (Lopes et al., 2019), making it highly relevant to the data-intensive operations of the hospitality sector.

Furthermore, GDPR grants data subjects a suite of enforceable rights, including the right to access, rectification, erasure (right to be forgotten), restriction of processing, data portability, and objection to automated decision-making (Granata et al., 2024; Biswal & Kulkarni, 2021). These rights necessitate the development of transparent data governance practices and responsive internal procedures, particularly in human resources and customer service departments where large volumes of employee and guest data are routinely processed (Vargas et al., 2021).

Non-compliance with GDPR carries severe financial penalties, up to 4% of an organization's global annual revenue or €20 million, whichever is higher (Debruyne et al., 2020; Tikkinen-Piri et al., 2017). This stringent enforcement mechanism has prompted many hospitality firms to undertake systemic changes, including overhauling privacy policies, redesigning data processing architectures, and minimizing data retention to reduce compliance risk (Mohan et al., 2019; Demirer et al., 2024). The regulation's emphasis on privacy by design and default further requires that data protection be integrated into the development of new systems and services from the outset (Biswal & Kulkarni, 2021; Amariles et al., 2020).

While ISO/IEC 27001 provides a strong foundation for information security, organizations seeking GDPR compliance may need to extend their control frameworks to address GDPR-specific requirements, particularly in personal data management and subject rights fulfillment (Diamantopoulou et al., 2020). The newer ISO/IEC 27552 standard specifically enhances the ISO 27001 framework to align with GDPR's privacy-centric approach, offering a structured pathway for integrating data protection into broader information security management (Tzolov, 2019).

PCI-DSS: Industry-Specific Security for Payment Card Data

In contrast to GDPR's broad focus on personal data privacy, the Payment Card Industry Data Security Standard (PCI-DSS) is a proprietary, industry-specific framework administered by the Payment Card Industry Security Standards Council (PCI SSC). Its primary objective is to reduce credit card fraud by establishing a baseline of technical and operational controls for entities that store, process, or transmit cardholder data (Helgadottir, 2019; Zhang, 2023).

PCI-DSS is mandatory for all organizations that accept branded payment cards from major schemes namely Visa, MasterCard, American Express, Discover, and JCB, regardless of transaction volume, making it particularly salient for the hospitality sector, which processes a high frequency of card-based transactions (Bulsara & Pandya, 2019). The standard outlines 12 primary requirements, subdivided into hundreds of specific sub-requirements, covering critical domains such as building and maintaining a secure network (e.g., firewalls, encryption), protecting cardholder data (e.g., masking, encryption in transit and at rest), maintaining a vulnerability management program (e.g., anti-virus, patching), implementing strong access control measures, regularly monitoring and testing networks and maintaining an information security policy.

Compliance with PCI-DSS is verified through annual assessments conducted by a Qualified Security Assessor (QSA) or internal security assessors (ISA), depending on the organization's transaction volume (Mohseni, 2013). Failure to maintain compliance can result in fines, increased transaction fees, or even the loss of card processing privileges, which can severely disrupt operations and damage customer trust (Sirigina, 2023).

Unlike GDPR, which emphasizes legal accountability and individual rights, PCI-DSS is technically prescriptive, focusing on specific controls to secure payment data. However, its implementation complements broader data protection goals by reinforcing technical safeguards such as encryption, access control, and continuous monitoring (Zhang, 2023). The evolving nature of payment technologies—such as contactless payments and mobile wallets—further necessitates ongoing security assessments and adaptive compliance strategies (Bulsara & Pandya, 2019).

ISO/IEC 27001: A Holistic Framework for Information Security Management

ISO/IEC 27001, jointly published by the International Organization for Standardization (ISO) and the International Electrotechnical Commission (IEC), provides a comprehensive, internationally recognized framework for establishing, implementing, maintaining, and continually improving an Information Security Management System (ISMS) (Disterer, 2013; Culot et al., 2021). Unlike the legally binding nature of GDPR or the prescriptive mandates of PCI-DSS, ISO/IEC 27001 offers a flexible, best-practice approach that can be tailored to an organization's size, sector, and risk profile (Kitsios et al., 2022; Panda & Alexander, 2019).

The standard is built upon the Plan-Do-Check-Act (PDCA) cycle, a continuous improvement model that enables organizations to systematically identify, assess, treat, and monitor information security risks (Torregosa et al., 2021; Disterer, 2013). A core principle of ISO/IEC 27001 is its risk-based approach, requiring organizations to conduct formal risk assessments and implement controls proportionate to the identified threats (Marhad et al., 2024; Fauzi & Lubis, 2021).

Annex A of the standard provides a catalog of 114 security controls across 14 domains—such as access control, cryptography, physical security, and incident management—aligned with the guidance in ISO/IEC 27002 (Kitsios et al., 2022). These controls address both technical and human factors, recognizing that organizational culture, employee awareness, and procedural rigor are as critical to security as technological safeguards (Alavi et al., 2014; Niescieruk et al., 2017).

Although ISO/IEC 27001 is not legally mandatory, its certification serves as a powerful signal of organizational commitment to information security, enhancing stakeholder trust and providing a competitive advantage (Sonkar, 2025). It also facilitates compliance with regulatory requirements such as GDPR and PCI-DSS by providing a structured framework for managing data protection and security controls (Tikanmaki et al., 2024).

For the hospitality industry, ISO/IEC 27001 offers a unifying framework that integrates security across decentralized operations, third-party vendors, and diverse service touchpoints. It enables organizations to move beyond compliance-driven security to a proactive, enterprise-wide culture of risk awareness and continuous improvement (Domínguez-Domínguez et al., 2023; Watkins, 2022).

While GDPR, PCI-DSS, and ISO/IEC 27001 differ in scope and enforcement, they are highly complementary and can be strategically integrated to form a robust cybersecurity posture in the hospitality sector. In brief, GDPR ensures legal compliance with data privacy rights and accountability, while PCI-DSS provides specific, actionable controls for securing payment data and ISO/IEC 27001 offers a holistic, risk-based management system that can encompass both regulatory and technical requirements. Together, these standards form a synergistic ecosystem that enables hospitality organizations to meet regulatory obligations, protect sensitive data, and build long-term resilience against evolving cyber threats.

For instance, an ISMS aligned with ISO/IEC 27001 can serve as the overarching structure within which GDPR compliance activities (e.g., data protection impact assessments) and PCI-DSS controls (e.g., network segmentation, encryption) are implemented and monitored (Diamantopoulou et al., 2020; Tzolov, 2019). This integrated approach not only enhances efficiency but also ensures consistency, reduces duplication, and strengthens overall resilience.

Moreover, the convergence of these frameworks supports a culture of security by design, where data protection is embedded into business processes, employee training, and technological infrastructure from the outset (Biswal & Kulkarni, 2021; El-Bably, 2021). This is particularly critical in an industry where customer trust, brand reputation, and operational continuity are intrinsically linked to data security. Table 1 presents a comparative analysis of GDPR, PCI-DSS, and ISO/IEC 27001, summarizing their key features such as scope, enforcement, focus, penalties and applicability.

Table 1. Comparison between GDPR, PCI-DSS and ISO/IEC 27001

Feature	GDPR	PCI-DSS	ISO/IEC 27001
Scope	Personal data protection in the EU	Securing cardholder data globally	Comprehensive ISMS framework
Enforcement	Regulatory (fines by DPAs)	Enforced by card brands via acquirers	Voluntary certification, though often contractually required
Focus	Legal compliance, individual rights	Technical and operational security of payment data	Risk-based information security management
Penalties	Up to €20M or 4% of revenue	Fines, loss of card processing ability	No direct fines, but reputational and contractual consequences
Applicability	Any organization handling EU residents' data	Any entity processing card payments	Any organization seeking structured security management

This comparative analysis highlights the critical importance of adopting a multi-layered, integrated approach to cybersecurity and data protection in the hospitality industry. While GDPR establishes a comprehensive legal foundation for personal data privacy, PCI-DSS delivers targeted safeguards for payment card data, and ISO/IEC 27001 provides a systematic, adaptable framework for managing information security risks.

METHODOLOGY

This study employed a systematic qualitative content analysis to examine data breach incidents within the global hospitality industry, with a specific focus on hotels and restaurants. Given the escalating frequency and severity of cyberattacks in this sector, and the frequent absence or delay of official disclosures from affected organizations, media reports serve as a critical and accessible source of real-world incident data (Kiyimba et al., 2018). Publicly reported incidents in reputable news outlets and cybersecurity-focused digital platforms often provide timely, detailed, and substantiated accounts of breaches, making them a viable and widely accepted data source in cybersecurity research.

To ensure comprehensive and geographically diverse coverage, data were systematically collected from both digital and mainstream media sources. Digital platforms included specialized cybersecurity news websites, industry blogs, and technology-focused publications, while mainstream sources encompassed internationally recognized news organizations such as BBC, Reuters, The Guardian, and CNN. The Google search engine was utilized as the primary retrieval tool, given its broad indexing capabilities and widespread use in academic media-based research (Kiyimba et al., 2018).

Search queries were constructed using the following keywords: "cyber attack in hotels", "cyber-attack in restaurants", "data breach in hotels", and "data breach in restaurants". These terms were selected based on their alignment with established cybersecurity lexicon and their frequent usage in prior academic studies analyzing digital threats within service-oriented industries. To enable a longitudinal analysis of the evolution of cyber threats, only incidents reported between 2009 and 2024 were included, providing a 15-year temporal scope that captures critical shifts in attack methodologies, technological adoption, and regulatory landscapes.

The initial search yielded over 500 results. A rigorous screening process was then applied to ensure data quality and reliability. Duplicates were removed, and articles were excluded if they lacked factual detail, originated from unverified or non-credible sources, were opinion-based without empirical grounding, or were not published in English. The final dataset comprised 50 confirmed data breach incidents, of which

17 involved hotel chains and 33 affected restaurant businesses. An incident was included in the analysis only if it met the following criteria: (1) it involved unauthorized access to customer data such as payment information, personal identification, passport details, or reservation records or to critical operational systems; and (2) the occurrence of the breach was corroborated by at least two independent, reputable sources to enhance validity and minimize the risk of misinformation.

To analyze the dataset, content analysis was employed to systematically extract, categorize, and interpret relevant information from textual media reports. As emphasized by Stalmirska and Camprubi (2022), content analysis enables researchers to identify recurring patterns, emergent themes, and contextual factors within large volumes of unstructured textual data, making it particularly suitable for studying cybersecurity events reported in public domains.

A mixed-methods analytical approach was adopted to ensure a comprehensive examination of the identified breaches. The qualitative component involved systematic coding and thematic categorization of each incident based on key attributes, including primary attack vectors (e.g., ransomware, phishing, malware, insider threats, third-party vulnerabilities); types of data compromised (e.g., financial, personal, operational); geographic location of the affected organization; size and organizational structure (e.g., multinational chain, independent establishment); response and mitigation strategies implemented post-incident (e.g., system shutdowns, customer notifications, forensic investigations). This thematic coding facilitated an in-depth exploration of the operational, technical, and managerial factors contributing to cybersecurity vulnerabilities in the hospitality sector. Concurrently, a quantitative component was conducted to generate descriptive statistics that enabled the identification of temporal and spatial trends. This analysis examined the frequency of breaches over time, their regional distribution (e.g., North America, Europe, Asia-Pacific), and their prevalence across subsectors (hotels vs. restaurants). By integrating numerical data with qualitative insights, the study achieved a robust and multidimensional characterization of the evolving cyber threat landscape. This triangulation of methods enhanced the validity and depth of findings, allowing for a more nuanced interpretation of patterns, escalation trends, and emerging risks.

It is acknowledged that reliance on media reports presents certain limitations, including potential journalistic bias, incomplete technical details, lack of forensic validation, and variable reporting standards across outlets. However, as supported by prior research, media-based content analysis remains a reliable and practical method for identifying and analyzing cybersecurity incidents, particularly in industries where mandatory public disclosure is inconsistent or legally non-binding. In the absence of centralized, publicly accessible breach registries for the hospitality sector, media sources provide one of the most feasible avenues for constructing a comprehensive incident database.

Thus, this methodological approach offers valuable insights into the scope, nature, and impact of cyber threats confronting hotels and restaurants globally. By systematically analyzing real-world incidents over a 15-year period, the study contributes to a deeper understanding of the vulnerabilities inherent in the hospitality ecosystem and lays the empirical foundation for evidence-based recommendations to enhance sector-wide cyber resilience.

FINDINGS AND DISCUSSIONS

The section presents a comprehensive analysis of the data collected descriptively and thematic analysis in the study, offering insights into the research questions. By critically examining the outcomes, this discussion aims to elucidate the implications of the findings, identify potential limitations, and suggest avenues for future research.

Descriptive Analysis

An analysis of documented cybersecurity incidents within the hotel industry reveals a diverse array of attack vectors and compromised data types. Among the seventeen identified breaches, the primary causal factors were categorized. Credential theft and social engineering tactics emerged as a significant threat, accounting for approximately 29% of incidents (n=5), exemplified by breaches at Marriott (2020), Otelier, and MGM Resorts (2023). Malware infections constituted another major category, representing 24% of breaches (n=4), affecting companies such as IHG, Hilton, Wyndham, and Prestige Software. Direct network attacks or unauthorized access, where the specific initial method was not detailed, accounted for 18% of cases (n=3), including the major Marriott breach (2014-2018), Shangri-La, and Huazhu incidents. Compromises stemming from third-party vendors or vulnerabilities were also prevalent, making up 18% of breaches (n=3), as seen with Sabre, Choice Hotels, and Dalmahoy Hotel. Lastly, 12% of breaches (n=2) resulted from unprotected servers or configuration errors, notably affecting Honotel Group and The Fullerton Hotel Sydney. These findings indicate that hotel data breaches are multifaceted, with no single dominant cause, although credential-based attacks and malware are prominent threats. Figure 1 below indicates an overview of reported data breach incidents in the hotel sector, illustrating the frequency and scope of cybersecurity events across major hotel chains.

Figure 1. Descriptive summary of data breach incidents in the hotel sector

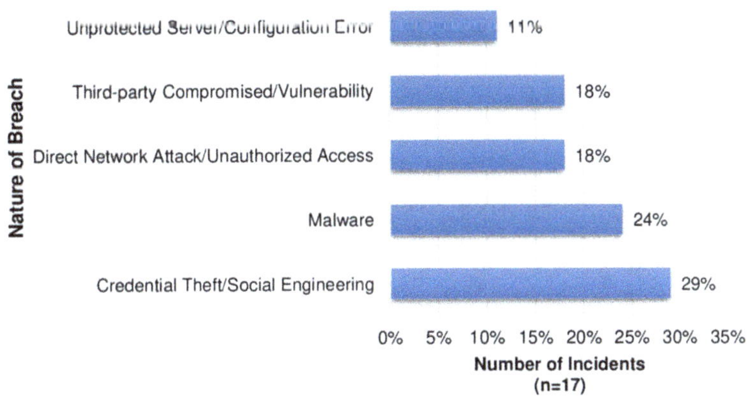

The analysis of data breaches within the restaurant sector highlights a pronounced focus on payment card data theft, primarily through Point-of-Sale (POS) system compromises. Out of the thirty-three identified incidents, malware, particularly POS-specific malware, was the overwhelmingly dominant attack vector, responsible for approximately 64% of breaches (n=21). This category includes widespread incidents affecting chains such as Zaxby's, Noodles & Co, Wendy's, Chipotle, Sonic, Darden Restaurants, Earl Enterprises, Landry's, Wawa, Checkers & Rally's, Hy-Vee, Yum! Brands, and Golden Corral. A broader category encompassing other methods such as web bugs, phishing, ransomware, and incidents with unspecified causes accounted for 24% of breaches (n=8), affecting Panera, Dunkin', DoorDash, McAlister's, Moe's, Schlotzsky's, Domino's India, McDonald's, Ahold Delhaize, Panda Express, Vero Foods, and Krispy Kreme. Credential stuffing or stolen credentials were cited as the primary cause in 6% of cases (n=2), impacting Dunkin' and Subway UK. Similarly, third-party compromises or vulnerabilities within shared infrastructure were identified as the main factor in 6% of breaches (n=2), specifically involving Wendy's and Focus Brands (McAlister's, Moe's, Schlotzsky's). This data underscores the restaurant industry's particular vulnerability to malware targeting payment processing systems, distinguishing its threat landscape from that of the hotel sector.

Figure 2. Descriptive summary of data breach incidents in the restaurant sector

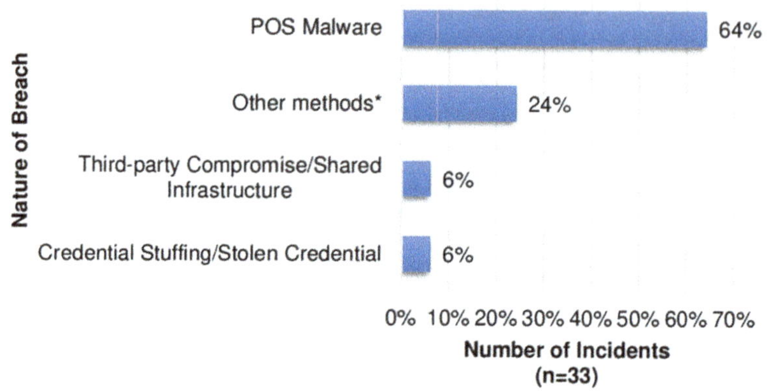

The findings of this study reveal a pervasive and escalating cybersecurity crisis within the global hospitality sector, particularly affecting hotels and restaurants. An analysis of recent data breaches demonstrates that the industry's rapid digital transformation, while enhancing operational efficiency and customer experience, has simultaneously expanded its attack surface, making it a prime target for cybercriminals. These findings align with the literature, which identifies the hospitality industry as uniquely vulnerable due to its data-intensive operations, decentralized IT infrastructures, and reliance on third-party vendors (Wynn & Lam, 2023; Wasserman & Wasserman, 2022). The discussion that follows synthesizes empirical evidence from recent breaches with scholarly insights to examine the nature of cyber threats, their root causes, financial and reputational consequences, and the strategic imperatives for mitigation.

The data indicate that cyberattacks in the hospitality sector are not isolated incidents but part of a systemic and recurring pattern. Major hotel chains including Marriott, Hilton, IHG, Hyatt, and MGM Resorts, have experienced multiple breaches over the past two decades, often involving the compromise of millions of guest records containing personally identifiable information (PII) such as names, addresses, passport numbers, and payment card details. The 2014–2018 Marriott-Starwood breach, which potentially affected 500 million guests, remains one of the largest data breaches in history and underscores the long latency period of undetected intrusions (Okoye et al., 2024). Similarly, the 2023 MGM Resorts breach, initiated through social engineering, resulted in over $100 million in losses, highlighting the financial toll of sophisticated attacks (Achuthan et al., 2024).

These findings corroborate the literature's assertion that the hospitality sector's digital ecosystem—comprising online booking systems, property management systems (PMS), point-of-sale (POS) terminals, and cloud-based platforms—is riddled with vulnerabilities (Quader & Janeja, 2021; Singh et al., 2024). The exploitation of third-party service providers, such as Sabre Hospitality Solutions and Otelier, further amplifies risk. The 2024 Otelier breach, which exposed 7.8 terabytes of guest data from major hotel chains, exemplifies how a single vendor compromise can cascade across multiple organizations (Lirosi, 2024). This supports the scholarly argument that third-party risk management is a critical, yet often neglected, component of cybersecurity in hospitality (Borkova et al., 2021).

The root causes of these breaches are multifaceted, encompassing technical, organizational, and human factors. Technically, outdated systems, misconfigured cloud storage (e.g., Honotel Group's unprotected server), and unpatched software create exploitable entry points. Organizationally, many hospitality firms operate with limited cybersecurity budgets, insufficient IT personnel, and fragmented security policies across geographically dispersed locations (Wynn & Lam, 2023; Al-Qarni, 2023). This structural weakness is exacerbated in franchise-based models, where individual operators may lack the resources or expertise to implement robust security measures (Hundal et al., 2025).

Human error remains a persistent vulnerability. The 2023 MGM Resorts breach, initiated by a phishing attack on an employee, illustrates how social engineering can bypass even technically sound defenses (Shutenko & Solovei, 2025). Similarly, the 2019 DoorDash breach originated from a phishing attack on a third-party provider, exposing 4.9 million users' data (Lirosi, 2024). These incidents affirm the literature's emphasis on human factors as a leading cause of breaches, necessitating comprehensive employee training and awareness programs (Khatri et al., 2023).

The financial and reputational impact of data breaches in the hospitality sector is substantial. Empirical evidence shows that breaches lead to direct costs—including forensic investigations, legal settlements, regulatory fines, and remediation efforts—often exceeding \$3.8 million on average (Markovic, 2025). The Wyndham Hotels case, which led to Federal Trade Commission (FTC) action, set a precedent for holding companies accountable for inadequate security practices (Johnson et al., 2018). Moreover, breaches trigger indirect costs such as stock price declines; Park et al. (2025) found that hospitality firms experience an average 1.9% negative market reaction post-breach, with hotel companies suffering greater losses than restaurants.

Reputational damage is equally significant. In a service-oriented industry where trust is paramount, breaches erode customer confidence and brand loyalty (Drake & Ridder, 2022). The spillover effect, where unbreached firms in the same sector also suffer reputational harm, further amplifies the collective risk (Park et al., 2025). This underscores the need for industry-wide cybersecurity standards and transparency in breach disclosure.

The evolving regulatory landscape, including the General Data Protection Regulation (GDPR), the Payment Card Industry Data Security Standard (PCI-DSS), and ISO/IEC 27001, imposes stringent requirements on data protection and compliance (Lirosi, 2024; Zhang, 2023). GDPR's extraterritorial reach and penalties of up to 4% of global revenue compel multinational hospitality firms to adopt privacy-by-design principles (Mangini et al., 2020). PCI-DSS mandates specific technical controls for securing payment data, while ISO/IEC 27001 provides a holistic framework for establishing an Information Security Management System (ISMS) based on risk assessment and continuous improvement (Disterer, 2013; Kitsios et al., 2022).

The integration of these frameworks offers a synergistic approach to cybersecurity. As Diamantopoulou et al. (2020) argue, an ISMS aligned with ISO/IEC 27001 can serve as the overarching structure within which GDPR compliance activities and PCI-DSS controls are implemented. This integrated model not only enhances compliance efficiency but also fosters a culture of proactive risk management, moving beyond reactive incident response to strategic resilience (Petersons, 2024; Abrahams et al., 2024).

Drawing on the literature, this discussion advocates for the adoption of integrated security frameworks, enhanced vendor risk management, continuous employee training, and transparent governance practices. Only through such a holistic strategy can the hospitality industry safeguard sensitive data, maintain consumer trust, and ensure sustainable digital evolution in an increasingly hostile cyber environment.

Thematic Content Analysis

A thematic content analysis of cybersecurity incidents in the hotel and restaurant sectors reveals four interconnected and critical themes: the nature and scope of cyber threats, root causes of vulnerability, financial and reputational consequences, and regulatory and strategic imperatives. The nature and scope of cyber threats demonstrate a shift from isolated attacks to systemic, large-scale breaches driven by sophisticated actors using malware, ransomware, social engineering, and third-party exploitation—evident in incidents such as the Marriott-Starwood breach affecting 500 million guests and the Otelier supply chain compromise impacting multiple hotel chains. These threats are facilitated by deep-rooted vulnerabilities, including outdated IT infrastructures, decentralized franchise models, misconfigured cloud storage (e.g., Honotel Group), and human error, as seen in the MGM Resorts phishing attack. The root causes highlight a persistent gap in cybersecurity investment, inadequate staff training, and overreliance on third-party vendors with weak security postures. These breaches carry severe financial and reputational consequences, including direct costs exceeding $100 million, class-action lawsuits (e.g., Wendy's $50 million settlement), stock price declines, and erosion of consumer trust, with research indicating an average 1.9% negative market reaction post-breach (Park et al., 2025). Finally, the evolving threat landscape has elevated cybersecurity to a strategic imperative, necessitating compliance with regulatory frameworks such as GDPR, PCI-DSS, and ISO/IEC 27001. Organizations must adopt integrated, proactive security strategies that combine technical controls, vendor risk management, employee awareness, and governance structures to build cyber resilience and safeguard the integrity of the hospitality industry.

Based on these findings, the study provided actionable and practical recommendations tailored to the operational realities of the hospitality industry. These recommendations were designed to enhance cybersecurity resilience, safeguard sensitive customer data, and support proactive risk management strategies. Ultimately, the research contributes to a deeper understanding of cyber threats in the hospitality sector and offers evidence-based guidance for organizations striving to strengthen their defenses in an increasingly interconnected and digitally dependent world.

SOLUTIONS AND RECOMMENDATIONS

The analysis of cybersecurity incidents within the global hospitality sector, encompassing hotels and restaurants, reveals a critical need for a strategic and integrated approach to cyber resilience. To address the multifaceted vulnerabilities and escalating threats documented over the past 15 years, a fundamental shift toward a Zero Trust Architecture (ZTA) is imperative. This model, predicated on the principle of "never trust, always verify," mandates continuous authentication and the enforcement of least-privilege access for all users and devices, thereby directly mitigating the prevalent risks of credential theft and social engineering, which have been identified as leading causes of breaches in the hotel industry.

To effectively navigate the complex regulatory and technical landscape, organizations should adopt a holistic security framework that synergistically integrates the General Data Protection Regulation (GDPR), the Payment Card Industry Data Security Standard (PCI-DSS), and ISO/IEC 27001. An Information Security Management System (ISMS) based on the risk-management principles of ISO/IEC 27001 can serve as the overarching structure. Within this framework, the specific technical controls of PCI-DSS for securing payment data can be systematically implemented, while the legal and procedural requirements of GDPR for personal data privacy can be rigorously enforced. This integrated approach promotes operational efficiency, reduces redundancy, and fosters a more cohesive and resilient security posture.

Given the persistent vulnerability of the human element, as evidenced by high-profile incidents initiated through phishing, a comprehensive and continuous employee cybersecurity training program is essential. This initiative must transcend one-time compliance exercises and evolve into an ongoing cultural endeavor, encompassing regular, role-specific modules on threat recognition, secure practices, and incident reporting to cultivate a pervasive culture of security from frontline staff to executive leadership.

The significant number of breaches originating from compromised third-party vendors, such as property management system providers and online travel agencies, necessitates the establishment of a formal and rigorous vendor risk management program. This requires conducting thorough security assessments prior to onboarding, mandating evidence of compliance with relevant standards, incorporating strong security clauses into contracts, and implementing continuous monitoring of vendor security postures to prevent cascading breaches.

To proactively identify and remediate technical weaknesses, such as unprotected servers and misconfigured cloud storage, organizations must conduct regular and comprehensive security assessments. These should include penetration testing, vulnerability scanning, and configuration audits to ensure that digital ecosystems are resilient against exploitation.

In recognition of the restaurant sector's pronounced vulnerability to Point-of-Sale (POS) malware, a specific focus on enhancing payment system security is warranted. This requires deploying advanced endpoint detection and response (EDR) solutions on all POS terminals, ensuring strict network segmentation, and maintaining rigorous patching and software hygiene to minimize the attack surface.

To mitigate the substantial financial and reputational damage associated with data breaches, which average over $3.8 million, every organization must develop, document, and regularly test a comprehensive incident response and communication plan. This plan must outline clear procedures for all phases of an incident and include a transparent strategy for timely notification of affected parties and regulators.

Finally, the persistent underinvestment in cybersecurity within the hospitality sector must be addressed by elevating cybersecurity to a strategic business priority. This requires a fundamental shift in resource allocation, including dedicated budgeting for security tools and personnel, and ensuring that cybersecurity is a standing agenda item for executive leadership and the board of directors. This top-down commitment is the cornerstone for driving the necessary cultural and operational changes to build long-term cyber resilience in an industry where customer trust is paramount.

CONCLUSION AND FUTURE RESEARCH DIRECTIONS

This study, which primarily examined historical cybersecurity incidents within the hospitality industry, identifies several critical avenues for future research to enhance the sector's proactive defensive capabilities. A comprehensive and systematic investigation is warranted to understand the real-time preparedness strategies employed by hospitality stakeholders, particularly focusing on the perspectives and practices of IT departments within hotel organizations and their external technology service providers.

In conclusion, the findings evidenced that cybersecurity in the hospitality sector is not merely a technical issue but a strategic imperative that intersects with legal, financial, and operational domains. The convergence of digital transformation, third-party dependencies, human vulnerabilities, and regulatory pressures demands a comprehensive, multi-layered approach to cyber resilience.

Future research should prioritize conducting in-depth interviews and qualitative surveys with key stakeholders, including Chief Information Security Officers (CISOs), IT managers, cybersecurity personnel, and technology vendors serving the hospitality sector. These investigations should explore the specific methodologies, tools, and protocols these professionals employ to anticipate, detect, and respond to cyber threats in real-time operational environments. Understanding the organizational culture surrounding cybersecurity, decision-making processes during potential breach scenarios, and the allocation of resources for threat intelligence and incident response capabilities would provide invaluable insights for developing more effective defensive strategies.

Research should also investigate the effectiveness of specific cybersecurity technologies and methodologies within the unique operational context of hospitality environments. This includes evaluating the real-world performance of network segmentation strategies, endpoint detection and response systems, multi-factor authentication implementations, and zero-trust architectures within actual hotel and restaurant operational settings. Additionally, exploring the human factors component through behavioral studies could provide insights into how employee training, awareness programs, and organizational policies translate into practical security outcomes. The development of predictive models for cybersecurity risk assessment specific to the hospitality industry represents another valuable research direction. By analyzing historical incident data in conjunction with current threat intelligence and organizational characteristics, researchers could create frameworks to help hospitality organizations better anticipate and prepare for likely attack vectors. This could include sector-specific threat modeling that accounts for the unique operational rhythms, seasonal variations, and guest interaction requirements inherent in hospitality environments. Finally, future research should examine the regulatory compliance landscape and its impact on organizational cybersecurity preparedness, particularly in light of evolving data protection requirements such as the EU General Data Protection Regulation (GDPR) and other regional privacy laws (European Commission, n.d.). Understanding how compliance mandates influence investment decisions, technology adoption, and overall security posture could provide crucial insights for policymakers and industry leaders seeking to enhance the sector's collective resilience against cyber threats. Such comprehensive research would bridge the gap between reactive incident analysis and proactive defense strategy, ultimately contributing to a more secure and resilient hospitality industry.

REFERENCES

Abrahams, T. O., Ewuga, S. K., Dawodu, S. O., Adegbite, A. O., & Hassan, A. O. (2024). A review of cybersecurity strategies in modern organizations: Examining the evolution and effectiveness of cybersecurity measures for data protection. *Computer Science & IT Research Journal*, *5*(1), 1–25. DOI: 10.51594/csitrj.v5i1.699

Achuthan, K., Ramanathan, S., Srinivas, S., & Raman, R. (2024). Advancing cybersecurity and privacy with artificial intelligence: Current trends and future research directions. *Frontiers in Big Data*, *7*, 1497535. DOI: 10.3389/fdata.2024.1497535 PMID: 39703783

Aksoy, L., Choi, S., Doğru, T., Keiningham, T. L., Lorenz, M. P., Rubin, D., & Tracey, J. B. (2022). Global trends in hospitality. *Journal of Business Research*, *142*, 957–973. DOI: 10.1016/j.jbusres.2021.12.068 PMID: 36540755

Alavi, R., Islam, S., & Mouratidis, H. (2014). A conceptual framework to analyze human factors of information security management system (ISMS) in organizations. In *Lecture Notes in Computer Science* (pp. 297–305). Springer. DOI: 10.1007/978-3-319-07620-1_26

Al-Qarni, E. A. (2023). Cybersecurity in healthcare: A review of recent attacks and mitigation strategies. *International Journal of Advanced Computer Science and Applications*, *14*(5), 135–140. DOI: 10.14569/IJACSA.2023.0140513

Alnajim, A. M., Habib, S., Islam, M., AlRawashdeh, H. S., & Wasim, M. (2023). Exploring cybersecurity education and training techniques: A comprehensive review of traditional, virtual reality, and augmented reality approaches. *Symmetry*, *15*(12), 2175. DOI: 10.3390/sym15122175

Alt, R. (2021). Digital transformation in the restaurant industry: Current developments and implications. *Journal of Smart Tourism*, *1*(1), 69–74. DOI: 10.52255/smarttourism.2021.1.1.9

Ali, S. M., Kim, D. J., & Kim, Y. G. (2020). The impact of cyber security breach on customer loyalty: Mediating role of consumer emotions. *Journal of Retailing and Consumer Services*, *57*, 102238. DOI: 10.1016/j.jretconser.2020.102238

Amariles, D. R., Troussel, A., & Hamdani, R. E. (2020). Compliance generation for privacy documents under GDPR: A roadmap for implementing automation and machine learning. arXiv. /arxiv.2012.12718DOI: 10.48550

Anwar, F. A., Deliana, D., & Suyamto, S. (2024). Digital transformation in the hospitality industry: Improving efficiency and guest experience. *International Journal of Management Science and Information Technology*, *4*(2), 428–437. DOI: 10.35870/ijmsit.v4i2.3201

Asimily Blog. (2025). *3 cyberattacks that devastated hospitality in 2023 and 2024*. Asimily. https://asimily.com/blog/3-cyberattacks-hospitality-2023-2024/

Biswal, S. P., & Kulkarni, M. S. (2021). Implications of GDPR on emerging technologies. *Revista Gestão Inovação e Tecnologias, 11*(4), 4898–4912. https://pdfs.semanticscholar.org/787c/1102d0a3150388ca36cab851a37f9446f6c8.pdf

Borkova, E. A., Temnova, N., & Plotnikov, V. (2021). Transition of businesses to online in the Covid-19 pandemic. *The European Proceedings of Social & Behavioural Sciences,* 65-72. DOI: 10.15405/epsbs.2021.12.03.9

Bulsara, H. P., & Pandya, E. A. (2019). Influence of demographic factors on security and privacy concerns in mobile payments. *International Journal of Innovative Technology and Exploring Engineering*, *9*(2), 5135–5138. DOI: 10.35940/ijitee.B8125.129219

Chalupa, S., & Petricek, M. (2020). The application of business process management in the hospitality industry: A case study. *IBIMA Business Review, 2020,* 1–11. DOI: 10.5171/2020.301930

Choi, S., Yeon, J., Song, H. J., & Hu, J. (2022). Information technology as a buffer against COVID-19. *Annals of Tourism Research*, *98*, 103527. DOI: 10.1016/j.annals.2022.103527 PMID: 36575669

Chorna, N., Korzh, N., Kiziun, A., Onyshchuk, N., & Antoniuk, K. (2024). The role of digital technologies in the transformation of the tourism business: Prospects for development and impact on the country's economy. *Journal of Interdisciplinary Research*, *14*(1), 136–140. DOI: 10.33543/140139136140

Culot, G., Nassimbeni, G., Podrecca, M., & Sartor, M. (2021). The ISO/IEC 27001 information security management standard: Literature review and theory-based research agenda. *The TQM Journal*, *33*(7), 76–105. DOI: 10.1108/TQM-09-2020-0202

Debruyne, C., Pandit, H. J., Lewis, D., & O'Sullivan, D. (2020). "Just-in-time" generation of datasets by considering structured representations of given consent for GDPR compliance. *Knowledge and Information Systems*, *62*(9), 3615–3640. DOI: 10.1007/s10115-020-01468-x PMID: 32647404

Demirer, M., Hernández, D. J., Li, D., & Peng, S. (2024). Data, privacy laws and firm production: Evidence from the GDPR. *SSRN. NBER Working Paper No. w32146.* DOI: 10.2139/ssrn.4731055

Diamantopoulou, V., Tsohou, A., & Karyda, M. (2020). From ISO/IEC27001:2013 and ISO/IEC27002:2013 to GDPR compliance controls. *Information and Computer Security*, *28*(4), 645–662. DOI: 10.1108/ICS-01-2020-0004

Disterer, G. (2013). ISO/IEC 27000, 27001 and 27002 for information security management. *Journal of Information Security*, *4*(2), 92–99. DOI: 10.4236/jis.2013.42011

Dominguez-Dominguez, R., Laguna, O. A. F., & Sánchez-Valdez, J. A. (2023). Exploratory analysis of a measurement scale of an information security management system. *arXiv*. /arXiv.2306.07367DOI: 10.48550

Drake, R., & Ridder, E. (2022). *Healthcare cybersecurity vulnerabilities.*, DOI: 10.19107/CYBERCON.2022.06

Efthimiou, S. G. (2024). The adaptation of tourism industry and COVID-19. *Theoretical Economics Letters*, *14*(6), 2081–2094. DOI: 10.4236/tel.2024.146103

El-Bably, A. Y. (2021). Overview of the impact of human error on cybersecurity based on ISO/IEC 27001 information security management. *Journal of Information Security and Cybercrimes Research*, *4*(1), 95–102. DOI: 10.26735/WLPW6121

European Commission. (n.d.). *Data protection.* https://commission.europa.eu/law/law-topic/data-protection_en

Fauzi, R., & Lubis, M. (2021). Assessment framework for defining the maturity of information technology within enterprise risk management (ERM). *International Journal of Advanced Computer Science and Applications*, *12*(10), 680–689. DOI: 10.14569/IJACSA.2021.0121075

Gadhi, A., Gondu, R. M., Chaudhary, H., & Abiona, O. (2024). Cyber resilience through real-time threat analysis in information security. *International Journal of Communications, Network and Systems Sciences*, *17*(4), 51–67. DOI: 10.4236/ijcns.2024.174004

Giannoukou, I. (2024). Revolutionizing hospitality: Strategic integration of innovation management embracing technological innovation for enhanced customer experiences. *Technium Business and Management*, *7*, 24–39. DOI: 10.47577/business.v7i.10585

Granata, D., Mastroianni, M., Rak, M., Cantiello, P., & Salzillo, G. (2024). GDPR compliance through standard security controls: An automated approach. *Journal of High Speed Networks*, *30*(2), 147–174. DOI: 10.3233/JHS-230080

Helgadottir, D. (2019). The interaction between Directive 2015/2366 (EU) on payment services (PSD2) and Regulation (EU) 2016/679 on general data protection (GDPR) concerning third party players. SSRN *Electronic Journal*. DOI: 10.2139/ssrn.3455428

Hundal, G. S., Rhodes, D. H., & Laux, C. (2025). Digital transformation of healthcare enterprises in the era of disruptions—A structured literature review. *Sustainability (Basel)*, *17*(13), 5690. DOI: 10.3390/su17135690

Hussein, H. S., Albadry, O. M., Mathew, V., Al-Romeedy, B. S., Alsetoohy, O., Kamar, M. A., & Khairy, H. A. (2024). Digital leadership and sustainable competitive advantage: Leveraging green absorptive capability and eco-innovation in tourism and hospitality businesses. *Sustainability (Basel)*, *16*(13), 5371. DOI: 10.3390/su16135371

ISO. (2022). *ISO/IEC 27001:2022 Information security, cybersecurity and privacy protection — Information security management systems — Requirements*. https://www.iso.org/standard/27001

Jamal, T., Kircher, J., & Donaldson, J. P. (2021). Re-visiting design thinking for learning and practice: Critical pedagogy, conative empathy. *Sustainability (Basel)*, *13*(2), 964. DOI: 10.3390/su13020964

Johnson, M. S., Kang, M. J., Lawson, T., & Singh, A. J. (2018). The impact of data breaches on hotel and restaurant firm stock returns. *The Journal of Hospitality Financial Management*, *26*(2), 75–86. https://core.ac.uk/reader/220129940

Jones, P., & Comfort, D. (2021). Corporate digital responsibility in the hospitality industry. *Athens Journal of Tourism*, *8*(1), 9–18. DOI: 10.30958/ajt.8-1-1

Khatri, S., Cherukuri, A. K., & Kamalov, F. (2023). *Global pandemics influence on cyber security and cyber crimes*. arXiv. /arXiv.2302.12462DOI: 10.48550

Kitsios, F., Chatzidimitriou, E., & Kamariotou, M. (2022). Developing a risk analysis strategy framework for impact assessment in information security management systems: A case study in IT consulting industry. *Sustainability (Basel)*, *14*(3), 1269. DOI: 10.3390/su14031269

Kiyimba, N., Lester, J. N., & O'Reilly, M. (2018). Utilising media and text-based sources. *Using naturally occurring data in qualitative health research: A practical guide*, 159–178. DOI: 10.1007/978-3-319-94839-3_7

Krabokoukis, T. (2023). Technology tools in hospitality: Mapping the landscape through bibliometric analysis and presentation of a new software solution. *Digital*, *3*(1), 81–96. DOI: 10.3390/digital3010006

Kumar, M. V. S., Khekare, G., & Sankriti, A. (2025). Enhancing knowledge management integrity through fake news detection: A hybrid LSTM-XGBoost approach for cybersecurity. In *Cybersecurity in Knowledge Management* (pp. 131–150). CRC Press., DOI: 10.1201/9781003498094-9

Lam, C. Y. T., & Law, R. (2018). Readiness of upscale and luxury-branded hotels for digital transformation. *International Journal of Hospitality Management, 79*, 60–69. DOI: 10.1016/j.ijhm.2018.12.015

Lanjewar, U., Khekare, G., & Wahi, A. (2024, December). *An in-depth review of machine learning, blockchain, and deep learning models for intelligent security and resilience enhancement in smart cities* [Conference session]. 2024 International Conference on Artificial Intelligence and Quantum Computation-Based Sensor Application (ICAIQSA), Nagpur, India. DOI: 10.1109/ICAIQSA64000.2024.10882264

Lirosi, M. (2024). *Cybersecurity: Hackers don't go on holiday, cyber attacks in tourism are growing*. First Online. https://www.firstonline.info/en/cybersecurity-hackers-don't-go-on-holiday-cyber-attacks-in-tourism-are-increasing/

Lopes, I., Guarda, T., & Oliveira, P. (2019). Implementation of ISO 27001 standards as GDPR compliance facilitator. *Journal of Information Systems Engineering & Management, 4*(2), 1–8. DOI: 10.29333/jisem/5888

de Magalhaes, M. (2021). Data protection regulation: A comparative law approach. *International Journal of Digital Law, 2*(2), 33–53. DOI: 10.47975/IJDL.magalhaes.v.2.n.2

Markovic, S. (2025). *Cyberattacks are draining millions from the hospitality industry*. Help Net Security. https://www.helpnetsecurity.com/2025/07/03/hospitality-industry-cybersecurity-challenges/

Marhad, S. S., Goni, S. Z. A., & Sani, M. K. J. A. (2024). Implementation of information security management systems for data protection in organizations: A systematic literature review. *Environment-Behaviour Proceedings Journal, 9*(SI18), 197–203. DOI: 10.21834/e-bpj.v9iSI18.5483

Mangini, V., & Tal, I., & Moldovan, A.-N. (2020). An empirical study on the impact of GDPR and right to be forgotten – organisations and users perspective. *Proceedings of the 17th International Conference on Availability, Reliability and Security*, 1–9. DOI: 10.1145/3407023.3407080

Mohan, J., Wasserman, M. F., & Chidambaram, V. (2019). *Analyzing GDPR compliance through the lens of privacy policy*. arXiv. /arXiv.1906.12038DOI: 10.1007/978-3-030-33752-0_6

Mohseni, M. (2013). *Has your organization compliance with ISMS? A case study in an Iranian bank.* arXiv. /arXiv.1303.0468DOI: 10.48550

Mulyana, R., Rusu, L., & Perjons, E. (2024). Key ambidextrous IT governance mechanisms for successful digital transformation: A case study of Bank Rakyat Indonesia (BRI). *Digital Business, 4*(2), 100083. DOI: 10.1016/j.digbus.2024.100083

Naldi, S., Maulina, E., Herawaty, T., & Irawati, R. (2022). Hospitality and tourism innovation: A systematic literature review. [Bisnis Dan Manajemen]. *BISMA, 14*(2), 94–109. DOI: 10.26740/bisma.v14n2.p94-109

Neisse, R., Steri, G., & Fovino, I. N. (2018). Blockchain-based identity management and data usage control (extended abstract). In: Hansen, M., Kosta, E., Nai-Fovino, I., Fischer-Hübner, S. (eds) *Privacy and Identity Management. The Smart Revolution. Privacy and Identity 2017.* IFIP Advances in Information and Communication Technology, vol 526. Springer, Cham. DOI: 10.1007/978-3-319-92925-5_15

Niescieruk, A., Księżopolski, B., Nielek, R., & Wierzbicki, A. (2017). How to train people to increase their security awareness in IT. In *Lecture Notes in Electrical Engineering* (pp. 12–17). Springer., DOI: 10.1007/978-981-10-5041-1_3

Okoye, C. C., Nwankwo, E. E., Usman, F. O., Mhlongo, N. Z., Odeyemi, O., & Ike, C. U. (2024). Securing financial data storage: A review of cybersecurity challenges and solutions. *International Journal of Science and Research Archive, 11*(1), 1968–1983. DOI: 10.30574/ijsra.2024.11.1.0267

Park, J., Shin, W., Kim, B., & Kim, M. (2025). Spillover effects of data breach on consumer perceptions: Evidence from the e-commerce industry. *Internet Research, 35*(1), 1–24. https://www.emerald.com/intr/article/35/1/1/1241722/Spillover-effects-of-data-breach-on-consumer. DOI: 10.1108/INTR-11-2022-0898

Panda, S., & Alexander, A. (2019). Implementation of information security management system (ISMS) aligned with ISO 27001. *International Journal for Research in Applied Science and Engineering Technology, 7*(5), 218–227. DOI: 10.22214/ijraset.2019.5034

PCI Security Standards Council. (2022). *Payment Card Industry Data Security Standard: Requirements and testing procedures (Version 4.0).* https://www.pcisecuritystandards.org

Petersons, E. (2024). *Cybersecurity challenges in the era of digitalization. SSRN.* DOI: 10.2139/ssrn.4723047

Quader, F., & Janeja, V. P. (2021). Insights into organizational security readiness: Lessons learned from cyber-attack case studies. *Journal of Cybersecurity and Privacy, 1*(4), 638–659. DOI: 10.3390/jcp1040032

Raissouni, K., Errabih, Z., Charroud, S., Raissouni, R., Raissouni, M. R., & Bourekkadi, S. (2023). Cybersecurity in the context of Moroccan energy companies. *E3S Web of Conferences, 412*, 01038. DOI: 10.1051/e3sconf/202341201038

Raki, A., Nayer, D., Nazifi, A., Alexander, M., & Seyfi, S. (2021). Tourism recovery strategies during major crises: The role of proactivity. *Annals of Tourism Research, 90*, 103144. DOI: 10.1016/j.annals.2021.103144 PMID: 36540883

Riasat, I., Shah, M., & Gönül, M. S. (2025). Strengthening cybersecurity resilience: An investigation of customers' adoption of emerging security tools in mobile banking apps. *Computers, 14*(4), 129. DOI: 10.3390/computers14040129

Rose, S., Borchert, O., Mitchell, S., & Connelly, S. (2020). *NIST special publication 800-207: Zero trust architecture*. National Institute of Standards and Technology., DOI: 10.6028/NIST.SP.800-207

Rupeika-Apoga, R., Petrovska, K., & Буле, Л. (2022). The effect of digital orientation and digital capability on digital transformation of SMEs during the COVID-19 pandemic. *Journal of Theoretical and Applied Electronic Commerce Research, 17*(2), 669–685. DOI: 10.3390/jtaer17020035

Sabourin, V. (2021). *Strategic management for the hospitality and tourism industry*. CRC Press., DOI: 10.1201/9781003105831

Shanti, R., Siregar, H., Zulbainarni, N., & Tony, T. (2023). Role of digital transformation on digital business model banks. *Sustainability (Basel), 15*(23), 16293. DOI: 10.3390/su152316293

Shastri, S., Wasserman, M. F., & Chidambaram, V. (2019). *GDPR anti-patterns: How design and operation of modern cloud-scale systems conflict with GDPR*. arXiv. /arXiv.1911.00498DOI: 10.48550

Shutenko, V., & Solovei, A. (2025). *Cybersecurity in the hospitality industry: 6 threats and solutions*. Techmagic. https://www.techmagic.co/blog/hospitality-cybersecurity

Sirigina, P. V. (2023). Digital payment security: A developer framework. *International Journal of Scientific Research in Computer Science Engineering and Information Technology, 9*(4), 664–675. DOI: 10.32628/CSEIT23564520

Singh, R., Gehlot, A., Akram, S. V., Thakur, A. K., Gupta, L. R., Priyadarshi, N., & Twala, B. (2024). Integration of advanced digital technologies in the hospitality industry: A technological approach towards sustainability. *Sustainable Engineering and Innovation*, *6*(1), 37–55. DOI: 10.37868/sei.v6i1.id208

Sonkar, N. (2025). *Scaling an ISO compliance practice: Strategic insights from building a $1m+ cybersecurity certification line*. arXiv. DOI: 10.48550/ARXIV.2505.11583

Spagnuelo, D., Bartolini, C., & Lenzini, G. (2020). Qualifying and measuring transparency: A medical data system case study. *Computers & Security*, *91*, 101717. DOI: 10.1016/j.cose.2020.101717

Stalmirska, A. M., & Camprubí, R. (2022). Conducting a systematic qualitative content analysis in hospitality and tourism research. In *Contemporary Research Methods in Hospitality and Tourism* (pp. 127–141). Emerald Publishing Limited. DOI: 10.1108/978-1-80117-546-320221009

Tikanmaki, I., Savolainen, J., & Ruoslahti, H. (2024). The role of standards in enhancing cybersecurity and business continuity management for organizations. *Information & Security: An International Journal*, *55*(1), 63–82. DOI: 10.11610/isij.5523

Tikkinen-Piri, C., Rohunen, A., & Markkula, J. (2017). EU general data protection regulation: Changes and implications for personal data collecting companies. *Computer Law & Security Review*, *34*(1), 134–153. DOI: 10.1016/j.clsr.2017.05.015

Torre, D., Alférez, M., Soltana, G., Sabetzadeh, M., & Briand, L. (2020). *Model driven engineering for data protection and privacy: Application and experience with GDPR*. arXiv. /arXiv.2007.12046DOI: 10.48550

Torregosa, J. T., Orong, M. Y., Ricalde, G. T., Amin, W. D., Lonzon, H. A., & Alcontin, R. B. (2021). Assessing the conformity level of information security management system of the higher education institutions: Basis for the development of policies and guidelines. *Mediterranean Journal of Basic and Applied Sciences*, *5*(1), 57–71. *SSRN*. DOI: 10.2478/picbe-2021-0050

Tsohou, A., Magkos, E., Mouratidis, H., Chrysoloras, G., Piras, L., Pavlidis, M., Debussche, J., Rotoloni, M., & Crespo, B. G. N. (2020). Privacy, security, legal and technology acceptance elicited and consolidated requirements for a GDPR compliance platform. *Information and Computer Security*, *28*(4), 531–553. DOI: 10.1108/ICS-01-2020-0002

Turluev, R., & Mutsurova, Z. M. (2021). Digital technologies: Problems and trends. *SHS Web of Conferences, 101*, 2006. DOI: 10.1051/shsconf/202110102006

Turukmane, A. V., & Khekare, G. (2023). Cyber quantum computing (security) using rectified probabilistic packet mark for big data. In *Quantum computing in cybersecurity* (pp. 1–15). Wiley Scrivener Publishing LLC., DOI: 10.1002/9781394167401.ch1

Turukmane, A. V., Khekare, G., Shelke, N., Sakarkar, G., & Buchade, S. (2024, December). *Evasion techniques in cybersecurity: An in-depth analysis* [Conference session]. 2024 International Conference on Artificial Intelligence and Quantum Computation-Based Sensor Application (ICAIQSA), Nagpur, India. DOI: 10.1109/ICAIQSA64000.2024.10882284

Tzolov, T. V. (2019). ISO 27552 as a model for establishment personal information management systems. *Proceedings of the 2019 International Conference on Information Technology*, 1–4. DOI: 10.1109/InfoTech.2019.8860898

Vargas, V. M., Budz, S., & Onete, B. (2021). The relationship between human resources activities and the general data protection regulation. *Proceedings of the International Conference on Business Excellence, 15*(1), 552–559. DOI: 10.2478/picbe-2021-0050

Verizon Business. (2024). *Data breach investigations report.* https://www.verizon.com/business/resources/reports/dbir/

Voronova, O., Khareva, V., & Khnykina, T. (2020). Modern information technologies in the hotel business: Development trends and implementation issues. *E3S Web of Conferences, 164*, 09017. DOI: 10.1051/e3sconf/202016409017

Warren, K. (2010). Weighing the option of biometrics in the hospitality industry. *Worldwide Hospitality and Tourism Themes*, *2*(1), 100–109. DOI: 10.1108/17554211011012630

Wasserman, L., & Wasserman, Y. (2022). Hospital cybersecurity risks and gaps: Review (for the non-cyber professional). *Frontiers in Digital Health*, *4*, 862221. Advance online publication. DOI: 10.3389/fdgth.2022.862221 PMID: 36033634

Watkins, S. G. (2022). *ISO/IEC 27001:2022*. IT Governance Publishing. DOI: 10.2307/j.ctv30qq13d

Wilson, G., Johnson, O., & Brown, W. L. (2024). *Exploring the impact of digital transformation on marketing strategies in the retail sector. Preprints*.Org. DOI: 10.20944/preprints202407.2371.v1

Wynn, M., & Lam, C. Y. T. (2023). Digitalisation and IT strategy in the hospitality industry. *Systems*, *11*(10), 501. DOI: 10.3390/systems11100501

Yoon, J., Shin, Y., & Kim, J. (2018). A study on the information security management index through analysis of EU-GDPR (European Union-General Data Protection Regulation). *Asia-Pacific Journal of Law Politics and Administration*, *2*(2), 13–32. DOI: 10.21742/ajlpa.2018.2.2.03

Zaman, R., & Hassani, M. (2020). On enabling GDPR compliance in business processes through data-driven solutions. *SN Computer Science*, *1*(4), 210. DOI: 10.1007/s42979-020-00215-x

Zhang, Y. (2023). Analysis of the digital transformation development path for travel enterprises. *Open Journal of Applied Sciences*, *13*(8), 1370–1385. DOI: 10.4236/ojapps.2023.138109

Chapter 6
From Data to Justice: Leveraging Digital Forensics in Cybercrime Investigations in Tourism and Hospitality

Razia Nagina
http://orcid.org/0000-0002-0305-8393
Lovely Professional University, India

ABSTRACT

This chapter analyzes digital forensics as an essential tool to combat cybercrime in tourism and hospitality operations. It evaluates every phase of digital forensics alongside the various evidence types and legal standards for evidence acceptance and technological obstacles investigators encounter. Through qualitative content analysis combined with multiple case studies, the chapter reveals how metadata alongside encryption and digital signatures affect cyber investigations. The study analyzes complex legal systems that exist throughout different jurisdictions including India and the U.S. and the UK while examining current solutions that use AI and blockchain analysis with cloud forensics. The chapter reveals that encryption protects data but creates difficulties for investigations and advanced analytics together with metadata enable investigators to reconstruct timelines and establish attributions. The chapter provides actionable guidance to improve forensic preparedness together with international collaboration for enhanced cybersecurity and digital tourism trust.

INTRODUCTION

The quick adoption of technology has transformed global interactions between people and businesses and public institutions in the digital era (Ruzimatjon, 2024).

DOI: 10.4018/979-8-3373-5826-0.ch006

The modern digital shift has created fresh security dangers for computer systems which include ransomware attacks and data breaches and identity theft and unauthorized system access (Jimmy, 2021; Verma & Shri, 2022). The mentioned problems demonstrate that conventional investigation methods fail to produce results which impacts both individuals and organizations and public institutions equally.

Traditional methods fail to stop borderless cybercrimes because digital systems have spread to all sectors including tourism and hospitality (Florido-Benítez, 2025). Digital forensics has become an essential investigative tool because of this transition. The organized way of finding, storing, analyzing, and showing electronic evidence for legal purposes (Vaghela et al., 2024). The system maintains data authenticity and integrity and court admissibility while defending against advanced cybercriminal methods that include data obfuscation and anonymization and encryption (Ibrahim et al., 2025).

Regulations establish strict guidelines for digital forensics to maintain evidence integrity which goes beyond the basic data recovery process. The court may reject evidence if it has not been handled appropriately according to Karagiannis & Vergidis (2021). The forensic tasks consist of recovering deleted data alongside fake transaction monitoring and log analysis to reconstruct cyber-event sequences according to Das et al. (2021). Through forensic processes it becomes possible to establish accountability and implement legal repercussions using digital fragments as trustworthy evidence.

Klasén et al. (2024) explain that the transformation represents a fundamental change in law enforcement practice because officers now depend on digital evidence from communications and transactions and geolocation data instead of traditional physical evidence. Digital forensics requires updated regulations alongside enhanced tools and professional development programs because of emerging threats (Lovell et al., 2022). The management of massive digital platform data represents one of the major challenges. Law enforcement officials face daily challenges with handling large volumes of information that include emails together with logs along with browsing history and encrypted files. The tourism sector faces this challenge most because businesses conduct their customer interactions primarily through digital channels (Dhande, 2024).

Cybercriminals generally use encryption methods to conceal their unlawful operations which emerge hindrances in conducting investigations (Phillips et al., 2023). In case direct proof is missing, investigators use timeline reconstruction methods to examine events. Investigators must use metadata analysis together with timeline reconstruction techniques to collect essential evidence when direct evidence is missing. The process of reconstructing events becomes difficult for investigators because anti-forensic methods modify or delete data (González Arias et al., 2024).

The complete process relies on ahead given several legal requirements. In order to sustain its integrity, it is required that evidence collection process should comply specific legal frameworks. It embraces maintenance of proper records and chain-of-custody documentation (Krzan, 2021). As the evidences collected and presented by forensic experts in courts directly impacts the legal verdicts and decisions due to their perceived clarity and credibility, thus forensic experts should deliver complex results to courts in unambiguous and understandable manner (Bakhtiar, 2023).

Digital forensics operates as an important resource for criminal investigations, national security operations, corporate regulatory compliance and civil case resolutions (Faqir, 2023). Digital forensics serves as a vital support to the tourism sector by assisting in detecting fraud while safeguarding booking platforms, payment networks and protecting customer details (Tariq, 2024; Das et al., 2025). Digital forensics relevance is clearly demonstrated in the 2017 WannaCry ransomware attack as in this case, forensic experts employ forensic techniques to identify offenders, their locations and assist victims recover their systems (Singh & Chopra, 2025; Rehman & Rassias, 2024)

Digital forensics needs continuous development by way of research, high-tech techniques and corresponding legislative revisions. Improved decryption capabilities, enhanced anti-forensic tools along with the effective processing of large datasets should be the primary research areas (Iyengar et al., 2025). Digital forensics transforms digital proofs into reliable and authentic legal documentation which makes it essential for justice systems and security-dependent industries such as tourism (Vala & Vekariya, 2024). The dynamic field's function in detecting cybercrimes, promoting justice, and implementing accountability measures in modern digital society is explained in the section that follows.

OBJECTIVES

- To explore the digital forensics process starting from collection to court presentation in Tourism and Hospitality.
- To study the kinds of digital evidence in cybercrime investigations in Tourism and Hospitality.
- To explore the lawful standards and challenges surrounding the admissibility and authenticity of Digital Evidence in Criminal Prosecutions.
- To find the challenges faced by digital forensic investigators and the emerging technologies used to overcome these hurdles in Tourism and Hospitality.

REVIEW OF LITERATURE

The tourism sector along with hospitality industry confronted a magnificent digital transformation in last decade due to increasing online booking platforms and mobile applications and smart technologies development for improving guest experiences. The digital transformation has established an ideal environment for cybercriminals to find weaknesses in digital systems that result in security breaches affecting tourism businesses with substantial financial losses and legal implications and reputation damage (Herke et al., 2025).

Traditional criminal investigation methods were originally considered suitable for handling tourism operational threats which primarily focused on physical safety and guest protection (Hua et al., 2020). The rising number of cyber incidents has exposed the limitations of conventional investigative tools. Digital forensics developed its own specialized field because of this void to deliver established protocols that secure digital evidence for courtroom use (Casino et al., 2022).

The volume of data and its sensitivity in tourism requires digital forensics as an essential component (Neo & Teo, 2022). Hotels, airlines and tour operators receive personal data from guests that contains financial details as well as travel records and identification papers (Fakir & Baydeniz, 2024). Data storage occurs throughout multiple interconnected platforms that include property management systems and loyalty programs together with cloud storage services and IoT devices found in smart rooms (Alam, 2021). The contemporary digital ecosystems develop a dual nature as they foster smooth guest services yet make businesses vulnerable to sophisticated cyber intrusions.

When managing the vast amounts of data generated by hospitality systems, digital investigations in the tourism industry pose a significant issue (Mariani & Baggio, 2022). The investigation requires the examination of extensive amounts of data which includes emails and logs as well as booking records and transaction histories and metadata (Harchandani et al., 2024). The investigation of large datasets requires both technical expertise and advanced analytical methods for detecting abnormal patterns which indicate cybercrimes (Ramya et al., 2025).

The process becomes more complex due to use of encryption. Encryption acts as double-purpose mechanism as it safeguards data while side-by-side acting as hindrance for data access. Encryption performs both functions by safeguarding guest transactions and acting as barrier at times when criminals employ it for hiding stolen data. Anti-forensic techniques such as data steganography, wiping and metadata manipulation impede the validation of evidence, enabling the process of extracting evidence more challenging (Asim et al., 2025).

According to recent studies, there is an increasing focus on using digital forensic techniques to examine ransomware attacks that target systems used by the tourism industry. Ransomware attacks lead to significant operational and financial damages because they block hotel systems and prevent access to electronic doors and disrupt payment systems and online reservation platforms (Kalinaki, 2024). When possible, digital forensic teams are asked to identify the points of entry, cryptocurrency payment trails, and the degree of the damage.

Digital forensics addresses both financial-gain cyberattacks as well as data breaches resulting from competitive espionage and hacktivism according to Mhara et al. (2024). The tourism sector has suffered massive data breaches which revealed extensive guest information leading to regulatory fines and legal actions according to Talukder et al. (2024). The investigation team needs to determine where these breaches started and what was accessed during unauthorized entry and measure the complete amount of data that was exposed.

The worldwide reach of tourism creates additional difficulties when conducting investigations. International hotel corporations together with worldwide travel platforms function in different legal territories which creates problems for evidence gathering and data movement and police agency partnership (Hutchings, 2021). The requirement for worldwide law enforcement collaboration and legal framework unification becomes clear because digital proof moves beyond national borders.

Contemporary technological advancements change the way forensic investigations are conducted. Machine learning and artificial intelligence are employed to automate the examination of evidence and reveal pattern of detection that are not identifiable by human experts (Singh et al., 2025). Besides offering improved decryption techniques for inaccessible material, quantum computing poses a potential hazard by breaking encryption systems (Ajala et al., 2024). The prevalence of cryptocurrency related cybercrimes in the tourism industry has enabled blockchain analysis crucial for tracking illicit money movements (Zan & Min, 2025).

Digital signatures exhibit a vital role in tourism operations reasoned most contracts and payment authorization and reservation confirmations presence as digital documents (Karthikeyan et al., 2026). Digital signatures are examined by forensic experts to ensure that transactions are genuine and to identify the persons involved in communication. It is too crucial for fraud investigations in the field (Daraojimba et al., 2023).

Digital forensics is a significant part of cybersecurity for business organizations in the tourism and hospitality sectors. As cyber threats become more complicated and last longer, the forensic field gets better and better. The literature asserts that tourism enterprises reliant on trust and fluid digital interactions must integrate robust digital forensic protocols into their security and crisis management frameworks.

OBJECTIVE 1: DIGITAL FORENSICS PROCESS: FROM COLLECTION TO COURT PRESENTATION IN TOURISM AND HOSPITALITY

As per Florido- Benítez (2024), cybercriminals are targeting the tourism and hospitality industry more and more because it has a lot of digital infrastructure, like reservation systems and customer databases, and payment gateways. Cybercrime attacks the damage both their businesses and the safety of travelers around the world are a big threat to hotel chains, their booking systems, travel agencies, and cruise lines.

The techniques applied for traditional investigations testimony deficient to manage the advanced digital threats which airlines, hotels, travel agencies, cruise lines and tourism boards encounter. Digital forensics acts as an important technique which makes investigators to transform unprocessed electronic data into lawfully acceptable proof (Thealla et al., 2024).

Digital forensics in tourism and hospitality needs an orderly process with various different phases. Each phase in the investigation process necessitates maintaining and preserving evidence virtue and integrity while transforming technical details into easily comprehensible information for lawful proceedings (Grimm et al., 2021). The next sections explore the fundamental digital forensic procedures for tourism and hospitality entities as they work to prevent cybercrime against their trust-based secured and streamlined operational environment.

A methodical process with various distinct stages or phases is required for Digital forensics in tourism and hospitality.

1. Identification

In digital forensics, identifying pertinent and relevant data is the foremost step. Potential evidence in the tourism and hospitality sector can be found in:

- Hotel property management systems (PMS)
- Booking platforms and channel managers
- Email servers and internal communications systems
- Mobile apps used for check-in or loyalty programs
- Cloud-based customer relationship management (CRM) tools
- Internet of Things (IoT) devices such as electronic door locks, smart thermostats, and in-room entertainment systems

For instance, The Marriott International data breach investigation required investigators to determine which systems held reservation records and passport information and payment card details from 500 million guests. The investigation proceedings needed system identification to seperate evidence while measuring the attack's full extent (Busra, 20024).

In an identical manner, investigators discovering a ransomware malware attack on a hotel in Europe swiftly located the back-office servers and electronic keycard system that were applied as primary evidence storage locations. Investigators had to instantly spotting the compromised systems since the ransomware attack prohibited visitors from entering their rooms until the ransom payment was made (Patsakis et al., 2024).

The proper system identification procedure facilitates investigators to fetch digital evidence while avoiding any systems that contain relevant data.

2. Collection

Once evidence sources are identified, the next step is collecting data in a way that preserves its integrity. In hospitality settings, this might involve:

- Creating forensic images of servers hosting reservation data
- Extracting logs from property management systems
- Capturing data from hotel Wi-Fi networks used by cybercriminals
- Downloading records from loyalty program databases

Experts utilize EnCase and FTK forensic tools to duplicate storage media contents with perfect precision. According to Nasir & Iqbal (2025), the investigators operate with duplicate data sets that preserve the original files for the presenting of court evidence.

When Sabre's system underwent a security incident, numerous hotels across the world were exposed by the SynXis reservation platform. During their comprehensive operation, the investigators had to gather data from distinct server sites while upholding the integrity of the evidence. According to Vinod (2022), the mechanism of collecting evidence has to be handled carefully because any flaw could compromise its lawful application and put companies at further danger of legal risks.

The hospitality industry poses unique challenges for data acquisition since systems that administer reservations and guest interactions run constantly, making non-disruptive data seizure challenging.

3. Preservation and Chain of Custody

In order to ensure that data stays unmodified from the moment it is collected till it is actually used in court, digital evidence preservation is indispensable. The chain of custody is a key idea in this context, which carefully records:

- Who accessed the evidence
- When and why it was accessed
- Any changes or actions done on the evidence

Incomplete, deficient or fragmented chain of custody documentation may provide defense attorneys the opportunity to raise concerns about the acceptance of the evidence.

For a major hotel chain breach investigation, investigators had to prerserve meticulous records of each server log and forensic image (Malik et al., 2024). In order to establish the breach timeline and assess company culpability in accordance with data protection standards under the EU GDPR, the documentation was an essential tool for regulators and courts (Labadie & Legner, 2023).

Inappropriate documentation and preservation practices can result in rejection of strong evidence.

4. Analysis

The most difficult stage of digital forensics is the analyzing stage. It entails sifting through enormous volumes of data to locate evidence of cybercrimes like:

- Skimming payment card details from hotel POS systems
- Stealing personal data from loyalty programs
- Planting ransomware on booking servers
- Hijacking Wi-Fi networks in tourist hotspots for credential theft

Specialized software helps investigators dig through logs, recover deleted files, and pick apart hidden metadata. Take the Marriott hack, for example. Forensic teams spotted some weird connections to outside servers and, after looking deeper, uncovered years of unauthorized access to sensitive data (Shandilya et al., 2024).

At a luxury resort, experts analyzed logs from the IoT door-lock system to figure out how hackers managed to get in and mess with room access credentials. By diving into the metadata in those logs, they pinned down exactly when and how the breach happened (Vardakis et al., 2024).

Encryption and anti-forensic tricks make things way harder for investigators. Attackers like to lock up stolen data with encryption and use anonymization to cover their tracks (González Arias et al., 2024). In response, forensic teams roll out advanced tools to crack encryption, dig up hidden connections, and piece together what happened by studying things like network activity and indirect evidence.

Following the uncovering of strange external server connections by forensic investigators, the Marriott hack exposed a lengthy history of unauthorized sensitive data access (Shandilya et al., 2024).

5. Correlation and Link Analysis

Digital crimes usually pull in all sorts of people, tools, and entry points. Investigators use correlation and link analysis to tie together bits of information that, on the surface, don't seem connected at all. Take a hospitality company dealing with fake online bookings, for example. Investigators can track those back to stolen reward points. That's where link analysis steps in—it helps make those hidden connections clear. Link analysis can connect:

- Login attempts from the same IP addresses
- Transactions funneling loyalty points to new accounts
- Emails between conspirators coordinating the fraud

Similarly, in phishing attacks targeting travel agencies, link analysis can help correlate malicious email campaigns with server logs, helping to identify the source of the attack (Shin et al., 2022).

By establishing connections between data fragments, investigators can create a clear narrative of how a crime unfolded—critical for presenting compelling evidence in court.

6. Presentation of Evidence

The last step is sharing your findings in court. For hospitality cybercrime cases, that usually means breaking down tricky technical evidence for a jury, a judge, or maybe some regulators—people who probably aren't tech experts.

Effective presentation includes:

- Simplified reports that translate technical jargon into everyday language
- Visual aids like charts, timelines, or network diagrams
- Clear explanations of how evidence links a suspect to criminal activity

Digital forensic experts need to defend their investigative procedures and discoveries when faced with cross-examination during testimony. Take the Marriott breach, for example. Forensic experts had to get up there and walk everyone through how the attackers slipped into the reservation systems and stuck around without getting caught. They had to lay out the whole timeline and show just how far the breach went, making sure regulators and the legal team understood every bit of it.

Evidence presentation quality directly affects the final outcome of a case since trust along with clear communication stands as the most essential factor.

The tourism and hospitality industry relies on digital forensics as its main defense against cybercrime threats according to Talukder et al. (2024). The combination of precise and transparent forensic processes must maintain legal defensibility while investigators uncover hidden evidence in complex hotel IT systems and present their findings in court according to Ferreira & Gromova (2024). Digital forensics continues to protect guest information and safeguard business reputation while delivering justice because the industry advances technologically and cybercriminals create new attack methods.

OBJECTIVE 2: EXPLORING THE TYPES OF DIGITAL EVIDENCE IN CYBERCRIME INVESTIGATIONS IN TOURISM AND HOSPITALITY

The modern tourism industry along with hospitality services functions as an essential part of digital systems in today's world. Hotels along with airlines and travel agencies and booking platforms maintain extensive databases which contain guest details and operational information (Gurgu et al., 2021). The sector attracts cybercriminals because of its digital dependence which allows them to steal financial resources and personal information and obtain competitive intelligence. The digital nature of hospitality crimes means investigators must rely on electronic proof to solve these cases (Pandey & Kapoor, 2025).

In cases like these, investigators look at everything from public records—emails, transaction logs—to private stuff like digital signatures, metadata, and encrypted files. Digging into this digital evidence really matters if you want to prosecute cybercrimes tied to tourism.

This chapter dives into real-world cases and examples from the industry, showing how different types of digital evidence have actually helped uncover cybercrimes against travel and hospitality businesses.

1. Metadata: The Silent Storyteller in Hospitality Forensics (Botwright, 2023)

Metadata—the "data about data"—is one of the quiet heroes in digital forensics. It provides hidden details about files or transactions, such as when they were created, modified, or accessed. In tourism and hospitality, metadata might include:

- Timestamps of booking confirmations
- GPS coordinates embedded in mobile check-in records
- Device details from hotel Wi-Fi logins
- Audit trails from property management systems (PMS)

Example: Marriott Data Breach

During a significant tourism sector cyberattack Marriott International found that hackers had accessed Starwood reservation data throughout 2014 until 2018. Metadata played a key role in figuring out when the attacks started, how long the unauthorized access lasted, and exactly what information the attackers deleted. Authorities used server log analysis and file timestamps to spot suspicious activity. These details proved crucial for legal cases and regulatory investigations (Aivazpour et al., 2022).

Example: Wi-Fi Metadata in Hotels

A posh resort in Spain found that its free Wi-Fi network was being used by a phishing attempt to target its visitors. Wi-Fi router data were analyzed by forensic specialists, who identified particular devices that were connected during the attack windows. Investigators were able to track cybercriminal machines throughout several lodging businesses in the area by combining MAC addresses and connection time metadata (Grechyn & McShane, 2021).

Cybercrime Context:

In hospitality, metadata can reveal how hackers navigate systems, plant malware, or extract data. It's particularly vital in:

- Proving unauthorized access to guest records
- Establishing timelines for fraud attempts
- Linking phishing emails to specific internal accounts

Even when attackers delete files or attempt to cover tracks, metadata often survives as silent proof of the crime.

2. Encrypted Data: Unmasking Hidden Threats

Encryption stands as a powerful tool for protecting visitor privacy and financial transactions. Hotels and travel websites rely on it to shield payment card numbers, PINs, and loyalty program details. Yet, the story doesn't end there. Hackers use encryption too—they mask their communications, conceal stolen data, and even lock up computers with ransomware (Sethi et al., 2024).

Example: Marriott's Starwood Breach (Continued)

In the Marriott hack, attackers got their hands on a lot of information—credit card numbers, passport numbers—the kind of data you really don't want to lose. Sure, much of it was encrypted, but investigators found that the attackers may have also grabbed the keys needed to unlock that encrypted data. So, what does this show? If you don't protect your encryption keys, encrypting the data alone won't keep it safe.

Example: Ransomware in a Hotel Chain

Back in 2020, a group of hackers hit a European hotel chain with ransomware. They locked down everything—payment terminals, booking systems, even electronic door locks. The attackers demanded Bitcoin to hand over the decryption keys. Forensic teams teamed up with cybersecurity experts, digging into the blockchain to trace the ransom payments. They also pulled encrypted files and picked apart the ransomware code. When they examined the hotel's old VPN system, they found a major security flaw. Fixing that didn't break the encryption, but it did help the hotel shore up its defenses going forward (Khadka, 2025).

Example: Kolkata – Fake Travel Agency Package Fraud

In April 2025, a fraudster in Kolkata posing as a travel agency operator offered cheap holiday packages to Southeast Asia. Victims transferred lakhs via GPay (e.g., 2.8 lakh) but never received tickets or confirmations. The scammer vanished after collecting the money, showcasing classic shell-account behavior and con-constructed booking websites (Ghosh, 2025).

Cybercrime Context:

Encryption complicates investigations but does not make evidence entirely invisible. Forensic experts can:

- Analyze malware code to reveal encryption routines
- Track cryptocurrency transactions linked to ransomware demands
- Identify encryption keys stored insecurely on compromised servers

Thus, even heavily encrypted data often leaves forensic clues that help investigators piece together the crime.

3. Digital Signatures: Verifying Authenticity in Digital Transactions

Digital signatures are cryptographic proofs attached to digital documents or transactions, confirming authenticity and origin. In hospitality, digital signatures are widely used in:

- Electronic booking confirmations
- Online contracts with vendors
- Secure payment processing
- Documenting internal approvals and audits

Digital signatures help protect both customers and businesses from fraud and repudiation (Rakhra et al., 2024).

Example: Hotel Supplier Contract Dispute

A vendor insisted they never signed a digital contract to sell high-end furnishings, and suddenly, a group of luxury hotels in Dubai was caught in a legal mess. Forensic investigators dug into the contract PDFs and the audit logs from the e-signature platform. They traced the vendor's digital credentials right back to the signed documents. That evidence backed up the hotels' claim—they had proof the vendor really did sign (Roberts, 2023).

Example: Airline Booking Scam

Fraudsters targeted a European airline with fake travel coupons that spread quickly online. Investigators relied on the digital signatures found in real e-tickets and receipts to spot the fakes. With that, they warned customers and tracked down where the bogus coupon codes started popping up on social media.

Example: Aadhaar Data and Tourism Services in India

The Indian Aadhaar data breach set off alarms for travel agencies that rely on biometric authentication, even though the incident wasn't about tourism directly. Many hotels and other hospitality businesses used Aadhaar information to speed up guest check-ins. When news broke about possible illegal access, digital signatures in transaction logs became a crucial tool. They let businesses figure out which data requests were legitimate and which ones came from suspicious sources (George et al., 2023).

Cybercrime Context:

Digital signatures provide certainty in an industry where trust is paramount. Forensic specialists can:

- Prove whether emails authorizing transactions were genuinely sent by hotel executives
- Verify online payment records in disputes with guests or vendors
- Authenticate contracts and prevent repudiation in legal conflicts

Digital signatures are increasingly vital in protecting hospitality businesses from sophisticated fraud and ensuring compliance with data protection laws.

In tourism and hospitality, digital evidence drives cybercrime investigations. Metadata uncovers timelines you can't see on the surface. Encryption hides information, but it also leaves behind forensic clues. Digital signatures prove the authenticity of transactions and documents—think about hotel operations, guest services, vendor contracts. As cyber threats grow more sophisticated, knowing how to pull, dissect, and present this evidence becomes crucial. It's what protects both companies and travelers in a world where everything's connected.

OBJECTIVE 3: LEGAL STANDARDS AND CHALLENGES SURROUNDING THE ADMISSIBILITY AND AUTHENTICITY OF DIGITAL EVIDENCE IN CRIMINAL PROSECUTIONS

Courts everywhere struggle to keep up with the pace of digital change. As cybercrime rises, judges and lawyers have to figure out what counts as evidence when it comes to electronic data (Nosál 2023). Digital evidence isn't like a physical object you can hold in your hand. It's far easier to alter, copy, or even fake, so people constantly worry about whether they can actually trust it. Courts have developed digital evidence standards to use in criminal proceedings yet each jurisdiction maintains distinct rules which creates difficulties for investigators and prosecutors (Stoykova 2023).

The next part studies criminal case digital evidence regulations in U.S. and Indian courts along with British standards. This paper also investigates important obstacles linked to digital evidence including methods to verify its integrity and procedures to maintain its chain of custody as well as its technical complexity when dealing with digital data.

1. Legal Standards in India

Digital evidence in India depends on the Indian Evidence Act of 1872 combined with the Information Technology Act of 2000 (IT Act) as its fundamental legal framework. Throughout the years the Indian judiciary has made important rulings that have defined specific rules affecting electronic evidence admissibility requirements.

a. Section 65B of the Indian Evidence Act, 1872 (Sonone et al., 2024)

Indian Evidence Act Section 65B regulates the court acceptance process for electronic evidence in Indian legal proceedings. A person who operates the device that generated the electronic record must issue a certificate for acceptance in court. The certificate needs to verify both the correct nature of the data and its unchanged form.

The Supreme Court established in Anvar P.V. v. P.K. Basheer (2014) that electronic evidence requires a certificate for admission in court. The Supreme Court overturned a previous ruling which permitted evidence without certification thereby strengthening the procedural requirements (Kapse, 2022).

b. The Information Technology Act, 2000

The Information Technology Act, 2000 along with its 2008 amendment sets forth rules for the recognition of electronic records and digital signatures. Courts accept electronic evidence including emails digital contracts and communications when proper authentication is established.

The courts must accept electronic records and digital signatures as valid under Section 85B until evidence shows otherwise. The presenting party must establish the authenticity of the evidence they introduce. Digital signatures receive certification authority approval to serve as secure electronic authentication methods according to Section 3.

Challenges in the Indian Legal System

The Indian system has a number of difficulties with regard to the admissibility and legitimacy of digital evidence, even with the legal protections in place. A major obstacle is the inconsistent interpretation of Section 65B by courts. There are discrepancies because some courts have accepted electronic evidence without requiring the certificate. Additionally, getting and presenting the certificate might be a difficult process, particularly if the material is kept on cloud servers located outside of India or if the evidence crosses many jurisdictions.

The integrity of digital evidence in India is further complicated by problems including electronic record manipulation, a shortage of skilled workers, and a deficient forensic infrastructure.

2. Legal Standards in the United States

The Federal Rules of Evidence (FRE) serve as the main governing foundation for the United States' well-established legal framework regarding the validity and admissibility of digital evidence. Because of a number of significant cases, the U.S. legal system has also generated extensive jurisprudence on digital evidence (Solanke, 2022).

a. Federal Rules of Evidence (Solanke, 2022)

All types of evidence, including digital evidence, are admissible in the United States under the Federal Rules of Evidence. A party wishing to admit an electronic document must provide the original or a copy, provided that the duplicate accurately conveys the information, in accordance with the Best Evidence Rule (Rule 1002). In actuality, this provision allows digital documents like computer files, emails, and texts as long as the party can prove their legitimacy.

Additionally, Rule 901 states that in order to prove authenticity, there must be enough proof to back up a conclusion that the item in question is what it claims to be. This regulation permits the employment of digital forensic specialists or technical experts to provide testimony regarding the methods used to gather, store, and examine digital evidence (Crothers, 2021).

b. Landmark Case: Lorraine v. Markel American Insurance Co. (Sibe & Kaunert, 2024)

Lorraine v. Markel American Insurance Co. (2007) stands out as a turning point for how U.S. courts handle digital evidence. In this case, the court took a close look at the rules for electronic evidence and spelled out exactly what standards apply, defining the following standards:

- Relevance: The proof needs to be pertinent to the argument.
- Authenticity: It must be demonstrated that the evidence is real and unaltered.
- Hearsay: The digital evidence must qualify as an exception to the hearsay rule if it is hearsay.

- Original Writing Rule: You have to provide the original or a precise copy.
- Probative Value: The evidence must be impartial and have probative value.

The decision set a strict threshold for the admission of digital evidence and emphasized the significance of appropriate authentication methods.

Challenges in the U.S. Legal System

The United States faces difficulties with the large amount of digital evidence, encryption, and anti-forensic tactics, even with a well-developed judicial system. It is frequently difficult for investigators to access encrypted material, which makes it difficult to gather comprehensive evidence. The U.S. court system also regularly faces jurisdictional concerns, especially when the evidence is kept in foreign nations or on cloud servers. As a result, there are now conflicts between privacy regulations and the need to gather important evidence for criminal cases.

3. Legal Standards in the United Kingdom

Based on common law principles, the UK has created its own framework for digital evidence admission. The Civil Evidence Act of 1995 and the Police and Criminal Evidence Act of 1984 (PACE) are the main regulating Laws.

a. The Police and Criminal Evidence Act 1984 (PACE) (Das & Sarkar, 2022)

Law enforcement organizations in the UK have the legal power to seize and examine electronic devices during criminal investigations under PACE. Section 69 of the Act makes computer evidence admissible in court unless someone can prove the system malfunctioned or the data got tampered with.

b. *Digital Evidence and Authentication*

The Civil Evidence Act 1995 spells out what counts as admissible electronic documents. Whoever wants to submit digital evidence has to show it came from a reliable system. That responsibility lands on the party bringing the evidence forward.

UK courts don't just stop at legislation—they pull from common law, too. When dealing with digital records, they look at principles like hearsay and best evidence. For things like emails, digital signatures, or online chats, courts usually expect some sort of certification or an expert to vouch for authenticity.

Challenges in the UK Legal System

Keeping digital evidence admissible isn't always easy. The rise of cloud storage—especially when servers sit outside the UK—makes it harder to guarantee access and data integrity. On top of that, the UK's Data Protection Act 2018, which mirrors the EU's GDPR, sets strict rules for handling personal data. These privacy requirements sometimes clash with the need to gather digital evidence, creating real challenges for investigators.

Key Challenges in Admissibility and Authenticity of Digital Evidence

No matter what the law says in different places, making sure digital evidence holds up in court isn't easy. There are still a number of obstacles to overcome in order to guarantee the validity and admissibility of digital evidence. Among these difficulties are:

- Chain of Custody: It is required to keep the evidence safe and unchanged from the moment someone collects it all the way to the courtroom. If anything breaks that chain—even a small mistake—the evidence can get thrown out.
- Issues of Jurisdiction: Data often sits on cloud servers overseas, so grabbing it means jumping through legal hoops, sometimes even dealing with diplomats. And when law enforcement needs proof but privacy laws say "no," things get complicated, fast.
- Encryption and Anti-Forensics: Cybercriminals aren't stupid—they use these tools to hide or destroy digital traces. That leaves investigators struggling to piece together what actually happened.
- Data Volume: The sheer volume of digital evidence is overwhelming, too. Cybercrime cases can dump mountains of data on investigators, who have to sift through it all on tight deadlines and, usually, with not enough help.
- Technical Expertise: Finally, there's the challenge of expertise. It's not just about knowing the tech—experts have to explain complex digital methods to judges and juries who might barely know how to use email. That's a tough job, but it's essential if digital evidence is going to stick.

OBJECTIVE 4: IDENTIFYING THE CHALLENGES FACED BY DIGITAL FORENSIC INVESTIGATORS AND THE EMERGING TECHNOLOGIES USED TO OVERCOME THESE HURDLES IN TOURISM AND HOSPITALITY

Tourism and hospitality have gone through a digital overhaul in recent years. Hotels and travel companies now rely on online booking platforms, mobile apps, digital payments, and smart rooms powered by IoT (Saber et al., 2025). This tech upgrade boosts guest experiences and streamlines operations, but it also opens the door to advanced cyber threats (Buhalis et al., 2019). Hospitality brands depend on trust and reputation, so any data breach can quickly become a disaster. That's why digital forensic investigators play a crucial role here—they protect customer data, secure business operations, and help keep reputations intact (Malik et al., 2024).

Forensic professionals in hospitality and tourism run into tough problems, especially with encryption and anti-forensic tactics. This chapter digs into how experts are dealing with these challenges right now, and what's coming next. It uses real-world case studies from both India and abroad to show how these solutions work in practice.

1. Overview of Digital Forensics and Its Challenges in Hospitality and Tourism

Digital forensics has become essential in tourism and hospitality, where a single breach can cost millions, land a company in regulatory trouble, and destroy a brand overnight (Busra, 2024). Investigators in this field track down, collect, secure, and analyze digital evidence from all sorts of systems, including:

- Property Management Systems (PMS) used by hotels to manage reservations and guest records.
- Point-of-Sale (POS) terminals that process payments in restaurants, spas, and shops.
- Loyalty program databases storing vast amounts of personal data about frequent travelers.
- Cloud-based platforms hosting booking systems for airlines, hotels, and travel agencies.
- Guest Wi-Fi networks, which are frequent targets for malware injection and phishing attacks.
- IoT devices embedded in smart rooms, like connected lighting, climate control, and voice assistants.

These systems streamline operations and let businesses tailor guest experiences, but they also catch the eye of cybercriminals looking for money or sensitive data. The tourism industry faces unique hurdles when it comes to investigations, mainly because it's a global business. Legal roadblocks pop up all the time—hotel chains and travel platforms cross borders, which complicates gathering evidence (Talukder et al., 2024). Add in the sheer volume of customer data and the nonstop flow of information in hospitality, and forensic investigators find it tough to get to the bottom of incidents.

2. Encryption Challenges in Digital Forensics (Singh & Chopra, 2025)

Encryption gives hospitality and tourism businesses a tough choice. On one hand, encrypting guest information and transaction data is crucial, especially to meet privacy laws like India's Digital Personal Data Protection Act and the European GDPR. On the other hand, these same encryption tools make forensic investigations after a breach much harder. So while guest data stays safe, finding out what went wrong—or who's at fault—can be next to impossible.

Full-Disk Encryption (FDE) (Götzfried & Müller, 2014)

Today's hotels go even further with security. They use full-disk encryption on front-desk computers and point-of-sale systems. That sounds like progress, but it's a double-edged sword. When ransomware struck a major European hotel group in 2018, investigators couldn't access reservation data because it was locked up with Windows BitLocker. Without administrative passwords, forensic teams couldn't get what they needed, which slowed everything down. The result? Operational chaos, especially at check-in and check-out, and guests felt the impact.

End-to-End Encryption (E2EE)

Hotel staff often rely on WhatsApp and Signal to stay in touch with suppliers, partners, and guests, as Bostrom (2021) notes. Both apps use end-to-end encryption, keeping conversations private. But this privacy can backfire. When fraud or insider threats crop up, investigators run into a wall. Take the 2022 case: An Indian hotel chain became the target of a booking theft scheme. Employees worked with outside accomplices to pull it off, but investigators hit a dead end. Essential chats happened on encrypted apps, and without access to the devices or cooperation from users, key evidence stayed locked away.

Ransomware and Encryption-Based Attacks

Ransomware is one of the scariest encryption threats out there. Attackers break into hotel networks, lock up files, and then demand cryptocurrency if you want your data back. Take Marriott International, for example—back in March 2020, they announced a breach that hit more than 5 million guests. It looked like ransomware was to blame. For discovering the mechanism used by attackers to assess Hotel's systems, forensic experts employed network logs along with traffic patterns despite encryption enabled it impossible to recover stolen data (Eluzor, 2024).

Then there's SpiceJet incidence happened in May 2022. Hackers went after their IT systems, and the whole thing messed up domestic flights all over India—delays, chaos, you name it. Investigators traced it back to a targeted breach (Baisley & Cherrat, 2023). Meanwhile, over in the UK, Travelex got slammed by the REvil ransomware in early 2020. That attack took down a bunch of their services and forced them to pay up just to get their data back (Crotty & Daniel, 2021). In both cases, digital forensic teams leaned on memory analysis and watched network traffic closely, since only the attackers had the private keys needed to unlock the encrypted files. Nobody else could decrypt anything without those keys.

3. Anti-Forensics and Obfuscation Techniques

Hospitality investigations are getting more difficult now days due to use of anti-forensic techniques to conceal digital evidence by Cybercriminals. These tactics serve to disrupt forensic tools while investigators must reconstruct incomplete digital trails.

Data Concealment and Manipulation

Attackers deployed POS malware during major hotel chain breaches at Hyatt Hotels and Starwood Hotels in 2015 to steal payment card data while staying undetected. The malware functioned stealthily within system memory and did not show evidence of log-wiping during reboot while producing minimal forensic traces. The investigation required payment processor data together with partial backups to determine attack timelines because attackers conceal their data to make discovery more challenging (Robinson, 2016; Zorz, 2015).

Metadata Tampering

File metadata stores information about file creation timestamps together with author information and device identification details (Schindler et al., 2024). Anti-forensic tools have the capability to modify this information. After a breach at a

European online travel agency hackers modified booking record timestamps to hide the exact time fraudulent transactions entered the system (Florido-Benítez, 2024). The forensic analysts determined the actual sequence of events by matching payment processor records with customer complaints.

Steganography

Steganography functions as a technique that conceals information through ordinary files which include images and audio files (Bamanga et al., 2024). Indian authorities discovered criminals using promotional images of luxury hotel packages to hide malicious scripts when they started investigating organized travel scams in 2021. The forensic investigation utilized pixel-level analysis to retrieve concealed payloads which enabled attackers to breach hotel booking websites and steal credit card information from customers.

Digging into cybercrime in tourism isn't simple. It needs the advanced investigation tools and a team of experts that knows what they're doing. Travelers face real risks, both to their privacy and sometimes even their safety, and it's up to investigators to keep up.

4. Emerging Technologies to Address Encryption and Anti-Forensics Challenges

Digital forensics in tourism and hospitality isn't standing still, either. Although itis tough yet criminals keep inventing new tricks. But technology keeps pushing forward, letting investigators find evidence no matter how well someone tries to hide it or encrypt it.

Artificial Intelligence (AI) and Machine Learning (ML)

AI and machine learning have changed the game of automated analysis of vast data. They crunch massive data sets, spot threats faster, and pick up on things people might miss. During the 2024 Ticketmaster breach, for example, AI tools caught credential stuffing attacks just by watching how people logged in (Senecal, 2024). Over in India, machine learning systems keep an eye on point-of-sale transactions and loyalty programs. They flag sneaky fraud that would look totally normal to a human.

Quantum Computing

Quantum computing is the next big emerging technology, and honestly, it's a double-edged sword. On one hand, quantum algorithms could tear through the encryption methods everyone uses today. At the same time, though, they give forensic teams a shot at unlocking evidence that was basically impossible to access before (Alghamdi, 2025). The big hospitality chains know what's coming. They are already working on quantum-resistant encryption to stay a step ahead of tomorrow's threats.

Cloud Forensics and Remote Acquisition

Hotels and travel companies rely on cloud tech these days for just about everything like booking systems, guest details, or any other that it can be named. When things go wrong, investigators use cloud forensics to pull data from platforms like AWS and Azure. It doesn't matter if the servers sit halfway around the world; legal orders open the door. Taking instance of 2023 case happened in Delhi: a fake travel agency was running a massive scam, and the key evidence lived on overseas cloud backups. Investigators uncovered bogus airline tickets, hotel booking fraud, and the working mechanism behind the same.

Blockchain Analysis

Cryptocurrencies are making things trickier. More hotels and travel agencies have started accepting crypto, which gives criminals new ways to cover their tracks. But tools like Chainalysis and Elliptic let investigators follow the money across blockchain networks. In Europe, authorities tracked Bitcoin from a ransomware attack against a luxury hotel straight to the criminals' wallets. Over in India, blockchain analysis helped crack down on crypto laundering tied to fake hotel booking sites—cybercriminals took deposits in crypto, then disappeared. Without these tools, a lot of this would stay hidden.

FINDINGS AND DISCUSSION

When you dig into the tourism and hospitality sector, it is quickly observed how vulnerable this sector is to cyberattacks. Hotels and tourism companies depend on digital systems for just about everything. So when something goes wrong like the Marriott breach or ransomware attacks on European hotel chains, it doesn't just mess up bookings or daily operations. It shakes customer trust too, which is every bit as valuable as money in this industry.

The chapter analysis discovered that hackers or cybercriminals know the basic mechanisms employed in tourism and hospitality sector with their pros and cons meticulously. They target the sector's web of connected systems, slipping in through things like property management software, loyalty program databases, and all those

IoT devices hotels love to use. Once inside, cybercriminals use some pretty advanced tricks. They move quietly through networks, grab data, and sometimes stick around for months or even years before anyone notices.

It is further found that encryption protects guest data, no doubt about it. But here's the thing—it also makes life a lot harder for forensic teams trying to untangle cybercrimes. Criminals don't just steal data; they hide it behind layers of encryption, then demand ransom, holding companies' hostage and grinding business to a halt. Full-disk and end-to-end encryption are everywhere now, and that just adds more walls for investigators who need answers fast.

The cybercriminals start looking for clues elsewhere. Metadata and network traffic suddenly become gold mines for such cybercriminals. Metadata, especially, is sneaky but powerful. It helps investigators spot odd logins and trace exactly how someone broke in and moved around inside a system. But attackers know this too. They'll mess with metadata—change timestamps, erase logs, anything to throw investigators off the scent. That's the risk: while metadata can shine a light on the truth, it can just as easily be twisted to hide it.

Forensic experts run into all kinds of problems, mostly because of presence of much data and it's often really complicated. In a typical case, forensic experts look at piles of files spread out across different systems. Investigators have to dig through endless transactions and conversations just to spot what might actually matter. All this really shows how important it is to have sharp analytical tools and people who actually know the ins and outs of the tourism and hospitality industry.

It is further examined that although cloud computing has become crucial in the operations of tourism and hospitality industry, but it's a mixed bag. For sure, it makes a lot of things easier for businesses, but it also brings its own headaches in terms of various potential associated risks. Investigators can pull the data they need using cloud forensic techniques, especially when the physical servers are sitting somewhere far away. Still, collecting evidence isn't easy. Jurisdiction issues and having to deal with third-party providers can slow things down and make the whole process a lot more complicated.

The modern and latest technologies is making a real difference for organizations facing tough problems right now. AI-powered analytics let investigators spot strange patterns buried in huge piles of data—stuff that points to fraud or shady activity in loyalty programs and payment systems. Then there's blockchain for them to curb such issues. Blockchain has become a go-to tool for tracking down ransom payments and following the trail of crypto-related fraud.

Lastly, in tourism and hospitality, it is found that digital forensics keeps changing because cybercriminals never stop coming up with new tricks. This industry is a bit of a special case. It's global, it deals with endless transactions, and everything hinges on customers trusting the brand. That's why it's so important for these businesses to stay ready and have real forensic know-how. That's how they protect their operations and their reputation.

SOLUTIONS AND RECOMMENDATIONS

The tourism and hospitality world has its own set of cyber headaches or risks, so entities can't afford to fall behind. If organizations want to strengthen your digital forensic game and keep its business running smoothly, check out these ten straightforward tips:

1. Integrate Digital Forensics into Cybersecurity Strategies

Establishment of digital forensic as a vital part of organizations' security framework that should work beyond mere incident recovery mechanism is required in tourism and hospitality sector. System designs should be integrated with forensic readiness for effectively locating evidence along with maintaining operational continuity.

2. Implement Advanced Logging and Monitoring

Tourism and hotel industry players should use advanced logging systems. Such robust systems should be able to track user authentication events, network connection detailed information, and comprehensive system activities. Such information acts as primary tool for investigating cyber incidents along with preserving unmodified or unbroken chain of evidence.

3. Train Staff in Forensic Awareness

It is suggested to train all frontline employees along with management and IT teams on the techniques to identify cybercrime indicators. They should also be given training for techniques of protecting digital evidence. Employees should be clearly informed about basic errors like rebooting hacked system that may lead to loss of vital forensic evidence.

4. Develop Incident Response Plans with Forensics in Mind

Development of comprehensive incident response plans are required by tourism and hotels business units. These plans should pin down the unambiguous methodology for forensic expert involvement and maintenance of digital evidence protection.

Such plans require to clearly mention responsibilities, communication systems, and compliance needs as well.

5. Invest in AI-Based Forensic Tools

Extensive data management needs of tourism and hospitality sector necessitate AI solutions deployment in the same. It is pretty understood that machine learning techniques can analyze enormous ranged logs for various anomalies. Such characteristics of machine learning assist forensic teams discover breaches more quickly. The other benefit of AI solutions is its ability to reveal those hidden patterns that even human investigators fail to detect.

6. Establish Secure Data Retention Policies

Tourism and hospitality organizations have to set clear rules for how long they keep digital records. They need to respect privacy laws but also hang on to the evidence they might need if something goes wrong. Customer trust is everything in this industry—if people don't feel safe, they'll just go somewhere else.

7. Leverage Cloud Forensics

For those using cloud services, it's smart to make sure cloud providers are ready to help right away if there's an investigation. The beauty of cloud platforms is that investigators can dig into data from anywhere, no matter where the devices are. Thus, it is suggested that tourism and hospitality undertakings should make partnership agreements with cloud providers for guaranteed spontaneous forensic support.

8. Adopt Blockchain Analysis for Cryptocurrency Tracking

Hotels and tourism entities are taking cryptocurrency now, which opens up new risks. To keep up, tourism companies need to work with blockchain analysis firms. These partners help track down shady transactions, ransomware payments, or anything illegal happening on the blockchain.

9. Foster Cross-Border Cooperation

Tourism runs on a global scale, so everyone involved has to work together across borders. That means tourism groups need to team up with international cybersecurity alliances, law enforcement, and legal experts to make sure they collect evidence that holds up under different countries' laws.

10. Prepare for Anti-Forensic Tactics

Investigators are always racing against criminals who keep coming up with new anti-forensic tricks. They need training and tools that can spot things like data wiping, hidden messages, and tampered metadata. Staying on top of the latest threat intelligence helps forensic teams keep up with the constantly changing tactics criminals use.

CONCLUSION AND FUTURE SCOPE

Digital technology changed the tourism industry in big ways—it made things easier for everyone, but it also opened the door to new cybersecurity problems. Sure, digital tools boost efficiency and make visitors happier, but they've also created new opportunities for cybercriminals. Investigators now use it to track down and analyze digital evidence. This kind of work is at the heart of cybercrime investigations.

Researchers keep finding that cyber threats aimed at tourism are constantly shifting and getting more complicated. The industry's digital systems work as both tools and targets—they help business, but they also give criminals a way to pull off ransomware attacks that can lock down hotel systems or leak travelers' private info. Tourism is complicated, and global rules don't always line up, so forensic experts have to develop skills that fit this unique environment.

It's not enough for tourism companies to bring in digital forensics only when there's a crisis. They need to weave these practices into everyday operations. New technology—think artificial intelligence, machine learning, blockchain analysis—lets forensic teams find and collect evidence faster. Cloud forensics adds another layer, since investigators can now reach important data from anywhere, without being tied to physical servers.

Looking ahead, researchers should figure out how to blend digital forensics with the latest tourism tech, like virtual reality, biometric security, and AI-driven services. Creating global standards for handling digital evidence is key. Tourism crosses borders, so international cooperation really matters.

At the end of the day, guest trust and strong security should be at the core of every tourism and hospitality business. Adopting digital forensics early, and using it in creative ways, helps these companies protect that trust—even as the digital world keeps getting more complicated.

REFERENCES

Aivazpour, Z., Valecha, R., & Chakraborty, R. (2022). Data breaches: An empirical study of the effect of monitoring services. *The Data Base for Advances in Information Systems*, *53*(4), 65–82. DOI: 10.1145/3571823.3571829

Ajala, O. A., Arinze, C. A., Ofodile, O. C., Okoye, C. C., & Daraojimba, A. I.Olakunle Abayomi AjalaChuka Anthony ArinzeOnyeka Chrisanctus OfodileChinwe Chinazo OkoyeAndrew Ifesinachi Daraojimba. (2024). Exploring and reviewing the potential of quantum computing in enhancing cybersecurity encryption methods. *Magna Scientia Advanced Research and Reviews*, *10*(01), 321–329. DOI: 10.30574/msarr.2024.10.1.0038

Alam, T. (2021). Cloud-based IoT applications and their roles in smart cities. *Smart Cities*, *4*(3), 1196–1219. DOI: 10.3390/smartcities4030064

Alghamdi, A. (2025). Quantum Cryptography: Implications for Digital Evidence in Criminal Investigations.

Asim, N., Osamor, J., Olajide, F., Iwendi, C., & Okeke, N. (2025, February). Detecting and Mitigating Anti-Forensic Techniques: A Comprehensive Framework for Digital Investigators. In *2025 AI-Driven Smart Healthcare for Society 5.0* (pp. 66-72). IEEE. DOI: 10.1109/IEEECONF64992.2025.10963229

Baisley, T., & Cherrat, Y. (2023). Cyber Threats and Engagements in 2022.

Bakhtiar, H. S. (2023). The role and nature of evidence: Forensic insight. *Jurnal Yuridis*, *10*(2), 10–22. DOI: 10.35586/jyur.v10i2.7072

Bamanga, M. A., Babando, A. K., & Mayer, J. (2024). *Recent advances in steganography*. IntechOpen.

Boström, P. (2021). Building and Evaluating a Full Disk Encrypted Secure Multiuser Operating Platform in Linux.

Botwright, R. (2023). *Malware Analysis: Digital Forensics, Cybersecurity, And Incident Response*. Rob Botwright.

Buhalis, D., Harwood, T., Bogicevic, V., Viglia, G., Beldona, S., & Hofacker, C. (2019). Technological disruptions in services: Lessons from tourism and hospitality. *Journal of Service Management*, *30*(4), 484–506. DOI: 10.1108/JOSM-12-2018-0398

Busra, M. M. (2024). An Economic Downfall: Fragile Data Management Systems a Major Security Threat for Sustainable Tourism.

Casino, F., Dasaklis, T. K., Spathoulas, G. P., Anagnostopoulos, M., Ghosal, A., Borocz, I., Solanas, A., Conti, M., & Patsakis, C. (2022). Research trends, challenges, and emerging topics in digital forensics: A review of reviews. *IEEE Access : Practical Innovations, Open Solutions, 10*, 25464–25493. DOI: 10.1109/ACCESS.2022.3154059

Crothers, D. J. (2021). The Wrong Road Taken: Social Media Content, Self-Authentication and Misapplication of the Business Records Rule. *North Dakota Law Review, 96*, 133.

Crotty, J., & Daniel, L. (2021). *Lessons from practice: insights on cybersecurity strategy for business leaders, from SMEs to global enterprises*. Open University.

Daraojimba, R. E., Farayola, O. A., Olatoye, F. M. O., Mhlongo, N., & Oke, T. T. L. (2023). Forensic accounting in the digital age: a US perspective: scrutinizing methods and challenges in digital financial fraud prevention. *Finance & Accounting Research Journal, 5*(11), 342–360. DOI: 10.51594/farj.v5i11.614

Das, G., Ali, Y. A., Singh, B., & Nag, K. (2025). Digital Forensics in E-Commerce: Investigating Online Payment Fraud and Data Breaches. *International Journal of Innovations in Science, Engineering And Management*, 262-268.

Das, P., & Sarkar, P. (2022). The Importance of Digital Forensics in the Admissibility of Digital Evidence. *NUJS J. Regul. Stud., 7*, 60.

Dhande, K. R. (2024). Fourth Industrial Revolution and the Role of Cyber Security: Technologies on the Travel and Tourism Industry and More Specifically Cyber Security in Travel Tourism. In *Corporate Cybersecurity in the Aviation, Tourism, and Hospitality Sector* (pp. 241-257). IGI Global.

Ebuzor, J. (2024). Understanding Customer Perception of Cyber Attacks: Impact on Trust and Security. In *Corporate Cybersecurity in the Aviation, Tourism, and Hospitality Sector* (pp. 83-111). IGI Global.

Fakir, F. Z., & Baydeniz, E. (2024). *The Future of Blockchain in Tourism and Hospitality: Global Insights*. Taylor & Francis. DOI: 10.4324/9781003521617

Faqir, R. S. (2023). Digital criminal investigations in the era of artificial intelligence: A comprehensive overview. *International Journal of Cyber Criminology, 17*(2), 77–94.

Ferreira, D. B., & Gromova, E. A. (2024). Digital Evidence: The Admissibility of Leaked and Hacked Evidence in Arbitration Proceedings. *International Journal for the Semiotics of Law-Revue internationale de Sémiotique juridique, 37*(3), 903-922.

Florido-Benítez, L. (2024). The cybersecurity applied by online travel agencies and hotels to protect users' private data in smart cities. *Smart Cities*, *7*(1), 475–495. DOI: 10.3390/smartcities7010019

Florido-Benítez, L. (2025). The role of cybersecurity as a preventive measure in digital tourism and travel: A systematic literature review. *Discover Computing*, *28*(1), 28. DOI: 10.1007/s10791-025-09523-3

George, A. S., Sagayarajan, S., Baskar, T., & Pandey, D. (2023). From paperwork to biometrics: Assessing the digitization of air travel in India through Digi Yatra. *Partners Universal International Innovation Journal*, *1*(4), 110–125.

Ghosh, D. (2025, April 15). *2 crore fraud case against fake travel agent*. Times of India. https://timesofindia.indiatimes.com/articleshow/120289096.cms

González Arias, R., Bermejo Higuera, J., Rainer Granados, J. J., Bermejo Higuera, J. R., & Sicilia Montalvo, J. A. (2024). Systematic review: Anti-forensic computer techniques. *Applied Sciences (Basel, Switzerland)*, *14*(12), 5302. DOI: 10.3390/app14125302

Götzfried, J., & Müller, T. (2014). Analysing Android's Full Disk Encryption Feature. *Journal of Wireless Mobile Networks, Ubiquitous Computing and Dependable Applications*, *5*(1), 84–100.

Grechyn, V., & McShane, I. (2021). "Seriously, Australia, why are you so stingy with Wi-Fi?": Customer satisfaction with Wi-Fi speed in Australian hotels and lessons for public Wi-Fi provision. *Journal of Hospitality and Tourism Technology*, *12*(4), 730–744. DOI: 10.1108/JHTT-01-2020-0025

Grimm, P. W., Grossman, M. R., & Cormack, G. V. (2021). Artificial intelligence as evidence. *Nw. J. Tech. & Intell. Prop.*, *19*, 9.

Gurgu, E., Zorzoliu, R. I., Pistol, L., Gurgu, I., Ungureanu, C., & Nae, G. (2021). The relationship between big datadriven technologies and performance management strategies applied to companies in the hospitality, tourism & travel industry. *Annals of Spiru Haret University. Economic Series*, *21*(4), 97–136.

Harchandani, R., Bansal, P., Jain, S., Sondhi, J. K., & Jacob, L. (2024). Big Data Paradigm in Cybercrime Investigation. In *Artificial Intelligence for Cyber Defense and Smart Policing* (pp. 91–109). Chapman and Hall/CRC. DOI: 10.1201/9781003251781-7

Herke, C., Tóth, D., & Perkumienė, D. (2025). The Role of Artificial Intelligence in Cybercrime in the Tourism Sector. In *Tourism and Heritage: Shaping Sustainable and Innovative Futures* (pp. 415–433). Springer Nature Switzerland. DOI: 10.1007/978-3-031-81485-3_17

Hua, N., Li, B., & Zhang, T. (2020). Crime research in hospitality and tourism. *International Journal of Contemporary Hospitality Management*, *32*(3), 1299–1323. DOI: 10.1108/IJCHM-09-2019-0750

Hutchings, A. (2021). Flying in cyberspace: Policing global travel fraud. *Policing: A Journal of* Ibrahim, F. M., Alawsi, H., & Mohammed, M. N. (2025). The Evolution of Cybercrime: Challenges and Advancements in Digital Forensics. In *Tech Fusion in Business and Society: Harnessing Big Data, IoT, and Sustainability in Business* (Vol. 2, pp. 455–464). Springer Nature Switzerland.

Iyengar, S. S., Nabavirazavi, S., & Hariprasad, Y. HB, P., & Mohan, C. K. (2025). Digital Forensics: Tools, Techniques, and Methodologies. In *Artificial Intelligence in Practice: Theory and Application for Cyber Security and Forensics* (pp. 89-137). Cham: Springer Nature Switzerland.

Jimmy, F. (2021). Emerging threats: The latest cybersecurity risks and the role of artificial intelligence in enhancing cybersecurity defenses. *Valley International Journal Digital Library*, *1*(2), 564–574. DOI: 10.18535/ijsrm/v9i2.ec01

Kalinaki, K. (2024). Ransomware threat mitigation strategies for protecting critical infrastructure assets. In *Ransomware Evolution* (pp. 120–143). CRC Press. DOI: 10.1201/9781003469506-10

Kapse, I. (2022). Digital Evidence: Admission, Tampering and Its Prevention. *Issue 1 Indian JL & Legal Rsch., 4*, 1.

Karagiannis, C., & Vergidis, K. (2021). Digital evidence and cloud forensics: Contemporary legal challenges and the power of disposal. *Information (Basel)*, *12*(5), 181. DOI: 10.3390/info12050181

Karthikeyan, P., Nachimuthu, P., Vadivelu, V., & Priyadharshini, S. (2026). Transforming Tourism: Exploring the Potential of Blockchain Technology. *Blockchain Technology for the Engineering and Service Sectors*, 307-343.

Khadka, K. (2025). Cybersecurity Challenges and Solutions in the Digital Transformation of Hospitality. *Available at SSRN* 5219742. DOI: 10.2139/ssrn.5219742

Klasén, L., Fock, N., & Forchheimer, R. (2024). The invisible evidence: Digital forensics as key to solving crimes in the digital age. *Forensic Science International*, *362*, 112133. DOI: 10.1016/j.forsciint.2024.112133 PMID: 39089208

Krzan, B. (2021). Admissibility of evidence and international criminal justice. *Rev. Brasileira de Direito Processual Penal*, *7*(1), 161. DOI: 10.22197/rbdpp.v7i1.492

Labadie, C., & Legner, C. (2023). Building data management capabilities to address data protection regulations: Learnings from EU-GDPR. *Journal of Information Technology*, *38*(1), 16–44. DOI: 10.1177/02683962221141456

Lovell, D., Vella, K., Muñoz, D., McKague, M., Brereton, M., & Ellis, P. (2022). Exploring technologies to better link physical evidence and digital information for disaster victim identification. *Forensic Sciences Research*, *7*(3), 467–483. DOI: 10.1080/20961790.2021.2023418 PMID: 36353313

Malik, A. W., Bhatti, D. S., Park, T. J., Ishtiaq, H. U., Ryou, J. C., & Kim, K. I. (2024). Cloud digital forensics: Beyond tools, techniques, and challenges. *Sensors (Basel)*, *24*(2), 433. DOI: 10.3390/s24020433 PMID: 38257526

Mariani, M., & Baggio, R. (2022). Big data and analytics in hospitality and tourism: A systematic literature review. *International Journal of Contemporary Hospitality Management*, *34*(1), 231–278. DOI: 10.1108/IJCHM-03-2021-0301

Mhara, M. A. A., Abdulrahman, A. A., & Baroud, A. A. (2024). Cyber attacks and threats: Study of the types of cyber attacks: Hacking, viruses, targeted attacks, and electronic espionage. *Int. J. Electr. Eng. and Sustain.*, 38-47.

Nasir, R., & Iqbal, W. (2025, May). Digital Forensics Showdown: Encase and FTK Head-to-Head. In *2025 5th International Conference on Innovative Research in Applied Science, Engineering and Technology (IRASET)* (pp. 1-6). IEEE.

Neo, H. F., & Teo, C. C. (2022). Biometrics in tourism: Issues and challenges. *Handbook of e-Tourism*, 1835-1849.

Nosál, J. (2023). Crime in the Digital Age: A New Frontier. In *The Implications of Emerging Technologies in the Euro-Atlantic Space: Views from the Younger Generation Leaders Network* (pp. 177–193). Springer International Publishing. DOI: 10.1007/978-3-031-24673-9_11

Pandey, P., & Kapoor, A. (2025). Cybercrime In The Digital Era: Impacts, Awareness, And Strategic Solutions For A Secure Future. *Sachetas*, *4*(1), 32–37. DOI: 10.55955/410004

Patsakis, C., Arroyo, D., & Casino, F. (2024). The malware as a service ecosystem. In *Malware: Handbook of Prevention and Detection* (pp. 371–394). Springer Nature Switzerland.

Phillips, A., Ojalade, I., Taiwo, E., Obunadike, C., & Oloyede, K. (2023). Cybersecurity tactics in mitigating cyber-crimes: A review and proposal. *Int. J. Cryptogr. Inf. Secur. IJCIS, 13.*

Rakhra, M., Singh, A., & Singh, D. (2024, March). Digital Signature Verification In Cloud Computing. In *2024 11th International Conference on Reliability, Infocom Technologies and Optimization (Trends and Future Directions)(ICRITO)* (pp. 1-6). IEEE. DOI: 10.1109/ICRITO61523.2024.10522372

Ramya, S., Smera, C., & Sandeep, J. (2025). Navigating Network Security: A Study on Contemporary Anomaly Detection Technologies. *Quantum Computing Models for Cybersecurity and Wireless Communications*, 183-199.

Rehman, S., & Rassias, M. (2024). Security Challenges in the 21st Century: Addressing Cybersecurity Threats in International Diplomacy.

Roberts, S. S. (2023). *International Investments in Luxury Real Estate: An Evaluation of International Real Estate Investors and Developers Entering a Cross-Continental Market* (Doctoral dissertation, Massachusetts Institute of Technology).

Robinson, T. (2016, January 15). *Hyatt discovers malware at 250 hotels.* SC Media. https://www.scmagazine.com/news/hyatt-discovers-malware-at-250-hotels

Ruzimatjon, Y. (2024). Digital technologies: How they are transforming our lives. *Web of Scientists and Scholars: Journal of Multidisciplinary Research, 2*(6), 73–79.

Saber, A. F., Helmy, S. H., & Abdel Gaber, M. H. (2025). The Role of Internet of Things in Improving Hotel Operations in Hospitality and Tourism Services and Its Impact on Customers Loyalty. *Journal of Tourism. Hotels and Heritage, 10*(1), 102–126. DOI: 10.21608/sis.2025.383006.1193

Schindler, S., Dembska, M., Bonnarel, F., Lacy, M., Johnson, M., & Desai, V. (2024). Data Documentation Beyond Provenance: Metadata, Research Data Management, FAIR Principles. In *Data-Intensive Radio Astronomy: Bringing Astrophysics to the Exabyte Era* (pp. 397–418). Springer International Publishing. DOI: 10.1007/978-3-031-58468-8_14

Senecal, D. (2024). *The Reign of Botnets: Defending Against Abuses, Bots and Fraud on the Internet.* John Wiley & Sons.

Sethi, S., Patil, R., Rani, S., Anjum, M., & Chaudhary, A. (2024, February). Decrypting Secrets: Deep Learning for Unmasking Malicious Traffic. In *2024 11th International Conference on Computing for Sustainable Global Development (INDIACom)* (pp. 1249-1254). IEEE.

Shandilya, S. K., Datta, A., Kartik, Y., & Nagar, A. (2024). A Study in Attack and Breaches. *Digital Resilience: Navigating Disruption and Safeguarding Data Privacy*, 279-309.

Shin, Y., Kim, K., Lee, J. J., & Lee, K. (2022). Focusing on the weakest link: A similarity analysis on phishing campaigns based on the att&ck matrix. *Security and Communication Networks*, *2022*(1), 1699657. DOI: 10.1155/2022/1699657

Sibe, R. T., & Kaunert, C. (2024). Digital Evidence, Digital Forensics, and Digital Forensic Readiness. In *Cybercrime, Digital Forensic Readiness, and Financial Crime Investigation in Nigeria* (pp. 57–83). Springer Nature Switzerland. DOI: 10.1007/978-3-031-54089-9_3

Singh, G., & Chopra, M. R. (2025). Security Challenges & Techniques to Prevent Cyber Crime Threats in Tourism Industry. *Management*, *5*(3), 35–40.

Singh, N., Khan, M. Z., Kaur, B., & Mishra, A. (2025). Revolutionizing Crime Investigation: The Role of Deep Learning in Forensic Intelligence. In *Forensic Intelligence and Deep Learning Solutions in Crime Investigation* (pp. 281-300). IGI Global Scientific Publishing.

Solanke, A. A. (2022). Digital forensics AI: On practicality, optimality, and interpretability of digital evidence mining techniques.

Sonone, S. S., Gawade, R. K., Hake, D. M., & Rathod, N. V. (2024). Admissibility of Electronic Record under Section 65B of The Indian Evidence Act Vis-à-vis Judicial Interpretation. *Int J Sci Res Sci & Technol. Jan-Feb, 11*(16), 36-41.

Stoykova, R. (2023). The right to a fair trial as a conceptual framework for digital evidence rules in criminal investigations. *Computer Law & Security Review*, *49*, 105801. DOI: 10.1016/j.clsr.2023.105801

Talukder, M. B., Hoque, M., & Kumar, S. (2024). Impact of Cybersecurity in the Aviation, Tourism, and Hospitality Industries. In *Corporate Cybersecurity in the Aviation, Tourism, and Hospitality Sector* (pp. 200-215). IGI Global.

Tariq, M. U. (2024). Data breach incidents and prevention in the hospitality industry. In *Corporate cybersecurity in the aviation, tourism, and hospitality sector* (pp. 181–199). IGI Global. DOI: 10.4018/979-8-3693-2715-9.ch010

Thealla, P., Nadda, V., Dadwal, S., Oztosun, L., & Cantafio, G. (Eds.). (2024). *Corporate cybersecurity in the aviation, tourism, and hospitality sector*. IGI Global. DOI: 10.4018/979-8-3693-2715-9

Vaghela, R., Gowda, V. D., Taj, M., Arudra, A., & Chopra, M. (2024). Digital evidence collection and preservation in computer network forensics. In *Handbook of Research on Innovative Approaches to Information Technology in Library and Information Science* (pp. 42–62). IGI Global Scientific Publishing. DOI: 10.4018/979-8-3693-0807-3.ch003

Vala, J. B., & Vekariya, V. M. (2024). The Role and Importance of Digital Forensics and Digital Evidence in Cyber Crime Detection. *International Journal of Life Sciences Biotechnology and Pharma Research, 13*(6), 413–420. DOI: 10.69605/ijlbpr_13.6.2024.80

Vardakis, G., Hatzivasilis, G., Koutsaki, E., & Papadakis, N. (2024). Review of smart-home security using the internet of things. *Electronics (Basel), 13*(16), 3343. DOI: 10.3390/electronics13163343

Verma, A., & Shri, C. (2022). Cyber security: A review of cyber crimes, security challenges and measures to control. *Vision (Basel)*, •••, 09722629221074760.

Vinod, B. (2022). Introduction to Hotel Revenue Management. In *Revenue Management in the Lodging Industry: Origins to the Last Frontier* (pp. 1–50). Springer International Publishing. DOI: 10.1007/978-3-031-14302-1_1

Zan, T. T., & Min, S. T. T. K. (2025). Cybercrimes and the illicit financial flows in Myanmar. *Journal of Academics Stand Against Poverty, 6*(1), 43–69.

Zorz, Ž. (2015, November 23). *PoS malware hit 54 Starwood luxury hotels*. Help Net Security. https://www.helpnetsecurity.com/2015/11/23/pos-malware-hit-54-starwood-luxury-hotels

Chapter 7

Digital Transformation and Cybersecurity in Hotels:
The Role of AI-Enabled Chatbots in Enhancing Guest Satisfaction and Loyalty

Shazia Waheed
http://orcid.org/0009-0002-2766-3683
Lovely Professional University, India

Sanjeev Kumar
http://orcid.org/0000-0002-7375-7341
Lovely Professional University, India

ABSTRACT

The hospitality industry experiencing rapid digital transformation, with technologies such as AI-enabled chatbots, cloud-based property management systems, and IoT-powered smart rooms reshaping service delivery and guest engagement. These innovations improve operational efficiency, personalization, and convenience; however, they also expose hotels to significant cybersecurity risks. The collection and storage of sensitive guest data, including financial information and personal identifiers, make hotels prime targets for cyberattacks such as ransomware, phishing, and data breaches. This chapter explores the intersection of digital transformation and cybersecurity in hotels, emphasizing the strategic role of AI-enabled chatbots

DOI: 10.4018/979-8-3373-5826-0.ch007

in enhancing guest satisfaction and loyalty. While chatbots deliver benefits such as responsiveness, personalization, and multilingual support, their integration introduces vulnerabilities that demand strong security measures.

1. INTRODUCTION

In recent decades, the hotel business in particular has been at the forefront of the digital transformation. Rapid technological advancements have changed how hotels run, engage with guests and add value throughout the guest's journey. Artificial intelligence (AI), self-service kiosks, and mobile applications are just a few examples of how the digital revolution has changed operational efficiency and transformed the experience of guests (Buhalis& Leung, 2018). AI-enabled chatbots have become one of the most important developments in this regard, giving hotels a strong instrument to engage guests instantly, individually, and affordably (Tussyadiah, 2020).However, hotels are also exposed to new risks as a result of digital transformation, especially in the area of cybersecurity. The enormous volume of sensitive data that hotels gather and retain, including as visitor personal information, payment information, and trip logs, makes them attractive targets for hackers (Zeng, Chen, & Lew, 2021). One of the top five businesses most commonly attacked by cyberattacks is the hospitality sector, with data breaches having serious financial and reputational repercussions, according to a Trustwave research from 2020. Because guest trust is essential to satisfaction and loyalty, the incorporation of digital technologies like chatbots must be balanced with strong cybersecurity safeguards.

Additionally, the COVID-19 pandemic has accelerated up hotel digitalization. Many hotels are using AI-driven technologies, like as chatbots, virtual concierges, and automated check-in systems, to reduce human contact while upholding high service standards in response to growing concerns about contactless interactions (Gretzel et al., 2020). These modifications are not short-term; rather, they are part of a longer-term trend toward service delivery that is facilitated by technology. But the extensive use of AI techniques begs important questions: How can hotels strike a balance between data security and personalization and efficiency? How do chatbots affect customer loyalty and happiness in light of cybersecurity issues. By examining the connections between cybersecurity, digital transformation, and AI-enabled chatbots in hotels, this chapter answers these queries. The chapter acknowledges cybersecurity as a critical enabler of trust and specifically looks into how chatbots might improve guest happiness and loyalty.

1.1 Digital Transformation in the Hotel Industry

According to Buhalis and Sinarta (2019), digital transformation in hotels involves more than just implementing new technologies; it also involves rethinking business models and procedures in order to maximize value production. Technology like artificial intelligence (AI), the Internet of Things (IoT), and big data analytics are changing how hotels communicate with their visitors. For instance, Marriott International has made significant investments in digital transformation projects, such as check-in mobile apps and chatbots powered by AI for customer service, while Accor has tried out AI-based personalization engines to predict visitor needs (Accenture, 2021). Chatbots with AI capabilities are an essential part of this change. Chatbots can effectively handle reservations, respond to inquiries, offer local recommendations, and handle complaints by mimicking human-like dialogues (Li, Bonn, & Ye, 2021). These features not only lessen employee workloads but also guarantee round-the-clock service availability, meeting the modern guest's demands for ease and speed. However, cybersecurity plays a critical role in the success of such digital efforts. Hotels that do not offer secure digital spaces run the risk of losing their reputation and business as guests become more conscious of the dangers of disclosing personal information online (Ali, Omar, & Bakar, 2021).

1.2 Cybersecurity as a Strategic Imperative for Hotels

Beyond technical security, cybersecurity in the hospitality industry is important for customer trust and brand image. Hotel cyber issues are not unusual. For example, over 383 million guests' records, including payment card and passport information, were made public by Marriott International's 2018 data breach (Information Commissioner's Office, 2020). These kinds of occurrences show how vulnerable hotels are in this age of digital revolution.

Furthermore, the potential attack surface grows as hotels use digital platforms and AI chatbots more frequently. IoT-enabled smart room vulnerabilities, ransomware, phishing, and malware attacks are examples of cyberthreats (Kansakar, Munir, & Shabani, 2019). Therefore, hotels should not consider cybersecurity as an afterthought but rather incorporate it into their digital strategy. Hotels can reassure visitors about the security of their personal information by implementing strong security measures, such as encryption, secure authentication, adherence to the Payment Card Industry Data Security Standard (PCI DSS), and General Data Protection Regulation (GDPR).

1.3 AI-Enabled Chatbots as a Driver of Guest Satisfaction and Loyalty

Hotel performance is largely dependent on guest satisfaction, which has historically been connected to physical facilities, staff interactions, and service quality (Chung & Koo, 2015). However, new factors influencing satisfaction have surfaced as digital service delivery has grown in popularity. Chatbots increase customer satisfaction by providing personalization, consistency, and responsiveness. They can help with bookings, answer often asked questions, and offer personalized suggestions based on guest profiles (Gnewuch, Morana, & Maedche, 2018). According to research, chatbot qualities including anthropomorphism, perceived intelligence, and usability greatly enhance the favorable experience of guests (Park & Kim, 2021). Chatbots improve customer satisfaction by lowering barrier in a customer's path and offering a human-like contact. Positive word-of-mouth, return business, and enduring relationships with hotel brands are all ways that happy guests are more likely to show their loyalty (Sweeney & Soutar, 2001). However, in the digital age, loyalty also depends on cybersecurity. Regardless of the caliber of chatbot interactions, guests are unlikely to stay loyal to hotels where their personal information is compromised (Luo & Homburg, 2007). Cybersecurity is therefore both a must and an enabler for using chatbots as a guest loyalty tool.

1.4 Purpose and Contribution of the Chapter

This chapter contributes to both academic literature and industry practice by examining the nexus between digital transformation, cybersecurity, and AI-enabled chatbots in hotels. Specifically, the chapter:

1. Explores how digital transformation has reshaped service delivery in hotels.
2. Analyses cybersecurity challenges and their implications for guest trust.
3. Investigates the role of AI-enabled chatbots in enhancing guest satisfaction and loyalty.
4. Provides practical recommendations for hotel managers and policymakers to balance innovation with data security.

The chapter adopts a holistic perspective, recognizing that digital transformation in hotels cannot be fully understood without considering cybersecurity risks and the role of AI tools in shaping guest experiences.

2. DIGITAL TRANSFORMATION IN THE HOTEL INDUSTRY

2.1 Understanding Digital Transformation in Hospitality

The term "digital transformation" describes the process of incorporating digital technologies into every aspect of company operations in order to significantly enhance customer value delivery and competitive advantage (Buhalis & Amaranggana, 2015). This shift in the hotel sector involves more than just implementing new technology; it also involves changing internal management procedures, guest interaction, and service delivery (Gretzel et al., 2015). Traditional, in-person guest service approaches are giving way to digitally enhanced operations that incorporate automation, personalization, and real-time data analytics in hotels (Mariani & Borghi, 2021).

Digital transformation in the hospitality industry can be defined as a process that uses cutting-edge technologies like artificial intelligence (AI), machine learning, big data, cloud computing, and the Internet of Things (IoT) to improve guest experiences, optimize operational efficiency, and boost profitability(Ivanov & Webster, 2019). Delivering exceptional guest satisfaction while meeting changing traveller expectations in a world that is becoming more digitally connected continues to be the major priority.

2.2 Drivers of Digital Transformation in Hotels

Several forces are driving hotels toward digital adoption:

I. **Changing Guest Expectations:** Today's guests, especially Gen Z and Millennials, expect smooth, customized, and technologically advanced experiences. Hotels must change to be relevant, from chatbots driven by AI for immediate service to smartphone check-ins(Li et al., 2021).

II. **Competitive Pressure:** The hospitality industry is more competitive than ever thanks to the growth of boutique hotels, international chains, and online travel agencies (OTAs). By providing distinctive guest-centric digital services, hotels may set themselves apart thanks to digital transformation (Sigala, 2018).

III. **Operational Efficiency:** Workflows are simplified, human error is decreased, and expenses are decreased with automation via AI, chatbots, and property management systems(Tussyadiah, 2020). AI chatbots, for example, can answer routine questions, allowing employees to concentrate on valuable guest encounters.

IV. **Data-Driven Insights:** These days, hotels use guest data analytics extensively to estimate demand, enhance pricing strategies, personalize services, and predict future market trends(Buhalis&Sinarta, 2019).

V. **Post-Pandemic Adaptations:** COVID-19 boosted up digital transformation by mandating contactless services. Digital room keys, chatbot-based help, and mobile check-ins become commonplace, permanently changing how guests engage with hotels (Gursoy & Chi, 2020).

2.3 Technologies Driving Transformation in Hotels

The following technologies are reshaping hotel operations:

- **Artificial Intelligence (AI) and Machine Learning:** Enabling predictive personalization, dynamic pricing, and guest interaction through chatbots(Mariani & Borghi, 2021).
- **Chatbots and Virtual Assistants:** Handling booking inquiries, room service requests, FAQs, and personalized recommendations 24/7(Lu et al., 2019).
- **Mobile and Contactless Technologies:** Facilitating mobile check-in/check-out, digital room keys, and contactless payments (Statista, 2022).
- **Big Data and Analytics:** Enhancing customer relationship management (CRM), demand forecasting, and revenue management (Buhalis&Amaranggana, 2015).
- **Internet of Things (IoT):** Smart rooms where guests can control lighting, temperature, and entertainment via mobile devices or voice commands (Ivanov et al., 2018).
- **Cloud Computing:** Supporting integrated property management systems accessible across hotel chains for consistency and efficiency (Gretzel et al., 2015).
- **Blockchain:** Emerging applications in secure payments, loyalty programs, and data protection(Kizildag et al., 2019).

2.4 Opportunities Created by Digital Transformation

Hotels benefit significantly from digital innovation:

- **Enhanced Guest Experience:** AI-powered personalization ensures guests feel valued and understood (Li et al., 2021).
- **Operational Cost Reduction:** Automation minimizes the need for human resources in routine tasks(Tussyadiah, 2020).
- **Increased Revenue:** Personalized upselling and dynamic pricing strategies drive higher revenues (Mariani & Borghi, 2021).
- **Brand Loyalty:** Tech-enabled convenience, combined with trust in data security, helps create loyal, returning customers(Sigala, 2018).

- **Sustainability:** Digital tools reduce paper use, optimize energy consumption, and promote eco-friendly operations (Buhalis&Sinarta, 2019).

2.5 Challenges of Digital Transformation in Hotels

Despite the benefits, hotels face several hurdles in implementing digital strategies:

- **High Implementation Costs:** Many small and mid-sized hotels struggle to invest in advanced technology infrastructure(Kizildag et al., 2019).
- **Cybersecurity Risks:** With increased reliance on guest data, the threat of cyberattacks and data breaches has grown significantly (Pencarelli, 2020).
- **Resistance to Change:** Employees and even guests may be hesitant to adopt fully digital experiences(Gursoy & Chi, 2020).
- **Integration Issues:** Legacy systems often clash with new digital platforms, creating inefficiencies (Ivanov & Webster, 2019).
- **Privacy Concerns:** Collecting and using guest data raises ethical and regulatory challenges, particularly under GDPR and other privacy laws (Mariani & Borghi, 2021).

2.6 The Evolving Role of AI in Hotel Digital Transformation

Artificial Intelligence (AI) has become the most important technology in the digital revolution of hotels. A major transformation in the way hotels engage with guests is being made possible by AI technologies, from chatbots that provide individualized guest care to predictive maintenance of hotel infrastructure(Lu et al., 2019). The forefront of digital guest engagement is represented by AI-enabled chatbots, that fill the gap between human-like service interaction and technology efficiency(Tussyadiah, 2020).

3. CYBERSECURITY IN HOTELS: CHALLENGES AND STRATEGIES

In the age of digital transformation, the hospitality sector is depending more and more on cloud-based platforms, digital services, and integrated technologies to improve guest satisfaction and operational effectiveness. Large volumes of sensitive guest information, such as payment details, behavioral insights, and personal identification, are being gathered and processed by hotels using AI-enabled chatbots and property management systems (PMS) (Berezina et al., 2016; Ivanov & Webster, 2019). In addition to increasing operational effectiveness and personalizing services, these technologies put hotels at serious danger for cybersecurity breaches. To protect visitor information, stay in compliance with regulations, and preserve brand reputation, it is crucial to prioritize strong cybersecurity (Simkin, 2021).

3.1 Types of Cybersecurity Threats

Data Breaches

One of the biggest cybersecurity risks facing the hotel industry is data breaches. They entail illegal access to private data kept in hotel databases, which frequently leads to the theft of guests' financial and personal data (Abomhara&Køien, 2015). Weak authentication, inadequate encryption, or hacked employee accounts can all lead to breaches.

One prominent example is the Marriott International hack in 2018, which exposed credit card information, travel history, passport numbers, and identities of almost 500 million visitors (Goodman, 2018). In addition to causing legal consequences and monetary fines, these violations seriously harm a hotel's reputation, which lowers attendance and trust.

I. **Ransomware Attacks:** Malware known as ransomware encrypts important hotel data or systems, making them unusable until a ransom is paid. Reservations, payment systems, and guest management services are just a few of the hotel operations that may be affected by these attacks (El Khoury et al., 2021). Hotels are particularly at risk, especially those with outdated IT systems or inadequate backups.
II. For example, a ransomware assault on a large hotel chain in 2020 resulted in the temporary closure of booking systems at several sites, which affected the firm's reputation and caused operational costs. Ransomware assaults frequently have a financial impact that goes beyond ransom payments and includes costs for system restoration, legal counsel, and fines from the government.
III. **Phishing Attacks:** The high level of staff engagement with email and web-based systems in the hospitality industry makes phishing assaults an ongoing danger. Phishing efforts are fraudulent emails or communications sent to employees with the intention of tricking them into downloading malware or disclosing login credentials (Chowdhury et al., 2020).

An attacker may gain access to critical visitor information or internal operating systems by breaching a hotel's network with just one successful phishing attempt. In order to reduce this risk, employee knowledge and training are essential.

Internet of Things (IoT) Vulnerabilities

Smart room controls, keyless access systems, and connected entertainment platforms are just a few examples of the IoT gadgets that hotels are using to improve the guest experience and provide convenience. Nevertheless, these gadgets frequently have fewer strong security measures and can act as ports of access for criminals (Roman et al., 2013).

IoT flaws may provide hackers the ability to control room access, intercept private data, or interfere with hotel operations. The increasing dependence on smart devices highlights the significance of continuous monitoring, device authentication, and secure network architecture.

Third-Party Vendor Risks

Hotels usually contract with outside companies to handle payment processing, cloud hosting, and IT support. Outsourcing increases flexibility and economy, but it also raises cybersecurity threats. The hotel's overall cybersecurity strategy may be weakened by vendors who use inadequate security measures or improper data handling procedures (Kshetri, 2017).

3.2 Impact of Cybersecurity Threats on Hotels and Guests

Financial Losses

Incidents involving cybersecurity can have serious financial consequences. Hotels are subject to fines, penalties, and compensation claims in addition to the immediate expenses of paying ransom in ransomware attacks or cleaning up after breaches (Berezina et al., 2016). For instance, violations of data protection laws such as the GDPR may lead to fines of up to €20 million or 4% of worldwide yearly income, whichever is greater (European Union, 2016).

I. **Operational Disruptions:** Hotel operations can get affected by cyberattacks. Hotel employees could not be able to manage reservations, access guest information, or process payments if PMS, booking engines, or payment systems are compromised (El Khoury et al., 2021). In addition to bothering visitors, this interruption may result in lower operational effectiveness and lost income.
II. **Reputational Damage:** The trust that guests have in hotels is directly related to their reputation. A hotel's reputation for protecting personal information may suffer from a cybersecurity attack, which could result in bad reviews, fewer repeat

businesses, and fewer reservations (Simkin, 2021). Frequently, the long-term harm to one's brand outweighs any short-term financial losses.

III. **Guest Safety and Privacy Concerns:** In certain situations, privacy and personal safety may be affected by breaches of guest data. For impacted customers, identity theft, financial fraud, or illegal entry to hotel rooms through IoT vulnerabilities can cause serious grief (Abomhara&Køien, 2015). Thus, cybersecurity must be a top priority for hotels for both operational and visitor welfare reasons as mentioned in the table 1.

Table 1. Impact of Cybersecurity Threats on Hotels and Guests

Type of Cybersecurity Threat	Impact on Hotels	Impact on Guests
Data Breach (Guest Data Theft)	Loss of customer trust, legal penalties, damage to brand reputation	Personal information (credit card, ID) may be stolen and misused
Ransomware Attack	Hotel operations disrupted (booking, payment systems blocked), financial losses	Guests may face delays, canceled reservations, or data exposure
Phishing Attacks	Employees tricked into revealing login details, leading to system compromise	Guests may receive fake emails or payment requests posing as the hotel
Malware/Virus Attack	Corruption of internal data and software systems	Possible data loss and privacy risks if devices are connected to hotel Wi-Fi
Wi-Fi Hacking	Unauthorized access to hotel network and sensitive information	Guests' online activities and personal accounts may be monitored or stolen
POS (Point of Sale) System Attack	Credit card fraud and financial loss for the hotel	Guests' payment details stolen during transactions
Insider Threats (Employee Misuse)	Data theft, privacy violations, and trust issues	Guests' personal data can be leaked or sold to third parties

3.3 Best Practices and Standards in Hotel Cybersecurity

Data Protection Regulations: GDPR

Strict guidelines for processing and retaining the personal data of EU citizens are mandated by the General Data Protection Regulation (GDPR) (European Union, 2016). Strong privacy policies, data encryption, breach reporting procedures, and access control measures must be put in place for hotels managing the data of EU visitors. In addition to ensuring legal conformity, compliance boosts consumer trust.

Payment Security: PCI DSS

Guidelines for the safe management of cardholder data are provided by the Payment Card Industry Data Security Standard (PCI DSS). To avoid financial fraud and data breaches, hotels that take credit card payments have to adhere to PCI DSS (PCI Security Standards Council, 2022). This involves putting in place safe payment gateways, encrypting cardholder information, and carrying out frequent security assessments.

Information Security Management: ISO/IEC 27001

An international standard for information security management systems (ISMS) called ISO/IEC 27001 aids businesses in recognizing, controlling, and reducing cybersecurity threats (ISO, 2013). By implementing ISO 27001, hotels can create risk assessment frameworks, implement incident response procedures, and rigorously secure information assets. Additionally, certification shows a dedication to cybersecurity excellence, which can improve a brand's reputation.

Cybersecurity Best Practices

i. **Employee Training:** Programs for staff members to get ongoing education lower the chances of social engineering and phishing attempts (Chowdhury et al., 2020).
ii. **Regular Updates and Patch Management:** Keeping network systems, PMS, and IoT devices updated stops known vulnerabilities from being exploited (Roman et al., 2013).
iii. **Network Segmentation and Access Control:** The impact of any breaches is minimized by limiting access to sensitive systems and isolating vital infrastructure (Abomhara&Køien, 2015).
iv. **Encryption and Secure Storage:** Unauthorized access is avoided by encrypting sensitive information about guests, such as payment details (Berezina et al., 2016).
v. **Incident Response Planning:** In order to minimize damage and downtime in the event of a breach, hotels should set up organized procedures (El Khoury et al., 2021).
vi. **Collaboration with Cybersecurity Experts:** Preparation against complex attacks is improved by collaborating with outside specialists for threat monitoring and penetration testing (Kshetri, 2017).

Integration with Emerging Technologies

It's critical to incorporate cybersecurity safeguards straight into AI-enabled chatbots and automated guest services as they expand. To protect visitor information, AI systems need to use data anonymization methods, stringent access control, and secure APIs (Ivanov & Webster, 2019). Hotels may develop technologically without compromising guest trust when AI is implemented securely.

4. AI-ENABLED CHATBOTS IN HOTELS

Artificial Intelligence (AI) technology has been rapidly incorporated into the hospitality sector to improve guest experience, operational efficiency, and service personalization. AI-enabled chatbots are one of these technologies that has revolutionized the hotel industry. They can answer questions from guests, make reservations, offer personalized recommendations, and speed operational procedures (Ivanov & Webster, 2019). Chatbots use cloud-based systems, machine learning, and natural language processing (NLP) to communicate with guests via messaging applications, websites, and mobile apps while providing round-the-clock support (Chung & Koo, 2015).The use of chatbots remains in line with the larger trend of digital transformation in the hospitality industry, where lodging establishments want to provide guests with smooth, effortless, and personalized experiences.

4.1 Functions and Applications of AI Chatbots in Hotels

I. **Guest Communication and Query Handling:** AI chatbots instantly respond to queries from guests, including those concerning amenities, services, and the availability of rooms. Hotels lessen the workload of front desk employees while maintaining timely and consistent communication by automating regular encounters (Tung & Law, 2020). For instance, chatbots that are coupled with messaging applications or hotel websites can respond to often requested questions, freeing up staff members to deal with more complicated demands.

II. **Booking and Reservation Management"** By allowing guests to check room availability, make reservations, and change reservations without human assistance, AI chatbots streamline the booking process (Ivanov et al., 2017). Certain smart chatbots can be incorporated with property management systems (PMS) to handle payments, provide real-time updates, and issue confirmations. Errors are decreased, operational effectiveness is raised, and the overall visitor experience is improved by this automation.

III. **Personalized Recommendations:** Chatbots can provide personalized recommendations based on guest interests, past reservations, and behavioral patterns by utilizing data analytics and machine learning (Gursoy et al., 2019). To increase engagement and possible revenue, chatbots can, for example, recommend restaurants, spa treatments, nearby attractions, or exclusive deals for every guest as discussed in the table 2.

Table 2. Functions and Applications of AI Chatbots in Hotels

Functions of AI Chatbots	Applications in Hotels
Customer Service Support	Answer guest queries instantly (room availability, check-in/out time, amenities, etc.)
Reservation Assistance	Help guests book rooms online and modify or cancel reservations easily
Personalized Recommendations	Suggest restaurants, spa services, or local attractions based on guest preferences
24/7 Availability	Provide round-the-clock assistance, even when staff are unavailable
Multilingual Communication	Interact with international guests in their preferred language
Feedback Collection	Collect reviews or feedback after stay to improve services
Complaint Handling	Quickly record and forward guest complaints to the right department
Marketing and Promotions	Share special offers, discounts, and loyalty programs through chat

Multilingual Support

Language limitations can make it difficult for hotels to provide services to their broad, international customer. Multilingual AI chatbots can communicate with guests in their native tongue, increasing inclusivity and accessibility (Ivanov & Webster, 2019). This feature increases guest happiness and increases the hotel's attractiveness to tourists from other countries.

Integration with IoT and Smart Services

IoT-enabled hotel equipment, including keyless entry systems, smart room controls, and in-room entertainment systems, can be interfaced with by chatbots (Roman et al., 2013). Chatbots allow guests to have a very convenient and customized stay by controlling lighting, ordering room service, and adjusting the temperature. This integration shows how AI-powered communication and intelligent hospitality solutions work together.

4.2 Benefits of AI Chatbots for Hotels

Operational Efficiency

By automating routine tasks like answering questions, managing reservations, and delivering information about services, AI chatbots simplify hotel operations (Chung & Koo, 2015). This enables employees to concentrate on higher-value tasks like organizing events, interacting with guests individually, and solving problems.

Cost Reduction

Hotels can lower labour expenses and operating overheads by automating repetitive procedures. Chatbots provide consistent service at a lesser cost than additional human labour because they work continuously without breaks or shift changes (Tung & Law, 2020).

Enhanced Guest Experience

Chatbots increase guest satisfaction by offering prompt answers, precise information, and personalized suggestions. Convenient round-the-clock assistance cuts down on wait times and guarantees guests feel appreciated during their stay (Ivanov & Webster, 2019).

Data Collection and Analytics

AI chatbots gather useful guest data, such as interaction habits, preferences, and commonly asked inquiries. Hotels can use this information to manage loyalty programs, optimize services, and conduct targeted marketing (Gursoy et al., 2019). For instance, information gathered from chatbot interactions can direct personalized advertising, discounts, and service enhancements.

Brand Differentiation

By using AI chatbots, hotels may stand out from the competition and improve their brand image by showcasing their technological innovation and sophistication. AI-enabled services are seen by customers as cutting edge, effective, and customer-focused, which enhances brand perception (Ivanov et al., 2017).

4.3 Challenges in Implementing AI Chatbots

Technical Limitations

Even with AI advancements, chatbots may still have trouble understanding complicated or unclear requests. Because natural language processing is rarely perfect, misinterpretations could result in inaccurate answers or upset guests (Chung & Koo, 2015). To increase accuracy, system updates and ongoing training are necessary.

Privacy and Security Concerns

AI chatbots manage private guest data, such as payment, behavioural, and personal details. Hotels may be vulnerable to breaches and non-compliance with regulations if they implement inadequate data security procedures (Simkin, 2021). Chatbots need to adhere to regulations like GDPR and PCI DSS, use encryption, and store data securely.

Resistance from Guests

AI-driven communication may not be preferred by all guests, especially in high-end or luxury service areas. To guarantee the happiness of all kinds of guests, hotels must strike a balance between automation and human help (Ivanov & Webster, 2019).

Integration with Legacy Systems

Integration issues may arise for hotels using outdated PMS or reservation systems. For chatbots to deliver accurate real-time information, they must seamlessly link with the current infrastructure, which might require a large investment in system changes (Tung & Law, 2020).

4.4 Best Practices for AI Chatbot Deployment

1. **User-Centric Design:** Chatbots should to be simple to use, responsive, and intuitive. The seamless interaction of guests is guaranteed by user experience design concepts (Gursoy et al., 2019).
2. **Multilingual and Context-Aware Functionality:** Accessibility and engagement are increased by offering context-aware responses and multilingual help (Ivanov & Webster, 2019).

3. **Data Privacy and Security:** Guest information is protected by the use of encryption, secure API integration, and adherence to PCI DSS and GDPR (Simkin, 2021).
4. **Continuous Learning and Updates:** To increase accuracy and relevance, machine learning models should be routinely trained using fresh visitor interaction data (Chung & Koo, 2015).
5. **Hybrid Support Models:** AI chatbots and human employees work together to efficiently address complex inquiries, ensuring that guests are satisfied at all service levels (Tung & Law, 2020).

4.5 Future Trends

1. **Advanced Personalization:** In order to deliver highly customized experiences and anticipate visitor demands before they are expressed, AI chatbots will increasingly use behavioural insights and predictive analytics (Ivanov & Webster, 2019).
2. **Voice-Enabled Interaction:** Convenience will be increased by integrating voice assistants, which will enable guests to engage with hotel services more naturally and hands-free (Gursoy et al., 2019).
3. **Emotional AI:** Through speech or text patterns, future chatbots may be able to identify the emotions of their users and modify their responses to produce more engaging and sympathetic exchanges (Chung & Koo, 2015).
4. **Seamless Omnichannel Integration:** Chatbots will function on a variety of platforms, such as social media, mobile apps, and in-room gadgets, guaranteeing standardized service delivery across all platforms (Tung & Law, 2020).

5. INTEGRATION OF CYBERSECURITY AND AI-CHATBOTS IN HOTELS

By facilitating smooth communication, individualized services, and effective operational management, the use of AI-enabled chatbots in hotels has completely changed how guests experience them (Ivanov & Webster, 2019). However, because chatbots handle sensitive guest data—such as payment details, personal identification, and behavioural patterns—across several platforms, this digital revolution presents new cybersecurity challenges.To make sure that technology advancements do not compromise operational integrity, guest confidence, or regulatory compliance, cybersecurity safeguards must be incorporated into AI chatbot deployment.

5.1 Cybersecurity Risks Associated With AI-Chatbots

Data Privacy and Protection Risks

AI chatbots gather, retain, and examine a great deal of visitor data, such as contact information, past reservations, preferences, and payment information. In the absence of strong security measures, this data may be intercepted, disclosed, or exploited, leading to security breaches that affect guest privacy and violate laws like GDPR and PCI DSS (Simkin, 2021; European Union, 2016).

Unsecured chatbot APIs or inadequate encryption, for instance, can provide hackers access to private information, which could result in identity theft, financial fraud, or harm to one's reputation. According to Ivanov and Webster (2019), hotels must incorporate encryption protocols, safe authentication methods, and strict access control in chatbot systems.

Threats from Cyberattacks

AI chatbots are at risk of ransomware, phishing, and virus attacks, just like any other linked system. To obtain access to hotel networks, interfere with operations, or control visitor interactions, attackers can take use of flaws in chatbot systems (El Khoury et al., 2021). Because chatbots frequently communicate with payment systems, PMS, and IoT devices, a compromised chatbot may act as a springboard for more extensive assaults. The necessity of thorough cybersecurity safeguards for all systems connected to AI chatbots is highlighted by this interconnectedness.

AI-Specific Vulnerabilities

According to Chung and Koo (2015), AI chatbots are prone to special vulnerabilities such aggressive assaults, in which input data is purposefully changed to trick AI models. Outdated or poorly trained models may unintentionally reveal sensitive information, misinterpret guest inquiries, or give inaccurate answers. Breach identification, model retraining, and ongoing monitoring are essential for reducing these hazards unique to AI.

5.2 Strategies for Secure AI-Chatbot Implementation

Data Encryption and Secure Storage

To stop unwanted access to private visitor data, it is essential to encrypt data both in transit and at rest (Berezina et al., 2016). Hotels should use encryption techniques and safe storage options to shield customer information, payment information, and interaction history from online attacks.

Compliance with International Standards

Hotels need to make sure AI chatbots follow international cybersecurity guidelines and standards, such as:

- **GDPR:** Enforces express consent, safeguards guest data privacy, and demands prompt breach reports (European Union, 2016).
- **PCI DSS:** Protects credit card data and payment processing (PCI Security Standards Council, 2022).
- **ISO/IEC 27001:**An information security management system (ISMS) is established by ISO/IEC 27001 to facilitate ongoing monitoring, risk assessment, and incident response (ISO, 2013).

Adherence to these guidelines not only reduces hazards but also strengthens guest satisfaction and legal responsibility.

Access Control and Authentication

Only authorized individuals and systems are able to access chatbot data and features thanks to stringent access control procedures. Role-based access control (RBAC) and multi-factor authentication (MFA) lower the possibility of unwanted manipulation and restrict exposure to insider threats (Abomhara&Køien, 2015).

Secure API Integration

In order to communicate with PMS, IoT devices, and outside services, AI chatbots frequently rely on APIs. Attackers cannot use integration points to gain access to hotel networks if these APIs are secured with authentication, encryption, and frequent monitoring (Roman et al., 2013).

Employee Training and Awareness

Employees using AI chatbots need to receive training on incident reporting, phishing detection, and cybersecurity best practices (Chowdhury et al., 2020). Knowledgeable staff members serve as the first line of defence against online attacks that target chatbots.

Incident Response and Monitoring

A strong issue response strategy designed especially for AI-chatbot systems should be kept up to date by hotels. Rapid reaction systems, anomaly detection, and real-time monitoring reduce the harm caused by ransomware attacks, breaches, and AI system malfunctions (El Khoury et al., 2021).

5.3 Benefits of Secure AI-Chatbot Integration

Enhanced Guest Trust and Satisfaction

When AI chatbots are used in a secure environment, guests can rest easy knowing that their information is safe. Chatbots that are safe, dependable, and responsive build trust and make for a better experience in general (Ivanov & Webster, 2019).

Operational Continuity

The probability of downtime or operational disruption due to hacking is decreased by secure chatbot systems. Constant and secure AI service guarantees smooth guest interaction and efficiently supports day-to-day hotel operations (Tung & Law, 2020).

Competitive Advantage

Hotels that successfully combine robust cybersecurity measures with AI chatbots stand out from the competition. According to Gursoy et al. (2019), guests are more inclined to select businesses that provide both cutting-edge AI-driven services and guarantees of data protection.

Data-Driven Insights with Safety

Without sacrificing privacy or breaking the law, hotels can use secure AI chatbots to gather, evaluate, and use guest data for marketing campaigns, individualized services, and operational enhancements (Chung & Koo, 2015).

5.4 Emerging Trends in Secure AI-Chatbot Deployment

a) **AI-Driven Threat Detection:** Real-time detection of suspicious activity by chatbots combined with AI-based security solutions can stop attacks and protect data (Ivanov & Webster, 2019).

b) **Privacy-Preserving AI:** By using strategies like federated learning and differentiated privacy, AI chatbots can learn from guest data without centrally keeping private information, improving security and compliance (Simkin, 2021).
c) **Blockchain Integration:** In chatbot systems, distributed ledger technology can guarantee data integrity, monitor interactions, and protect transactions (Tian, 2016).
d) **Adaptive Security Protocols:** According to Chowdhury et al. (2020), AI chatbots have the potential to employ dynamic security measures that adapt to changing threats and offer proactive defence against new breaches.

6. ENHANCING GUEST SATISFACTION AND LOYALTY THROUGH AI AND SECURE DIGITAL SERVICES

Two of the most important factors influencing success in the hospitality industry are guest satisfaction and loyalty. According to Sweeney and Soutar (2001), hotels that offer outstanding service quality, trust, and personalized experiences are more likely to encourage repeat business and favorable word-of-mouth. A revolutionary change in the way hotels provide services while safeguarding guest information is represented by the combination of strong cybersecurity procedures with AI technology, especially chatbots that are powered by AI.

6.1 AI-Enabled Chatbots and Guest Satisfaction

Personalized and Immediate Service

AI chatbots provide personalized, real-time communication that speeds up response times and cuts down on wait times. At any time, guests can request amenities, make reservations, or ask questions about services, and they will receive prompt, personalized answers (Gursoy et al., 2019). This is in line with the increasing demand for quickness in hospitality services, especially from Gen Z and millennial tourists (Tussyadiah& Park, 2018).

Usability and Convenience

Guest happiness is significantly impacted by how AI chatbots are regarded to be usable i.e., perceived usability. Guests from a variety of backgrounds can interact with ease thanks to user-friendly interfaces, intuitive designs, and multilingual capabilities (Chung & Koo, 2015). Guest satisfaction is greatly increased when services are easy to use and accessible, particularly for foreign visitors who could encounter language problems.

Anthropomorphism and Emotional Engagement

Conversational tone and natural language processing are examples of anthropomorphic qualities that make an interaction more human-like and encourage emotional connection (Luo & Homburg, 2007). According to research, when AI chatbots demonstrate empathy and adjust to complexities of conversations, guests report better levels of satisfaction (Park & Kim, 2021). This emotional bond helps foster long-term commitment in addition to providing immediate satisfaction.

6.2 Role of Cybersecurity in Guest Trust and Satisfaction

Trust as a Foundation for Satisfaction

While usability and chatbot intelligence improve user experiences, confidence in safe data handling is just as crucial. Guests share private information that could seriously undermine confidence, such as credit card numbers, passport information, and travel schedules (Simkin, 2021). Therefore, secure chatbot systems are the foundation of customer satisfaction, guaranteeing that convenience does not come at the price of security.

Transparency and Compliance

Hotels that make clear that they follow cybersecurity guidelines like GDPR, PCI DSS, and ISO/IEC 27001 are more trusted by guests (European Union, 2016; PCI Security Standards Council, 2022; ISO, 2013). Transparency about the use and security of data builds trust and gives guests peace of mind that their privacy is a primary concern (Chowdhury et al., 2020).

Impact on Service Continuity

When chatbot services are disrupted by cyberattacks, it might lead to delays or inaccurate information, which can significantly impact the customer's experience. On the other hand, strong cybersecurity procedures provide continuous service availability, protecting customer satisfaction (El Khoury et al., 2021).

6.3 From Satisfaction to Loyalty

Satisfaction as a Driver of Revisit Intention

Numerous studies have demonstrated that satisfied guests are more likely to stay at the same hotel again and refer others to it (Chung & Koo, 2015; Sweeney & Soutar, 2001). When AI chatbots are safe and dependable, they consistently provide convenience, customisation, and emotional involvement, which increase the likelihood that users will return.

Building Emotional Loyalty

Emotional attachment is the foundation of loyalty, which extends beyond practical fulfilment. According to Luo and Homburg (2007), guests are more likely to form emotional loyalty toward a hotel if they feel both well-served and protected. In the luxury hospitality industry, where emotional experiences frequently surpass transactional value, this is especially crucial (Tung & Law, 2020).

Reducing Switching Intentions

Trust is damaged and switching intentions rise when hotels do not protect guest data, even when service quality is generally excellent (Gursoy et al., 2019). AI chatbots, on the other hand, increase loyalty and lower perceived risks when combined with cybersecurity measures.

6.4 Synergistic Role of AI and Cybersecurity

Creating Secure Personalization

In order to provide personalized assistance, AI depends on customer information, which cybersecurity makes sure is secure. Innovation and trust are balanced because of the way these two domains work together to guarantee that personalization doesn't compromise privacy (Ivanov & Webster, 2019).

Enhancing Competitive Advantage

Hotels that combine cutting-edge AI with robust cybersecurity are distinctive as creative yet dependable businesses. This dual ability gives the company a competitive edge and attracts tech-savvy tourists who appreciate both safety and digital ease (Tian, 2016).

Reinforcing the Service-Profit Chain

The service-profit chain model suggests a connection between profitability, guest satisfaction, service quality, and employee satisfaction (Heskett et al., 1994). In addition to improving guest experiences, secure AI chatbots lighten staff workloads so they can concentrate on higher-value activities, which boosts overall profitability and brand strength.

6.5 Future Outlook: Secure AI for Sustainable Loyalty

The future of hospitality lies in the fusion of AI innovation and cybersecurity resilience. Key developments include:

- **AI-Powered Sentiment Analysis** –Emotional recognition in real time to improve satisfaction and customize answers.
- **Blockchain-Loyalty Programs** –Long-term loyalty is strengthened by reward systems that are safe, open, and unbreakable (Tian, 2016).
- **Federated Learning for Privacy** –Locally trained AI models on devices improve personalization while lowering the danger of centralized data breaches (Simkin, 2021).
- **Sustainability-Linked Digital Trust** –Hotels that include safe and sustainable AI methods will stand out as eco-conscious travellers demand more responsible use of technology (Tussyadiah& Park, 2018).

In the digital age, increasing guest satisfaction and loyalty requires a complete strategy that incorporates safe digital offerings rather than merely implementing AI-enabled chatbots. While cybersecurity guarantees trust, transparency, and continuity, AI chatbots offer personalization, convenience, and emotional involvement. When combined, these components strengthen the intention to return, lessen switching behaviours, and foster emotional loyalty.

In a time when guests have greater expectations than ever for ease, personalization, and digital trust, hotels that combine AI innovation with cybersecurity resilience will be better positioned to prosper. In addition to increasing guest satisfaction and loyalty, secure AI creates the groundwork for the hospitality industry's long-term competitiveness and sustainable growth.

7. CASE STUDIES – SUCCESSFUL IMPLEMENTATION OF AI AND CYBERSECURITY IN HOTELS

7.1 Marriott International: Integrating Chatbots with Secure Guest Data Management

One of the biggest hotel chains in the world, Marriott International, has led the way in implementing AI-powered guest communication technologies. Guests can request services like housekeeping, late checkout, and dinner reservations through the "ChatBotlr," which is linked into the Marriott mobile app (Marriott International, 2017).

Cybersecurity Measures

Marriott has made significant investments to comply with GDPR and PCI DSS standards because of the size of its operations and the sensitive nature of guest data. In order to assure real-time threat detection after a significant data breach in 2018, Marriott cooperated with cybersecurity firms, upgraded its encryption processes, and implemented two-factor authentication (Simkin, 2021).

Impact on Guests

Due to quicker service answers and less dependence on interactions at the front desk, guests expressed greater satisfaction (Ivanov & Webster, 2019). More significantly, in the wake of the breach, Marriott strengthened customer loyalty by being open and honest about its improved cybersecurity procedures.

7.2 Hilton Hotels: AI Chatbots for Personalized Loyalty Engagement

In collaboration with IBM Watson, Hilton unveiled its AI-powered "Connie" chatbot, which bears the name of its founder, Conrad Hilton. Connie improves the visitor experience by offering tailored hotel information, loyalty program updates, and local recommendations (Hilton Worldwide, 2016).

Cybersecurity Measures

Hilton incorporates Connie into its Hilton Honors loyalty program, which contains transaction records and private guest preferences. Hilton uses secure API gateways,

ISO/IEC 27001-compliant security systems, and ongoing chatbot interaction monitoring to safeguard this data (ISO, 2013).

Impact on Guests

Connie's capability to offer personalized suggestions increased anthropomorphism and perceived intelligence, which in turn boosted visitor engagement (Park & Kim, 2021). Hilton improved customer satisfaction and emotional loyalty among returning customers, especially among its loyalty program members, by implementing visible cybersecurity safeguards.

7.3 Accor Hotels: Balancing Innovation and Data Protection

The French international hospitality group Accor has implemented AI-powered chatbots for a number of its brands, ranging from the high-end Sofitel to the low-cost Ibis. These chatbots help with reservations, support requests, and travel advice in multiple languages (Accor, 2019).

Cybersecurity Measures

Accor's chatbots are bound by GDPR requirements, which is important because the company handles guest data throughout the EU. The team uses privacy-by-design, frequent penetration testing, and end-to-end encryption to reduce chatbot interaction vulnerabilities (European Union, 2016).

Impact on Guests

Accor reported higher levels of guest satisfaction, particularly among foreign visitors who take use of the round-the-clock, multilingual chatbot assistance. Additionally, its proactive approach to cybersecurity strengthens confidence, which is crucial in markets where privacy concerns are more pressing (El Khoury et al., 2021).

These case studies show how the hospitality sector is negotiating the relationship between cybersecurity resilience and AI innovation. Although AI-enabled chatbots increase satisfaction, convenience, and customisation, these advantages can only be maintained with strong cybersecurity safeguards in place.

The experiences of Marriott, Hilton and Accorhighlight the value of both trust and innovation. In addition to improving client pleasure, hotels that strike a balance between these factors also gain a competitive edge and maintain long-term loyalty.

8. CHALLENGES AND FUTURE DIRECTIONS

With technology like AI-enabled chatbots, cloud-based property management systems, and IoT-driven smart rooms, the hospitality sector has enthusiastically embraced digital transformation. Hotels are now vulnerable to ongoing cybersecurity threats as a result of the integration of these technologies. Although the implementation, enforcement, and innovation of international standards like GDPR, PCI DSS, and ISO/IEC 27001 offer a foundation for enhanced resilience, difficulties still exist (Cheng & Kapoor, 2022). The main cybersecurity and digital transformation issues that hotels are experiencing are examined in this part, along with possible future paths that could improve operational effectiveness, resilience, and trust.

8.1 Key Challenges in Cybersecurity for Hotels

Rapidly Evolving Cyber Threats

Many hotels are unable to keep up with the rapid evolution of cyber threats. Attackers are always coming up with new ways to get into systems, including as ransomware-as-a-service, AI-powered attacks, and complex phishing schemes (Symantec, 2021). Hotels frequently find it difficult to keep their security up to date, which leaves gaps that can be exploited.

Legacy Systems and Integration Issues

According to Yun et al. (2020), a large number of hotels still use outdated property management systems (PMS) that were not created with contemporary cybersecurity concerns in mind. Security flaws arise when these outdated systems are integrated with more recent technology, including cloud-based solutions or Internet of Things devices. Outdated software, for instance, might not support MFA or encryption, making it a perfect target for hackers.

Resource Constraints

Investments in cybersecurity demand significant human and financial resources. Small and medium-sized hotels frequently lack the funds to employ cybersecurity experts or implement cutting-edge technologies, even while large hotel chains may set aside significant sums for security (PwC, 2020). Smaller firms are more exposed to hazards as a result, leading to a digital divide.

Human Factor Vulnerabilities

Human error is still a significant cybersecurity concern in spite of technical developments. Employees might unintentionally click on harmful links, create weak passwords, or handle visitor data improperly (Krombholz et al., 2015). It is especially challenging to maintain constant training and awareness in hotels with frequent employee turnover.

Regulatory Complexity and Compliance Gaps

Regulatory compliance is made more difficult by the worldwide nature of the hospitality industry. Hotels that operate in several jurisdictions are required to continuously adhere to the CCPA in California, the GDPR in Europe, and other regional data privacy legislation. Hotels are exposed to financial and reputational risks as a result of this complexity, which frequently leads to inconsistent compliance (European Commission, 2018).

Balancing Guest Convenience with Security

Instant Wi-Fi, smartphone check-ins, and one-click payments are all examples of the smooth digital experiences that guests expect. Strict security protocols, however, have the potential to complicate these procedures. Hotels must strike a balance between security and convenience because too strict measures can irritate visitors (Gursoy et al., 2019).

9. CONCLUSION

Today's hospitality industry is going through a significant digital transformation, incorporating cutting-edge technology like cloud-based management systems, biometric check-ins, AI-enabled chatbots, and IoT-powered smart rooms to improve guest experiences and boost operational effectiveness. These developments have completely changed the way hotels operate and engage with their guests, allowing for unheard-before levels of cost-effectiveness, convenience, and personalization. However, there are serious cybersecurity threats brought forth by this digital transformation that cannot be ignored. Data security is a critical issue since the same technologies that enable hotels to run more efficiently and provide greater guest service also increase the attack surface for bad actors. In this regard, cybersecurity has become not merely a technological requirement but also a vital component of customer loyalty, trust, and the industry's long-term competitiveness.

Hotels deal with a variety of cybersecurity issues. Threats that are constantly changing, like ransomware, phishing, and sophisticated malware, surpass conventional defenses, exposing weaknesses. A lot of hotels continue to use old property management systems that were never intended to survive contemporary cyberattacks, and combining them with new digital solutions frequently results in additional security flaws. Due to resource limitations, smaller hotels in particular are unable to engage expert staff or invest in advanced cybersecurity technology, which leads to uneven levels of protection across the business. The human element is still a significant weakness, which leads to these problems. Employee errors, such as using weak passwords, falling for phishing schemes, or improperly managing visitor data, continue to be a regular point of entry for hackers.The situation is made more difficult by regulatory complexity, as hotels that operate internationally must comply with local data protection legislation as well as frameworks like the Payment Card Industry Data Security Standard (PCI DSS), the EU's General Data Protection Regulation (GDPR), and ISO/IEC 27001. Hotels must simultaneously strike a balance between security procedures and guest convenience since too strict policies run the danger of compromising the smooth digital experience that guests are coming to anticipate more and more.

Despite these challenges, the hospitality industry has started implementing a number of best practices and compliance frameworks that systematically address cybersecurity issues. PCI DSS protects financial transactions, GDPR prioritizes the protection of personal data and guest consent, and ISO/IEC 27001 provides a comprehensive framework for managing information security risks. In addition to these legal obligations, hotels are progressively putting into practice sensible safeguards including strong encryption, multi-factor authentication, frequent security assessments, staff development, and incident response plans. These precautions are essential tools for building trust and proving a hotel's dedication to protecting the financial and personal data of its guests, not just technical ones. As a result, compliance and proactive security measures are now both strategic advantages for promoting guest loyalty and operational requirements.

Looking ahead, modern technologies and fresh strategies that address new threats will influence hotel cybersecurity in the future. By enabling real-time anomaly identification and predictive threat avoidance, artificial intelligence and machine learning will lessen the need for human monitoring. Outdated perimeter-based defences will be replaced by zero-trust security frameworks, which guarantee that no user or device is trusted by default. While biometric authentication techniques promise to improve security and convenience by facilitating smooth guest access to services, blockchain offers promise for tamper-proof data storage and transparent, secure transactions. Additionally, rather than viewing training as a one-time event, hotels may develop a strong cybersecurity culture among their staff by integrating knowledge and safe practices into everyday operations.Developing uniform defenses for international hotel chains will also require industry-wide standardization initiatives and international cooperation.

Ultimately, cybersecurity has evolved from a minor technical issue to a determining element in customer loyalty, brand reputation, and guest trust. In a time when data breaches can result in permanent damage to a hotel's reputation, safeguarding sensitive data has become just as crucial as offering luxurious services or physical comfort. Transparency about data management is becoming more and more important to guests, who will choose hotels that can ensure both digital safety and personalized assistance. Strong cybersecurity is therefore both a prerequisite for compliance and a competitive advantage for hotels.

In general, the hotel industry is at a turning point. Although digital transformation presents hotels with previously unheard-of chances to improve guest experiences and optimize operations, it also exposes them to intricate and constantly changing cybersecurity threats. The industry's capacity to balance innovation and security, protection and convenience, and technical resilience and human awareness will determine its destiny. In addition to protecting their operations, hotels that are successful in integrating cybersecurity into the core of their digital strategies will also foster long-lasting guest loyalty and trust, guaranteeing long-term success in the risky digital age.

REFERENCES

Abomhara, M., & Køien, G. M. (2015). Cyber security and the internet of things: Vulnerabilities, threats, intruders and attacks. *Journal of Cyber Security and Mobility*, *4*(1), 65–88. DOI: 10.13052/jcsm2245-1439.414

Accenture. (2021). *Digital transformation in hospitality: Unlocking growth opportunities*. Accenture. https://www.accenture.com

Accor. (2019). *Accor digital innovation and chatbot integration*. Accor Group. https://group.accor.com

Ali, A., Omar, R., & Bakar, A. A. (2021). Cybersecurity awareness in the hospitality industry: An exploratory study. *Journal of Hospitality and Tourism Technology*, *12*(4), 675–690. DOI: 10.1108/JHTT-10-2020-0274

Berezina, K., Cobanoglu, C., Miller, B. L., & Kwansa, F. A. (2016). Cybersecurity in the hospitality industry: Past, present, and future. *Cornell Hospitality Quarterly*, *57*(4), 370–380. DOI: 10.1177/1938965515624013

Buhalis, D., & Amaranggana, A. (2015). Smart tourism destinations: Enhancing tourism experience through personalization of services. In Tussyadiah, I., & Inversini, A. (Eds.), *Information and communication technologies in tourism 2015* (pp. 377–389). Springer., DOI: 10.1007/978-3-319-14343-9_28

Buhalis, D., & Leung, R. (2018). Smart hospitality—Interconnectivity and interoperability towards an ecosystem. *International Journal of Hospitality Management*, *71*, 41–50. DOI: 10.1016/j.ijhm.2017.11.011

Buhalis, D., & Sinarta, Y. (2019). Real-time co-creation and nowness service: Lessons from tourism and hospitality. *Journal of Travel & Tourism Marketing*, *36*(5), 563–582. DOI: 10.1080/10548408.2019.1592059

Cheng, M., & Kapoor, B. (2022). Digital transformation and cybersecurity challenges in the tourism and hospitality sector. *Tourism Management Perspectives*, *41*, 100947. DOI: 10.1016/j.tmp.2021.100947

Chowdhury, N., Gkioulos, V., Olsen, R., & Petersen, S. A. (2020). Phishing attacks: Scenarios and defense mechanisms. *Computers & Security*, *97*, 101947. DOI: 10.1016/j.cose.2020.101947

Chung, N., & Koo, C. (2015). The use of social media in travel information search. *Telematics and Informatics*, *32*(2), 215–229. DOI: 10.1016/j.tele.2014.08.005

El Khoury, P., Kassar, A., & Tohme, M. (2021). Ransomware in hospitality: Threats, challenges, and solutions. *Journal of Information Security and Applications, 60*, 102887. DOI: 10.1016/j.jisa.2021.102887

European Commission. (2018). *General Data Protection Regulation (GDPR).* Official Journal of the European Union. https://gdpr-info.eu

European Union. (2016). *General Data Protection Regulation (GDPR): Regulation (EU) 2016/679.* Official Journal of the European Union. https://eur-lex.europa.eu/eli/reg/2016/679/oj

Gnewuch, U., Morana, S., & Maedche, A. (2018). Towards designing cooperative and social conversational agents for customer service. *Information Systems and e-Business Management, 16*(3), 491–511. DOI: 10.1007/s10257-017-0364-4

Goodman, M. (2018, November 30). Marriott discloses massive data breach affecting 500 million guests. *The New York Times.*https://www.nytimes.com

Gretzel, U., Fuchs, M., Baggio, R., Hoepken, W., Law, R., Neidhardt, J., Pesonen, J., Zanker, M., & Xiang, Z. (2020). e-Tourism beyond COVID-19: A call for transformative research. *Information Technology & Tourism, 22*(2), 187–203. DOI: 10.1007/s40558-020-00181-3

Gretzel, U., Sigala, M., Xiang, Z., & Koo, C. (2015). Smart tourism: Foundations and developments. *Electronic Markets, 25*(3), 179–188. DOI: 10.1007/s12525-015-0196-8

Gursoy, D., & Chi, C. G. (2020). Effects of COVID-19 pandemic on hospitality industry: Review of the current situations and a research agenda. *Journal of Hospitality Marketing & Management, 29*(5), 527–529. DOI: 10.1080/19368623.2020.1788231

Gursoy, D., Chi, C. G., Lu, L., & Nunkoo, R. (2019). Consumers acceptance of artificially intelligent (AI) device use in service delivery. *International Journal of Information Management, 49*, 157–169. DOI: 10.1016/j.ijinfomgt.2019.03.008

Heskett, J. L., Jones, T. O., Loveman, G. W., Sasser, W. E.Jr, & Schlesinger, L. A. (1994). Putting the service-profit chain to work. *Harvard Business Review, 72*(2), 164–174.

Hilton Worldwide. (2016). *Hilton introduces "Connie" the robot concierge powered by IBM Watson.* Hilton Newsroom. https://newsroom.hilton.com

Information Commissioner's Office. (2020). *Marriott International fined for data breach.* ICO. https://ico.org.uk

ISO. (2013). *ISO/IEC 27001: Information technology — Security techniques — Information security management systems — Requirements.* International Organization for Standardization. https://www.iso.org/isoiec-27001-information-security.html

Ivanov, S., & Webster, C. (2019). Adoption of robots, artificial intelligence and service automation by travel, tourism and hospitality companies – A cost-benefit analysis. *International Journal of Contemporary Hospitality Management, 31*(7), 2510–2528. DOI: 10.1108/IJCHM-05-2018-0370

Ivanov, S., Webster, C., & Berezina, K. (2017). Adoption of robots and service automation by tourism and hospitality companies. *Revista Turismo & Desenvolvimento (Aveiro), 27/28*, 1501–1517.

Ivanov, S., Webster, C., & Garenko, A. (2018). Young Russian adults' attitudes towards the potential use of robots in hotels. *Technology in Society, 55*, 24–32. DOI: 10.1016/j.techsoc.2018.06.004

Kansakar, P., Munir, A., & Shabani, N. (2019). Technology in hospitality industry: Prospects and challenges. *IEEE Consumer Electronics Magazine, 8*(3), 60–65. DOI: 10.1109/MCE.2019.2892245

Kizildag, M., Dogru, T., Zhang, T., Mody, M. A., Altin, M., & Ozturk, A. B. (2019). Blockchain and smart contracts: Applications in travel, tourism, and hospitality. *Journal of Hospitality and Tourism Technology, 10*(3), 410–422. DOI: 10.1108/JHTT-02-2019-0026

Krombholz, K., Hobel, H., Huber, M., & Weippl, E. (2015). Advanced social engineering attacks. *Journal of Information Security and Applications, 22*, 113–122. DOI: 10.1016/j.jisa.2014.09.005

Kshetri, N. (2017). The emerging role of big data in key development issues: Opportunities, challenges, and concerns. *Big Data & Society, 4*(2), 1–20. DOI: 10.1177/2053951717726557

Li, M., Bonn, M. A., & Ye, B. H. (2021). Hotel digitalization and customer engagement: The role of artificial intelligence technologies. *International Journal of Hospitality Management, 94*, 102876. DOI: 10.1016/j.ijhm.2020.102876

Lu, L., Cai, R., & Gursoy, D. (2019). Developing and validating a service robot integration willingness scale. *International Journal of Hospitality Management, 80*, 36–51. DOI: 10.1016/j.ijhm.2019.01.005

Luo, X., & Homburg, C. (2007). Neglected outcomes of customer satisfaction. *Journal of Marketing, 71*(2), 133–149. DOI: 10.1509/jmkg.71.2.133

Mariani, M. M., & Borghi, M. (2021). Customers' evaluation of AI-enabled services in tourism: The role of anthropomorphism, intelligibility, and transparency. *Annals of Tourism Research, 91*, 103313. DOI: 10.1016/j.annals.2021.103313

Marriott International. (2017). *Marriott's ChatBotlr makes service easier.* Marriott News Center. https://news.marriott.com

Park, E., & Kim, K. J. (2021). Can an AI chatbot be a customer's friend? *Service Business, 15*(4), 529–548. DOI: 10.1007/s11628-021-00451-0

PCI Security Standards Council. (2022). *PCI DSS: Payment Card Industry Data Security Standard.*https://www.pcisecuritystandards.org

Pencarelli, T. (2020). The digital revolution in the travel and tourism industry. *Information Technology & Tourism, 22*(3), 455–476. DOI: 10.1007/s40558-019-00160-3

PwC. (2020). *Global digital trust insights survey 2020.* PwC. https://www.pwc.com

Roman, R., Zhou, J., & Lopez, J. (2013). On the features and challenges of security and privacy in distributed internet of things. *Computer Networks, 57*(10), 2266–2279. DOI: 10.1016/j.comnet.2012.12.018

Sigala, M. (2018). Social media and customer engagement in the hotel industry. *International Journal of Hospitality Management, 77*, 183–185. DOI: 10.1016/j.ijhm.2018.07.009

Simkin, L. (2021). Cybersecurity risks in hospitality: Balancing digital innovation and guest trust. *Journal of Business Research, 136*, 242–250. DOI: 10.1016/j.jbusres.2021.07.045

Statista. (2022). *Mobile check-in and digital key adoption in hotels worldwide.* Statista. https://www.statista.com

Sweeney, J. C., & Soutar, G. N. (2001). Consumer perceived value: The development of a multiple item scale. *Journal of Retailing, 77*(2), 203–220. DOI: 10.1016/S0022-4359(01)00041-0

Symantec. (2021). *Internet security threat report 2021.* Symantec. https://www.broadcom.com

Tian, F. (2016). An agri-food supply chain traceability system for China based on RFID & blockchain technology. *13th International Conference on Service Systems and Service Management (ICSSSM),* 1–6. DOI: 10.1109/ICSSSM.2016.7538424

Trustwave. (2020). *2020 Global security report.* Trustwave. https://www.trustwave.com

Tung, V. W. S., & Law, R. (2020). The potential for tourism and hospitality experience research in human–robot interactions. *International Journal of Contemporary Hospitality Management*, *32*(11), 3509–3523. DOI: 10.1108/IJCHM-09-2019-0792

Tussyadiah, I. P. (2020). A review of research into automation in tourism: Launching the annals of tourism research curated collection on artificial intelligence and robotics in tourism. *Annals of Tourism Research*, *81*, 102883. DOI: 10.1016/j.annals.2020.102883

Tussyadiah, I. P., & Park, S. (2018). Consumer evaluation of hotel service robots. In Stangl, B., & Pesonen, J. (Eds.), *Information and communication technologies in tourism 2018* (pp. 308–320). Springer., DOI: 10.1007/978-3-319-72923-7_24

Yun, J. J., Zhao, X., Jung, K., & Yigitcanlar, T. (2020). The culture for open innovation dynamics. *Sustainability*, *12*(1), 1–21. DOI: 10.3390/su12010290

Zeng, Z., Chen, X., & Lew, A. A. (2021). Managing big data in the hospitality and tourism industry: Potential applications and challenges. *Tourism Management*, *83*, 104247. DOI: 10.1016/j.tourman.2020.104247

Chapter 8
Securing the Digital Journey:
Cybersecurity Threats, Vulnerabilities, and Digital Forensics Solutions in Modern Tourism Infrastructure

Vipin Singh
http://orcid.org/0000-0001-5566-0151
Vellore Institute of Technology, India

Nimisha Maheshwari
Vellore Institute of Technology, India

Sandeep Singh Rana
Vellore Institute of Technology, India

Ganesh Khekare
http://orcid.org/0000-0002-1687-4699
Vellore Institute of Technology, India

ABSTRACT

Virtual onset of tourism industry has revolutionized how people plan their trips, book them, or even experience them. Yet at the same time this has also opened the realm up to threats and vulnerabilities such as cybersecurity threats which has never been seen like this before. This chapter also investigates the intricate empirical system of cybersecurity in the contemporary architecture of tourism, reviewing the multidimensional threats that affect hospitality systems, booking systems, payment

DOI: 10.4018/979-8-3373-5826-0.ch008

systems and customer data databases. The study will be able to discern the most important gaps in security by performing extensive research based on the existing vulnerabilities, the new threat vectors, and digital forensics solutions, therefore, suggesting an evidence-based set of recommendations that could considerably increase the cybersecurity resilience of tourism organizations. Characteristic features of the findings are that tourism companies have adopted the use of digital technologies to improve customer experiences and efficiency in operations

INTRODUCTION

The tourism sector is already one of the biggest sectors of the global economy as it yields about 10.4 percent of world output and it employs more than 330 million globally (Dhande, 2024). The industry has been going through a digital revolution, which has drastically changed the way of conducting industries and by the way, travelers interact with tourism facilities (Buhalis, 1998). Online reservation systems to metro applications to smart rooms in a hotel to online payment systems; technology has taken over the face of modern tourism infrastructure making customer experiences smooth and operation easy and efficient.

Nevertheless, the digital revolution has provided great attack surface to cybercriminals. The information that tourism organizations handle including sensitive personal and financial information is enormous and thus they are a juicy target of a number of risks posed by cyber related attacks (Paraskevas, 2022). These vulnerabilities are worsened by the fact that the industry operates using linked systems, third party service providers, and outdated infrastructure. The recent series of large-scale cyber-attacks on hotel chains, airlines, and travel user-cantered booking systems have revealed the utter priority of an advanced security surveillance both outside and inside the cyber-world in the touristic industry. The data breaches that involved the Marriott International of 500 million guests and a breach in British Airways that involved 380,000 payments transactions are an indicative of cyber threats to the tourism infrastructure (Ebuzor, 2024).

The COVID-19 pandemic boosted the digital transformation of tourism as digital health certificates and contactless technologies become a cure to safe travel (Wang, & Abbas, et al.,2022). This quick pace of digitization which has gone through on many occasions without proper security analysis has opened new avenues and widened the threat arena. Tourism organizations have become targets of adversaries that are much more sophisticated and use such tools as advanced persistent threats, ransomware attacks, and social engineering, which are specifically aimed at exploiting the specifics of operation in the industry. The threat landscape has further been complicated by rise of nation-state actors that use nation-state tourism infrastructure as a source of intelligence gathering (Fjäder, 2014).

Increased penetration of mobile tourism apps and Internet of Things (IoT) devices in smart hotels has led to a multiplicative growth of the entry points that can be used by cybercriminals (Saber, & Helmy, et at., 2025). Studies suggest that there is a lack of reasonable protective measures installed on tourism-based mobile applications, and most of them do not have appropriate encryption and authentication procedures. In the same manner, the presence of different kinds of IoT sensors, smart locks, and automated systems in the hospitality sector has resulted in new avenues of attack that traditional security tools are unable to deal with.

The economic cost of cybersecurity breaches to tourism organizations has been in a state of crisis where the mean price of a data breach to the hospitality sector surpasses above 4.2 million dollars on an annual basis. Small and medium-sized tourism business ventures have an uneven playing field since they usually do not possess the capital or the skills to develop extensive cybersecurity measures (Zeqiri, & Ben Youssef, et at., 2025). The seasonality of work in tourism also makes security even more of a problem, because when you change the subject of temporary work, when they are hired once and then fired, they come with their own security vulnerabilities, which could not originally have been offered.

Digital forensic has become a major field of study in conducting investigations, collecting evidence, and learning the tactics of an attack on the tourism infrastructure (Adel, 2020). To respond to cyber incidents and contain threats, it is now important to incorporate forensic capacity in cybersecurity measures as the threats evolve in sophistication and frequency. The peculiarities of digital investigations in tourism industry, such as maintaining data evidence in distributed cloud infrastructures and processing large transaction volumes, demand special forensics practices and applications.

The regulatory environment in which cybersecurity in tourism operates has only got more complicated over time where organizations must respond to several areas of jurisdiction as well as make operations efficient (Babikian, 2023). The rise of technologies, like artificial intelligence, blockchain, and quantum computing, opens and poses threats to cybersecurity in tourism that should be actively evaluated and addressed on a strategy level. In this chapter, the relationship between cybersecurity and digital forensics in the tourism scenario was discussed and the direction of future design regarding the safety of the digital tourism environment was thoroughly examined.

OBJECTIVES

- To Investigate the present day cybersecurity threat environment.
- To Examine the very flaws that are present in the tourism technological systems.
- To Evaluate digital forensics controls in incident recovery and evidence preserving in tourism.
- To Assess the impact of cyber incidents on the tourism businesses.
- To Determine the future cybersecurity demands such as AI, blockchain, IoT.

LITERATURE REVIEW

Cybersecurity Evolution and History of Tourism

The crossroads between cyber security and tourism has transformed a lot in the last 20 years. The initial research of this field concentrated more on non-sophisticated data protection strategies and the conventional IT security issues. The preliminary extensive studies on the information security risks in the hospitality segment have identified the vulnerability of the hotel systems to unauthorized access and leak of information (Chen, & Fiscus, 2018).

The appearance of online travel agencies (OTAs) and direct booking websites changed the situation with risk (Lee & Min, 2021). A study has been conducted on how the digitalization of tourism services brought new vulnerabilities, while technological innovation offered an opportunity to increase the security of tourism services. Such research underlined the dual character of technology, which contributes to security as well as a source of emergent threats.

Contemporary Threat Landscape Analysis

The academic literature available has reported a major increase in volume of cyber threats against tourism infrastructure in the recent past. Very complex calculations of cybersecurity incidents in the sphere of hospitality indicated that reports of attack on this sphere increased by 300 percent in 2020-2022(Ghaderi et al., 2024). The most popular type of threat reported by research was ransomware closely followed by payment card industry (PCI) breaches and customer data theft.

More details accessed the geographical concentration of cyber-attacks to tourism bodies. Certain results revealed that the Asia-Pacific tourism companies suffered the most attacks due to the fast rate of digitalization and the lack of investment in security. Research also showed that small and medium tourism businesses (SMTEs) had been disadvantaged because of insufficient funds to be used in cybersecurity.

Tourism Systems

Many researchers have undertaken an extensive study of system-level vulnerabilities concerning the tourism infrastructure. Extensive evaluations revealed numerous property management systems (PMS) weaknesses, with 78 percent of the surveyed hotels contributing to the use of old software versions that are prone to security attacks. It was shown through analysis that default passwords, lack of encryption of data during transmission, and poor access controls were common.

Long-term investigations were carried out on weaknesses in mobile tourism apps. The analysis of 150 most popular travel apps indicated a great number of security gaps such as lack of data encryption, poor authentication features, and excessive requests of permissions. The study has found out that 62 percent of travel apps examined allowed the sensitive user data to be stored in a readable form, which put even millions of travelers at risk of having privacy compromised.

Digital Forensics in the Context of Tourism

Digital forensics use in cybersecurity incidents in tourism is of immense academic concern. Cyber-attacks on the hotel reserving system have particular forensic systems that are designed to investigate them. The methodologies were capable of using timeline analysis, network traffic investigation and log file correlation to recover the sequences of an attack as well as the perpetrators.

A study was done on cloud-based forensics in terms of the tourism and uses of Software-as-a-Service (SaaS) services. Research solved the problems specific to evidence gathering in distributed cloud environments and provided new ways of evidence preservation in distributed cloud environments, across jurisdictions, and service providers (Karagiannis & Vergidis, 2021).

REGULATORY AND COMPLIANCE FRAMEWORKS

The field under consideration has been the focus of academic literature that defines the regulatory environment of tourism cybersecurity. General Data Protection Regulation (GDPR) formulated by the European Union has had far reaching considerations on the tourism organizations(Anastasiadou,2006). The studies recorded the compliance issues of international firms in the tourism industry working in more than one jurisdiction having different regulatory requirements (Dodds & Joppe, 2005).

Tourism cybersecurity researchers have paid special attention to the Payment Card Industry Data Security Standard (PCI DSS). Research compared PCI DSS compliance level of tourism merchants, and the result showed that only 34 percent of the tested organizations whose compliance was full. Resource limitation and technical challenges were directed as the main challenges to compliance and compliance management.

New Technologies and Problems of the Future

Modern study has embarked on the issue of cybersecurity and emerging technologies in tourism (Ghaderi et al., 2026). Research papers looked at the security issues related to use of artificial intelligence in tourism recommendation systems. Possible weak points in machine learning algorithm were identified e.g. the adversarial attacks, techniques that poison the data and can affect the integrity of the system.

A number of researchers have examined the potential of blockchain technology to improve tourism cybersecurity . In-depth discussion was conducted on how blockchain could be used in the secure identity verification scheme, tamper-proof booking system and decentralized payment system. The studies emphasized the use of blockchain in tourism in terms of its security advantages and challenges associated with its implementation (Rashideh, 2020).

Table 1. Compiled from multiple academic sources cited in Literature Review (2018-2025)

Research Area	Key Findings	Research Gaps Identified
Threat Landscape Evolution	300% increase in cybersecurity incidents (2020-2022); Ransomware as primary threat vector	Limited research on emerging threat actors and attack sophistication
Vulnerability Assessment	78% of hotels use outdated PMS software; 62% of travel apps store unencrypted data	Insufficient analysis of IoT device vulnerabilities in smart tourism
Digital Forensics Applications	Specialized frameworks needed for tourism infrastructure; Cloud forensics challenges identified	Limited forensic tools are designed specifically for tourism environments
Regulatory Compliance	Only 34% of tourism organizations maintain PCI DSS compliance; GDPR compliance challenges are widespread	Cross-border regulatory harmonization is insufficiently addressed
Emerging Technologies	AI/ML vulnerabilities in recommendation systems; Blockchain potential for secure transactions	Quantum computing implications for tourism security are unexplored

continued on following page

Table 1. Continued

Research Area	Key Findings	Research Gaps Identified
Framework Effectiveness	Existing frameworks are inadequate for tourism-specific challenges; the TCMM model proposed	Industry-specific risk assessment methodologies are underdeveloped
Small Enterprise Challenges	SMTEs disproportionately affected; Resource constraints limit security investments	Cost-effective security solutions for SMTEs require further research
Incident Impact Analysis	Average incident costs $3.2 million; Prolonged operational disruptions are common	Long-term economic impact on the tourism ecosystem is insufficiently quantified

Source – Author's Own

Cybersecurity Frameworks

Recent academic studies have focused on the development of cybersecurity frameworks specific to tourism. TCMM offers an effective framework of tourism cybersecurity evaluation and maturity as well as its enhancements in tourism institutions. It includes the industry-specific risk factors and workability standards to provide unique security advice (Gander,& Hartley, & Powell, et at., 2011). .

The effectiveness of the available cybersecurity frameworks when implemented in the context of tourism was studied. Comparative analysis of NIST Cybersecurity Framework, ISO 27001, and industry-specific guidelines has shown a gap in covering tourism-specific challenges like seasonal employment, integrations with third-party systems, and customer-oriented system needs.

The literature review shows that there is a strong evolution of the current research regarding tourism cybersecurity that has advanced beyond mere data protection to elaborate threat analysis. Nevertheless, there are still crucial gaps in the IoT vulnerabilities, multi-border regulatory standards, and cost-efficient solutions to the small businesses which demand dedicated future research.

Conceptual Framework for Tourism Cybersecurity Management

In the light of the holistic survey of cybersecurity issues in contemporary tourism infrastructure, the current study presents an interim organizational conceptual model that will deal with the complex nature of tourism cybersecurity management. Tourism cybersecurity resilience framework (TCRF) is a comprehensive concept that offers insight into the management and perception over this topic of cybersecurity in the tourism setting.

Framework Components

The TCRF is a complex of four.

Layers 1: Environmental Context The background layer includes all the external forces that shape tourism cybersecurity such as regulatory and industry provisions, threat environment development, and technology matures. The green environment serves as the background in which any choice in cybersecurity should be considered.

The most important of them are:

- Regulatory compliance needs (GDPR, PCI DSS, industry-related regulations)
- Threat intelligence and trend of the attack
- Technological innovation and arising security challenge
- Collaboration in the industry and information sharing processes

Layer 2: **Organizational Capabilities** The second level concerns internal capabilities that tourism organizations will have to build to manage cybersecurity risks. This incorporates governing structures, risk management, technical abilities, and human resources.

Key elements include:

- Strategic planning and cybersecurity governance
- Risk evaluation and risk management tools
- Technical infra-structure and security controls

The human resource potential and training systems

Incident response and continuity planning businesses

Layer 3 Operational Integration The third layer concerns the operationalization of cybersecurity measures in tourism operations. It can appreciate the fact that successful cybersecurity is not a separate entity, but must be incorporated in the business processes.

The areas of integration are:

- Customer service / customer engagement processes
- Third party vendor management and control Third-party vendor management and oversight
- PMS, POS, IoT device operational technology security
- Security of data and privacy
- Threat detection and constant surveillance

Layer 4: Resilience and Adaptation The highest layer lies on the response of the organisation in overcoming cyber incidents and changing threats. This incorporates technical resilience as well as the ability of organizational learning.

Resilience includes such components as:

- Incident detection and remedying abilities
- The planning of business continuity and disaster recovery
- Organizational learning and knowledge management
- Iterative refinement and change processes
- Stakeholder management and crisis communication

Feedback Loops and Framework Interactions

The TCRF focuses on the dynamism of communication between the layers, and the essence of having feedback loops to enhance improvement all the time. Adjustments to organizational capabilities are implemented as a reaction to the environmental changes and affect the strategy of integration and resilience operation.

The framework has included some important feedback mechanisms:

Threat Intelligence Feedback: information about arising threats and means of attack receives flowed back to the environment during the creation and maintenance of organizational capabilities and operational security processes.

Incident Learning Feedback: Lessons learned due to security incidents lead into organizational skills and workflow procedures and the capability to become more resilient in the future.

Feedback of Regulatory Compliance: Alterations in the regulatory needs will catalyze changes in the organizational capacities and the working practices.

Performance Measurement Feedback: The security performance monitoring constantly gives information about how to enhance all framework layers.

Methodology of Implementation of a Framework

The adoption of TCRF would feature a systematic way that helps tourism organizations to disclose their actual cybersecurity situation and come up with a specific course of action designed to enhance it:

Phase 1: Current state assessment. Organizations should carry out a detailed analysis of their potential in all layers of their framework. This entails the vulnerability assessment, risk analysis and capability gaps study.

Phase 2: Target State Definition Target states are formulated on each layer of the framework based on the results of the assessment and organizing objectives.

This entails the establishment of deliberate cybersecurity objectives and measures of performance.

Phase 3 Gap Analysis and Prioritization The gap between the current and target states is analyzed, and areas to be improved upon are identified as priority areas. Implementation priorities are determined by resource limitations and priorities of risk.

Phase 4: Implementation planning. Plans are developed in detail for each of the priorities, including timeline, resources, and success measures. Plans take into consideration technical and organizational issues of enhancing cybersecurity.

Phase 5: Implementation The implementation activities take place based on the arranged plans, and continuous monitoring of the progress and performance is carried out. Consistent reviews are necessary in order to make sure the implementation is close to the planned execution, as well as adjustments according to the updated situation.

Phase 6: Continuous Improvement Within the framework, continuous improvement takes place due to regular reassessment, lessons integrated, and adaptation to new threats and technologies discovered.

Validating the Framework and Metrics

The TCRF adopts an overall framework for measuring the effectiveness of the framework and comparing cybersecurity performance:

Leading Indicators: A set of indicators which predict the future performance of security, including the rate of vulnerabilities corrected, the rate level of security training activities and the accuracy of threat detection.

Lagging Indicators: These are metrics that are used to record the real-life security performance, e.g. the number of incidents, the time it takes to recover after an incident and how much the incident would cost.

Operational Metrics: Measurements of daily security activities, such as system availability, user satisfaction, and compliance levels.

Strategic Metrics: This is a strategy measures that evaluate the effectiveness of cybersecurity investments in general, its compliance with the business objectives.

The framework's effectiveness is validated through regular assessments that compare actual performance against established benchmarks and industry standards. This validation process ensures that the framework remains relevant and effective in addressing evolving cybersecurity challenges.

FINDINGS AND DISCUSSIONS

Critical Vulnerabilities in Tourism Infrastructure

Modern tourism infrastructure analysis indicates that there are some important vulnerability areas that give major security risks. These are the industry-related weaknesses due to the complex technological environment of the industries, which contains legacy systems, third party integrations and customer facing applications.

These include vulnerabilities to legacy systems.

The tourism organisations often have heterogeneous environments integrating new cloud-based with old on-prem ones. In most hotels, the property management systems (PMS) is still being taken care of by old software platforms, which are not up to date. The study reveals that 45 percent of consulted tourism organizations work to produce PMS software that has been out of support by the vendors leading to unpatched vulnerability which cybercriminals can take advantage of.

Another crucial area of vulnerability is point-of-sale (POS) systems. A lot of the tourism facilities are using very old POS terminals which do not have the encryption feature and are deployed using unsupported operating systems. These systems are interrelated so that there is a possibility of getting an entry into the network infrastructure through a compromise in one terminal.

Risks of Third-Party Integration

An increase in the attack surface is seen with an industry such as the tourism industry which needs third party service providers. Channel managers, payment processors, online travel agents (OTAs) as well as reservation systems must be integrated with the core systems of tourism operators. Every entry point during integration puts forth the capability of an entry point by the cybercriminals.

The vulnerability of channel manager systems has been a special issue, with these systems typically demanding large volumes of inventory and price data. In the research, the researchers involved found numerous cases of the breached channel managers giving an attacker rights to a number of hotel properties at the same time, outlining the ripple effect of thirdparty vulnerabilities.

Weaknesses on Customer-Facing Applications Weaknesses

Mobile apps and online booking systems are the key touch-points a tourism organization enjoys with customers. Nonetheless, most of such apps have serious security flaws where they uncover delicate customer information.

The incidences of lack of sufficient input validation, insecure data storage, weak authentication mechanism, and session management are common.

Threat Actor Landscape and Attack Methodologies

As the threat landscape appears in the forms of cybersecurity targeting tourism infrastructure is represented by a variety of threat actors of varying motives and capabilities. It is important that their presence and techniques of operation become understood so that effective defence mechanisms could be formulated.

Established Cybercriminal gangs

Advanced groups of cybercriminals pose the greatest risk to the tourist infrastructure. Such groups usually use some advanced persistent threat (APT) tactics, where they can keep long-standing access to compromised systems without being caught. The top of their motives is the amount of money they earn, using ransomware attacks and stealing payment card data as well as customer identities.

The study found that there are a number of well-known cybercriminal organizations whose main target are the tourism organizations. The malware and exploitation methods exploited by these groups in most cases are custom-designed to hospitality sector attacks and tourism infrastructure. They often perform the reconnaissance in large scale, where they research on the system of target organizations and determine the most suitable attack planes.

Insider Threats

The risk of a tourism organization caused by insider threats is high, given both the low employee retention rates and seasonality of the staffing employed in the tourism industry. People working in malicious insiders with proper access to the systems can circumvent conventional security provisions and wreak havoc before they are detected.

The analysis found out that the percentage of insider threats in terms of cybersecurity incidents in the tourism organizations is about 28 percent. These threats include as small as employees stealing the customer information in order to make money, and as extreme as a disgruntled employee destroying systems as he/she quits their job. The complexity of the issue is somewhat increased by the necessity to grant access to the system to some temporary workers during the peak seasons, which also provides more opportunities to engage in malicious activity.

Nation-State Actors

Cyber espionage, which is sponsored by governments, is directed more and more at tourism bodies and for those whose activity is directed to geopolitically exposed areas (Buchanan, 2020) . Such actors usually want intelligence gathering opportunities and they will use the infrastructures in tourism as one to keep track of a certain individual or group.

The study recorded various cases of high society attackers that used nation-state groups to breach hotel systems and spy on how personnel communicate or perform in the hotel. These kind of attacks are usually accompanied by very advanced methods that aim at creating a continued access without being detected by the standard security solutions.

Financial Consequences

The direct financial damages of cyber incident are ransoms, devastation of systems, counts of fines the regulatory authorities slap on a company, and suit expenses(Tahmasebi,2024). The study shows that the average cost of a cybersecurity attack to the tourism organizations stands at about 3.2 million whereas the bigger organizations incurring a proportionate higher cost.

Attacks through ransomware have been especially damaging and some organizations have paid in excess of $1 million to regain operations after ransom was paid. Nevertheless, the recovery time is likely to be extended, and the costs involved in reconstructing the system and enhancing security are likely to be higher even in those cases when the organizations follow the strategy of paying their ransoms.

Operational Disruptions

The effect of cyber incidents often leads to major operational disruption which has a wide range of effects compared to direct financial implication. The unavailability of hotel reservation systems can deny them new bookings and affect the reservation of old customers resulting to customer dissatisfaction and possible loss of income (Spanaki & Durmishllari, 2019).

The studies had witnessed incidences by which cybercrimes had made tourism entities go back to manual procedures making their operations far more inefficient.

These interruptions might last days or months, especially when companies do not have comprehensive plans of attack response and other types of support.

Reputational Damage

The aftermaths of cyber incidents on reputations can be long-term effects in relation to tourism organizations. Customer confidence is a key essence in the tourism business and any customer data breach may greatly affect an organization and its standing on the market.

This can be turned into a nightmare because social media and online review sites increase reputational harm as all the negative experiences broadcast at a high rate to potential customers. The study shows that following major cyber-incidents, tourism organizations tend to undergo long-term losses in the booking of customers and the market share.

Digital Forensics Posabilities and Difficulties

There are definite issues connected with the peculiarities of tourism industry and its IT base, that has to be taken into account when the digital forensics capacities are implemented in the tourism organizations.

Problems of Preserving Evidence

The vulnerability of evidence preservation is a common issue in tourism organizations because the agencies are always in a position to provide services continuously, and hence have difficulty in retaining evidence. Log files and other temporary data can be automatically purged by many systems and useful forensic evidence can be destroyed.

Tourism infrastructure is distributed, with systems in many geographical sites and probably many cloud providers, thus making evidence collection and preservation harder (Huang & Chen,2022). The management of the forensic process among various jurisdictions and the various providers of service also necessitates specific skills and greater planning.

Challenges of Time Line Reconstruction

The problem of reconstructing timelines of attacks in the tourism setting proves quite tricky to manage because of the many connections between various systems and the sheer amount of business-related traffic. However, to be able to detect the malicious actions along with the normal operational processes that have to be carried out by the tourism business, some advanced analytical methods and a good knowledge of business processes that have to be undertaken by the tourism business are required.

The study discovered that a few instances have failed because forensic investigation has been impeded by the capability of adequate logging and monitoring. Most tourism groups do not have centralized logging packages, and it is hard to correlate the events in different systems, and find patterns of attack (Krügel et al., 2001).

Resource and Skills Limitation

Majority of tourism organizations do not have in-house digital forensics, and they depend on external consultants to conduct incidents investigation and evidence analysis. Such a dependence may lead to slow response and escalate costs in case of security incidents.

The network of tourism operations is particularly specialized, so the investigation needs a forensic agent who combines knowledge about cybersecurity and the operations of the tourism business. This particular set of skills is rather scarce in the workforce of cybersecurity professionals and it restricts the number of available professionals.

Regulatory Compliance and Regulations

The regulatory environment in tourism cybersecurity is also still changing and this poses a challenge on organizations with operations in two or more countries.

Data Protection Regulations and GDPR

The General Data Protection Regulation or GDPR of the European Union has exerted serious influence on cybersecurity needs of tourism organizations (Amoo, & Atadoga, &Osasona, et at., 2024). The heavyweight data protection rules and the huge penalty regime of the regulation have compelled organizations to re-evaluate their cybersecurity programs to be compliant with the regulation.

Some of the compliance issues are application of suitable technical and organizational measures, privacy impact assessments, and management of comprehensive data on data processing. According to the research, GDPR compliance is a challenge to most tourism organizations because of the intricacy of their data processing tasks and the forthcoming usage of numerous third-party processors.

PCI DSS Compliance

Intense focus has been on the Payment Card Industry Data Security Standard (PCI DSS) compliance, which is a challenge to tourism organizations. The requirements of the standard that the payment should be processed securely, network security and periodic testing of security, mostly involve significant investment on technology and skills.

The study also indicated that most of the smaller tourism organizations are incapable of performing PCI DSS compliance and being able to sustain the same because of the limited resources and complexity of technology. Failure may lead to a massive financial fine and the inability to conduct payment processing.

Industry-Specific Regulations

In different jurisdictions, there are cybersecurity policies that focus on tourism and issues particular to the industry. These policies tend to concentrate on secured data about customers, reservation system security framework, and reporting of incidents.

The uncoordinated state of tourism-specific regulation poses an opportunity whereby the organizations concerned with international operations deal with compliance difficulties. Issues of compliance to numerous jurisdictions involve thorough knowledge of the differences in the requirements and ability to introduce proper controls.

Remedies and Prescriptions

Deriving on the overall analysis of the threats, vulnerabilities and challenges associated with the present day tourism infrastructure, the evidence-based recommendations are forwarded that can be used to improve security status of tourism organizations:

Recommendation 1: Zero Trust architecture Implementation

Each tourism organization is recommended to use a Zero Trust security model in which there is no implicit trust and all transactions and access requests must be repeatedly verified. This practice is especially important to tourism industry because of its integration ecosystem of third party and customer facing applications.

The Zero Trust practice must also encompass network segregation to isolate important systems like property management systems and payment processors. Multi-factor authentication should be required on all user accounts, not only employees, vendors, partners. As well, companies need to conduct continuous monitoring and behavioral analytics to identify abnormal activities that can show security breaches.

The given recommendation targets the inherent problem of perimeter-based security systems that are not suitable to the contemporary tourism infrastructure.

Recommendation 2: Establish Comprehensive Vulnerability Management Program

Tourism organizations need to adopt a systematic program on reducing vulnerability, and the program should manage the specific problematic areas of their technological environment. It involves the creation of habitual vulnerability scans of every system, such as legacy apps and third-party integrations.

Priorities should be set on vulnerability in terms of how they may affect the operation of the tourism business and customer information. Vulnerability scanning tools need to be automated to continuously poke at systems to see whether they have picked up new vulnerability in the past. Also, companies are advised to launch vulnerability disclosure programs in which good hackers can report the security vulnerabilities.

The patching management procedures should be simplified so that the security patching can be implemented in time at the least cost to the operations. It is more so in the case of tourism organizations where availability of systems should be 24/7 to be able to serve its international clients across time-zones.

Recommendation 3: Build Specific Incidents Response Capabilities in the Field of Tourism

Special teams dealing with tourism systems and business processes should be formed in the tourism organizations to respond to incidents. Such teams ought to have members of ITs, operations, legal and customer service departments to make sure they have adequately handled incidents.

Specific tourism scenarios that the incident response plan must bear in mind include compromising the reservation system, breaking the payment processing system and breaching customer data. Tabletop exercises ought to be done on a regular basis to exercise response procedures and in finding ways of improvement.

Organizations are also supposed to enter into partnerships with specialized digital forensics suppliers with knowledge in tourism infrastructure. Contracted deals with forensics can really fasten the task of response in cases of security breaches.

Recommendation 4: Apply Advanced Threat Detection and Response Systems

Organizations that deal with tourism ought to implement Security Information and Event Management (SIEM) solutions that have tourism-based use cases as well as correlation rules. Such systems are to be combined with all important infrastructure elements, such as property management systems, booking systems, and payment processors.

Machine learning and artificial intelligence should also be implemented to detect nuance patterns of attacks that would not be detected using the conventional rule-based applications. Threat intelligence feeds should be integrated to provide real-time information about emerging threats targeting the tourism industry. This intelligence should be used to update detection rules and proactively defend against known attack techniques.

Recommendation 5: Strengthen Third-Party Risk Management

As the tourism business has a strong tie with third-party supplier of services, third party risk management programs should be conducted at the organization. This will involve carrying out comprehensive security checks on all the vendors before their engagement with the company and continuous security checks of the security postures of the vendors.

The agreements should have particular-the liability and cybersecurity provisions in the contract. The vendors are supposed to hold rightful cybersecurity insurance and be able to show that they have worked in accordance with security guidelines.

Organizations need to develop frameworks of vendor security rankings based on aspects like: security certificates, history of the institution, and compliance. Security reviews with the vendors should be conducted regularly in order to guarantee that they are also continuing to comply with the security requirements.

Recommendation 6: Increase Worker Cybersecurity Education and Consciousness

Tourism organizations should take an initiative to invest in an elaborate cybersecurity training program that suits the different skills and values of individuals within their workforce. Training must focus on the threats present in the industry like social engineering attacks to the customer service representatives, and the phishing attacks manipulating the theme of tourism.

Training that is simulated needs to be incorporated to determine how workers will verify any kinds of security threats and react to these dangers. Through periodical phishing exercises, it would be possible to determine weak employees and give them special tutorials.

The fact that the turnover rate in tourism is high demands the introduction of efficient onboarding procedures, which involve the mandatory induction on cybersecurity to all of the newly hired workers. The efforts within awareness should remain in a continuous form and ensure that cybersecurity is in the top of minds of all members of staff.

Recommendation 7: Data Protection and Privacy by Design Recommendation

Privacy-by-design should be embraced and used in tourism organizations so that data protection considerations should be incorporated into all system development and business affairs. This involves adopting the data minimization concepts of gathering only a required amount of customer information and instituting a definite data storage policy.

All sensitive data need to have encryption both in the resting stage and in transit. The payment details of customers ought to be tokenized to lower chances of data leakage. Moreover, companies are supposed to use data loss prevention (DLP) products to avoid the departure of data in case of unauthorized access.

All the new processes and systems that have to deal with the customer data should have routine privacy impact assessment done on them. These reviews are supposed to define any possible privacy threats and put the right mitigation strategies.

Recommendation 8: Provide Industry Scope Cybersecurity Intensity

Tourism bodies are expected to seek industry-wide cybersecurity efforts that enable threat information sharing and other collaborative defense opportunities. The industry associations ought to form working groups on cybersecurity that formulate best practices and attempts responses.

Industry-specific information sharing and analysis centers (ISACs) should be created to promote the flow of real-time threat intelligence to tourism industry. These centers will allow the smaller organizations to have access to threat intelligence and the expertise of security to their organizations that they could never get otherwise.

A partnership between the government and the rest of the tourism ecosystem should be established to counter the problem of cybersecurity. Threat intelligence and incident response capabilities can be offered by government agencies and best practice and resources can be obtained through industry partners.

Recommendation 9: Create Cyber Insurance And Risk Transfer Plans

Tourism organizations are encouraged to consider the possibilities of acquiring a broad cyber insurance policy that will reflect their risk profile and business needs. Insurance plans must cover business interruption, data breach response cost, regulatory fines and cost of managing reputation.

What should be included in vendor agreements and customer contracts is risk transfer strategies. Liability allocation to cybersecurity incidents, when third-party systems or services are involved, should be properly defined by organizations.

Insurance policies must be reviewed regularly in order to cover the organization considered from the perspective risk profile alteration. The insurance providers must be chosen depending on knowledge of tourism industry risks and their capacity to provide a proper cover.

Recommendation 10: Invest in Cybersecurity Research and Development

The tourism organizations ought to invest into research and development of cybersecurity that deals with emerging threats and technologies. These would involve collaboration with academic institutions and vendors of cybersecurity to come up with new security solutions.

New technologies like quantum computing, artificial intelligence, and blockchain are to be considered in terms of their possible usage to promote cybersecurity in the area of tourism. Organization should also consider the security implication of embracing the emerging technologies and should also take concerted risk aversion measures.

Cybersecurity labs/ cybersecurity centers of excellence internal projects should be created to promote cybersecurity innovation and knowledge exchange in the organization. These facilities may become the focus points of the cybersecurity research and development work.

FUTURE RESEARCH DIRECTIONS AND THE CONCLUSION

The current survey of these cybersecurity threats, vulnerabilities and the digital forensics applications in a modern tourism infrastructure provides a profound understanding of how sound cyber protective approaches are extremely crucial through safeguarding the digital tourism ecosystem. The results indicate that although tourism organizations have effectively deployed the digital technologies to improve efficiency and customer experiences, most of them have been susceptible to the advanced cyber threats based on the lack of sufficient security interventions and risk management strategies.

The study has also highlighted various areas of major concern where cybersecurity is particularly an issue to the tourism organizations. The vulnerability of the legacy systems, the risk of third-party systems integration, as well as the weaknesses of applications present to the customers all form immense surfaces on which the cybercriminals deliberately attack. Supplementing the threat of cybercriminal organized groups lie state-based threat actors that add another dimension of the sophistication of threats that affect tourism infrastructure.

The operational and financial costs of cyber incidents on tourism organizations are immense and they keep on increasing. This may result in long term financial losses, business interruptions and, reputational loss that can severely hurt the viability of organizations and their presence in the market. The study shows that companies that have been proactive on cybersecurity programs will have much low incident costs and quick recovery time in comparison to those that have been reactive.

The implications of digital forensics in tourism organizations should be greatly enhanced to deal with the peculiarities of the investigation of cyber incidents in distributed, complex environments. The nature of the industry in which it operates, as well as the technological support requires certain special expertise and tools to preserve the evidence, to create a timeline and analyze a given incident.

The regulatory environment of tourism cybersecurity remains in a state of flux, which poses compliance issues to the extend that most organizations have a wide range of jurisdictions of operation. Managing to adopt all-inclusive cybersecurity frameworks that capture the unique needs of the industrial field as well as upholding the regulatory compliance is a major challenge that most tourism establishments are still struggling with.

The ten recommendations listed in this chapter give a guide towards improving the resilience of cybersecurity in tourism organizations. The suggestions are related to technical fields of cybersecurity as well as to organizational perspective of a problem because efficient security must be considered on the basis of combined technology, processes, and people.

Future Research Direction

There are a few domains that can be used to develop further in the field of tourism cybersecurity in order to tackle new challenges:

Machine Learning and AI Security

Since tourism organizations are taking up AI and ML technologies to serve their customers better through recommendations and optimize operations, studies are required to analyse and address the security risks involved in using AI and ML technologies. Future research must focus on adversarial attacks on tourism AI systems, data poisoning methods and the security of the automation of decision-making processes.

One should also research the uses of AI and ML technologies to defend against cyber-attacks in tourism-related settings. Among this is the formulation of tourism specific algorithm associated with threat detection, automation in incidence response, and security/management of smart orchestration algorithms.

Implication of quantum Computing

Quantum computing is considered as a challenge and an opportunity to cyber-security in tourism. There is a need to evaluate quantum threat to existing encryption systems applied at the tourism infrastructure and devise quantum-resistant cryptography.

Moreover, the possible implementation of quantum computing to increase the touristic area of cybersecurity must be discussed.

Blockchain and Distributed Ledger Technologies

The implications of digital forensics in tourism organizations should be greatly enhanced to deal with the peculiarities of the investigation of cyber incidents in distributed, complex environments. The nature of the industry in which it operates, as well as the technological support requires certain special expertise and tools to preserve the evidence, to create a timeline and analyze a given incident.

The regulatory environment of tourism cybersecurity remains in a state of flux, which poses compliance issues to the extend that most organizations have a wide range of jurisdictions of operation. Managing to adopt all-inclusive cybersecurity frameworks that capture the unique needs of the industrial field as well as upholding the regulatory compliance is a major challenge that most tourism establishments are still struggling with.

The ten recommendations listed in this chapter give a guide towards improving the resilience of cybersecurity in tourism organizations. The suggestions are related to technical fields of cybersecurity as well as to organizational perspective of a problem because efficient security must be considered on the basis of combined technology, processes, and people.

Future Research Direction

There are a few domains that can be used to develop further in the field of tourism cybersecurity in order to tackle new challenges:

Machine Learning and AI Security

Since tourism organizations are taking up AI and ML technologies to serve their customers better through recommendations and optimize operations, studies are required to analyse and address the security risks involved in using AI and ML technologies. Future research must focus on adversarial attacks on tourism AI systems, data poisoning methods and the security of the automation of decision-making processes.

One should also research the uses of AI and ML technologies to defend against cyber-attacks in tourism-related settings. Among this is the formulation of tourism specific algorithm associated with threat detection, automation in incidence response, and security/management of smart orchestration algorithms.

Implication of Quantum Computing

Quantum computing is considered as a challenge and an opportunity to cybersecurity in tourism. There is a need to evaluate quantum threat to existing encryption systems applied at the tourism infrastructure and devise quantum-resistant cryptography.

Moreover, the possible implementation of quantum computing to increase the touristic area of cybersecurity must be discussed.

Behavioral Cybersecurity Research

It is important to have the human factors of tourism cybersecurity as part of building security awareness training programs. Further study ought to look at the psychological forces that affect cybersecurity practice in tourism settings, such as effects of travel stress, cultural variance, and time tension.

They would also need to research the creation of individual security awareness that has the ability to be streamed to fit the particular learning style and risk factor. Gamification and Virtual Reality as the method of training in the field of cybersecurity is a study potential in tourism terms.

The situation in the cybersecurity of tourism is bound to transform with the appearance of new technologies and more advanced tools of attacks used by the threat actors. The security and resilience of the digital tourism ecosystem will involve ongoing research and collaborative activities among these institutions i.e. academia, industry and government agencies. The suggestions and the research directions that are depicted in this chapter offer the basis of further development of the field and complex nature approaches to cyber security issue tackling, which may occur in the context of the modern tourism infrastructure

REFERENCES

Adel, A. (2020). *Developing a Digital Forensic Capability for Critical Infrastructures: An Investigation Framework.* Auckland University of Technology.

Amoo, O. O., Atadoga, A., Osasona, F., Abrahams, T. O., Ayinla, B. S., & Farayola, O. A. (2024). GDPR's impact on cybersecurity: A review focusing on USA and European practices. *International Journal of Science and Research Archive, 11*(1), 1338–1347. DOI: 10.30574/ijsra.2024.11.1.0220

Anastasiadou, C. (2006). Tourism and the European Union. In *Tourism in the new Europe: the challenges and opportunities of EU enlargement* (pp. 20–31). CABI. DOI: 10.1079/9781845931179.0020

Babikian, J. (2023). Navigating legal frontiers: Exploring emerging issues in cyber law. *Revista Española de Documentación Científica, 17*(2), 95–109.

Buchanan, B. (2020). *The hacker and the state: Cyber attacks and the new normal of geopolitics*. Harvard University Press.

Buhalis, D. (1998). Strategic use of information technologies in the tourism industry. *Tourism Management, 19*(5), 409–421. DOI: 10.1016/S0261-5177(98)00038-7

Chen, H. S., & Fiscus, J. (2018). The inhospitable vulnerability: A need for cybersecurity risk assessment in the hospitality industry. *Journal of Hospitality and Tourism Technology, 9*(2), 223–234. DOI: 10.1108/JHTT-07-2017-0044

Dhande, K. R. (2024). Fourth Industrial Revolution and the Role of Cyber Security: Technologies on the Travel and Tourism Industry and More Specifically Cyber Security in Travel Tourism. In *Corporate Cybersecurity in the Aviation, Tourism, and Hospitality Sector* (pp. 241-257). IGI Global.

Dodds, R., & Joppe, M. (2005). *CSR in the tourism industry?: The status of and potential for certification, codes of conduct and guidelines.* IFC.

Ebuzor, J. (2024). Understanding Customer Perception of Cyber Attacks: Impact on Trust and Security. In *Corporate Cybersecurity in the Aviation, Tourism, and Hospitality Sector* (pp. 83-111). IGI Global.

Fjäder, C. (2014). The nation-state, national security and resilience in the age of globalisation. *Resilience, 2*(2), 114–129. DOI: 10.1080/21693293.2014.914771

Gander, P., Hartley, L., Powell, D., Cabon, P., Hitchcock, E., Mills, A., & Popkin, S. (2011). Fatigue risk management: Organizational factors at the regulatory and industry/company level. *Accident; Analysis and Prevention, 43*(2), 573–590. DOI: 10.1016/j.aap.2009.11.007 PMID: 21130218

Ghaderi, Z., Beal, L., & Houanti, L. (2026). Cybersecurity threats in tourism and hospitality: Perspectives from tourists engaging with sharing economy services. *Current Issues in Tourism*, 1–16.

Huang, H. Y., Ku, E. C., & Chen, C. D. (2022). Cloud infrastructure enhancing product competitive advantage of tourism SMEs on online consumption values of tourists. *Business Process Management Journal, 28*(4), 1146–1163. DOI: 10.1108/BPMJ-05-2022-0246

Karagiannis, C., & Vergidis, K. (2021). Digital evidence and cloud forensics: Contemporary legal challenges and the power of disposal. *Information (Basel), 12*(5), 181. DOI: 10.3390/info12050181

Krügel, C., Toth, T., & Kerer, C. (2001, December). Decentralized event correlation for intrusion detection. In *International Conference on Information Security and Cryptology* (pp. 114-131). Berlin, Heidelberg: Springer Berlin Heidelberg.

Lee, S. K., & Min, S. R. (2021). Effects of information quality of online travel agencies on trust and continuous usage intention: An application of the SOR model. *The Journal of Asian Finance, Economics and Business, 8*(4), 971–982.

Li, Z., Wang, D., Abbas, J., Hassan, S., & Mubeen, R. (2022). Tourists' health risk threats amid COVID-19 era: Role of technology innovation, Transformation, and recovery implications for sustainable tourism. *Frontiers in Psychology, 12*, 769175. DOI: 10.3389/fpsyg.2021.769175 PMID: 35465147

Paraskevas, A. (2022). Cybersecurity in travel and tourism: a risk-based approach. In *Handbook of e-Tourism* (pp. 1–24). Springer International Publishing. DOI: 10.1007/978-3-030-05324-6_100-1

Rashideh, W. (2020). Blockchain technology framework: Current and future perspectives for the tourism industry. *Tourism Management, 80*, 104125. DOI: 10.1016/j.tourman.2020.104125

Saber, A. F., Helmy, S. H., & Abdel Gaber, M. H. (2025). The Role of Internet of Things in Improving Hotel Operations in Hospitality and Tourism Services and Its Impact on Customers Loyalty. *Journal of Tourism. Hotels and Heritage, 10*(1), 102–126. DOI: 10.21608/sis.2025.383006.1193

. Spanaki, M. Z., & Durmishllari, B. (2019). Technology and Tourism-The Case of the Online Hotel Booking: How Satisfied do the Guests Feel From the Online Reservations' Platforms?.

Tahmasebi, M. (2024). Cyberattack ramifications, the hidden cost of a security breach. *Journal of Information Security*, *15*(2), 87–105. DOI: 10.4236/jis.2024.152007

Zeqiri, A., Ben Youssef, A., & Maherzi Zahar, T. (2025). The Role of digital tourism platforms in advancing sustainable development goals in the Industry 4.0 era. *Sustainability (Basel)*, *17*(8), 3482. DOI: 10.3390/su17083482

Chapter 9
Investigating and Mitigating Cybercrime in Tourism:
Digital Forensics Approaches for Data Breaches, Fraud, and Identity Theft

Sushil Bhardwaj
http://orcid.org/0000-0001-5184-3866
RIMT University, India

Devinder Singh Anand
Chandigarh University, India

Gurpreet Kaur
Chandigarh University, India

Rohit Markan
http://orcid.org/0000-0001-9525-422X
CGC Jhanjeri, Mohali, India

ABSTRACT

The rapid digital transformation of the tourism sector certainly has rendered things more accessible and convenient, but it has also hosted the industry into a bunch of cybercrime-related issues including data breaches, booking fraud, phishing, malware, and identity theft. These threats can even seriously undermine customer trust, generate operational problems, and can lead to significant financial and reputational damage. This chapter concerns the use of digital forensics in the tourism industry

DOI: 10.4018/979-8-3373-5826-0.ch009

by introducing its basic principles, practical tools, and investigative techniques. The chapter also discuss about strategies for uncovering breaches and tracing fraudulent transactions alongside with the legal, ethical, and regulatory responsibilities. The chapter pivots on real-life case studies to underline how the forensic knowledge can build up the solid wall in compliance, and proactively lead enterprises to cyber risk management. Ultimately, it underscores the need for innovative approaches to safeguard digital trust in a globally connected tourism ecosystem.

INTRODUCTION

The tourism sector has been fundamentally dependent on global interconnectivity, communication, and information exchange since its inception. It has demonstrated a fast-paced evolution that has transformed the sector to a digital one completely. Nowadays, tourists have to rely on nearly all the online platforms, mobile Apps, and digital payment methods for their journey facilities; starting from booking a flight, and reserving a hotel to going through airport check-in procedures and paying for services at a foreign place. This move to digital platforms has come with benefits such as ease, speed, and customization, but it has as well posed some new challenges. Currently, their business activities involve the handling of a large amount of customer and financial data, thus they have become attractive targets for digital offenders (Gong et al., 2022). Nowadays, such threats as booking frauds, phishing attacks, ransomware, the installation of malware, and identity theft have been happening often. To really reflect the graveness of the issue we need to know first about the digital evolution of tourism, the reason behind the sector as an appealing target for cybercrime (Kazaure et al., 2023), and the effect of breaches on both tourists and entrepreneurs.

The Digital Evolution of Tourism

As the name implies, travel has been primarily a human-centered industry relying on face-to-face communication, hard copies, and personal contacts all of which are almost entirely replaced by digital formats. In the good old days, travelers used to insert paper tickets, make cash payments, and talk to travel agents, but today, almost every process has shifted to digital means. For instance, airlines are issuing electronic boarding passes, hotels are providing their customers with digital check-in facilities, while browsers are loading mobile apps with entire trips (Riadi et al., 2023). Cloud computing from another side allows companies to keep customer transaction records and booking details on multi-locations distributed systems (Ombu, 2023).

Social media is a digital marketing tool that companies can use to reach specific customers with ads instantly.

The digital shift has not only revolutionized customer expectations but also radically transformed how business is conducted. Travelers no longer have the problem of information asymmetry but are able to access prices, customer reviews and personalized travel recommendations at once. Cost-cutting, streamlined processes, and the ability to expand globally are the main benefits businesses derive from the new system. However, every step of digital progress also introduces new vulnerabilities. Online payments, user accounts, and personal information entered into booking systems all become potential entry points for cybercriminals (Tevdoradze et al., 2024). Systematically, the challenges of tackling the cyber threats by the tourism sector are the volume of data involved, the scope of digital channels, and the involvement of third parties (Adams, 2024). The vast amount of personal data accessible to cybercriminals is one of the speedy side effects of the digital shift. The value of such information goes beyond the immediate misuse of data. For instance, personal credentials that are sold on the black market can be obtained to perpetrate more serious crimes like identity theft. Thus, even though making the sector digital has opened a lot of doors it has simultaneously created a platform for high risk.

Common Cyber Threats Facing the Tourism Sector

Cybercrime in tourism manifests in various forms, each uniquely designed to take advantage of the weaknesses in the technical infrastructure or human factors. The most important threats consist of booking fraud, phishing attacks, ransomware, malware intrusions, and identity theft.

Booking fraud has become increasingly common as reservations move online. Cybercriminals tend to use stolen credit card information to book rooms or build counterfeit websites that resemble legitimate travel portals. At times travelers might lose the money paid for flying tickets or accommodation which do not exist, and as for businesses, they face disputes and lose reputational credibility (Hua et al., 2020). The dependence on third-party booking intermediaries heightens the accountability issue, hence providing additional gaps for fraudsters to dwell on. *Phishing attacks* are another persistent threat. Emails have always been tourism companies' mainstream communication channels whether they are about reservations, itineraries, or promotional offers. Cybercriminals capitalize on this trust to send messages that appear to come from a reliable source (Wyatt, 2023). Without even noticing it, travelers enter their payment information on a fake site, while employees of the companies may click on links that start the weapons in systems. The simplicity and credibility of phishing attacks make them so efficient. *Ransomware* attacks are a class of threats that are extremely detrimental. These attacks use software to lock or encrypt files within a company, thus they pay a ransom to get the files back. For hotels, this could mean losing access to reservation systems and even digital room key platforms. For airlines, disruptions to ticketing or flight scheduling can ground operations. A very shortsighted way to see it is the high season losses which affect the margins, thus straining the businesses to give in to demands. Various channels introduce *malware* like compromised web pages, and infected emails, and encrypted public Wi-Fi networks. When implanted malware can either pull out information, track the user, or make channels for long-term power. For instance, a customer that connects to Wi-Fi at a hotel might unintentionally leak sensitive files to an attacker. Or, a booking engine might only invisibly extract consumer credit card details during a transaction. Lastly, yet not the least *identity theft* tends to be one of the major consequences. Credit card companies and service providers handle a plethora of private identifiers every day, these include camera ids and bank card details (Gruber et al., 2022). Criminals victoriously use that data to acquire other people's ids, execute fraud, or even to do illegal things in someone else's name. And thus, travelers have their part as well which is emotional damage and financial loss, with the latter resulting in extended recovery times. For the businesses, there is also the erosion of trust, tarnished brand reputation, and can even involve punitive measures under the data protection acts. Each case of these threats stresses a significant defect: dependence on digital trust. In the industry of tourism unlike in others, mistakes sometimes cause immediate consequences. Thus if clients cancel reservations, make unauthorized charges, or if there is a failure in systems that directly imply a poor service to them then the need for resilience prevails.

Table 1. Mapping Cyber Threats to Digital Forensic Objectives in Tourism

Cyber Threat	Forensic Focus	Key Evidence	Strategic Outcome
Booking Fraud	Transaction analysis	Payment and booking logs	Fraud prevention
Phishing	Access traceability	Email headers, login logs	Credential protection
Ransomware	Malware analysis	Encrypted files, memory data	Service recovery
Data Breaches	Access reconstruction	Server and network logs	Compliance assurance
Identity Theft	Activity correlation	Account and device logs	Trust restoration

The Table 1 shows the major cyber threats affecting the tourism sector and the corresponding digital forensic focus for each threat. It highlights how forensic evidence supports strategic outcomes such as fraud prevention, service recovery, regulatory compliance, and trust restoration.

Critical Analysis of Cybercrime Dynamics in the Tourism Sector

The tourism sector exhibits a distinctive cyber risk profile when compared with domains such as banking or healthcare. While financial institutions operate within tightly regulated and centralized security frameworks, tourism systems are highly distributed and dependent on multiple third-party platforms. Online travel agencies, payment gateways, cloud service providers, and destination management systems collectively form an interconnected ecosystem. This structural fragmentation significantly expands the attack surface, making coordinated security enforcement difficult.

A critical weakness lies in the seasonal and event-driven nature of tourism transactions. During peak travel seasons, organizations prioritize service availability and speed over rigorous security checks. Cybercriminals exploit this pressure by launching phishing campaigns, automated booking fraud, and ransomware attacks when monitoring capacity is strained. Unlike sectors with stable transaction volumes, tourism experiences sudden spikes that reduce the effectiveness of anomaly-based detection systems.

Another important factor is the imbalance between digital growth and forensic preparedness. Many tourism organizations invest heavily in customer-facing technologies such as mobile applications and digital payments but underinvest in forensic readiness. As a result, breaches are often detected late, evidence is inadequately preserved, and incident response remains reactive. This contrasts sharply with sectors like banking, where forensic logging, audit trails, and regulatory compliance are embedded into system design.

Human factors further intensify cyber risk. Tourism employees frequently handle sensitive data but often lack specialized cybersecurity training. High workforce turnover and reliance on temporary staff weaken organizational memory and security culture. Consequently, social engineering attacks remain highly effective in this sector.

From a strategic perspective, cybercrime in tourism should not be viewed solely as a technical problem but as a governance and risk management challenge. The absence of standardized forensic frameworks across tourism enterprises limits collective resilience. Without integrating digital forensics into cybersecurity strategy, tourism organizations remain vulnerable not only to repeated attacks but also to regulatory and reputational fallout. A shift from descriptive awareness to analytical risk governance is therefore essential for sustainable digital tourism operations.

Consequences and the Growing Urgency

The effects of cybercrime are not restricted to financial loss alone in the tourism sector. They reach the core of the industry: trust, reliability, and customer satisfaction.

The *financial impact* is the first that people notice. Companies incur losses from fraudulent payments, ransom payments, and system repair costs. The stress is added by the costs of investigation, legal action, and floor insurance rates among other things (Oginni et al., 2017). Coupled with such issues is the fact that, in many ransomware cases, companies that pay get their data back partially or sometimes even lose it again. *Reputational harm* has often a mark more damaging and longer-lasting than the aforementioned. The whole trip sector is mostly deeply based on customers' trust. Once customers transfer their faith into other companies that are seen as safer, it takes just one misconduct like a data breach to start the snowballing effect. This will be the fastest to reach out to media and social networks causing a negative reputation which in turn will lower the number of tourists (Dinesha, 2023). The process of rebuilding one's reputation is way enormous than the task of recovering from financial loss.

Regulation also is a burden. With the coming of the global data laws such as the GDPR in Europe, businesses undergo rigorous following of the practices concerning the storing and processing of data. The penalties for breaches can result in multimillion-dollar fines especially with the security technologies that have been neglected discovered (Fianyi et al, 2016). A multinational network in the tourism sector is even more difficult to manage because of such regulation.

OBJECTIVES

The primary aim of this chapter is to provide readers with a clear conceptualization of the role of digital forensics in the investigation and mitigation of cybercrime in the tourism sector. It is a gateway to the comprehension of essential concepts, challenges, and best practices while at the same time giving a practical input for the adoption of the practices in the industry.

Main objectives are:

a) *Present the extent by which tourism is increasingly dealing with cyber threats:* Describe the categories of cybercrime which are primarily targeted to hospitality organizations, such as online booking fraud, data breaches, malware attacks, and identity theft.

b) *Describe digital forensic techniques:* Provide detailed accounts of evidence collection, analysis, and reporting that follow a structured approach and are useful for organizations that wish to conduct investigations on cyber incidents.
c) *Describe the tools and technologies that forensic use:* Show the software, hardware, and analytical techniques involved in digital forensics to track malware and preserve evidence of it.
d) *Talk about preventive and corrective strategies:* Illustrate how information obtained from forensic inquiries can be of assistance in developing security measures, regulations, and staff training.
e) *Explore the legal, ethical, and regulatory aspects:* Elaborate on the data protection laws that tourist companies have to conform to and the moral principles they have to adhere to while performing forensic investigations.
f) *Exhibit cyber incident cases:* Demonstrate the practical utilization of digital forensics in tourism through real-life examples, and draw the necessary insights and best practices.
g) *Promote continuous improvement and innovation:* Motivate readers to consider new tools and methods in fighting cybercrime in tourism through the use of forensic technology.

FUNDAMENTALS OF DIGITAL FORENSICS

Digital forensics (Chowdhury et al., 2024) is, by all means, a staple in the battle against cybercrime. It is the section of study that gains its strength from its focus on the methods of identifying, collecting, preserving, analyzing, and presenting digital evidence in a way that is both right according to the laws and accurate. When it comes to the tourism industry, where the organizations deal with a huge amount of personal, financial, and travel-related data, its role becomes a matter of great importance (Lyu et al.,, 2022). The lack of digital forensics could mean that the companies would not be able to retrace the attack, know who was behind it, or make the relevant suggestions against it. This part of the text refers to the main principles which influence the forensic investigations, reveals techniques which lead to accuracy, integrity, and trustworthiness in these processes.

The Role and Principles of Digital Forensics

Essentially, digital forensics is a practice that expresses the process of decomposing random jumbled digital tokens into coherent, credible evidence (Paraskevas, 2020). Cyber incidents, for instance, a case of cut duplicates, involuntary entry, or invasion of malware, create imprints in devices, networks, or logging files. These traces might be as simple as a suspicious login entry in a server log or as complex as malicious code hidden in a device's memory. When pieced together, they provide a narrative of how an attack unfolded.

Collection, Preservation, and Chain of Custody

The first step of forensic investigations is *collection*, which is a process of identifying and securing potential evidence. In the tourism sector, sources of evidence could be online booking systems, hotel management systems, airline websites, payment gateways, or even personal devices used by the employees (Nikkel, 2020). Because digital information can be manipulated or erased in a very short time, the crucial thing during this step is to act fast and be careful.

When the evidence is available, it must be preserved so as to keep its credibility intact. Preservation is the process where accidental changes, alterations, sabotages, or corruption are avoided. Write-blockers are a popular device that is employed to prevent changes in data made by storage devices. They allow investigators to read devices without changing any data. Like this, the original data is safeguarded from any modifications.

The chain of custody is the most vital part of the process, which is a documented history of every action performed with the evidence. It indicates who had access to the evidence, when it was handled, and in what conditions it was stored. A well-defined chain of custody protects the evidence from being suspected of manipulating and affirms it stays valid in the court. For instance, if investigators create a forensic image of a hotel booking database, every later move—copying, analyzing, and reporting—has to be logged very carefully.

In addition to preservation, it is also very much connected to the practice of*forensic imaging*, where investigators, instead of having direct access to the original media, create a bit-level copy of the digital media. Instead of the original devices, they do the analysis on these forensic images. This way the original source is protected. The original source remains untouched while at the same time allowing investigators to look for deleted files, hidden records, or unusual activity. For the tourism industry, creating images forensically could be a way to detect fraudulent reservations or unauthorized accesses without causing any harm to the original system.

INSTRUMENTS AND TECHNIQUES OF DIGITAL FORENSIC INVESTIGATION

Digital forensics is not a concept; it is a discipline that depends heavily on the tools and methods that make it possible to transform raw digital data into meaningful evidence. After the cyberattack, investigators cannot afford luxury of guesswork or the application of universal IT methods. They are armed only by reliable special tools targeting the recovery of deleted files, localization of hidden network traffic, and tracking the gestures of malicious code. In sectors such as tourism, where the interest is in targeting enormous customer databases, e-commerce booking, and global networking, this is not a facility but a must-have kit. Contemporary technology provides a range of tools that now form the arsenal of the criminal investigator. They can be used to recover data, analyze volatile memory, discover mobile devices, monitor network traffic, detect malware, and log file analysis. Concurrently, there are recent developments such as AI-powered forensic platforms that open up new avenues for swiftness and accuracy.

Established Methodologies and Core Software

At the heart of digital forensics lies the task of preserving and recovering evidence. Investigators often begin with data recovery, as attackers frequently attempt to erase traces of their activities. Arresters likely start with recovering the data which is troublesome for abusers to tidy traces of their actions. Advanced forensic software such as EnCase, FTK (Forensic Toolkit), or the open-source platform Autopsy is designed to retrieve deleted or hidden files. Therefore, these programs do not just restore files; they can also reconstruct metadata showing when files were created, modified, or accessed. In the context of tourist businesses, this might disclose fraudulent changes in booking records or unauthorized SQL queries run by the intruders.

Disk imaging is yet another fundamental practice. Rather than running on a compromised site, investigators copia et imperfection total at the bit level. All of your files, including those that have been deleted or overwritten, will be preserved with the help of tools such as X-Ways Forensics or ProDiscover.

Memory forensics is equally important as with the disks storing permanent data a lot of malicious activities occur in volatile memory which disappears when the system is powered down. Moreover, the mobile forensics sector has really taken off. Today, smartphones can not only save money but can also become the tool of choice for employees in their own free time during the working day. Various tools such as Cellebrite and Oxygen Forensic Detective allow for the extraction of messages, call logs, location data, and application activity. In the context of tourism, this may help track fraudulent payment attempts made through wallets on mobile devices or phishing messages sent via apps to guests.

Specialized Techniques: Networks, Malware, and Logs

While recovering data and imaging disks can provide smoking guns, many attacks make their most significant marks by dynamic rather than static activity. For this reason, investigators increasingly rely on techniques that analyze networks, malware, and logs—domains where the digital footprints of attackers often remain hidden.

Network traffic analysis is one of the most revealing approaches. Every online interaction, from a guest connecting to hotel Wi-Fi to a booking request reaching an airline's database, generates packets of data. By capturing and examining these flows, investigators can identify unusual communication patterns, unauthorized access attempts, or large transfers of sensitive information. Tools such as Wireshark or commercial platforms like NetWitness allow deep inspection of network activity. For example, in a suspected breach of a travel agency's reservation system, traffic analysis may uncover that large volumes of customer data were sent to an unfamiliar external server during off-peak hours, pointing directly to data exfiltration.

Malware detection and analysis represents another key area. Cybercriminals often rely on custom malware to infiltrate systems, encrypt files, or quietly extract information. Forensic investigators use sandboxing tools like Cuckoo Sandbox, Ghidra, or IDA Pro together with reverse engineering software to study the malicious code in a safe environment. Through their studies, they come to realize not only how the code behaves but also whether it contacts command-and-control servers or whether it plants backdoors.

Log analysis completes the triad of specialized techniques. Almost every digital system records logs: login attempts, file access, error messages, and system updates. These logs act like a diary of system activity, offering investigators a timeline of events. By carefully analyzing them, patterns emerge that reveal the attacker's path. Tools such as Splunk or the ELK Stack (Elasticsearch, Logstash, and Kibana) make it possible to handle the immense volume of logs produced daily. For example, in the aftermath of a phishing campaign targeting customers of a resort chain, log analysis might show that attackers used stolen credentials to access internal systems from specific IP addresses at unusual times.

Emerging Innovations: AI-Assisted Platforms and Future Tools

As cybercrime grows in sophistication, traditional forensic tools, though effective, can struggle to keep up with the sheer speed and scale of modern incidents. This has led to the rise of AI-assisted forensic platforms, which enhance detection and investigation by automating parts of the process and identifying patterns that might escape human analysts. Artificial intelligence (Mandayam, 2025) can be applied in several ways. Machine learning algorithms (Baroto et al., 2024) are trained to detect anomalies in vast datasets, such as unusual login behavior or suspicious spikes in network traffic. Natural language processing helps sift through unstructured evidence like emails or chat logs, identifying keywords or sentiment that signal malicious intent. AI also assists in correlating disparate data sources, piecing together a clearer narrative of how an attack unfolded. For tourism businesses, which often generate data across global locations and multiple platforms, these AI-driven capabilities are transformative. Imagine a multinational hotel chain where millions of transactions occur daily. An AI-assisted forensic system can scan these logs in real time, flagging anomalies within minutes. Such speed allows organizations to contain breaches before they spread, rather than reacting after the damage has been done.

Beyond AI, automation, and cloud forensic tools are reconfiguring the field. Automation frees investigators to focus on interpretation by cutting down the amount of time needed for repetitive tasks like hash verification or log correlation (Hayes et al., 2020). Cloud solutions allow for collaborative forensic investigation across jurisdictions, which is an advantage for tourism companies operating internationally. Different investigators can securely access the same forensic data, thus speeding up the response.

Another promising area of research is the application of blockchain for forensics integrity. Blockchain's immutability can be used in evidence management, which entails that every single action on a piece of evidence is permanently recorded and verifiable (Al-E'mari et al., 2024). This reinforces the chain of custody, which is particularly relevant in the case of border-crossing tourism where there might be several parties concerned.

FRAUD AND IDENTITY THEFT MITIGATION

Fraud and identity theft are some of the most damaging types of cybercrime in tourism. Every stage of travel whether booking tickets, checking into hotels, or paying for services—involves the exchange of personal and financial data. This wealth of information makes the sector an attractive target for cybercriminals who exploit weak defenses to steal credit card details, manipulate bookings, or impersonate legitimate travelers. For businesses, the fallout covers everything from financial loss to reputational damage and regulatory sanctions (Ashqar et al., 2024). For cardholders, the aftermath can be more personal which includes stealing funds, damaging their credit scores, and protracted recovery.

Digital forensics walks with illuminated feet in solving these crimes by exposing how they are conducted and assisting companies to deal with them. The implementation of preventive measures is also very important in controlling these incidents before they escalate. This section will consider how forensic techniques track financial fraud and identity theft in the tourism industry, the impact on the tourism sector and how to mitigate future risks.

Forensic Techniques for Investigating Fraud and Identity Theft

Digital forensic, when a fraud or identity theft occurs, is the digital-forensic tracking application that we will include the ability to perform means of tracing activity, uncovering evidence, and identifying responsible parties. Investigations often start with the analysis of the transactions. The forensic experts need to study booking records, payment logs, and financial trails to spot the anomalies in the transactions (Baroto, 2024). For example, a booking that shows details that do not match like a customer address in one country and a payment card registered in a different country, or a device that has failed to process several payments repeatedly.

Log analysis as another core technique. Every interaction with a booking platform, mobile application, or payment gateway incurs logs. The investigator needs to analyze login histories, IP addresses, and timestamps so that he will determine if the access was legitimate or not (Amato et al., 2020). For instance, if a customer account is accessed from different countries within minutes, then forensic evidence may indicate the use of the compromised credential.

In phishing-driven theft cases, investigators look at email headers and metadata. These details identify the servers on which phishing emails were sent and can often be connected to known phishing campaigns. Likewise, forensic imaging of infected devices can identify malware used to steal passwords or monitor user activity. Identity theft investigations are also based on correlation analysis, where data from different sources—payment systems, travel records, and communication logs—are combined to trace the criminal activities. For example, when a fraudulent airline ticket is acquired with a stolen identity, forensic analysis may connect the IP addresses of the purchase with the prior phishing campaigns targeting the same area.

Preventive Strategies for Reducing Risk

Although forensic investigation is essential following an event, the best strategy for tackling fraud and identity theft is to prevent it from occurring in the first place. The tourism organizations can adopt a mix of the technological, procedural, and human-centered measures.

Multi-factor authentication (MFA) is one of the strongest defenses. By requiring users to provide additional verification—such as a fingerprint, one-time code, or biometric check—MFA significantly reduces the risk of account takeovers. For example, a traveler who wants to access their airline account from a new router is likely to confirm the login through a mobile code, which Denis prevents the attacker because he has no login credentials.

Encryption plays a similar but equally important part. The shield of camera network security protocol in the distorted images crypto-graphic key. Stolen data cannot be read without the right keys to decrypt it.

Fraud monitoring systems add another layer of defense. These systems utilize machine learning to scrutinize the transactional patterns in real time. If an unusual booking is detected such as ten reservations made from the same device among a few applications, the system is already able to flag the transaction. Continuous monitoring also helps in the area of fraudulent use of loyalty points or sudden spikes in unusual account activities.

The *staff training and awareness* program can further help in tightening protection. Employees who are aware of the phishing or social engineering threats are less likely to get the malware mail or through malicious calls. Training can be more helpful for the front-line employees in hotels or travel agencies, where they may directly handle the sensitive data.

To sum up, the organizations should prepare for incidents by planning for them. These plans include among others, the steps to take to detect fraud, notify affected customers, and work with forensic experts in investigating. A clear plan cut down on confusion during the crises and increases the recovery rate.

Building Trust through Resilient Practices

Fraud and identity theft not only bring about financial losses but also the customer trust, which is a key factor in the tourism sector. A traveler who has a negative experience of identity theft after booking through a site may not choose to experience the services of that company, regardless of some compensation given. Thus the measures should be aimed not only at stopping crime but also at restoring trust.

Transparency plays an important role here. When breaches occur, organizations that communicate clearly explaining what happened, what steps are being taken, and how customers are being supported—tend to retain more goodwill. Along with these services, the perpetrator of the crime can also extend free credit monitoring or identity recovery service to the victim as a further expression of the concern for their welfare. Resilience also comes from collaboration. Tourism enterprises are to work with payment processors, cybersecurity firms, and even with competitors to share knowledge about fraud trends (Ghaderi, 2024). The industry-wide cooperation upholds that new threats are detected on time and addressed collectively. For instance, if several hotels observe the same fraudulent listings from a certain IP range, they can share the information and block the future attempts across the entire sector. For the most part, the means of addressing fraud and identity theft are through creating an environment where travelers and businesses feel secure. The combination of powerful preventive measures along with effective forensic investigations enables the tourism organizations to prove that they take threats seriously and they can respond vigorously whenever the incidents arise.

LEGAL, ETHICAL, AND REGULATORY CONSIDERATIONS

It is not right to think of digital forensics as only a technical process. The implementing of them happens only in the context of laws, ethical codes, and regulatory prescriptions. The highly sensitive data that tourism companies deal with, such as payment details and customer passport records, makes compliance and accountability the priority. Lack of respect for the either legal or ethical boundary can lead to the blocking of some of the investigations, loss of customer trust, or putting companies at risk of huge fines. This section will deal with the legal frameworks governing the forensic work, the ethical duties lawyers must observe, and the regulatory duties that dictate how the digital evidence is collected and used.

Legal Compliance in Digital Forensics

The law is the backbone of every forensic investigation. Evidence collected or handled in a manner that is not legally compliant can be excluded from court, even if it is technically correct. This is of particular importance to the tourism industry, where compliance can sometimes involve both national laws and international regulations. These are multiplied because hotels operate across borders and take care of customers from all corners of the world. A very important issue is the General Data Protection Regulation (GDPR) of the European Union. GDPR imposes strict conditions on the collection of personal data and requires the user to provide clear consent, be transparent, and secure it properly. If a data breach were to occur, the organization has to inform the regulators within 72 hours and give the precise details of the incident.

Another critical one is the Payment Card Industry Data Security Standard (PCI DSS). It is a regulation that applies to any business that processes payments through credit cards. This includes hotels, airlines, and travel agencies that fit directly into the scope of PCI DSS (Florido-Benítez, 2024). PCI DSS necessitates strict procedures of how cardholder data is stored, accessed, and transmitted. When forensic investigations involve the theft of payment data, they must follow PCI DSS guidelines to secure the evidence, thus, the company shows its due diligence in protecting financial data. There are local laws as well that come into play. Data protection laws, consumer rights laws, and cybercrime laws differ from country to country, and multinational tourism companies often have to navigate a patchwork of overlapping requirements. The forensic experts must keep in mind these differences if they want their methods to be admissible in different jurisdictions.

Ethical Responsibilities in Forensic Practice

While laws provide the official framework, ethical issues refer to the manner in which forensic work is done. Digital forensics involves the use of highly personal information such as the disclosures of trip itineraries, financial records, or even private communications which places the investigators in a position of trust. It follows that the observing of ethical codes is a paramount obligation together with the observing of technical procedures. A front-most ethical responsibility is privacy protection. The investigatory personnel should be the people who check and disclose the information that probably is relevant to the case alone. For example, if a forensic picture of a hotel database is the one that includes customer payment records and personal correspondence, data solely related to the breach shall be analyzed. Accessing or exposing unrelated information would constitute an ethical violation, even if it is technically possible.

A further ethical consideration involves the handling of digital evidence. Investigators must avoid altering or manipulating data, even if it is unintentional. Evidence must be presented truthfully and objectively, without prejudice toward specific outcomes. Within the tourism sphere that gathers up millions of travelers, the objectivity is essential. The ethical method makes sure that the conclusions are credible both in court and in the public eye. The last ethical responsibility is professional competence. Forensic specialists have to keep their knowledge about the newest technology and laws up to date.

Regulatory Oversight and Industry Obligations

From the legal compliance and ethical standards, the tourism industry has to deal with a growing number of regulatory obligations. These regulations are designed not just to protect customers, but also to ensure that the industries adopt consistent and high-quality practices in security and forensics. The regulators are now requiring incident reporting. The tourism companies that are affected must notify the authorities within a structured time and sometimes provide forensic reports that cover the incident's scope. This will show the firm is taking the appropriate measures to investigate, contain the situation, and minimize the damage. Without the right forensic processes, organizations may face challenges that lead to fines or more oversight (Cassidy et al., 2024). Retention policies are also important to shape forensic actions. Many jurisdictions name the timeline of how long a customer is informed and the conditions under that the information must be deleted. The exact conditions the forensic investigators must not contradict when collecting the evidence. Retaining unnecessary personal data is a compliance risk for the companies even after the investigation is over. The global tourism challenge of cross-border regulation also exists. A European hotel may welcome guests from Asia, America, and Africa, which means that any investigation could involve data subjects to multiple legal systems.

CASE STUDIES OF CYBER INCIDENTS IN TOURISM

Real-world case studies help translate theory into practice. Technical definitions and procedures forensics are the base, but it is often through older incidents that one sees the necessity of cyber resiliency. The tourism industry which includes airlines, hotels, and online travel agencies has had a number of notorious breaches in the past decade. These incidents brought to the front both the fragility of digital platforms and the essential role of the forensic examination in finding out what happened and showing how the problems can be solved to prevent attacks from occurring again.

This section examines four illustrative cases: a breach that took place at a worldwide hotel chain, a cyberattack on an online travel agency, a ransomware incident which affected an airline, and a phishing driven fraud campaign directed towards regional tourism businesses. Each instance shows how forensic methods were practiced; what problems the investigators got as well as the lessons taken from these incidents.

Breach at Global Hotel Chain: Guest Data Exposed

One of the most discussed cyber incidents in the tourism sector is a breach case that occurred at a hotel chain that felt this data loss that affected a few million customers. The assailants broke into the company's reservation database and got hold of records which had the names of the customers, passport numbers, credit card details, and travel histories.

Investigative Process: The forensic investigation got started at a time when the company realized the so-called abnormal events were happening in its booking platform. A log was built up telling that the fraud indexes were repeated for settings in the database that were later pointing to data transfer; even the team got the impression of data exfiltration. Forensic teams at once made forensic imaging of the servers to recover the state of the system at intrusion time. Together, log analysis and network traffic monitoring helped them to reconstruct the sequence of the attack. Evidence that log files were tracked showed that the attackers had obtained credentials through a login of a vendor that was compromised.

Challenges: The breach was so serious that it became very hard for the organization to locate the entire path of data exfiltrated. The intruders were able to maintain the access for a long time hidden which increased the volume of stolen data. The first step in ascertaining the stolen files was a massive job that engaged the time and effort of many forensic investigators, as it included several databases. Another challenge nested within compliance, as the firm had to meet permissions in different states and countries. Complying with GDPR and other data protection laws mandated thorough documentation that specified the time of the breach, what data was compromised, and how the company reacted to it.

Lessons Learned: The case brought to light that it is of primordial importance to monitor any third-party access. Although the hotel chain had high internal security protocols, the breach utilized the vendor system's weak point. Certainly, the forensic evidence showed that more monitoring of third-party access as well as stricter access controls could have eased the risk. Attacks were not even visible in the beginning, and thus longer stay offended the tourist company more, came due to failure in breach detection at right time.

Cyberattack on an Online Travel Agency: Fake Bookings and Fraud

An online travel agency (OTA) experienced a coordinated cyberattack involving fraudulent bookings made through its platform. Attackers used stolen payment card details to create thousands of reservations, later reselling them to unsuspecting travelers at discounted rates. The OTA faced financial losses, chargeback disputes, and reputational harm when customers discovered their bookings were invalid.

Investigative Process: The forensic response concentrated mainly on the transaction analysis. Investigators reviewed paying records and distinguished the right transactions from the fraudulent ones. They could quicken the process: most fake bookings originated from some IP addresses and they were often routed to anonymizing via proxies. Forensics backtracked to diagnose the scripts once they could track back to them, they realized the scripts had been automating the booking process just like that.

The mode of operation of the fraud included attackers using the OTA's imaginary booking servers. In particular, they succeeded in exploiting a vulnerability found in the payment gateway through an integration model, which let them pass the security checks. After receipt of the blueprints of the system flaws, the OTA patched their loophole and they could shield off the new fraud.

Challenges: The major problem in this case was the high number of fraudulent transactions committed. It took a lot of time and diligent effort to sift through the numerous bookings to find genuine customers. Another issue was the cross-border operations between many of the fraudulent payments that had been processed in the countries that were outside the OTA's headquarters. Getting concerned payment processors and banks on the same page prolonged resolution.

Lessons Learned: The OTA gained the knowledge that it is important for the booking process to have a fraud monitoring system that is real-time, enabling detection of unusual booking patterns before the transactions are processed. This incident, on the other hand, also pointed out that it is required to use stronger authentication measures at the time of booking to prevent the automated scripts that steal the platform. From the standpoint of forensics, the case proved again that the analysis of transaction logs and server imaging have the power to show clear paths from a security breach to mitigation.

Phishing Campaign Going On To Regional Tourism Companies

A small network of tourism businesses, such as local hotels and travel agencies, had a phishing epidemic whereby they fell victim to a campaign that infected their computer system. Attackers pretended to be a government tourist association, sending emails for account verification. Several members of the consortium inadvertently complied with the request making the attackers gain access as well to their booking platforms and financial records.

Investigative Process: Forensic analysis identified the emails' header as the entry point which showed that the phishing emails had been sent through the compromised servers that were located abroad. The track of broken credentials used to enter booking systems was also reconstructed by log analyses. Inside, attackers were able to change reservations redirect payments and take away the customer details.

In the case of some organizations, the forensic imaging of the systems that were infected showed key logging malware that had been additionally downloaded once the intruders got access. This way, more credentials were captured and thus the theft was wider for the company.

Challenges: A significant issue was that cybersecurity resources were limited within smaller companies. Many of them did not have IT staff which was a problem for rapid response. Coordination was another task, as the concerted action affected a number of firms simultaneously, meaning that the detectives had to collect and coordinate different pieces of information from different sources.

Lessons Learned: This case highlighted the vulnerability of small and medium-sized tourism businesses, which are often less prepared for sophisticated cyberattacks. It also reinforced the need for industry-wide collaboration. Sharing forensic findings across affected businesses helped uncover the full scale of the campaign and accelerated response. Moreover, it is also necessary to have the preventive measures such as basic cybersecurity practices like employee training and using multi-factor authentication.

BUILDING A CYBER-RESILIENT ECOSYSTEM IN TOURISM

Cyber resilience is one of the most important goals to be pursued by the tourism sector. It is resilience, rather than traditional security which is focused just on preventing attacks, that should be the focal point of the tourism industry. Resilience protection at the very basis is to make sure that services as available as possible, data security is ensured and customers are confident even in the presence of ICT attacks. The insights provided by the forensic investigation teach valuable lessons which organizations can use to build a stronger security posture and become proactive in their security. The tourism industry, by means of policies, training, audits, response planning, and continuous monitoring, can be set up as an integrated ecosystem of defense.

Organizational Policies and Governance

Strong organizational policies are the beginning of the road to resilience. Companies in the tourism sector, whether they are big hotel chains or small travel agencies, have to lay out the cybersecurity framework with definitive responsibilities, standards, and procedures. Forensic investigations often bring to light breaches that may be caused by not only technical problems but also due to weakly defined or poorly enforced policies.

Effective governance also needs the commitment of leadership. The cybersecurity of the business should be linked to the business, and not considered as a technical problem. It is essential for boards and senior managers to be regularly informed about risks, compliance requirements, and forensic findings. By embedding cybersecurity into corporate governance, organizations create accountability at every level.

Employee Training and Awareness

The most sophisticated technical protection can be disrupted if staff have not been properly trained. Studies on forensic investigations show often that human errors enable incidents; for instance, clicking on phishing links or misconfiguring systems, or mishandling data. In Tourism, where the staff handle customer personal data alone and interact with them extremely high, employee awareness becomes a defensive line.

In the training programs, practical topics like recognizing phishing emails, establishing strong passwords and reporting suspicious activity constitute the core. Yet another important part is the role-specific training; for instance, staff dealing with payment information ought to be acquainted with PCI DSS requirements, while customer service staff should have the knowledge about the importance of safeguarding of the personal identifiers.

Security Audits and Continuous Monitoring

The Resilient Systems are the ones that are regularly tested and updated. Security audits offer the company a systematized viewpoint of the security of an organization, which is the main tool for the identification of the gaps that hackers can exploit before they are found. Hardware failure and other vulnerabilities found in ports and records often highlight the areas where audits were inadequate, such as unpatched software or weak access controls.

Audits can include internal reports as well as independent third-party penetration testing. External auditors are an independent body that adds value and know-how, helping the companies to compare themselves with the industry standards. Real-time visibility, addressed by continuous monitoring, is the shadow of audit. Advanced monitoring multiplies network, user, and log traffic to shadow anomalies (Tok et al., 2022). For example, a sudden increase in the booking transactions of a hotel that is entirely booked on a specific date or by multiple logins from faraway regions may be a signal of a fraud attempt. In some situations, combining the monitoring with automatic alerts, the enterprise can react fast and, often, solve the problems before they escalate.

FUTURE DIRECTIONS AND INNOVATIONS

As the tourism industry embraces the digital continuum, it continues to face a new range of threats. Cybercriminals are becoming more decentralized and are able to utilize cloud resources to build up a botnet for a certain period of time only. In this environment for digital forensics to be effective it must remain dynamic. It will have to forecast the risks, acquire high-tech gear, and orient itself towards forward-looking practices that foster digital trust. The forensic future in the tourism sector will be built on the successful cooperation between the human hand and smart tools (Afolabi et al., 2021) that will facilitate detection, reaction, and prevention.

AI-Driven Threat Detection and Analysis

Artificial intelligence (AI) is not just the face of the shift; it is also the mind. Hyper-modern cybersecurity and digital forensics depend on AIs (Bhardwaj, 2025). Regulation detecting a threat has always been through imposition of the rules: saw, failed login attempts, blocked to known malicious IP addresses. However, there is a better way than it. AI is the answer here, for it will help the systems to learn from the datasets available to them and not only to learn normal patterns but also to identify anomalies in real time (Bhardwaj, 2025).

When it comes to the tourism industry, the tools driven by AI can read millions of booking transactions, email communications, or network logs first, detect all kinds of signs of fraud or intrusion, and then present insightful information to the user (Suryal et al., 2024). An example is the case when an AI system connects the dots and discovers that guests were booking from different places but they were using the same devices which had identical digital fingerprints. Apart from that, an AI can track the use of cards for example, that have been repeatedly used on several accounts.

In addition to that, forensic investigations can take advantage of the fact that AI can do less practical work. Tasks such as log parsing, malware classification, and correlating evidence across multiple systems can be completed faster and with fewer errors. This reduces investigation time and allows human experts to focus on higher-level analysis. The time to come will see the introduction of the AI robotic aspect in the forensic workflow, which will help keep pace with the speed and the breadth of the cyber threats in the tourism sector.

Blockchain-Based Security and Trust

Among the newest promising ideas is the use of blockchain technology. The tourism industry is heavily reliant on digital transactions, especially transactions that cover every aspect of travel, such as booking, paying, and even the use of digital currency (Abdelhamed, 2023). One of the things surrounding each transaction is that it involves multi-intermediary which acts as the independent risk factor identifying fraud or manipulation. Blockchain is a minimalist ledger that is decentralized and each transaction is registered visibly and immutably (Rashideh, 2020).

Two main advantages that blockchain provides digital forensics are as follows. First, they have a way of showing the faulty audit trail as eliminator in the future. This feature helps to confirm whether the transaction is genuine or not. For example, if a passenger claims that a booking or payment is wrong, forensics can use the blockchain as a base-truth source. Second, it can be used for identity verification which will free blockchain from impersonation and identity theft risks. For example, the blockchain, which is based on security, would eliminate the need for travelers to exchange personal information with different airlines, hotels, and agencies each time.

The tourism industry has seen the deployment of blockchain-based loyalty programs and ticketing systems at an early stage (Erol et al., 2022). The next step would be to chain blocks not only for processes but also for the forensic evidence which in turn would be safe from demolition. Placing forensic records on a blockchain would help the investigators to show integrity of the evidence and sustain their trust in the procedures where the court relies on.

Predictive Analytics and Proactive Risk Management

In the traditional approach, forensic investigations deal with understanding events after they have happened, but the future looks like predictive analytics (Kumar, 2024)- the forecasting of risks before they become crises. Predictive systems are based on historical data, threat intelligence, and machine learning models which help to estimate the possibility of the attack and point out the most vulnerable systems.

In the area of tourism, the organizations could use predictive analytics to forecast the peak times of fraud activities during the festivals or big events that usually boost sales. The bad incidents that have occurred earlier like data breaches could add some inputs into the predictive models that are to be employed (Bhavsar et al., 2022). For example, the models could point out the jamming attack campaigns such as the ones that target only certain regions. If they identify these problems early enough organizations can fortify themselves in good time.

Active risk management is about the testing of system vulnerabilities as well. Renovation through the threat modeling process is a real example of this. The companies are looking into the scenario of what-ifs and defining the vulnerabilities that they themselves could create. For instance, a hotel and airline booking system would be infected by ransomware while the hotel payment gateway would be breached. These scenarios will be informed by forensic insights so the companies can understand the situation better and thus they can improve their incident response effort and reduce the attack surface.

Strategic and Governance-Oriented Innovations in Tourism Forensics

Beyond technological advancements, future innovation in digital forensics for tourism must emphasize organizational integration and sector specific governance. Forensic capabilities should no longer operate as isolated technical functions but be embedded within enterprise risk management, operational planning, and decision making structures. Tourism organizations will increasingly be expected to demonstrate forensic readiness through predefined evidence handling procedures, standardized incident documentation, and alignment with international compliance frameworks.

Another critical direction involves strengthening inter organizational cooperation. As tourism ecosystems rely heavily on third party vendors, payment processors, and platform providers, future forensic investigations will require coordinated data sharing agreements and interoperable forensic standards. This collaborative approach will improve response speed and reduce investigative blind spots created by fragmented ownership of digital infrastructure.

Capacity building will also shape future developments. The growing complexity of digital evidence necessitates specialized training for tourism professionals, legal teams, and technical staff to interpret forensic findings effectively. Developing sector focused forensic competencies will support informed decision making during incidents and enhance accountability.

Ultimately, innovation in digital forensics should be evaluated not only by technological sophistication but by its ability to reduce recurrence of incidents, support regulatory compliance, and restore stakeholder confidence. Such an outcome driven approach will position digital forensics as a strategic enabler of resilience and trust in the evolving tourism landscape.

CONCLUSION

The tourism sector is in the hub of global networking, digital convenience, and turbulence. As this chapter has shown, the sector's increasing reliance on online platforms, mobile applications, and digital payment systems has created both opportunities and vulnerabilities. Cybercriminals exploit these vulnerabilities through booking fraud, phishing campaigns, ransomware, malware, and identity theft, leaving businesses exposed to financial loss, reputational harm, and regulatory penalties. In this environment, digital forensics emerges as an indispensable discipline, enabling organizations to not only investigate incidents but also to strengthen their long-term resilience.

The implementation of certain principles ensures consistency of the work done in the field. The completeness of the process by forensic imaging and the chain of custody brought about both technical rigor and legal defensibility. These practices do not belong to the realm of specialized technicians; they give the tourism businesses a structured way to respond when their systems are compromised or data is stolen. The use of forensic software, advanced log analysis, network monitoring, and malware detection to recover data has been discussed. These tools endow the investigators with the capability of tracing root causes through unauthorized access and aggregating timelines to spot the systems that have been breached. The latest trends, such as AI-supported facilities forensics and the use of blockchain to provide evidence, show the way to the rapid progress in and the future of forensic research. This allows the reading of digital forensics not as a lineal progress of adaptation and growth, but as an active transformation in relation to an evolving landscape of threats.

The cases show how theory becomes practice. The cases of cybercrime in hotels, online travel agencies, and airlines have been the brightest examples of the reality of such a world. They have also shown the issue of territorial jurisdiction, their capability to prolong their stay in a particular sector, and the issues of limited resources in some of the companies. Meanwhile, this has further highlighted some key lessons learned: watching the third parties, developing staff, backing up, and collaborating across the board are important things. Each case demonstrates the practical relevance of forensic investigation as a reactive and preventive measure, respectively.

Adherence to frameworks such as GDPR and PCI DSS is crucial for protecting customer data from breaches and being punished severely. Ethical responsibilities are another side of the equation as things like privacy respect and transparency, are significantly important, because a loss of trust from mishandled information or cover-up of breaches would be serious. Organizational strategies such as employee awareness, continuous monitoring, security audits, and incident response planning prevent forensic practices from being isolated as single-time actions but become part of the business as usual. With time the goal is to reshape passive response into a state of resilience. The sole focus of digital forensics has been to arm the tourism sector with the capabilities needed to conduct thorough investigations; however, the greater worth is in the formulation of the defenses and the strategies run in a proactive mode. The drawn-out effect is not just fortified cybersecurity levels but the digital transformation of the tourism sector becoming more sustainable.

The study has provided a comprehensive exploration of how digital forensics supports the investigation, prevention, and mitigation of cybercrime in tourism. Along with that, it has mixed the ground level theoretical principles with actual-world examples and stressed the importance of ethical and legal frameworks as well. Through achieving a technology-governance-and-human-awareness merger, the tourism industry can build a cyber-resilient ecosystem. Such resilience will not only protect businesses and customers but will also maintain the trust that the whole sector depends on.

REFERENCES

Abdelhamed, M. (2023). *Electronic signature and its role in securing transactions in the tourism sector. Journal of Tourism, Hotels and Heritage*. Print., DOI: 10.21608/sis.2023.220851.1148

Adams, T. (2024). Trends, challenges and opportunities of engaging digital forensics for cybercrime investigations. *Advances in Multidisciplinary and Scientific Research Journal, 15*(1), 1–12. DOI: 10.22624/AIMS/CISDI/V15N1P1

Afolabi, O. O., Ozturen, A., & İlkan, M. (2021). Effects of privacy concern, risk, and information control in a smart tourism destination. Journal of Tourism. *Ekonomska Istraživanja, 34*(1), 3119–3138. DOI: 10.1080/1331677X.2020.1867215

Al-E'mari, S., Sanjalawe, Y., Makhadmeh, S. N., & Alqudah, H. (2024). Digital forensics meets blockchain: Enhancing evidence authenticity and traceability. *International Conference on Cybersecurity Research*, 1–6. DOI: 10.1109/ICCR61006.2024.10532961

Amato, F., Castiglione, A., Cozzolino, G., & Narducci, F. (2020). A semantic-based methodology for digital forensics analysis. *Journal of Parallel and Distributed Computing, 138*, 172–177. DOI: 10.1016/j.jpdc.2019.12.017

Ashqar, R. I., Ashqar, H. I., & Ramos, C. M. Q. (2024). *Identity and access management in tourism and hospitality*. In Springer International Publishing., DOI: 10.1007/978-3-031-44131-8_32

Baroto, W. A. (2024). Advancing digital forensic through machine learning: An integrated framework for fraud investigation. *Asia Pacific Fraud Journal, 9*(1), 1–16. DOI: 10.21532/apfjournal.v9i1.346

Bhardwaj, S., Sharma, I., & Kaur, G. Rohini, & Sharma, S. (2025). Personalization in tourism marketing based on leveraging user-generated content with AI recommender systems. In M. Valeri, S. Shah, & B. Al-Ghazali (Eds.), Redefining Tourism With AI and the Metaverse (pp. 317–346). IGI Global Scientific Publishing. DOI: 10.4018/978-8-3693-8482-4.ch010

Bhardwaj, S., Sharma, I., Mahendru, S., Kaur, R., & Sharma, S. (2025). Exploring the role of AIoT in data privacy and security. In Tariq, M. (Ed.), *Merging Artificial Intelligence With the Internet of Things* (pp. 75–102). IGI Global Scientific Publishing., DOI: 10.4018/979-8-3693-8547-0.ch003

Bhavsar, K. A., Patel, A. M., & Parikh, S. M. (2022). Approaches to digital forensics in the age of big data. In *International Conference on Computing for Sustainable Global Development* (pp. 449–453). DOI: 10.23919/INDIACom54597.2022.9763231

Cassidy, A. A. T. J., Fuad, A., & As Shofy, M. U. A. (2024). Emerging trends and challenges in digital crime: A study of cyber criminal tactics and countermeasures. *TechComp Innovations*, *1*(1), 38–45. DOI: 10.70063/techcompinnovations.v1i1.25

Chowdhury, R. H., & Mostafa, A. (2024). Digital forensics and business management: The role of digital forensics in investigating cybercrimes affecting digital businesses. *World Journal of Advanced Research and Reviews*, *23*(2), 1060–1069. DOI: 10.30574/wjarr.2024.23.2.2438

Dinesha, H. A., & Jayanthila, D. (2023). Forensics: Cybercrime investigation analysis in social networks. *Journal of Digital Security*, *1*(2), 20. DOI: 10.26634/jds.1.2.20377

Erol, I., Neuhofer, I. O., Dogru, T., Oztel, A., Searcy, C., & Yorulmaz, A. C. (2022). Improving sustainability in the tourism industry through blockchain technology: Challenges and opportunities. *Tourism Management*, *93*, 104628. DOI: 10.1016/j.tourman.2022.104628

Fianyi, I. (2016). Curbing cyber-crime and enhancing e-commerce security with digital forensics. arXiv: Cryptography and Security. https://www.arxiv.org/abs/1610.08369

Florido-Benítez, L. (2024). The cybersecurity applied by online travel agencies and hotels to protect users' private data in smart cities. *Smart Cities*, *7*(1), 475–495. Advance online publication. DOI: 10.3390/smartcities7010019

Ghaderi, Z., Béal, L., Hall, C. M., Zaman, M., Rather, R. A., & Som, A. P. M. (2024). Cybersecurity and smart tourist destinations resilience. *Tourism Recreation Research*, •••, 1–17. DOI: 10.1080/02508281.2024.2434791

Gong, Y., & Schroeder, A. (2022). A systematic literature review of data privacy and security research on smart tourism. *Tourism Management Perspectives*, *44*, 101019. DOI: 10.1016/j.tmp.2022.101019

Gruber, J., Voigt, L., Benenson, Z., & Freiling, F. C. (2022). Foundations of cybercriminalistics: From general process models to case-specific concretizations in cybercrime investigations. *Forensic Science International Digital Investigation*, *43*, 301438. DOI: 10.1016/j.fsidi.2022.301438

Hayes, D., & Kyobe, M. (2020). The adoption of automation in cyber forensics. IEEE International Conference on ICT and Automation for Sustainability, 1–6. DOI: 10.1109/ICTAS47918.2020.233977

Hua, N., Li, B., & Zhang, T. (2020). Crime research in hospitality and tourism. *International Journal of Contemporary Hospitality Management, 32*(3), 1299–1323. DOI: 10.1108/IJCHM-09-2019-0750

Kazaure, A. A., Jantan, A., & Yusoff, M. N. (2023). Digital forensics investigation approaches in mitigating cybercrimes: A review. *Journal of Information Science Theory and Practice, 11*(4), 14–39. DOI: 10.1633/JISTaP.2023.11.4.2

Kumar, M. (2024). A comprehensive framework for preventing digital arrest scams: Integrating predictive crime script models, cognitive resilience, advanced forensics, and public awareness. International Journal of Advanced Research in Science. *Tongxin Jishu*, •••, 736–745. DOI: 10.48175/IJARSCT-18796

Lyu, J., Khan, A. A. F., Bibi, S., Chan, J. H., & Qi, X. (2022). Big data in action: An overview of big data studies in tourism and hospitality literature. *Journal of Hospitality and Tourism Management, 51*, 346–360. DOI: 10.1016/j.jhtm.2022.03.014

Mandayam, R. (2025). The impact of artificial intelligence on digital forensics. *International Journal of Innovative Research in Engineering & Multidisciplinary Physical Sciences, 13*(1), 231816. Advance online publication. DOI: 10.37082/IJIRMPS.v13.i1.231816

Nikkel, B. J. (2020). Fintech forensics: Criminal investigation and digital evidence in financial technologies. *Forensic Science International Digital Investigation, 33*, 200908. DOI: 10.1016/j.fsidi.2020.200908

Oginni, O. S. (2017). Towards black box forensic cybercrime investigation model (BBFCIM): Beyond the rule of thumb. In Global, I. G. I. (Ed.), (pp. 168–187)., DOI: 10.4018/978-1-5225-1031-4.ch010

Ombu, A. (2023). Role of digital forensics in combating financial crimes in the computer era. *Journal of Forensic Accounting Profession, 3*(1), 57–75. DOI: 10.2478/jfap-2023-0003

Paraskevas, A. (2020). *Cybersecurity in travel and tourism: A risk-based approach.* Springer Nature., DOI: 10.1007/978-3-030-05324-6

Rashideh, W. (2020). Blockchain technology framework: Current and future perspectives for the tourism industry. *Tourism Management, 80*, 104125. DOI: 10.1016/j.tourman.2020.104125

Riadi, I., Yudhana, A., Pramuja, G., & Fanani, I. (2023). Mobile forensic tools for digital crime investigation: Comparison and evaluation. *International Journal of Safety and Security Engineering, 13*(1), 11–19. DOI: 10.18280/ijsse.130102

Suryal, A., Vishwakarma, P., & Malik, A. (2024). Impact of artificial intelligence in digital forensics: A review study. Social Science Research Network. DOI: 10.2139/ssrn.4492420

Tevdoradze, S., Mushkudiani, Z., Tevdoradze, N., & Tevdoradze, N. (2024). The effect of criminal activity on tourism. *Axali Ekonomisti*, *19*(01), 25–31. DOI: 10.36962/NEC19012024-04

Tok, Y. C., & Chattopadhyay, S. (2022). Identifying threats, cybercrime and digital forensic opportunities in smart city infrastructure via threat modeling. *Forensic Science International Digital Investigation*, *45*, 301540. DOI: 10.1016/j.fsidi.2023.301540

Wyatt, B. (2023). 50 dark destinations: Crime and contemporary tourism. *Journal of Heritage Tourism*, *1–2*(5), 730–731. Advance online publication. DOI: 10.1080/1743873X.2023.2210431

KEY TERMS AND DEFINITIONS

Chain of Custody: The chain of custody is the paper trail that shows evidence is seized, held, controlled, transferred, analyzed, and disposed of. It is a significant principle in the digital forensics domain and can be considered as a precondition for the legal admissibility and integrity of the evidence.

Cybercrime: Cybercrime poses a challenge in the tourism industry when criminals commit crimes via digital pathways. Enormous threats arise, such as the use of unauthorized credit card information for booking flights in online booking fraud, hacking into databases, malware attacks, and identity theft.

Data Breach: A data breach is an incident of security where confidential, sensitive, or protected data is accessed or exfiltrated without authorization. This may be an instance of this kind where a hotel, airline, or a travel agency's website is breached leading to the exposure of data from their customers.

Digital Forensics: Digital forensics is the discipline in forensic science that concern with the investigative proofing of digital incidents, such as breaches of data, fraud, and identity theft, through the systematic collection of evidence, preservation, analysis, and reporting digital evidence to cyber incidents Like the ones listed above. It can be a blueprint for firms to read how the hack happened, who did it, and what countermeasures should be taken. The intention is to offer defense systems that make criminals abandon such actions.

Forensic Imaging: Forensic imaging refers to the exact, bit-for-bit creation of a storage device image without any changes to the original filesystem at all. This process will ensure that the original data is not lost, providing investigators with an image to work from, which is the very ethos of the process. The forensic image's integrity is the heart of a trustworthy investigation.

GDPR (General Data Protection Regulation): GDPR refers to the EU legal requirements for data protection and privacy of all individuals within the EU and EEA areas. It also deals with the dynamics of transferring personal data outside the EU and EEA zones. Tour companies are to be aware that compliance with GDPR and other data protection laws are imperative not only for legal requirements but also for ethical considerations, besides, they properly handle digital evidence during forensic investigations.

Online Booking Fraud: Online booking fraud is a small-scale type of cyber incident where the activities which are illegitimate are done by the use of online fishing travel booking platforms. Reservations can be placed with the help of stolen credit cards, famine bookings can be made, or booking systems can be manipulated for monetary benefit.

Chapter 10

Impact of Social Media and Cyber Reputation on Educational Institutions and Tourism:

Crisis Management Strategies

Samiul Biswas
http://orcid.org/0000-0003-2542-7847
Lovely Professional University, India

ABSTRACT

In the digital age, social media serves as both a powerful asset and a potential threat to educational institutions and tourism. This study explores the dual impact of social media and cyber reputation on institutional operations, emphasizing the importance of strategic crisis management. While social media enhances branding, student engagement, alumni networking, and tourism visibility, it also exposes institutions to risks such as viral misinformation, cyberbullying, data breaches, and online defamation. To mitigate these threats, the study proposes a three-phase crisis management framework: pre-crisis planning, immediate response, and post-crisis evaluation. Key recommendations include establishing digital media policies, creating media monitoring teams, and integrating cybersecurity measures. Effective management of social media and cyber reputation is vital for preserving public trust, ensuring stakeholder confidence, and sustaining long-term institutional credibility in tourism within an increasingly interconnected digital landscape.

DOI: 10.4018/979-8-3373-5826-0.ch010

INTRODUCTION

In the 21st century, digital technology, especially social media, has impacted schools and travel a lot. There are various ways for schools and businesses in the tourism industry to talk to people, promote their brands, and talk to people who are interested in what they do. Some of these are LinkedIn, Facebook, Instagram, Twitter (now X), and YouTube. People used to use it to communicate to each other on the side, but now it's the major means for people to talk to each other, promote businesses, and find out about emergencies (Veletsianos, 2020). People in these locations construct and battle for institutional identities in real time (Manca & Ranieri, 2016).

People can instantly share information on Facebook and Twitter, two social media sites. This means that news can get around quickly, no matter if it's good or harmful. People's opinions of a business or tourism company based on how it looks and works online are called its "cyber reputation." It has become a serious issue that affects public opinion, admissions, customer choices, funding, stakeholder trust, and even policy decisions (Wiedmer, 2011; Fertik & Thompson, 2010). A single tweet, picture, or video can go viral and influence how people feel about places or groups of people all around the world (Boyd, 2014; Coombs, 2015).

People's reputations improve over time based on their actions or the actions of an organization in the past. Cyber reputation, on the other hand, is continually evolving and getting better. It is influenced by both official communication and public discourse, including student or tourist reviews, alumni and visitor anecdotes, and media criticism (Coombs, 2015; Wang & Kandampully, 2020). This means that groups and organizations can no longer tell people what they think of them. These days, students, graduates, visitors, influencers, journalists, and online groups (Kietzmann et al., 2011) all work on their reputations. This shift from one-way to two-way communication is a major shift from how public relations used to work.

Social media can be enjoyable, but it can also be risky. Cyberbullying, slander, disseminating false information, and publishing private information without permission are all common concerns in both education and tourism (Boyd, 2014; Hinduja & Patchin, 2014). In most cases, institutions don't control what happens online; instead, they adapt to it. A single viral post from a student, a disgruntled client, or a whistleblower can ruin a company's brand and make it impossible for them to make money. It can also get bad press and make people mad. In both cases, taking too long to respond or not handling replies well can make things worse, which can hurt your reputation and your finances in the long run (Coombs & Holladay, 2012).

When social media makes it impossible to recognize the boundary between business and personal life, it's also tougher to deal with an issue. It's easy to connect personal posts from students, professors, travel agents, or tourists to businesses or travel brands. People's views on some brands may shift (Veletsianos & Kimmons, 2013). It's hard to deal with companies and photos when personal expression and official representation come together, such when offensive or controversial information becomes viral. News releases and print ads don't work well for topics that change quickly on the internet these days. To handle a crisis properly, we need to be able to talk to one other online swiftly, clearly, and sensibly (Coombs, 2015; Veletsianos, 2020).

Social media conversations can cause people to become enraged and make snap decisions. This is what coordinated online boycotts and "cancel culture" are all about. The relationship between schools and tourism businesses may be negatively impacted by this type of negative news, which is awful because reputation and trust are crucial. It may also mean fewer visits, fewer students, or even litigation (Gillespie, 2018; Marwick & Boyd, 2011). Talking to people online is more important than ever because algorithms may make things more popular and feelings can spread. Having effective public relations is not enough if you want your firm to survive and grow over time. You should think about your online persona as well.

This chapter discusses how tourism and education simultaneously manage their online reputations, social media, and crisis situations. The first chapter talks about what an internet reputation is and how it affects people and businesses. Then it speaks about real-life challenges and circumstances to highlight how crucial it is to maintain a strong online presence and how easy it is to lose it. This three-step method can help groups and organizations get ready for a crisis, deal with it, and think about it after it happens. People will be better at handling problems that occurs online (Coombs, 2015; Holloway, 2012).

This part also has some fascinating plans and policy suggestions, but solely for tourism and education. Some of these are getting ready for crisis communication, which means educating spokesmen how to talk to people online and setting together teams for social media (Wang & Kandampully, 2020). The chapter also argues that schools should educate digital citizenship and media literacy and that tourists should learn how to stay safe online (Ribble, 2012; Sharma & Verma, 2019).

Lastly, businesses and groups that want to get more tourists need to know how to utilize social media securely, with a plan, and in a way that works. This is incredibly significant because digital impressions typically arrive before real ones. You need to be responsible, seek for guidance, and use digital technology the appropriate way to have a solid online reputation and be ready for anything. As the number of digital spaces grows, businesses need to take care of their online presence so they can stay strong and compete with other businesses around the world.

OBJECTIVE

To examine the influence of social media and online reputation on public perceptions of educational institutions and tourism organizations, and to develop effective crisis management strategies to protect their integrity during digital crises.

LITERATURE REVIEW

People talk to each other differently at school and on vacation now that they utilize social media. Veletsianos (2020) discusses the significance of platforms such as Facebook, Instagram, and YouTube in influencing institutional perceptions and fostering public engagement. Wiedmer (2011) contends that this technological innovation has created cyber reputation, wherein a company's online presence dramatically effects public perception, decision-making, and institutional efficacy. When people talk to other people in person, their reputations get better over time. But a person's internet reputation can change quickly because of reviews from people who don't know them, viral content, and exposure that is dependent on algorithms.

Coombs (2015) talks about the pros and cons of social media. It can help people become involved and inform others about it, but it can also be dangerous because it can spread lies and abuse. Because social media is interactive, corporations can't control stories once they are out in the open. Boyd (2014) talks on how quickly negative things may spread on social media. This underscores how crucial it is for schools and tourist destinations to have strong strategies for what to do in case of an emergency. Because things can spread so quickly online, even tiny problems can affect an institution's reputation a lot. If the school doesn't answer or gets it wrong this is very important.

Manca and Ranieri (2016) look at how digital tools have changed the way teachers teach. They focus on the pros and cons of watching what students do online. They found that everyone in the school needs to improve their tech skills: teachers, students, and managers. People behave and expect from service providers differently because of social media, say Wang and Kandampully (2020). This means you need to be more open about your business and quickly answer question.

To the talk, Holloway (2012) adds by making a list of the most important parts of a plan for how to talk to people in a disaster. He also thinks that businesses should do more than just deal with problems as they come up. Keep an eye on what people do online and be ready for anything that could happen. Make a list of the people who have a stake in the matter. Some people think that a person's online reputation is something important that they should value. Fertik and Thompson (2010) talk about this idea. They think it's a very important but hard to measure kind of wealth. It could change how schools work together, how they handle funding, and how they try to get kids from other countries to come to their schools.

Recent research suggests that digital citizenship and ethical media usage are increasingly vital skills for managing an organization's online presence. Sharma and Verma (2019) believe that students and professors often get into online fights that can ruin their reputations because they don't know enough about digital literacy and media ethics. who's why groups who engage with visitors and students are more likely to train their staff and students how to use media safely and responsibly.

The research shows that most people agree that social media offers unique chances for exposure, outreach, and involvement. But institutions also need to prepare ready in a different way. This entails being able to use technology, recognizing what values are important, being able to relate to people clearly, and being ready to respond fast in an emergency. People act differently online, the algorithms that operate platforms change, and the culture of the internet changes, therefore you should always check the rules and policies. This is very important in fields like tourism and education where how things look is very important.

Table 1. Key Scholarly Contributions on Social Media, Cyber Reputation, and Crisis Management in Education and Tourism

Author(s)	Focus Area	Key Contribution
Veletsianos (2020)	Social media in education and tourism	Highlights the transformative role of platforms like Facebook, Instagram, and YouTube in institutional communication, branding, and stakeholder engagement.
Wiedmer (2011)	Cyber reputation	Introduces the concept of cyber reputation as a critical factor influencing public perception and institutional outcomes.
Coombs (2015)	Social media risk and crisis communication	Discusses the dual nature of social media—its power to engage and its potential to spread misinformation and damage reputation.
Boyd (2014)	Virality and crisis escalation	Emphasizes how negative incidents can go viral rapidly, increasing the need for immediate and strategic crisis management.
Manca & Ranieri (2016)	Digital tools in education	Examines how digital engagement reshapes teaching, learning, and institutional communication; advocates for increased digital competence.
Wang & Kandampully (2020)	Social media in tourism	Shows how real-time engagement, transparency, and consumer interaction redefine service expectations and brand storytelling.
Holloway (2012)	Crisis management framework	Proposes structured communication plans, including scenario planning and digital monitoring, for effective crisis response.

continued on following page

Table 1. Continued

Author(s)	Focus Area	Key Contribution
Fertik & Thompson (2010)	Strategic value of cyber reputation	Argue that digital reputation is a form of institutional capital influencing partnerships, recruitment, and credibility.
Sharma & Verma (2019)	Digital literacy and ethical behaviour	Recommend integrating media literacy into education to manage reputational risks posed by students' and staff's online behaviour.

CONCEPTUAL FRAMEWORK

Figure 1. Conceptual framework showing the relationship among social media, cyber reputation, institutional/tourism perception, crisis trigger, and crisis management phases.

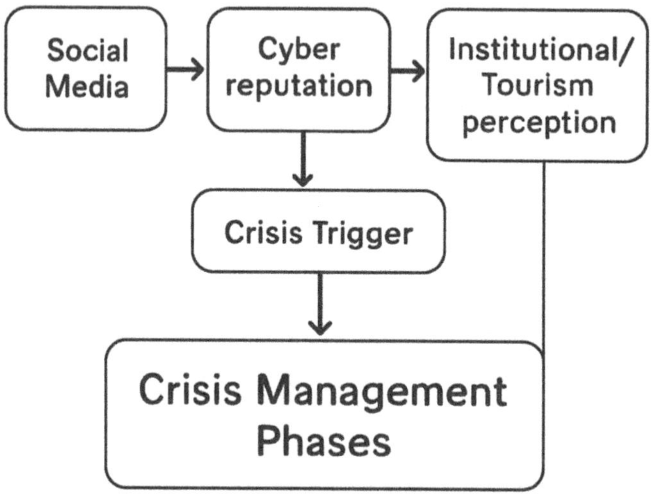

IS SOCIAL MEDIA BENEFICIAL OR HARMFUL FOR TRAVEL AND SCHOOLS?

For schools and the travel industry, social media may be both beneficial and negative. It includes a lot of wonderful tools for getting people to know you, getting them engaged, and developing a brand. But technology poses a lot of huge difficulties, especially when people don't use it in a sensible or moral way (Wang

& Kandampully, 2020). Social media has had a stronger impact than ever before because both businesses depend on trust, reputation, and communication.

Schools and businesses in the tourism industry may now show the world who they are in ways that were never possible before. Schools, colleges, universities, and tourist locations can effectively show off their distinctive beliefs, cultures, offerings, and success stories by routinely and creatively posting digital content (Wang & Kandampully, 2020). Videos that show off student life or campus infrastructure, posts that show off staff achievements, and travel reels that show off tourist spots all make a website more interesting.

People are more inclined to keep in touch and be honest when they can communicate to each other on Facebook, Instagram, X (previously Twitter), and WhatsApp in real time. It makes it easy for colleges and institutions to talk to one other about tests, events, admissions, and grades. Tourism companies should also tell about bargains that are only good at specific times of the year, safety restrictions, and what their consumers think of their services. These posts will make both new and old guests happy. This entertaining manner of talking to people creates trust and gets students, alumni, tourists, families, and local communities involved (Manca & Ranieri, 2016).

People can also feel better about themselves when they use social media. People might just talk about and enjoy things like school rankings, student accomplishments, teacher research publications, or the wonderful moments they had at school. For example, former students can stay in touch through LinkedIn groups, assist their schools thrive, or be a mentor to other students. Review services like TripAdvisor, Google Reviews, and the comments sections of Airbnb can help businesses by giving them important feedback. This input can help them get better and change the opinions of others who are thinking about going to school or visiting.

But social media can be bad, especially if people don't use it the right way or for the wrong reasons. It's not good to share information that isn't true or is misleading. Wang and Kandampully (2020) say that false or unverified information about admissions, test dates, teacher behaviour, tourist safety, or service quality can hurt a school or business's reputation. When people see wrong information online, they get mad, complain, or break the rules.

Another big problem is giving out personal or private information without asking first. If someone shares test papers or videos from the classroom without permission, they could get in a lot of trouble with the law and with their morals (Manca & Ranieri, 2016). In the tourism industry, similar breaches of guest data, internal staff communication, or payment records can violate privacy, break data protection laws, and put businesses at risk of lawsuits or fines.

Kids can fight, bully, say racist things, or complain about tourists, and professionals can act badly online, and it spreads quickly. They can also lie and make things worse. If these links aren't addressed promptly and well, they could affect the reputation of the school or travel service provider as a whole (Hinduja & Patchin, 2014). For example, one negative picture, tweet, or video might make a lot of people angry, which could cause difficulties in the news, government investigations, or demands for boycotts.

CYBER REPUTATION IN EDUCATIONAL INSTITUTIONS AND TOURISM

Cybersecurity threats make things a lot less safe. Hackers are getting into hotel reservation systems, school databases, and university research portals more and more often. These kinds of breaches not only hurt businesses, but they also take personal or financial information. After that, businesses may have to deal with lawsuits, government investigations, and a lot of people who want the business to lose faith in it.

Schools and businesses in the tourism industry can use social media to connect with each other and market themselves, but they need to be careful, responsible, and plan ahead. You need to do things to make sure you get the most out of social media and stay safe. This means that there should be clear rules for how to talk to each other online, what to do in an emergency, and a promise to be honest online. Students and staff should also get training on a regular basis. These companies need to be smart and fair in order to keep doing well in a digital world that is changing quickly.

Institutions must also understand that interacting with people online is no longer a choice or a minor issue; it is now a significant component of their identity and the level of trust stakeholders place in them. Companies of all sizes should pay attention to how quickly and extensively social media is expanding these days, since most individuals meet new people online. Not only at work, but also in the whole community, which includes students, professors, travellers, alumni, and service workers, schools and tourism groups need to keep getting better at using technology.

It's clear that digital connections need to be real, honest, and flexible. When something goes wrong, stakeholders should get prompt answers, honest communication, and true responsibility. Over time, schools that don't achieve these standards could lose students, money, clients, or faith, and their reputation could suffer.

In this case, it's very important to promote a culture of responsible digital citizenship. Companies shouldn't teach stakeholders about digital ethics and media literacy. Instead, they should provide them the tools they need to be outstanding brand champions instead of someone who potentially ruin the company's reputation. Moving from reactive control to proactive empowerment is a huge step toward making online communities safer.

Lastly, schools and other organizations need to stay up with how digital technologies and online cultures are changing. Following the rules, keeping an eye on digital traces, and working with experts in digital communication, public relations, and cybersecurity will be very crucial. The education and tourism industries can turn social media into a long-term asset that strengthens community ties, increases global visibility, and reinforces the values they want to uphold by using strategic foresight, making policies that include everyone, and acting ethically.

Digital or cyber reputation is what people think about a business or group based on how it looks and works online. Cyber reputation is particularly essential these days because more and more individuals are meeting new people online for the first time. This is especially true for jobs like teaching and tourism, where people need to trust, believe in, and see them. There are a lot of digital touchpoints that help build this reputation, such as institutional websites, social media activity, search engine results, online reviews, interactions with stakeholders, faculty or staff behaviour in online spaces, and media coverage (Wiedmer, 2011; Fertik & Thompson, 2010).

People who go to school, parents, instructors, lawmakers, and even employers all make decisions about the school based on its internet reputation. Students do more than just go to school or look at pamphlets these days. They don't attend to school in person or look at stuff like brochures. They don't utilize things like test scores or graduation rates to figure out how good a school is. Instead, they look at factors like student reviews, instructor profiles, how well-known their research is, and reviews on sites like Quora or Reddit. Parents utilize digital openness to find out if a school is safe, has excellent policies, and teaches well. This is especially true if the parents are from a different country. The way people think about a university online also affects how it hires faculty and works with other schools. A website that isn't up to date or a digital war that isn't over yet can make good applicants not want to apply.

People also choose to go somewhere based on how easy it is to find online. Many people look at hotel reviews, travel blogs, YouTube vlogs, Instagram pictures, and posts from people they follow before they decide where to go on vacation. A bad story on social media about how safe it is, how clean it is, how good the service is, or how rude people are could keep a lot of people from going. A good story about the same thing, on the other hand, can make a lot of people want to know more. People are more interested in what other travellers say about their trips than in official travel ads because trips are becoming more personalized and based on experiences.

Their online name has an effect on how much they sell in both cases. If you are well known online in the education field, you can get more students, work with schools in other countries, make more money, get study grants, get gifts from former students, and get sponsors. More bookings, endorsements from well-known brands, repeat visits, and links to foreign sites like Booking.com or Airbnb could all be good for the tourism business. But if you have a bad name online, you could lose all of these advantages very quickly. It's also hard to get back a bad name.

Your internet reputation isn't fixed; it shifts all the time and can be switched around by sudden events. If you don't handle a complaint or bad post well, it could ruin years of work you put into your image. What if a teacher is mean, there is a fight on campus, or a guest has a bad experience and posts about it on social media? There could be a lot of hashtags, complaints, and even protests online. "Cancel culture" is when people online attack famous people or groups after saying bad things about them or thinking they have flaws. It is possible for this to happen even if there isn't enough proof.

People and groups that spend a lot of time online are usually better at figuring things out. People are more inclined to help and understand organizations when they need it if they have been honest and open online in the past. People who are interested in these groups trust them and give them the benefit of the doubt. This helps them get well quickly and doesn't tarnish their reputation as much when things go wrong.

Cyber photographs have a huge effect on the law, morals, and the government. Data breaches, faculty misconduct, plagiarism, discrimination, and service failures are all examples of viral events that could compel the government take action, lead to legal proceedings, or have regulators look more closely at the situation (Coombs, 2015). For instance, education boards or accrediting bodies might check into schools, and booking sites in other countries might place tourism enterprises on a blacklist or pull them off the list. The GDPR in Europe and India's Digital Personal Data Protection Act imply that businesses are now in responsible of how they use technology and protect customer data.

Schools and businesses that cater to visitors need to do more to preserve their internet reputations in order to solve these enormous concerns. This is what it means We are putting together a group of digital communicators whose job it is to watch what people do online, judge it, and respond to it. I use tools like Google Alerts, Social Mention, and Brand24 to check my internet presence and images every month. We can stop incorrect information and tales that grow out of hand by making it easier for individuals to complain. We are making it clear how students, workers, and business partners should use social media. We wish to share good news via talking to the media, meeting notable individuals, and using networks of former students. We're adding seminars and training for staff on digital citizenship and media literacy to assist people be more responsible online.

Finally, a company's cyber reputation is now a vital aspect of its strategy that is needed for its success, the trust of its stakeholders, and the brand's identity. In a world where everything is digital and everyone is linked; tourism and education groups need to do more than merely preserve their online reputations. They also need to improve it. You can't merely talk to do this. You should know how to communicate to lawyers, do public relations, be honest, use technology, and get involved in your community. Using digital tools that are consistent, real, and responsible is the only way for businesses to build strong online identities that can handle the problems of today's online world.

CRISIS MANAGEMENT FRAMEWORK FOR EDUCATIONAL INSTITUTIONS AND TOURISM

When everything is linked, problems with social media can emerge rapidly and without warning. They can harm the way schools and tourism businesses do business, as well as their reputations and integrity. Both industries care a lot about their reputations, so businesses need to have a full crisis management plan that covers all three main parts of crisis management: before, during, and after the crisis (Coombs, 2015; Wang and Kandampully, 2020).

Pre-Crisis Phase: Prevention and Preparedness

You should be ready for a problem and do everything you can to keep it from happening. It's all about being ready for calamities and stopping them before they happen. First, schools and tourist attractions need to create clear guidelines about how to use social media and other digital forms of communication that everyone can comprehend. You should know what sort of behaviour is allowed online, what kind of content is moral, what the regulations are for privacy, and what happens if you break them. Everyone who works at, goes to, or visits the school should know how to observe these rules (Coombs, 2015).

One of the most important things to do right now is to get together with other individuals to mend and monitor over digital problems. The group should use social listening platforms like Hootsuite, Mention, or Brand watch to keep an eye on student or tourist groups, chats, hashtags, reviews, and digital news sites. If businesses can notice indicators of anger, complaints, or inaccurate information early on, they can fix problems before they get worse.

When things don't go as planned, institutions need to learn how to talk to people. People should talk about things like who is in charge of what, how to gain permission, how to talk to each other, how to establish contact lists, and who should speak for the group. They should undertake practice drills or simulations on a regular basis to make sure everyone is ready and to teach teams how to act swiftly. If people are ready for things to go wrong, such a data leak, a viral complaint, or a service breakdown, they might be able to keep calm and not cause delays.

Crisis Phase: React and Keep Things Under Control

The institution falls into the active crisis phase as soon as a crisis starts. The most critical things to accomplish here are to move rapidly, speak properly, and do as little harm as possible. If you make a mistake, owning up to it right away demonstrates that you are responsible and helps people trust you. If you don't answer quickly away or deny something, people may become more sceptical, receive more media attention, and ruin your reputation even worse (Holloway, 2012).

Institutions should give out regular updates that are based on facts and use official channels including press releases, verified social media accounts, institutional websites, and direct email. Messages should be prepared in a style that is appropriate for the individuals who will read them, such as students, parents, staff, tourists, the media, and business partners from foreign nations. The core principle should still be the same, though.

Different parts of the company need to work together when something goes wrong. People who work in public relations get messages from people who don't work for the company. If you work in IT, you need the internet or tech to get things fixed. Talk to someone in the administration or guest services office if you're having issues. To keep people honest and from bothering each other, lawyers need to watch out for them. Tourists, students, and business partners from other countries should feel welcome at schools and companies that work with people from other countries. These places should know about cultural differences.

Another thing that affects where people go is how simple it is to find online. Before choosing where to go on vacation, a lot of people read hotel reviews, travel blogs, YouTube vlogs, Instagram photos, and posts from people they follow. Many people might not go if they read a bad post on social media about how safe, clean, helpful, or rude the staff is. A good story, on the other hand, can get people interested in learning more. Travel ads aren't as interesting to people as what other travellers have to say about their trips. This is because trips are becoming more specific and based on experiences.

In either case, their online name changes how much they sell. You can get more students, work with schools in other countries, make more money, get study grants, get gifts from past students, and get sponsors if you are well known in the field of education online. There could be more bookings, repeat visits, and links to foreign sites like Booking.com or Airbnb, all of which are good for the tourist business. You could lose all of these benefits very quickly, though, if you have a bad name online. Also, a bad name is hard to get back.

Post Crisis Phase: Recovery and Institutional Learning

Your image on the internet isn't set in stone; it changes all the time and can be shattered by sudden events. An angry customer or bad review could ruin years of work you put into your image if you don't handle it well. If a teacher is mean, there's a fight on campus, or a guest has a bad time and talks about it on social media, what should be done? There might be a lot of concerns, hashtags, and even protests on the web. There is something called "cancel culture" where people attack well-known people or groups online after saying bad things about them or believing they are flawed. Even though there isn't enough proof, this could happen.

The texts were sent to certain people, but did they really get them? Did you forget to include any significant teams of people? What did digital sites do when they were full? People who have a stake in the matter should be asked what they think. This includes students, parents, graduates, tourists, and business partners from other countries. You can use polls, forms, or town halls to find out what people think. By being honest, people can find problems, fix trust issues, and figure out how to do better next time (Manca and Ranieri, 2016).

The study shows that we need to change how we handle crises. It's possible that you need to change the rules, improve the technology, and teach the staff more. Institutions should also think about telling everyone what they've learned and what they're going to do to make sure it doesn't happen again.

It's important for schools that offer educational tourism or programs with other countries to get back in touch with their foreign advisors, embassies, host schools, and cultural exchange groups. They might trust them more if the school keeps an eye on them. People may feel safer, more professional, and more ready for the world if this is done. The school may also look better.

It is easy for a business to fix problems with their online presence or image if they have a good plan for what to do in a crisis. For this reason, you should always be ready, before, during, and after the post. Anyone from anywhere in the world can leave a review. People who work together to get back on their feet, be open with each other, and be proactive about digital governance are more likely to have a better image, more trust from stakeholders, and a stronger sense of resilience when they come out of a crisis.

RESULTS AND DISCUSSIONS

The results of this study show that social media has a big and changing effect on how people in the tourism and education sectors see institutions and the public. This material talks about five main principles that are based on research, case studies, and theories. These include the dual potential of social media, the growing strategic importance of cyber reputation, the urgent need for organized crisis management protocols, the impact of regional and cultural factors, and the rise of digital citizenship and ethics as institutional priorities.

Schools and tourism companies have modified the way they speak to people since social media became a part of their professions. People utilize Facebook, Instagram, LinkedIn, X (previously Twitter), and YouTube to keep up with business news, discuss their triumphs, market their programs, and meet new people. If tourism businesses want to stay relevant and competitive, they need to be able to talk to one other online in real time. This is especially true for firms that rely on seasonal clients and their brand. People can talk to each other directly on social media, without having to go through traditional gatekeepers like newspapers or travel businesses. This can help schools and other groups send messages to more people and make it easier for people to get messages from schools and other groups.

However, the instruments that assist groups in telling their tales may also work against them. Groups should use caution while engaging in these activities since they may present opportunities for expansion and exposure. People claimed that data breaches, poor user-generated material, viral schemes, and misleading information might all have negative consequences. Additionally, because of the way social media operates, inflammatory or contentious tales can spread swiftly—often more quickly than official news or updates. This type of issue is more common in groups without defined guidelines, ongoing oversight, or contingency preparations. People are more prone to have false information shared about them in public, have their stories misinterpreted, or have their reputations harmed.

The study discovered that your internet reputation has a huge impact on how well you do at school and on vacation. People used to communicate to each other in person to make themselves look better. Cyber reputation, on the other hand, changes swiftly and is dependent on how people act online. If you want to gain more students, tourists, staff, money, or collaborate with other countries, you need to have a strong web presence right now. When students are trying to determine whether to go to school or travel, they usually check at the school's website first and sometimes only.

In the future, individuals who are interested in going to college or traveling will need to have a broad understanding of computers and the internet. The interviews and the analysis of the relevant literature both demonstrated this. This includes the opinions of their friends and other significant people in their lives, as well as reviews found on the internet and the amount of time they spend on social media. The reputation of an individual can be damaged by a number of factors, including events that take place or the opinions and beliefs of other people. In addition, the images that are posted online have a significant impact on the number of alumni who participate, the level of trust that contributors have, and the dependability of partners. As a result of this, a great number of companies make use of various technologies in order to monitor their reputation and plan how they will market their brand. More people will trust you, and they will continue to be with you. People have also observed that businesses that have conducted themselves in an honest manner on the internet in the past have a "reputational cushion" that makes it easier for them to deal with issues. Individuals have faith in those businesses, which is the reason behind this

Many companies arc aware that they must have an online presence; yet, they are not prepared for the challenges that can be brought about by social media. It is possible that negative events will take place, such as data breaches, complaints that go viral, and public backlash following posts that are perceived to be contentious, if individuals do not respond promptly, if messages are not clear, or if there are no preparations in place for dealing with crises. When it came to digital strategy, businesses that lacked a well-defined plan would frequently wait until something negative occurred before taking any action to prevent it. When this happened, people's interest in the damage rounds decreased because they took longer to complete overall.

Before, during, and after the crisis, we used the three-step crisis management strategy. This plan was utilized in both real life and fake life occurrences. According to the findings of the study, businesses were more effective at handling crises and repairing their reputations when they had clear policies, digital reaction teams, spokespeople who had been educated to communicate with the media, and the ability to rehearse. In many cases, individuals who were unable to effectively collaborate with others or lead in a digital manner were found to have violated the law, garnered a great deal of attention from the media, and lost the trust of stakeholders. People have a tendency to believe that teams do not get along. In situations where there were issues with technology or occupations that were unclear, it was more difficult for people to communicate with one another. It was abundantly evident that teams need to collaborate with one another, that emergency plans are essential, and that all administrative staff members need to continue their education on digital risk.

The data also demonstrates that the influence of social media on businesses might differ depending on the location of the firm as well as the culture that the business originates from. There was a higher likelihood of internet scandals occurring in schools in India due to the fact that a greater number of people in Indian towns had smartphones, the internet, and utilized technology in the classroom. People in the region who are concerned about student groups, the media, and civil society all keep a careful eye on these organizations. On the other side, tourism businesses located in geographically isolated or economically disadvantaged regions are unable to promptly address online complaints or misleading information because they lack the appropriate tools, sufficient staff, or a social media presence that is sufficiently established.

People's backgrounds in terms of culture have a significant impact on the degree to which they comprehend new information. It is important to keep in mind that something that may be humorous or casual to some people in one culture or country may not be humorous or casual to other people. It is necessary for businesses that are interested in collaborating with individuals from different nations to discover methods that will not be detrimental to their reputations. There are also variations in the manner in which catastrophes are documented and the responses that people have to them, depending on factors such as the language, caste, or gender of the individuals involved, as well as the events and languages that are prevalent in the region.

Lastly, the sessions demonstrated that both the people who work for institutions and the groups they work for as a whole need to learn more about digital citizenship and ethics. It's incredibly crucial to create a culture of ethical digital participation since what students, graduates, tourists, staff, and even casual spectators put online can affect how other people regard a school or institution. A lot of people said that schools should teach students how to stay safe online. They should not only write legislation, but they should also get involved, teach, and set a positive example.

Everyone who took part in the study thought it was very important for youngsters to learn about digital ethics and how to utilize the media at school, in job training programs, and when they talk to people in the community. They will learn how to tell if something they see online is accurate, how to identify digital footprints, how to fight cyberbullying, how to keep their personal information safe, and how to be nice to people online. People assumed that groups that advocate moral behaviour online will not only preserve their own reputations, but also make the internet a better place for everyone. Some schools have also begun to create useful digital records that demonstrate things like how the community is involved, how staff members have assisted, how kids have done well, or how tourism could be better. This is done to help people who desire to write stories online.

This means that a business needs to know how to handle its online presence, social media, and emergencies. It's not just a part of a business; it's often the most important and obvious part. In today's digital world, there are both risks and opportunities. Businesses need to know how digital impact works, spend money to get ready, and be honest and do the right thing to gain trust.

This study shows that businesses and schools that deal with tourists need to quickly and carefully think about how they use digital tools, especially social media. It also has suggestions for how to make laws better. The digital world is getting bigger, faster, and harder to deal with. Companies need to change how they deal with emergencies, talk to each other, and work with the government. More and more people are using the same websites to help or hurt their identities. Because of this, groups and schools need to be ready for anything that could go wrong with their computer.

There should be a clear policy for how to use digital communication at work. This policy should make it clear what employees can and can't do, how to respond, how to protect data, and what will happen if they break the rules. This kind of rule shouldn't be in place for long or come from the top. Students, professors, staff, lawyers, communication experts, and IT experts should all look at it and change it all the time. Being honest makes sure it's good and follows the rules. It also makes people think that everyone is responsible for keeping online spaces safe.

For this to operate, schools need to set up distinct committees for digital governance or crisis response that will be in charge of the complete school year or tourism year. People on these teams should know a lot about a lot of various topics, such law, communication, public relations, IT, student support services, and international affairs (if the institution is connected to the rest of the world). Their major duty should be to use real-time tools to keep an eye on what's going on online, locate and research new dangers, deal with how people act during a crisis, and complete reviews after the event. These organizations should also be able to make choices immediately away, without all the red tape that slows things down and makes them worse.

Having a plan for handling a crisis is just as important as being prepared, responding promptly, and considering what transpired after the crisis. There should always be a strategy in place for how to approach individuals in institutions who are struggling. Examples of appropriate public speech, guidelines for workplace communication, what to do in the event of an emergency, and contact information for news or emergencies should all be included. By conducting frequent simulations or "mock crisis drills," businesses can assess their readiness and develop the trust and collaboration necessary to handle issues when they arise. Things won't become worse if you know who is speaking, what they are saying, and when they are saying it.

It's also crucial to keep in mind that all of your children should be able to utilize and comprehend technology. Regular training through orientation courses, workshops, and other programs should be provided to instructors, office workers, tourists, and students. In these classes, children should learn how to behave on social media, how to handle cyberbullying, how to protect their data, and how to be honest. Because the threats associated with the internet are constantly evolving, you should repeat this type of preparation. It should always teach you something fresh. Media literacy should also be taught in schools, particularly to those who wish to pursue careers in communication, business, service, or education. People can avoid issues and enhance their reputations without even trying if they are taught how to be wise and responsible online.

It's not simply that schools and tourism firms don't get along that they have a poor online reputation. Because of this, people will remember you for a very long time. It affects things like your enrolment, relationships, and how others see you. To monitor your online presence, you can utilize media tracking services, Google

Alerts, or software that looks at people's sentiments. This can assist you in monitoring your reputation over time, identifying negative behaviours, and determining when others are mentioning you. Not only can these audits help us address issues, but they can also facilitate communication, make things easier, and ensure that we are better engaging the public.

Rules should be developed with input from local and national tourist and education organizations. Everyone must follow their instructions. The government and organizations that accredit schools and other organizations should mandate that they educate their pupils about internet safety, social media policies, and any issues they may have had in the past with negative things occurring online. Everyone in the organization could do things correctly if there were guidelines for protecting online identities and digital risk assessments were required to ensure the quality of the work. More adjustments could be made to the amount of public funds and assistance provided, particularly to organizations that assist the underprivileged or vulnerable.

Regulators should also consider how various locations and technological platforms affect people's ability to use the internet. To effectively engage in the digital ecosystem, organizations operating in rural or isolated places could require modifications to their physical space, training materials in a particular language, or technical assistance. These groups, particularly those with limited resources and personnel, may benefit from the establishment of consortium-based crisis response networks, public-private partnerships, or centralized digital training canter.

As a last resort, the organization ought to consider establishing digital ethics as a long-term objective. Businesses must not only address the issue but also educate individuals on appropriate, helpful, and courteous technology use. By living this lifestyle yourself, you can model it for others. By sharing positive digital stories, participating in civic discussions, endorsing student-led digital campaigns, or simply being kind and forthright when they receive criticism, institutions can help to make online discussions more civil and courteous.

The last issue is that the concepts aren't only about modifying technology; they also propose that schools and hotels should use the internet in a totally different way. It's not simply about lousy communication or short-term variances in how individuals see things. It's crucial to be trustworthy, able to bounce back, and keep institutions alive in a world where pixels and platforms often define how people view things. By planning for everything from how to handle social media to how to protect their online reputation to being ready for a disaster, businesses can keep their identity in the future and make the internet a better place for everyone.

CONCLUSION

These days, when everything is connected online, how a school or tourism group seems online is incredibly significant, maybe even more so than how outstanding its services or academics are. People may view, comment about, and remember your brand in many different ways on social media. It might make your gains a lot bigger or start a calamity right now. Because online platforms are easy to get to, happen in real time, and are often hard to foresee, institutions' reputations are no longer reliant simply on official stories. Instead, they are built by a collection of influential people from all over the world, including students, graduates, tourists, critics, and others.

In order to effectively respond to disasters, the tourism and education industries need to develop comprehensive, long-term, and proactive strategies that involve multiple disciplines. These plans ought to be focused on being truthful, prompt in responding, and courteous while using the internet. It is necessary for you to have knowledge of other nations, to be proficient with computers, to have the ability to communicate with people in a short amount of time, and to be able to get along with individuals from a variety of backgrounds. Today, governments are required to devise strategies for how to communicate with the general public, examine their public image on a regular basis, and recruit professionals to work on digital teams.

Children, teachers, workers, and others who provide services should all be taught how to use technology in a secure manner so that they can become responsible digital citizens. These abilities can assist groups of people in learning how to utilize the internet in a manner that is both secure and intelligent. They also prevent the spread of misinformation and encourage conversation that is courteous and beneficial. Nothing that people say on the internet should be taken seriously by educational institutions. It would be more beneficial for them to purchase equipment that can handle the randomness of online chats and assist individuals in developing trust in one another.

These findings also demonstrate that a company can improve its appearance by demonstrating that it is responsible, welcoming, and open to transitioning. Businesses have the potential to gain a great deal of knowledge and improve their performance if they are able to handle unexpected events. By incorporating digital ethics into their policies, companies may safeguard their identities while also demonstrating that they are robust, trustworthy, and forward-thinking leaders in their industry. People can also use them to communicate with one another and experiment with new things.

It is true that the internet has both positive and negative aspects. A greater number of connections and challenging tasks are available in the world. When it comes to being successful, businesses and organizations will understand the significance of being online, being prepared for everything, and being able to make effective use of social media.

REFERENCES

Boyd, D. (2014). *It's complicated: The social lives of networked teens*. Yale University Press.

Coombs, W. T. (2015). *Ongoing crisis communication: Planning, managing, and responding* (4th ed.). SAGE Publications.

Coombs, W. T., & Holladay, S. J. (2012). *The handbook of crisis communication*. Wiley-Blackwell.

Fertik, M., & Thompson, D. (2010). *Wild West 2.0: How to protect and restore your online reputation on the untamed social frontier*. AMACOM.

Gillespie, T. (2018). *Custodians of the Internet: Platforms, content moderation, and the hidden decisions that shape social media*. Yale University Press.

Hinduja, S., & Patchin, J. W. (2014). *Cyberbullying: Identification, prevention, and response*. Cyberbullying Research Center.

Holloway, J. (2012). Crisis communication in the digital age: Social media's role in crisis communication. *Journal of Business Continuity & Emergency Planning*, *6*(1), 84–92. PMID: 22948108

Kietzmann, J. H., Hermkens, K., McCarthy, I. P., & Silvestre, B. S. (2011). Social media? Get serious! Understanding the functional building blocks of social media. *Business Horizons*, *54*(3), 241–251. DOI: 10.1016/j.bushor.2011.01.005

Manca, S., & Ranieri, M. (2016). Facebook and the others: Potentials and obstacles of social media for teaching in higher education. *Computers & Education*, *95*, 216–230. DOI: 10.1016/j.compedu.2016.01.012

Marwick, A. E., & Boyd, D. (2011). To see and be seen: Celebrity practice on Twitter. *Convergence (London)*, *17*(2), 139–158. DOI: 10.1177/1354856510394539

Ribble, M. (2012). *Digital citizenship in schools: Nine elements all students should know* (3rd ed.). ISTE.

Sharma, P., & Verma, R. (2019). Digital literacy and ethical practices among university students: A study of online behaviour and institutional reputation. *Journal of Media and Communication Studies*, *11*(4), 35–45. DOI: 10.5897/JMCS2019.0641

Sharma, R., & Verma, S. (2019). Digital literacy and online behavior: A pedagogical approach for ethics in the digital age. *Journal of Education and Learning*, *8*(4), 100–109.

Veletsianos, G. (2020). *Learning online: The student experience*. Johns Hopkins University Press. DOI: 10.1353/book.73824

Veletsianos, G., & Kimmons, R. (2013). Scholars and faculty members' lived experiences in online social networks. *The Internet and Higher Education*, *16*, 43–50. DOI: 10.1016/j.iheduc.2012.01.004

Wang, Y., & Kandampully, J. (2020). Building service brand equity through social media in tourism and hospitality: The role of digital engagement. *Journal of Services Marketing*, *34*(4), 463–472. DOI: 10.1108/JOSM-11-2019-0342

Wiedmer, T. (2011). The world of cyber reputation: Avoiding the pitfalls. *Delta Kappa Gamma Bulletin*, *77*(3), 24–27.

Wiedmer, T. (2011). The role of social media in shaping public perception of institutions. *Journal of Educational Administration*, *49*(4), 386–410. DOI: 10.1108/09578231111146416

Chapter 11
Protecting Tourist Data in Online Booking Platforms:
Challenges and Solutions

Jyoti Prakash
http://orcid.org/0000-0002-7892-6052
Institute of Technology and Management, Dehradun, India

Urvashi Kumari
http://orcid.org/0009-0002-6542-6726
Sushant University, India

Pooja Malhotra
Galgotias University, India

Minakshi Memoria
King Khalid University, Abha, Saudi Arabia

ABSTRACT

Online booking platforms have become integral to modern tourism, offering convenience and exposing travellers to significant cybersecurity risks. Sensitive data such as personal details, payment credentials, and travel itineraries are increasingly vulnerable to threats like phishing, ransomware, data breaches, and insider misuse. Protecting tourist data requires a multi-layered approach, combining secure encryption protocols, blockchain-based transaction verification, and AI-driven threat detection systems. Strong authentication mechanisms, such as biometrics and two-factor authentication, further enhance security and reduce fraud. However, challenges persist in balancing user convenience with robust safeguards, ensuring

DOI: 10.4018/979-8-3373-5826-0.ch011

compliance with global data protection regulations, and managing evolving threats in a highly digitalised tourism ecosystem. This chapter explores the key vulnerabilities of online booking systems, evaluates current protective strategies, and suggests sustainable solutions for safeguarding tourist trust.

INTRODUCTION

In the past two decades, internet booking platforms have dominated worldwide travel and hospitality industries. These platforms—ranging from global online travel agencies (OTAs) such as Booking.com and Expedia to region-specific portals and direct booking engines of hotels and airlines—enable tourists to conveniently plan, book, and manage their trips (Talwar et al., 2020). The increasing reliance on digital channels, accelerated further by the COVID-19 pandemic, has shifted consumer behavior toward contactless, real-time, and mobile-friendly booking solutions (Gretzel et al., 2020). However, this digital convenience comes with heightened risks, particularly regarding the protection of sensitive tourist data, including personally identifiable information (PII), payment credentials, travel preferences, and geolocation details.

RISE OF ONLINE BOOKING PLATFORMS

By democratizing travel services, internet booking platforms have transformed tourism. Tourists may compare costs, read reviews, and make educated judgments on these platforms, increasing transparency and competition (Zeqiri et al., 2025). According to Louati et al. (2024), personalization has been further improved with the use of AI, ML, and big data analytics, which allow for the customization of offers to specific visitors according to their digital footprints. This customization enhances the user experience and boosts firms' income, but it also gathers and processes a lot of data, which raises worries about data abuse and spying.

Tourism is a data-intensive sector: every online transaction generates vast amounts of personal and financial information. Booking a hotel room or a flight typically requires details such as name, email address, passport information, credit card numbers, and even biometric identifiers when integrated with advanced authentication systems (Fan et al., 2022). This makes online booking platforms lucrative targets for cybercriminals, who exploit vulnerabilities to access and monetize stolen data.

NATURE OF TOURIST DATA AND ITS VALUE

Tourist data is not merely transactional but also contextual and behavioural. Beyond basic PII, online platforms track user behaviour, including search history, travel preferences, loyalty program participation, and spending habits. Combined with geolocation data from mobile devices, these insights provide comprehensive digital profiles of tourists (Li et al., 2018). Such data is valuable not only for enhancing customer experiences but also for secondary uses like targeted advertising, cross-selling, and strategic planning by destination management organizations (DMOs).

Issues of ownership, privacy, and ethical usage have been brought to light by the high digital economy value of visitor data. According to Karadayi-Usta (2024), the data breach that occurred at Marriott International in 2018 exposed the personal information of over 500 million visitors. This individual's information included credit card details and passport numbers. These kinds of instances bring to light the absolute need of implementing stringent data security procedures within the tourist industry.

CYBERSECURITY THREAT LANDSCAPE IN ONLINE TOURISM PLATFORMS

A broad variety of cybersecurity risks have emerged as a result of the fast digitalization of the tourist industry. Several different types of cyberattacks may be launched against online booking systems, including the following methods:

1. **Data Breaches:** Hackers exploit vulnerabilities to gain unauthorized access to sensitive customer data.
2. **Phishing Attacks:** Cybercriminals use fake booking emails or websites to steal user credentials (Al-Khouri, 2012).
3. **Ransomware:** Critical booking systems are locked down until a ransom is paid, disrupting operations and damaging trust.
4. **Insider Threats:** Employees with access to customer databases may misuse or leak information.
5. **Third-Party Risks:** Integrations with payment gateways and marketing partners increase vulnerabilities if those systems are compromised.

The interconnectedness of global tourism platforms amplifies these risks, as one breach in a partner system can cascade across the entire value chain (Khan et al., 2021).

REGULATORY AND ETHICAL CONSIDERATIONS

In light of these threats, regulatory agencies and governments have implemented robust data protection systems. According to Buhalis and Sinarta (2019), a significant number of tourist operators, particularly small and medium-sized firms (SMEs), have difficulties in complying with these rules owing to a lack of resource availability, both financially and technically.

Ethical concerns further complicate the landscape. Tourists often provide personal data without fully understanding how it will be used or stored. Issues of informed consent, algorithmic bias in personalized recommendations, and the commodification of personal data underscore the tension between technological advancement and consumer rights (Milano et al., 2021).

IMPORTANCE OF TRUST IN TOURISM PLATFORMS

Trust is a fundamental determinant of consumer behavior in online tourism. Tourists are less likely to book through platforms they perceive as insecure or untrustworthy (Amaro & Duarte, 2015). Protecting tourists' information is, then, crucial for staying competitive and for meeting regulatory requirements. Customers are more likely to trust and remain loyal to a brand that has strong data protection measures, clear privacy policies, and obvious security features (Cheung & To, 2017).

Trust also extends to destination branding. A secure digital environment reassures international tourists, particularly those from regions with high data protection awareness, such as Europe and North America. Conversely, recurring data breaches can tarnish a destination's reputation, leading to long-term declines in arrivals and revenue.

RESEARCH GAP AND RATIONALE FOR THE STUDY

Although literature on cybersecurity and e-commerce are abundant, research specifically addressing tourist data protection in online booking platforms remains fragmented. The majority of research ignores the specific characteristics of tourist data, such as its international scope, integration with various stakeholders, and increased sensitivity as a result of travel documentation, in favour of more general discussions of cybersecurity or e-commerce (Mishra et al., 2022). According to Bratić et al. (2025), this study intends to address the lack of research in the field by offering a thorough examination of the problems and potential solutions related to safeguarding tourist data. It does this by combining findings from studies on tourism.

OBJECTIVES OF THE CHAPTER

This chapter seeks to:

1. Examine the nature and value of tourist data in online booking platforms.
2. Analyze the cybersecurity threat landscape specific to the tourism sector.
3. Evaluate regulatory frameworks and ethical considerations in data protection.
4. Explore technological and managerial solutions to safeguard tourist data.
5. Provide recommendations for tourism stakeholders to build resilient and trustworthy booking ecosystems.

PROBLEM STATEMENT

With the advent of easy-to-use internet booking systems, the travel business has seen a dramatic shift, catering to the needs of travellers all over the world. These platforms act as digital intermediaries that connect travellers with airlines, hotels, tour operators, and ancillary service providers. The convenience of instant bookings, competitive pricing, and personalized recommendations has driven their popularity, making them central to the digital tourism ecosystem (Buhalis & Law, 2008). On the other hand, this technological innovation has simultaneously brought forth a number of complicated difficulties with regard to the safeguarding of tourists data.

The core problem lies in the dual nature of tourist data. On one hand, data is the lifeblood of online booking platforms, enabling personalization, efficiency, and competitiveness. On the other, the same data, when inadequately protected, becomes a liability that exposes both tourists and businesses to severe financial and reputational damage. The sensitivity of tourist data—encompassing personally identifiable information (PII), payment credentials, biometric data, geolocation details, and travel history—makes it a high-value target for cybercriminals (Fan et al., 2022). Unlike other sectors, tourism data often includes cross-border elements, such as passport details and visa information, thereby amplifying the stakes of a potential breach.

Tourism cybersecurity incidents show these platforms' susceptibility. Nearly 500 million customers' personal details, including passport and credit card information, were exposed in the most massive data breach ever in 2018 at Marriott International (Isaak & Hanna, 2018). Such high-profile breaches reveal systemic weaknesses in data governance, technological safeguards, and corporate accountability. They also underscore the broader issue of eroding consumer trust in digital booking systems. When tourists perceive booking platforms as insecure, they may revert to traditional offline channels or choose competitors perceived as safer (Cheung & To, 2017).

Cyber threats are becoming more complex, which is a major aspect of the issue. According to Al-Khouri (2012), online booking systems are always at risk of being targeted by phishing, malware, ransomware, denial-of-service assaults, and even insider threats. Many third-party connections in the tourist value chain are susceptible to hacking attacks. One security hole in the industry's network might have far-reaching consequences for many different parties (Khan et al., 2021). For example, a breach in an airline's reservation system can compromise hotel and tour booking information when data is shared through global distribution systems (GDS). This interconnectedness complicates responsibility and accountability, as breaches may originate from external partners beyond the direct control of a booking platform.

Problems with regulations and jurisdiction only make matters worse. U.S. and European data protection laws like California's Consumer Privacy Act and the General Data Protection Regulation (GDPR) place heavy burdens on companies with respect to data security, consent, and data processing (Conduah et al., 2025). Although these regulations improve consumers' rights, small and medium-sized tourist businesses (SMEs) have a harder time complying since they don't have the capital or manpower to set up sophisticated cybersecurity systems (Concord Technologies Inc., 2024).

Ethical considerations further complicate the landscape. Tourists often provide personal data without fully understanding the extent of its collection, storage, and secondary uses. The growing reliance on AI-driven personalization raises concerns about algorithmic bias, surveillance, and the commodification of private data (Milano et al., 2021). While personalization enhances convenience, it also entails continuous tracking of user behaviour, which can erode privacy if not managed transparently. Many sites don't make data use restrictions clear, leaving travellers misinformed about data sharing (Satiti & Udin, 2025). Information asymmetry increases mistrust and tourist resistance to digital surveillance (Wider et al., 2023).

Another dimension of the problem lies in the reputational and economic consequences of data insecurity. Tourism thrives on trust, and destinations as well as service providers rely heavily on positive brand perception to attract visitors (Amaro & Duarte, 2015). Repeated incidents of data breaches can tarnish the image of booking platforms and destinations, discouraging tourists from engaging with them. Moreover, the financial burden of regulatory fines, legal settlements, and cybersecurity investments further strains companies, particularly SMEs that already operate on narrow margins. Thus, failure to adequately protect tourist data not only undermines consumer trust but also threatens the financial viability of businesses and the competitiveness of entire destinations.

The topic of safeguarding tourist data is still understudied, even though it is of paramount relevance. The current body of research mostly ignores the specific challenges faced by the tourist industry in favour of more broad discussions about e-commerce security. Because of its international scope, interaction with many stakeholders, and increased sensitivity as a result of trip documentation, tourism data necessitates sector-specific approaches (Kim and colleagues, 2019). Furthermore, while technical solutions such as encryption, blockchain, and AI-based anomaly detection are being explored (Fan et al., 2022), their adoption is uneven and often limited by cost, scalability, and technical expertise. There is also insufficient discussion about how these technological innovations can be effectively integrated with regulatory frameworks and ethical practices to build a holistic approach to data protection.

The core problem, therefore, can be articulated as follows: while online booking platforms are indispensable for the growth and digitalization of global tourism, they face mounting challenges in protecting sensitive tourist data from increasingly sophisticated cyber threats, regulatory complexities, and ethical dilemmas. The inadequacy of current safeguards not only exposes tourists to risks of identity theft, fraud, and privacy invasion but also threatens consumer trust, business sustainability, and the long-term competitiveness of the tourism industry. Addressing this problem requires a multidisciplinary approach that integrates technological innovation, regulatory compliance, ethical responsibility, and consumer awareness. Without urgent and comprehensive solutions, the digital foundations of tourism risk becoming liabilities rather than assets in an increasingly data-driven global economy.

LITERATURE REVIEW

According to Çinar (2020), there is a growing need for research in the fields of regulatory studies, cybersecurity, information systems, and tourism management to address the safety of tourist data inside online booking platforms. A growing body of literature explores themes ranging from the digitization of tourism and consumer trust in online platforms to the cybersecurity threat landscape, regulatory compliance, and technological innovations aimed at ensuring secure data environments. This review critically examines existing scholarship to highlight progress made, persisting challenges, and gaps that necessitate further inquiry.

Digitization of Tourism and Online Booking Platforms

The digital revolution has profoundly reshaped the tourism industry. Early studies emphasized how information and communication technology (ICT) transformed service delivery, providing tourists with tools to search, compare, and book travel services more efficiently (Chorna et al., 2024). According to Xiang et al. (2015), online booking platforms have become the main intermediates, replacing conventional travel agencies. These platforms include both worldwide giants like Expedia and Booking.com as well as direct booking systems, which are used by hotels and airlines.

Wang et al. (2016) stated that most common way for tourists to interact with booking platforms is via their mobile devices, thanks to the widespread availability of apps for these devices. According to Arora and Thota (2024) and Kumar et al. (2024), platforms may now provide individualized services by combining big data analytics with AI and machine learning. This allows for the customization of suggestions according to user data. Concerns about data abuse and security breaches arise from the fact that customization is highly dependent on gathering and processing sensitive customer information. Digitalization boosts competitiveness, but it also makes platforms more vulnerable due to the increased amount of sensitive data they manage (Li et al., 2018).

Nature and Value of Tourist Data

Data collected from tourists includes a broad variety of personal and financial details. Data collected may include names, addresses, passport numbers, and other forms of personally identifiable information (PII), as well as information on payments, travel preferences, geolocation, and loyalty program membership (Fan et al., 2022). Because tourists often engage with systems spanning countries, the data generated by this industry is inherently cross-border, which adds another layer of complexity to the regulatory landscape.

The literature emphasizes that tourist data may be seen as a strategic advantage and a possible liability. Data, according to Gretzel et al. (2020), may play a role in strategic destination management, predictive analytics, and improved customer experience. On the other side, vacationers are vulnerable to scams, identity theft, and spying due to insufficient security. When visitors are in the dark about the full scope of data collecting, ethical concerns around ownership and consent arise, according to scholars like Milano et al. (2021).

Additional evidence of its significance is the monetary and public-relations worth of tourism data. A single security breach has the potential to cause substantial financial losses, regulatory fines, and the loss of confidence from consumers (Khan et al., 2021). The fact that 500 million customer data were stolen in the 2018 Marriott International hack is indicative of the magnitude of the danger (Isaak & Hanna, 2018).

Cybersecurity Threats in Tourism Platforms

Cybercriminals target tourism platforms because of the sensitive and large amounts of data they process. A wide variety of cybersecurity dangers have been identified in several research. Some examples of these risks include vulnerabilities, denial-of-service attacks, insider threats, malware, ransomware, and phishing (Al-Khouri, 2012).

Research on case studies such as British Airways (2019) and EasyJet (2020), which suffered breaches affecting hundreds of thousands of customers, demonstrates how attackers exploit vulnerabilities in online booking systems to access financial and personal information (BBC News et al., 2020). Scholars also note the growing sophistication of attacks, with criminals increasingly targeting mobile booking apps and exploiting weaknesses in multi-factor authentication (Kim et al., 2019).

A further factor that makes the situation worse is the interdependence of the tourist value chain. It is common practice for online booking platforms to link with global distribution systems (GDS), as well as airlines, hotels, and vehicle rental companies (Elphick, 2025). According to Khan et al. (2021), a compromise in the system of one partner might have a cascading effect throughout the network, putting many other platforms' data at risk. For the purpose of data security, this interconnectedness makes responsibility and accountability more difficult to achieve.

Regulatory and Legal Frameworks

Regional and international legislative frameworks have a significant impact on the management of visitor data. The most important is the EU's General Data Protection Regulation, which mandates that businesses protect customers' personal information while keeping it legitimate, transparent, and safe (Voigt & Von dem Bussche, 2017).

In developing nations with less developed institutional capacity, there is a lack of consistency in monitoring compliance and sanctioning infractions, even while regulatory frameworks do exist (Kim et al., 2019). The regulatory framework is not uniform, which leaves opportunities for fraudsters to exploit.

Consumer Trust and Behavioural Studies

Consumer trust is a recurring theme in the literature, with numerous studies demonstrating its centrality in online booking behaviour. Amaro and Duarte (2015) found that tourists' intention to purchase online is strongly influenced by perceptions of security and trustworthiness. Cheung and To (2017) similarly concluded that perceived data protection measures directly shape e-tourism adoption.

The loss of trust following breaches can have long-term repercussions for both platforms and destinations. Isaak and Hanna (2018) argue that the erosion of trust is not easily reversible, as consumers often shift to competitors perceived as more secure. Studies also suggest that transparency in privacy policies and visible security features, such as HTTPS protocols and encryption, positively influence trust (Milano et al., 2021).

Furthermore, cultural differences shape consumer attitudes toward data privacy. Research by Li et al. (2018) shows that consumers in Western countries often exhibit stronger concerns about privacy compared to those in Asia, where convenience may outweigh privacy considerations. These differences highlight the importance of contextualizing strategies for building trust in diverse markets.

Technological Innovations for Data Protection

A significant strand of literature focuses on technological solutions for protecting tourist data. Encryption remains a cornerstone, ensuring that data is protected during transmission and storage (Al-Khouri, 2012). Multi-factor authentication and tokenization are widely adopted to secure payment processes.

The most recent research investigates cutting-edge technologies like as blockchain, which promises to store data in a decentralized and tamper-resistant manner, hence eliminating dependence on centralized databases that are susceptible to security breaches (Ansar et al., 2024). Using AI and ML, fraudulent transactions may be prevented in real-time by detecting abnormalities (Eren et al., 2025). A lot of money, technological know-how, and user buy-in are needed for these technologies, so academics warn that they aren't a magic bullet.

Research also highlights the digital divide, with SMEs often struggling to implement cutting-edge solutions due to cost constraints (Buhalis & Sinarta, 2019). This uneven adoption creates vulnerabilities in the broader tourism ecosystem, as cybercriminals may exploit weaker actors in the value chain.

Ethical and Social Dimensions

Ethical concerns around data usage in tourism are studied by academics alongside regulatory and technological aspects. Issues of openness, justice, and permission arise when tourist data is monetized. While recommender systems are great for customization, Milano et al. (2021) claim that they might also contribute to algorithmic biases and make consumers less independent.

According to Gretzel et al. (2020), the COVID-19 pandemic not only hastened the digitalization of tourism, but it has also socialized new types of monitoring, including contact-tracing applications. These new discoveries show how individual rights to privacy are at odds with public health and safety concerns. A lack of customer knowledge is also hinted to in the literature.

According to Kim et al. (2019), many tourists sign agreements without fully comprehending the data sharing and use policies. Because of this knowledge gap, informed consent is limited, and booking platforms should be more forthright in their communications.

RESEARCH GAP

Despite extensive scholarship, several gaps remain. First, much of the literature examines cybersecurity in general e-commerce contexts without fully addressing the unique features of tourism, such as cross-border data flows and integration across multiple stakeholders. Second, while regulations like the GDPR are widely studied, there is limited research on how developing countries approach data protection in tourism. Third, although technological innovations like blockchain and AI are frequently discussed, empirical studies on their real-world implementation in tourism remain scarce. Finally, more research is needed on consumer awareness and education, as behavioural aspects are critical to ensuring data protection in practice.

FINDINGS AND DISCUSSION

The analysis of literature and industry practices reveals several key findings regarding the challenges of protecting tourist data in online booking platforms and the potential solutions being explored. These findings underscore the centrality of data protection in maintaining consumer trust, sustaining business competitiveness, and ensuring the long-term viability of digital tourism ecosystems. This section discusses the findings across four interrelated domains: the criticality of tourist data as both an asset and liability, the escalating sophistication of cyber threats, the uneven adoption of regulatory and technological measures, and the implications for consumer trust and industry sustainability.

Tourist Data as an Asset and a Liability

One of the most significant findings is the dual role of tourist data as both a strategic asset and a source of vulnerability. Online booking platforms increasingly depend on personal data to provide personalized services, dynamic pricing, and targeted marketing (Tussyadiah & Miller, 2019). This data-driven personalization enhances customer satisfaction and strengthens competitive positioning. Iyelolu et al., (2024) found that Booking.com employs artificial intelligence algorithms to boost conversion rates by analyzing user search behavior and tailoring suggestions to the user's preferences.

However, the same data that drives growth also becomes a liability when improperly protected. The Marriott International breach in 2018 illustrates the catastrophic consequences of data insecurity, compromising passport details and payment credentials of nearly 500 million guests (Isaak & Hanna, 2018). This case demonstrates that while data enhances business value, its mishandling can result in irreparable reputational damage and costly regulatory penalties. The finding aligns with Li et al. (2018), who argue that organizations must strike a balance between leveraging data for competitive advantage and safeguarding it against misuse.

Sophistication and Interconnectedness of Cyber Threats

The findings highlight that cyber threats to tourism platforms are not only increasing in volume but also growing in sophistication. Traditional threats such as phishing, ransomware, and malware remain pervasive (Al-Khouri, 2012), but attackers now employ advanced tactics such as AI-driven social engineering and exploitation of third-party vulnerabilities. The EasyJet data breach in 2020, which affected nine million customers, was linked to sophisticated hackers targeting booking systems to access financial and personal data (Khan et al., 2021).

The interconnectedness of tourism platforms amplifies these risks. Booking platforms often rely on global distribution systems (GDS), payment gateways, and third-party service providers, creating complex networks where a breach in one node can compromise the entire system (Buhalis & Sinarta, 2019). This interconnectedness complicates accountability. For instance, when British Airways suffered a cyberattack in 2019 that exposed data of 500,000 customers, questions emerged about whether the responsibility lay with the airline, the booking platform, or third-party vendors (Voigt & Von dem Bussche, 2017).

These findings suggest that the tourism sector faces systemic vulnerabilities that cannot be addressed through isolated measures. A coordinated, multi-stakeholder approach is necessary to strengthen resilience across the ecosystem.

Uneven Adoption of Regulatory and Technological Safeguards

Another critical finding is the uneven adoption of data protection regulations and technologies across regions and organizational sizes. Developed economies have implemented robust data protection frameworks such as the GDPR and CCPA, mandating transparency, accountability, and enhanced consumer rights (Voigt & Von dem Bussche, 2017). These regulations have forced larger platforms and multinational companies to invest heavily in compliance mechanisms, including encryption, anonymization, and incident response systems.

Gossling and Reinhold (2024) state that small and medium-sized organizations (SMEs), which make up a significant number of tourist industries, sometimes have difficulties in complying with regulations owing to the fact that they are frequently constrained by financial and technological restrictions. Many SMEs lack dedicated IT departments or cybersecurity expertise, making them vulnerable entry points for attackers. This regulatory asymmetry creates weak links in the tourism value chain, as cybercriminals can exploit less-protected entities to access larger networks,

Some technological advancements that might be considered as remedies include blockchain technology, multi-factor authentication, and anomaly detection powered by artificial intelligence (Shevchuk et al., 2025). In contrast to centralized systems that may be breached, blockchain stores booking data decentralized and tamper-proof. Lack of understanding, scalability issues, and expense restrict uptake. Although sophisticated technologies are promising, their implementation is inconsistent and generally unavailable to smaller firms (Eren et al., 2025).

Consumer Trust as a Determinant of Digital Tourism

Trust emerges as a recurring theme in both scholarly and industry evidence. Studies consistently demonstrate that tourists' willingness to use online booking platforms is strongly influenced by their perception of data security (Amaro & Duarte, 2015; Cheung & To, 2017). Transparent privacy policies, visible security certifications, and robust data protection mechanisms enhance consumer trust. Conversely, data breaches lead to long-lasting erosion of confidence, with tourists often switching to competitors perceived as safer (Isaak & Hanna, 2018).

The findings also indicate cultural differences in how trust and privacy are valued. Research by Li et al. (2018) shows that consumers in Europe and North America express higher sensitivity to privacy concerns compared to consumers in Asia, where convenience and affordability often outweigh data protection considerations. This suggests that strategies for building trust must be context-specific, balancing global regulatory compliance with local consumer expectations.

Trust is not only a determinant of individual consumer behaviour but also a factor in destination branding. Destinations associated with secure digital ecosystems are more likely to attract international tourists, particularly from regions with strict privacy norms (Gretzel et al., 2020). Conversely, repeated breaches can damage the reputation of entire destinations, reducing competitiveness in the global tourism market.

DISCUSSION: TOWARD A HOLISTIC APPROACH

All things considered, the results show how critical it is to secure consumer information in online booking systems in a comprehensive manner. technology, legislative, ethical, and behavioural aspects all contribute to the issue, making a purely technology approach inadequate.

First, the dual role of tourist data as an asset and liability necessitates a paradigm shift in data governance. Organizations must move from reactive compliance to proactive stewardship, treating data protection as a strategic priority rather than a regulatory burden (Milano et al., 2021).

Second, the interconnectedness of the tourism ecosystem requires coordinated action. Stakeholders including booking platforms, airlines, hotels, payment providers, and regulators must collaborate to establish standardized protocols and shared responsibility mechanisms. The current fragmentation undermines collective resilience, leaving the sector vulnerable to cascading breaches.

Third, addressing regulatory and technological asymmetries is crucial. Policymakers should design capacity-building initiatives to support SMEs in adopting affordable cybersecurity solutions. Public-private partnerships could play a role in subsidizing technologies like blockchain and AI to ensure inclusivity across the tourism value chain (Khan et al., 2021).

Transparency and education are final requirements for regaining and preserving the confidence of consumers. Information on the collection, usage, and protection of tourists' personal data have to be communicated to them in easy-to-understand language. According to Lin et al., (2022), competitive advantage is more likely to be gained by platforms that make it clear that they are committed to protecting users' privacy in a market that is becoming more data-conscious.

SOLUTION AND RECOMMENDATION

The findings indicate that safeguarding tourist data on online booking platforms requires a multi-pronged approach, integrating technological innovation, regulatory compliance, organizational governance, and consumer empowerment. The following recommendations outline actionable strategies for strengthening data protection and ensuring the resilience of digital tourism ecosystems.

Strengthen Data Governance and Privacy-by-Design

The booking systems of tourist groups should include privacy-by-design and data reduction principles. According to Cavoukian (2011), privacy-by-design means that security features should not be seen as afterthoughts but as integral parts of platforms. Businesses may greatly lessen their vulnerability to data breaches if they anonymize critical information and simply gather the bare minimum of data needed.

Invest in Advanced Encryption and Authentication

End-to-end encryption and tokenisation are necessary to protect payment and identification data (Fan et al., 2022). Additionally, implementing multi-factor authentication (MFA) and biometric verification can strengthen user access security. Such measures not only reduce vulnerability to unauthorized access but also build consumer trust in the platform's security standards (Al-Khouri, 2012).

Adopt Blockchain for Secure Transactions

Decentralised and tamper-proof blockchain technology might secure booking transactions and client data (Khan et al., 2021). Its distributed ledger reduces reliance on vulnerable centralized databases. Tourism businesses should pilot blockchain-based systems for booking confirmation, payment processing, and loyalty program management to enhance transparency and trust.

Enhance Cybersecurity Training and Awareness

According to Buhalis and Sinarta (2019), human mistake continues to be the top source of security breaches, especially in small and medium-sized enterprises (SMEs) with low technological knowledge. Regular cybersecurity training for employees including phishing detection, passwords hygiene, and incident response should be institutionalized. Similarly, educating tourists on safe browsing and booking practices can reduce risks of social engineering attacks (Cheung & To, 2017).

Implement Continuous Monitoring and AI-Driven Threat Detection

Protective measures that are reactive and static are no longer adequate. In the event of suspicious actions, such as strange login habits or fraudulent booking attempts, anomaly detection systems that are backed by artificial intelligence have the ability to deliver real-time notifications (Milano et al., 2021). Platforms have the ability to identify breaches before they become large-scale intrusions if they integrate predictive analytics into their security operations.

Strengthen Collaboration Across Stakeholders

The interconnected nature of booking platforms demands collaborative solutions. Industry stakeholders—including airlines, hotels, payment providers, and regulators—should establish standardized cybersecurity protocols and data-sharing agreements (Gretzel et al., 2020). Multi-stakeholder partnerships can ensure collective resilience, while information-sharing platforms such as Computer Emergency Response Teams (CERTs) can enhance response to cross-border threats.

Ensure Regulatory Compliance and Support for SMEs

Full compliance, nevertheless, is usually out of reach for SMEs due to a lack of resources. Governments and trade groups should incentivize small and medium-sized enterprises (SMEs) to implement cost-effective cybersecurity measures by offering them toolkits, technical help, and financial incentives. Without exposing any links in the value chain, this method eliminates regulatory imbalance and makes it more secure (Rawindaran, et al.,2023).

Establish Transparent Communication with Consumers

Tourists are becoming more and more demanding that their data be gathered and utilized in a transparent manner. Booking platforms should publish clear, accessible, and multilingual privacy policies, backed by visible security certifications (Amaro & Duarte, 2015). Transparent breach notifications also help maintain consumer trust, demonstrating accountability even during crises (Isaak & Hanna, 2018).

Develop Incident Response and Recovery Frameworks

Preparedness is as crucial as prevention. Platforms should design robust incident response frameworks including data backup strategies, recovery plans, and post-breach audits (Li et al., 2018). Regular simulations of cyberattack scenarios can improve readiness and minimize downtime during actual breaches.

Promote Ethical Use of Data and Consumer Empowerment

Beyond compliance, companies must commit to the ethical use of consumer data. Practices such as informed consent, data portability, and the option to opt-out of profiling respect consumer autonomy (Milano et al., 2021). By giving visitors, the ability to govern their own data, not only is ethical stewardship ensured, but also the legitimacy of the brand is increased in an industry that is very competitive.

CONCLUSION AND FUTURE RESEARCH

Web booking systems have transformed the tourist sector, giving travellers and companies new options. Modern tourism relies on these platforms for real-time access to accommodations, flights, and activities. This simplicity has made tourist data collecting, storage, and use vulnerable. According to Florido-Benítez (2024), tourist data may be a strategic advantage for companies but also a danger if it is managed improperly or leaked.

The chapter demonstrates that cyber threats targeting tourism platforms are increasingly sophisticated, often exploiting the complex interdependencies between booking systems, payment gateways, and third-party vendors (Khan et al., 2021). The sector's fragmented structure exacerbates vulnerabilities, as smaller enterprises with limited resources struggle to maintain compliance with stringent data protection standards (Buhalis & Sinarta, 2019). This asymmetry not only weakens the resilience of the broader ecosystem but also creates avenues for attackers to infiltrate high-value targets indirectly.

Another important conclusion is the centrality of consumer trust. Tourists' willingness to engage in online transactions hinges on perceptions of privacy, security, and organizational transparency (Cheung & To, 2017). Data breaches, such as those experienced by Marriott, British Airways, and EasyJet, have shown that reputational damage often outlasts the immediate financial penalties (Isaak & Hanna, 2018). According to Gretzel et al. (2020), safeguarding visitor data is crucial for maintaining global competitiveness and destination branding, in addition to being a legislative necessity.

From a solutions perspective, the discussion highlights the need for multi-dimensional interventions. Technological measures such as encryption, blockchain, and AI-powered threat detection must be complemented by robust governance practices, ethical data use, and continuous consumer engagement (Fan et al., 2022; Milano et al., 2021). Furthermore, building collaborative frameworks across stakeholders is critical to addressing systemic risks and ensuring shared accountability (Voigt & Von dem Bussche, 2017).

In sum, this chapter concludes that the protection of tourist data is a multifaceted challenge that transcends technology. It requires coordinated action across technical, organizational, regulatory, and behavioural domains. In addition to endangering consumers, ignoring these problems might undermine digital tourism platforms' legitimacy and viability in the long run.

FUTURE RESEARCH

While this chapter has identified key challenges and potential solutions, it also uncovers several gaps that warrant further academic inquiry and industry experimentation. Future research should focus on the following directions:

1. Cross-Cultural Perspectives on Data Privacy

Current literature highlights regional differences in consumer attitudes toward privacy, with Western tourists exhibiting greater concern than their Asian counterparts (Li et al., 2018). Future studies should conduct comparative analyses across diverse cultural contexts to understand how local norms, legal regimes, and trust perceptions shape data security expectations. Such insights will enable platforms to design culturally adaptive strategies for consumer engagement.

2. Blockchain and Emerging Technologies in Tourism Security

Blockchain technology has great potential as a decentralized and immutable database system (Fan et al., 2022), but there is little indication that it works in large-scale tourist applications. Future research should explore pilot projects and case studies examining blockchain's scalability, interoperability, and cost-effectiveness in securing booking systems. Similarly, the role of quantum computing, edge AI, and zero-trust architectures should be explored as next-generation security paradigms.

3. SME-Centric Cybersecurity Models

Although small and medium-sized enterprises (SMEs) play an important role in the tourist value chain, they are mostly ignored in the contemporary research and policy discussions, which concentrate on major platforms. Research in the future should concentrate on making security solutions for SMEs that are easy to use, scalable, and affordable (Md Ramli et al., 2022). This includes exploring the potential of cloud-based security-as-a-service models, cooperative security clusters, and government-subsidized digital literacy programs (Buhalis & Sinarta, 2019).

4. Ethical Dimensions of Data Governance

The ethical implications of data collection, profiling, and behavioural targeting remain underexplored in the tourism context (Milano et al., 2021). Future studies should assess how practices such as predictive analytics, biometric identification, and cross-platform data sharing align with principles of informed consent, fairness, and autonomy. The integration of ethical frameworks into platform governance will be critical for building consumer trust and legitimacy.

5. Consumer Education and Behavioural Research

Tourists themselves play a pivotal role in data security, yet limited research has explored how awareness campaigns, nudges, and interface design can improve safe booking practices (Cheung & To, 2017). Future research should adopt behavioural science approaches to test interventions that encourage stronger password practices, safer payment methods, and informed consent decision-making.

6. Post-Breach Recovery and Trust Rebuilding

While existing literature focuses heavily on breach prevention, there is less attention on how companies and destinations can recover from cyber incidents. Research should examine strategies for restoring consumer confidence post-breach, including transparent communication, restitution policies, and brand rehabilitation efforts (Isaak & Hanna, 2018). This line of inquiry will be increasingly relevant as breaches become inevitable despite preventive measures.

7. Global Harmonization of Data Protection Policies

The current regulatory environment is fragmented, with variations between GDPR, CCPA, and other regional laws creating compliance challenges for multinational platforms (Voigt & Von dem Bussche, 2017). Future research should explore the feasibility of harmonized global standards for tourism data protection, potentially under the auspices of international organizations such as UNWTO or OECD. Comparative studies can highlight best practices and inform policymaking toward standardization.

8. Longitudinal Studies on Trust and Security Practices

Organizational practices and customer sentiment are often studied in empirical studies that only record data from a particular moment in time. In order to monitor the changes in platform reputation, security, and trustworthiness brought about by industry events, legislative shifts, or technology uptake, future studies should use longitudinal approaches. We can learn more about the dynamics of digital tourists' conduct from these types of investigations (Chandra et al., 2010).

The transformation of tourism into a digital-first industry has amplified the urgency of safeguarding tourist data. As booking platforms continue to expand globally, the stakes of data protection will only grow higher. Addressing these challenges requires not only technological innovation but also interdisciplinary research that integrates perspectives from information systems, law, ethics, and consumer psychology. Future research must prioritize inclusivity, ensuring that solutions are accessible not only to large corporations but also to the SMEs that form the backbone of the tourism sector.

Ultimately, protecting tourist data is not a static goal but an evolving process. As cyber threats grow in complexity, regulatory frameworks adapt, and consumer expectations shift, continuous inquiry and innovation will be required to keep pace. The sustainability of the digital tourism ecosystem depends on our ability to transform data protection from a reactive compliance requirement into a proactive, ethical, and trust-building practice.

REFERENCES

Al-Khouri, A. M. (2012). Data protection issues in a cloud computing environment. *European Journal of Law and Technology*, *3*(2), 1–15.

Amaro, S., & Duarte, P. (2015). An integrative model of consumers' intentions to purchase travel online. *Tourism Management*, *46*, 64–79. DOI: 10.1016/j.tourman.2014.06.006

Ansar, K., Ahmed, M., Helfert, M., & Kim, J. (2024). Blockchain-Based Data Breach Detection: Approaches, Challenges, and Future Directions. *Mathematics*, *12*(1), 107. DOI: 10.3390/math12010107

Arora, S., & Thota, S. R. (2024). Using Artificial Intelligence with Big Data Analytics for Targeted Marketing Campaigns. *International Journal of Advanced Research in Science Communication and Technology*, *4*(3), 593–602. DOI: 10.48175/IJARSCT-18967

BBC News. (2019). British Airways faces record £183m fine for data breach. https://www.bbc.com/news/business-48905907 (accessed on 04-09-2025)

BBC News. The Guardian, & Symantec. (2020). The British Airways cyber-attack. BBC News. https://usercontent.one/wp/www.compliancepartners.com/wp-content/uploads/2024/11/Case-Study-British-Airways.pdf?media=1738570254 (accessed on 03-09-2025)

Bradač Hojnik, B., & Huđek, I. (2023). Small and Medium-Sized Enterprises in the Digital Age: Understanding Characteristics and Essential Demands. *Information (Basel)*, *14*(11), 606. DOI: 10.3390/info14110606

Bratić, M., Marić Stanković, A., Pavlović, D., Pivac, T., Kovačić, S., Surla, T., Čerović, S., & Zlatanov, S. (2025). New Era of Tourism: Innovative Transformation Through Industry 4.0 and Sustainability. *Sustainability (Basel)*, *17*(9), 3841. DOI: 10.3390/su17093841

Buhalis, D., & Law, R. (2008). Progress in information technology and tourism management: 20 years on and 10 years after the Internet. *Tourism Management*, *29*(4), 609–623. DOI: 10.1016/j.tourman.2008.01.005

Buhalis, D., & Sinarta, Y. (2019). Real-time co-creation and nowness service: Lessons from tourism and hospitality. *Journal of Travel & Tourism Marketing*, *36*(5), 563–582. DOI: 10.1080/10548408.2019.1592059

Cavoukian, A. (2011). Privacy by design: The 7 foundational principles, *Information and Privacy Commissioner of Ontario*. Retrieved from https://www.ipc.on.ca (accessed on 03-09-2025)

Chandra, S., Srivastava, S. C., & Theng, Y. (2010). Evaluating the Role of Trust in Consumer Adoption of Mobile Payment Systems: An Empirical Analysis. *Communications of the Association for Information Systems, 27*, 561–588. DOI: 10.17705/1CAIS.02729

Cheung, C., & To, W. M. (2017). The influence of perceived trust on e-tourism adoption: An empirical study. *Journal of Information Technology & Tourism, 17*(3), 329–348.

Chorna, N., Korzh, N., Kiziun, A., Onyshchuk, N., & Antoniuk, K. (2024). The Role of Digital Technologies in the Transformation of the Tourism Business: Prospects for Development and Impact on the Country's Economy. *AD Alta: Journal of Interdisciplinary Research, 14*(1), 136–140. DOI: 10.33543/140139136140

Cinar, K. (2020). The Digital Revolution: Impact on Tourism Education. *Journal of Tourism and Gastronomy Studies, 8*(4), 2417–2443. DOI: 10.21325/jotags.2020.719

Conduah, A. K., Ofoe, S., & Siaw-Marfo, D. (2025). Data privacy in healthcare: Global challenges and solutions. *Digital Health, 11*, 20552076251343959. DOI: 10.1177/20552076251343959

Elphick, D. (2025, July 23). Hotel guide to Global Distribution System (GDS). SiteMinder. https://www.siteminder.com/r/global-distribution-system/ (accessed on 04-09-2025)

Eren, H., Karaduman, Ö., & Gençoğlu, M. T. (2025). Security and Privacy in the Internet of Everything (IoE): A Review on Blockchain, Edge Computing, AI, and Quantum-Resilient Solutions. *Applied Sciences (Basel, Switzerland), 15*(15), 8704. DOI: 10.3390/app15158704

Fan, Z., Wu, F., & Cao, Z. (2022). Blockchain-based secure data sharing for online booking platforms. *Information Systems Frontiers, 24*(2), 361–377.

Farhad, M. A. (2024). Consumer data protection laws and their impact on business models in the tech industry. *Telecommunications Policy, 48*(9), 102836. DOI: 10.1016/j.telpol.2024.102836

Florido-Benítez, L. (2024). The Cybersecurity Applied by Online Travel Agencies and Hotels to Protect Users' Private Data in Smart Cities. *Smart Cities, 7*(1), 475–495. DOI: 10.3390/smartcities7010019

Gössling, S., & Reinhold, S. (2024). Accelerating small and medium sized tourism enterprises' engagement with climate change. *Journal of Sustainable Tourism, 33*(5), 840–857. DOI: 10.1080/09669582.2024.2350659

Gretzel, U., Fuchs, M., Baggio, R., Hoepken, W., Law, R., Neidhardt, J., Pesonen, J., Zanker, M., & Xiang, Z. (2020). e-Tourism beyond COVID-19: A call for transformative research. *Information Technology & Tourism, 22*(2), 187–203. DOI: 10.1007/s40558-020-00181-3

Ho, F. N., Ho-Dac, N., & Huang, J. S. (2023). The Effects of Privacy and Data Breaches on Consumers' Online Self-Disclosure, Protection Behavior, and Message Valence. *SAGE Open, 13*(3), 21582440231181395. DOI: 10.1177/21582440231181395

Isaak, J., & Hanna, M. J. (2018). User data privacy: Facebook, Cambridge Analytica, and privacy protection. *Computer, 51*(8), 56–59. DOI: 10.1109/MC.2018.3191268

Iyelolu, T. V., Agu, E. E., Idemudia, C., & Ijomah, T. I. (2024). Leveraging Artificial Intelligence for Personalised Marketing Campaigns to Improve Conversion Rates. *International Journal of Engineering Research and Development, 20*(8), 253–270.

Karadayi-Usta, S. (2024). Cybersecurity Risks Analysis in the Hospitality Industry: A Stakeholder Perspective on Sustainable Service Systems. *Systems, 12*(10), 397. DOI: 10.3390/systems12100397

Khan, S., Nicholson, B., & Tsoukas, H. (2021). Vulnerabilities in global value chains: A case study of the tourism sector. *Journal of Business Research, 124*, 240–252.

Kim, J., Kim, S., & Nam, C. (2019). Data privacy concerns and the adoption of mobile tourism applications. *Sustainability, 11*(19), 5209.

Kumar, V., Ashraf, A. R., & Nadeem, W. (2024). AI-powered marketing: What, Where, and how? *International Journal of Information Management, 77*, 102783. DOI: 10.1016/j.ijinfomgt.2024.102783

Li, M., Fang, Y., & Lim, K. H. (2018). Institutional antecedents and consequences of information reuse: A cross-country investigation. *Journal of Management Information Systems, 34*(4), 1098–1133.

Lin, X., Huang, X., Liu, S., Li, Y., Luo, H., & Yu, S. (2022). Competitive Price-Quality Strategy of Platforms under User Privacy Concerns. *Journal of Theoretical and Applied Electronic Commerce Research, 17*(2), 571–589. DOI: 10.3390/jtaer17020030

Louati, A., Louati, H., Alharbi, M., Kariri, E., Khawaji, T., Almubaddil, Y., & Al-dwsary, S. (2024). Machine Learning and Artificial Intelligence for a Sustainable Tourism: A Case Study on Saudi Arabia. *Information (Basel), 15*(9), 516. DOI: 10.3390/info15090516

Md Ramli, A., Asby, P. N. K., Mohd Noor, H., & Afrizal, T. (2022). Challenges of SME in The Tourism Industry: A review. *Environment-Behaviour Proceedings Journal, 7*(21), 249–256. DOI: 10.21834/ebpj.v7i21.3721

Milano, S., Taddeo, M., & Floridi, L. (2021). Recommender systems and their ethical challenges. *AI & Society, 36*(1), 105–113.

Mishra, A., Alzoubi, Y. I., Gill, A. Q., & Anwar, M. J. (2022). Cybersecurity Enterprises Policies: A Comparative Study. *Sensors (Basel), 22*(2), 538. DOI: 10.3390/s22020538

Shevchuk, R., Martsenyuk, V., Adamyk, B., Benson, V., & Melnyk, A. (2025). Anomaly Detection in Blockchain: A Systematic Review of Trends, Challenges, and Future Directions. *Applied Sciences (Basel, Switzerland), 15*(15), 8330. DOI: 10.3390/app15158330

Stati, A., & Udin, U. (2025). The Impact of Digital Transformation on the Development of the Tourism Industry: Bibliometric Analysis. *International Research Journal of Multidisciplinary Scope, 6*(1), 603–616. DOI: 10.47857/irjms.2025.v06i01.02510

Talwar, S., Dhir, A., Kaur, P., & Mantymaki, M. (2020). Why do people purchase from online travel agencies (OTAs)? A consumption values perspective. *International Journal of Hospitality Management, 88*, 102534. DOI: 10.1016/j.ijhm.2020.102534

Tussyadiah, I., & Miller, G. (2019). Perceived impacts of artificial intelligence and responses to positive behavior change intervention. *Computers in Human Behavior, 92*, 13–24.

Voigt, P., & Von dem Bussche, A. (2017). *The EU General Data Protection Regulation (GDPR): A practical guide*. Springer. DOI: 10.1007/978-3-319-57959-7

Wang, D., Xiang, Z., & Fesenmaier, D. R. (2016). Smartphone use in everyday life and travel. *Journal of Travel Research, 55*(1), 52–63. DOI: 10.1177/0047287514535847

Wider, W., Gao, Y., Chan, C. K., Lin, J., Li, J., Tanucan, J. C. M., & Fauzi, M. A. (2023). Unveiling trends in digital tourism research: A bibliometric analysis of co-citation and co-word analysis. *Environmental and Sustainability Indicators, 20*, 100308. DOI: 10.1016/j.indic.2023.100308

Xiang, Z., Du, Q., Ma, Y., & Fan, W. (2015). Characteristics of online reviews: Evidence from the hospitality industry. *International Journal of Hospitality Management, 43*, 77 83.

Zeqiri, A., Ben Youssef, A., & Maherzi Zahar, T. (2025). The Role of Digital Tourism Platforms in Advancing Sustainable Development Goals in the Industry 4.0 Era. *Sustainability (Basel), 17*(8), 3482. DOI: 10.3390/su17083482

Chapter 12
Securing Destinations:
How Can Cybersecurity and Digital Forensics Enhance Trust in Modern Tourism Systems?

Swati Sharma
http://orcid.org/0000-0003-2949-2363
Amity University, Noida, India

Bruno Barbosa Sousa
http://orcid.org/0000-0002-8588-2422
Polytechnic University of Cavado and Ave, Portugal & UNIAG, Portugal

Shelley Duggal
http://orcid.org/0000-0002-8932-9675
Amity School of Hospitality, Amity University, Noida, India

Akshita Tiwari
http://orcid.org/0000-0002-5167-6794
Amity University, Noida, India

ABSTRACT

The tourism sector is depending more on digital platforms, smart infrastructure, and data-driven services in the era of digital transformation (Ma, C., T. Somrak, 2025). The use of digital forensics and cybersecurity to improve trust and resilience in contemporary tourism systems is examined in this study (Zhang, J., 2025). The main research question is: How can cybersecurity and digital forensics be combined to enhance user trust, security, and dependability in contemporary travel platforms and smart destinations? A systematic literature review along with the case study analysis of cyber incidents in the tourism sector (for example breaches of airline

DOI: 10.4018/979-8-3373-5826-0.ch012

booking systems), as well as the expert interviews with cybersecurity specialists in tourism business made an entire mixed-methods toolkit. The findings indicate that despite its importance in vulnerability analysis and proactive future attack prevention, post-incident forensics is largely overlooked; most tourism systems do not possess advanced threat detection capabilities (Buhalis & Sinarta, 2019; Tandon et al., 2022).

1. INTRODUCTION

Recent years have seen the travel and tourism industry undergo a profound shift owing to the rapid advancement of technologies like artificial intelligence, the Internet of Things, cloud systems, and mobile applications. As noted by Buhalis and Amaranggana (2015), this advancement has given rise to smart tourism ecosystems where digitised platforms integrate travel services, customise user experiences, and optimise operations to maximum efficiency. Travel promotion, management, and enjoyment has been revolutionised by technology, including real-time booking systems, AI-powered travel assistants, and virtual tours. As seamless travel integration grows, tourism enterprises seek to gain a competitive edge by harnessing advanced and cloud-based infrastructure and are prioritising data-driven services (Ma & Somrak, 2025). This growing dependence, however, increases susceptibility to cybersecurity threats. Online travel agencies, hotel management systems, and airline reservation systems face a surge in data breaches, identity theft, and service disruption, highlighting an urgent need for enhanced cyber resilience in the sector as noted by Tandon et al. (2022). Given the importance of these considerations, it is quite unfortunate that most modern travel agencies do not have the capabilities to detect and manage sophisticated cyber threats. Particularly digital forensics and post-event analysis is still not widely used despite being critical for identifying gaps and reinforcing system defences (Zhang, 2025). Additionally, user trust, which is vital for digital interaction, is significantly influenced by security measures such as payment encryption and secure authentication (Buhalis & Sinarta, 2019). This chapter addresses cybersecurity and digital forensics within the context of contemporary tourism. It focuses on the effect of integrating these domains on the reliability, security, and credibility of digital tourism platforms and smart destinations. This study applies a mixed-methods design comprising a systematic literature review, case study analysis, and expert interviews to generate relevant insights for policy makers, destination managers, and stakeholders in the tourism sector. The primary research puzzle for this investigation is: In what ways can digital forensics and cybersecurity enhance security, reliability, and trust of users in modern travel platforms and smart destinations?

By tackling this issue, the chapter adds to the larger conversation about safe and sustainable digital travel in a time when trust, privacy, and resilience are essential for success rather than optional.

2. LITERATURE REVIEW

2.1 The Evolution of Digital Infrastructure in Tourism

Digitalisation is adopted by the travel & tourism sector, which changed and transformed traditional service delivery to technology-enabled systems fand also facilitated hyper-personalized experiences, real-time interactions, and predictive analytics. IoT, cloud computing, big data analytics, and mobile platforms have all been put together to create smart tourism, which makes travel services more dynamic and connected (Buhalis & Amaranggana, 2015). Travellers now plan, book, and enjoy their trips primarily through digital platforms like augmented reality (AR) tools, mobile apps, online travel agencies (OTAs), and chatbots driven by artificial intelligence (Gretzel et al., 2015). These innovations not only enhance customer satisfaction but also increase operational efficiency and global competitiveness among destinations.

Smart infrastructure now underpins a growing number of destinations, characterized by sensor networks, open data platforms, and interoperability among transport, accommodation, and entertainment systems (Ma & Somrak, 2025). As digital infrastructure becomes a foundational component of tourism, the sector must also grapple with associated risks, particularly regarding cybersecurity and data protection.

Table 1. Critical Literature Review

Author(s) & Year	Main Area Discussed	Key Contributions	Identified Research Gaps
Paraskevas (2020)	Cybersecurity risk management in travel & tourism	Highlights growing cyber risks due to digital dependence of tourism systems; proposes risk-based cybersecurity strategies for tourism organisations.	Does not empirically examine trust outcomes; digital forensics and post-incident recovery mechanisms are not addressed.
Florido-Benítez (2024)	Cybersecurity in OTAs, hotels, and smart destinations	Identifies vulnerabilities in online travel agencies and smart tourism infrastructures affecting data privacy and operational security.	Limited empirical validation; absence of discussion on forensic investigation and its role in rebuilding tourist trust.
Florido-Benítez (2025)	Systematic review of cybersecurity research in tourism	Demonstrates increased scholarly attention post-COVID-19; emphasizes preventive cybersecurity approaches for tourism resilience.	Weak integration of digital forensics; lack of frameworks linking cybersecurity practices directly to trust enhancement.
Buhalis & Leung (2023)	Smart tourism systems and data security	Discusses cybersecurity challenges in smart tourism ecosystems involving IoT, AI, and big data platforms.	Trust is treated implicitly; no focus on forensic readiness or evidence-based accountability after cyber incidents.
Sharma & Gupta (2025)	Cybersecurity readiness in India's tourism sector	Reveals low awareness, policy gaps, and limited preparedness among tourism stakeholders in emerging markets.	Focuses on threats rather than solutions; excludes digital forensics and trust restoration strategies.
Casey & Turnbull (2023)	Digital forensics and cyber investigations	Explains how digital forensics supports breach investigation, evidence preservation, and accountability across sectors.	Lacks sector-specific application to tourism; trust implications for tourists and destination branding remain unexplored.

The reviewed literature in **Table 1** indicates that while cybersecurity has emerged as an important concern in modern tourism systems—particularly with the rise of online travel agencies, smart destinations, and data-driven service platforms—research remains largely fragmented and prevention-oriented. Most studies emphasize risk identification, system vulnerabilities, and technical safeguards, but rarely extend their analysis to trust as a measurable outcome for tourists, service providers, or destinations. Digital forensics, despite its critical role in post-incident investigation, accountability, and transparency, is largely absent from tourism-focused research (Florido-Benítez, L. 2025). Existing forensic studies are predominantly generic or law-enforcement-centric and fail to contextualize tourism's complex digital ecosystems. Furthermore, empirical evidence linking cybersecurity and forensic readiness to trust recovery, destination reputation, and consumer confidence is notably scarce, especially in emerging tourism markets. This reveals a significant research gap and highlights the need for integrated, interdisciplinary frameworks that position cybersecurity and digital forensics as strategic trust-building mechanisms in modern tourism systems.

2.2 Common Cyber Threats in Tourism

Tourism organizations are increasingly vulnerable to cyber threats due to the high volume of personal, financial, and behavioural data they process. Common threats include phishing attacks targeting travelers and staff, ransomware incidents that lock critical booking or operational systems, and Distributed Denial of Service (DDoS) attacks that disrupt websites or customer interfaces (Tandon et al., 2022). The airline and hospitality sectors have experienced some of the most severe breaches, with notable cases involving millions of compromised customer records.

These attacks not only cause financial and reputational damage but also erode consumer confidence in digital tourism systems. According to Sharma et al. (2021), many tourism companies lack dedicated cybersecurity teams or comprehensive protocols for threat detection, making them attractive targets for cybercriminals. As online payment systems, loyalty programs, and contactless technologies become more widespread, the attack surface continues to expand.

2.3 Importance of Cybersecurity and Digital Forensics in Other Sectors

Cybersecurity and digital forensics have long been critical in sectors such as finance, healthcare, and national security, where the protection of sensitive data is paramount. In these fields, proactive cybersecurity measures—such as penetration testing, multi-factor authentication (MFA), and intrusion detection systems (IDS)—are standard practice (Srinivas & Deepa, 2020). To investigate breaches and guarantee adherence to legal requirements, digital forensics—the science of locating, conserving, and evaluating digital evidence—is essential (Casey, 2011).

These industries show how combining forensic preparedness and cybersecurity can improve breach attribution, speed up recovery, and increase organisational resilience. Although handling similarly sensitive data, the tourism industry has been slower to implement such strict frameworks. The knowledge gained from these established industries provides important insights for enhancing digital safety in travel systems (Zhang, 2025).

2.4 Gaps in Current Tourism Cybersecurity Practices

Despite the growing digital sophistication of tourism services, the industry exhibits considerable gaps in cybersecurity preparedness. Buhalis and Sinarta (2019) note that many tourism businesses—especially small and medium enterprises (SMEs)—lack dedicated security budgets, staff training, or incident response plans. A reactive rather than proactive approach to cybersecurity prevails, often with outdated infrastructure and minimal encryption protocols in place (Kaur et al., 2024).

Furthermore, the use of third-party vendors and cloud services without sufficient due diligence introduces additional vulnerabilities. Post-incident forensics is rarely employed, which hampers learning from breaches and improving future defenses (Tandon et al., 2022). These gaps underscore the need for a sector-wide shift toward a security-by-design approach, incorporating digital forensics as a preventive and investigative tool.

2.5 Trust and Customer Perception in Digital Tourism Services

The success of digital tourism platforms is largely dependent on consumer trust. Travellers' willingness to interact with platforms frequently depends on how secure they believe the platforms to be, and they are becoming more conscious of the risks to their digital privacy (Buhalis & Sinarta, 2019). In addition to protecting users, features like MFA, transparent privacy policies, and secure payment gateways serve as indicators of reliability.

According to research by Lee and Song (2021), user loyalty and satisfaction in online travel transactions are highly influenced by perceived security. Consumer perceptions can also be influenced by open and honest communication both during and after cyber incidents. Customers are more inclined to share personal information and use digital services with confidence when they think a company takes cybersecurity seriously (Zhang, 2025).

2.6 Recent cyber attacks in Travel & Tourism Industry

Recent global incidents highlight that cyberattacks in the tourism ecosystem are becoming more frequent, sophisticated, and disruptive. In 2025, major European airports experienced a targeted attack on automated check-in systems, leading to extensive flight disruptions and cascading effects on tourism travel schedules and local economies. This shows how attacks on critical travel infrastructure can rapidly affect thousands of travelers and hospitality services that rely on timely arrivals and departures. At the same time, the industry faces massive volumes of automated web attacks, especially in the Asia-Pacific hotel and travel booking sectors, driven by bots and web application vulnerabilities that probe systems for weaknesses.In India, the hospitality and tourism sectors are among the top targets of malware and ransomware campaigns, with industry reports showing millions of malware attacks concentrated in healthcare and hospitality sectors in 2024, underlining significant risk exposure due to rapid digitization and limited cybersecurity resources in some firms. Specific cases, such as the fake payment link scam at a luxury hotel in Mumbai and the Otelier cloud platform data breach affecting booking platforms for major hotel brands, illustrate how both direct and third-party supply chain vulnerabilities can compromise sensitive guest data and financial information as **Table 2**. Global scams using AI-powered fake booking sites or phishing campaigns further demonstrate how attackers exploit user trust to harvest credentials and payment details across the travel customer journey

2.7 Protecting Destinations from Cyber Threats

To safeguard tourism destinations and hospitality systems, stakeholders must adopt a multi-layered cybersecurity strategy:

1. Strengthen Infrastructure and Risk Assessment: Regular penetration testing, vulnerability scanning, and patch management should be institutionalized to identify and fix weak points in booking systems, hotel PMS, OTA integrations, and IoT devices.
2. Employee & Traveler Awareness: Training staff and informing travelers about phishing, fake sites, and social engineering reduces the success rate of credential theft and fraud.
3. Incident Response & Forensics: Establishing clear cyber incident response playbooks along with digital forensics capabilities helps organisations detect, analyse, and recover quickly from breaches, preserving evidence and limiting reputational damage.
4. Regulatory & Industry Collaboration: Sharing threat intelligence, complying with data protection regulations, and collaborating with national cybersecurity agencies improves collective resilience.
5. Third-Party Security Governance: Hotels and travel companies should enforce security standards across third-party providers (e.g., cloud platforms, CRM vendors) to prevent supply chain compromises.

Together, these measures can enhance trust among tourists and partners, maintain operational continuity, and build a stronger defensive posture against evolving cyber threats.

Table 2. Summary of Recent cyber Attacks in Tourism & Hospitality Industry

Case / Location & Year	Type of Attack	Impact on Tourism / Hospitality Sector	Source
European Airports (2025)	Cyberattack on check-in systems	Disrupted check-ins, flights delayed/cancelled, affecting travelers and tourism flows in Europe	(travelandtourworld.com)
Mumbai Five-Star Hotel (India, 2025)	Fake payment link scam impersonating hotel	Guests received fraudulent links, potential theft of payment info, hotel alerted police	(The Times of India)
APJ Web Attacks on Hotels & Travel (2022-23)	Over 1.15 billion web attacks vs hotel & travel sites	Highlights massive volume of bot/web attacks on hotel and travel booking systems	(eHotelier Insights)
India Malware & Hospitality Attacks (2024)	Malware & ransomware incidents target hospitality sector	Hospitality among top attacked sectors in India with millions of malware attacks	(The Economic Times)
Otelier Cloud Breach (2024)	Data breach of hotel management platform	Exposed large amounts of guest data from major hotel chains	(Cesar Ritz Colleges)
Phishing and Fake Booking Scams (Global, 2025)	AI-powered fake sites, phishing emails	Travelers tricked into entering credentials or payment info	(travelandtourworld.com)
Revinate CRM Compromise (Global, 2024)	CRM data leak used for phishing	Guest booking details used to send scam emails to customers	(Reddit)

3. RESEARCH METHODOLOGY

3.1 Mixed-Methods Approach

A mixed-methods approach allows for a thorough understanding of how to use cybersecurity and digital forensics to improve resilience and trust in tourism systems. Assessing technological, operational, and human elements within the scope of digital threats requires both quantitative and qualitative insights (Yigit et al., 2026). While in-depth qualitative interviews reveal industry perceptions and operational gaps regarding digital risk management, quantitative case study data captures underlying patterns of vulnerability and threat. This triangulation enhances findings by addressing the validity and comprehensiveness of the issues and their causes (Creswell & Plano Clark, 2017).

As with many other fields within cybersecurity, the interdisciplinary nature of the field allows for different types of data to be integrated, closing the gap between academic frameworks and practical industry problems.

3.2 Systematic Literature Review Process

A systematic literature review (SLR) was conducted to establish a foundational understanding of digital threats, cybersecurity practices, and forensic readiness in the tourism industry. The review followed PRISMA guidelines (Preferred Reporting Items for Systematic Reviews and Meta-Analyses) to ensure transparency and replicability.

Databases searched included Scopus, Web of Science, IEEE Xplore, and ScienceDirect, using keywords such as "cybersecurity in tourism", "digital forensics hospitality", "smart tourism cybersecurity", and "tourism data breaches". The inclusion criteria were:

a) Peer-reviewed articles and reports from 2015 to 2025
b) English language
c) Studies focused on digital threats, cyber incidents, or security frameworks in tourism or related service sectors

After screening 186 articles and applying relevance filters, 48 high-quality sources were selected for full review. These included empirical studies, case reports, and conceptual frameworks relevant to the intersection of tourism, technology, and cybersecurity.

3.3 Case Study Selection and Analysis Framework

To understand the real-world application of cybersecurity and forensic practices, the study analysed three prominent case studies involving cyber incidents in tourism:

1. **Airline Booking System Breach (2018)** – involving theft of passenger data from a global airline
2. **Hotel Chain Data Breach (2020)** – breach of loyalty program and reservation data
3. **Online Travel Platform Ransomware Attack (2022)** – operational shutdown and extortion demand

These cases were selected based on their global relevance and media coverage, availability of public and technical incident reports, involvement of customer data and system vulnerabilities. The analysis used a cyber incident response framework, examining attack vector and timeline, Breach containment and recovery actions, Use (or absence) of forensic investigation, Impact on brand reputation and customer trust and Lessons learned and system improvements.

Data was coded thematically to identify recurring issues, such as delayed breach detection, lack of forensic readiness, and communication failures.

3.4 Semi-Structured Interviews: Participant Selection and Themes Explored

To complement the literature and case data, semi-structured interviews were conducted with 10 cybersecurity professionals working in or with tourism enterprises (e.g., airlines, OTAs, hotels, and tech vendors) (Shah IA, Jhanjhi NZ, Brohi S.2024). Participants were selected using purposive sampling to ensure industry expertise and direct experience with security implementation in tourism systems. Interviewees included Chief Information Security Officers (CISOs),IT risk managers, Cybersecurity consultants, Digital compliance officers.

Interviews lasted 45–60 minutes and followed a flexible guide that covered the following themes:

a) Current cybersecurity practices and challenges
b) Attitudes toward digital forensics and breach response
c) Organizational barriers to better security adoption
d) Perceived relationship between visible security measures and customer trust
e) Recommendations for improving cyber resilience in tourism

All interviews were transcribed and analyzed using thematic coding, enabling the identification of cross-cutting issues and expert insights that supplemented findings from the literature and case studies.

4. FINDINGS AND ANALYSIS

The mixed-methods approach provided a multi-dimensional understanding of the cybersecurity landscape in tourism:

The systematic literature review laid the foundation by identifying broad patterns, current practices, and known challenges. It helped frame the theoretical gaps and set benchmarks for comparison with field data. The case study analysis offered real-world validation of the literature findings. In all three cases analyzed, a lack of forensic response and communication failure post-breach were consistent, reinforcing the need for forensic readiness and customer transparency. The semi-structured interviews brought forth rich qualitative data that contextualized the challenges and strategies from industry experts' perspectives. Recurring themes across interviews validated literature and case insights, while also highlighting internal organizational struggles not well-documented in academic literature. Triangulation of these three methods enhanced the reliability of findings, ensuring that insights were grounded in both academic and practical realities.The integrated analysis suggests a clear disconnect between the digital sophistication of customer-facing tourism services and the underlying cyber defense mechanisms. This gap presents a risk not just to data privacy and system integrity but also to user trust and long-term brand equity.

The findings reveal that while tourism organizations are digitally advanced in customer-facing functions, they are often lagging in back-end cybersecurity infrastructure. Interviews and literature confirm a widespread lack of real-time threat monitoring systems, with many enterprises relying on outsourced IT vendors without internal capabilities to detect or respond to complex cyber threats.

Honestly, digital forensics just keeps getting sidelined. Every time there's a big breach, you'd think companies would jump on it, dig deep, figure out what went wrong, right? Nope. Either they drag their feet or just do the bare minimum, mostly 'cause they don't have a real plan, their people aren't trained up, or nobody's bothered to set basic protocols in place. So, yeah, they miss out on learning from the mess and end up just as vulnerable next time. From talking to customers, it's wild how much simple stuff—like two-factor authentication, encrypted payments, or telling users when stuff goes sideways—makes people stick around. **Table 3** spelled it out: if a company's upfront when disaster strikes, their reputation takes way less of a hit.

But man, the internal problems are everywhere. Especially with small and mid-sized tourism businesses. They're running on shoestring cybersecurity budgets, half the staff barely knows how not to click on phishing emails, and everyone's juggling a bunch of vendors with zero clarity on who's responsible for what. The result? Security is a total patchwork, and nobody's got the big picture. Finally, the literature and expert insights highlight the need for future-readiness, including the integration of AI for predictive threat detection, securing IoT infrastructures in smart destinations, and complying with global cybersecurity standards.

Table 3. Themes & Sub- Themes

Theme	Sub-Themes	Sources	Key Insights
1. Cybersecurity Gaps in Tourism	- Lack of real-time monitoring- Inadequate incident response- Weak authentication systems	Literature Review Case Studies Interviews	Tourism enterprises are often reactive, with limited investment in proactive cyber defense.
2. Underutilization of Forensics	- Absence of forensic readiness plans- No structured post-breach investigation- Limited staff knowledge	Case Studies Interviews	Digital forensics is rarely integrated into cybersecurity protocols, weakening long-term resilience.
3. Trust and Customer Perception	- Importance of visible security (e.g., MFA, SSL)- Transparency after breaches- Data privacy concerns	Interviews Literature Review	Consumers associate visible security features with platform reliability and are more loyal to transparent brands.
4. Organizational Challenges	- Limited budgets for cybersecurity- Low cybersecurity awareness among staff- Fragmented vendor management	Interviews	Internal constraints are a major barrier to implementing advanced security frameworks.
5. Future-Readiness Needs	- Need for AI-based threat detection- Integration of IoT and blockchain security- Regulatory alignment	Literature Review Interviews	Smart tourism systems require updated, scalable, and interoperable security infrastructure.

5. RECOMMENDATIONS

As smart tourism systems evolve through technological integration, ensuring cybersecurity and forensic preparedness becomes foundational to sustainable operations and customer trust. This section provides targeted recommendations in three key areas: enhancing cybersecurity readiness, advancing digital forensics capabilities, and implementing organizational strategies that foster resilience and response agility.

5.1 Enhancing Cybersecurity Readiness

1. Real-Time Threat Monitoring and Response

The absence of real-time cyber threat monitoring has been identified as one of the tourism industry's most serious weaknesses. Attack surfaces have increased dramatically as tourism platforms become more digitally integrated, from cloud-based reservation systems to IoT-driven smart destination features. By putting Security Information and Event Management (SIEM) systems into place, travel agencies can gather and examine logs from all areas of their IT infrastructure, identify irregularities, and instantly send out alerts to security teams (Srinivas & Deepa, 2020).

Additionally, intrusion prevention systems (IPS) and intrusion detection systems (IDS) are essential tools for spotting and thwarting malware intrusions, system configuration errors, and unauthorised access attempts. According to Tandon et al. (2022), these technologies aid in shortening the duration of breaches and lowering the monetary and reputational expenses linked to extended exposure. Additionally, real-time monitoring facilitates adherence to regional frameworks and international data protection laws like the GDPR, which demand timely breach detection and reporting.

The tourism environment is dynamic, especially during times of high traffic (holidays, festivals, etc.). To safely manage peak usage, continuous monitoring needs to be flexible, scalable, and integrated with automated response protocols.

2. Use of AI and Machine Learning in Anomaly Detection

Traditional rule-based security systems struggle to keep up with the sophistication and volume of modern cyber threats. In contrast, AI and machine learning (ML) algorithms can analyze massive datasets in real time, identifying suspicious patterns that deviate from normal user behavior—such as fraudulent bookings, irregular login locations, or unexpected data flows (Zhang, 2025). These tools can detect unknown (zero-day) threats that may otherwise go unnoticed.

For example, AI systems can be trained to recognize bot-driven DDoS attacks or fake review manipulations on tourism platforms. Moreover, ML-enhanced threat intelligence feeds can prioritize alerts based on risk levels, allowing security teams to respond more effectively and avoid alert fatigue (Ma & Somrak, 2025). The predictive capabilities of AI also enable tourism businesses to move from reactive to proactive cybersecurity, anticipating vulnerabilities before they are exploited.

Despite their potential, AI systems must be implemented with caution. Bias in training data, lack of explainability, and overreliance on automation can introduce new risks. Therefore, a hybrid approach—where AI augments but does not replace human oversight—is recommended.

3.Integration of Multi-Factor Authentication and Data Encryption

Securing access and data is paramount in a digital tourism environment where transactions, identities, and sensitive preferences are processed daily. Multi-Factor Authentication (MFA) is a proven measure that dramatically reduces the risk of unauthorized access, even if credentials are compromised. MFA solutions—combining passwords with biometric scans, SMS codes, or authentication apps—should be mandatory for both users and internal staff accessing administrative systems (Lee & Song, 2021). Additionally, end-to-end encryption ensures that data is unreadable to unauthorized parties during transmission and storage. Customer information, including passports, credit cards, and personal travel itineraries, must be encrypted both at rest (e.g., in cloud storage) and in transit (e.g., during bookings). Encryption not only protects users but also strengthens legal compliance and platform credibility. Organizations should also perform regular encryption audits and vulnerability scans to identify and patch weak encryption protocols or outdated software libraries.

5.2 Advancing Digital Forensics Capabilities

Forensic-Readiness Planning

Digital forensics involves the collection, preservation, analysis, and presentation of digital evidence following a cyber incident. Forensic-readiness refers to an organization's preparedness to conduct effective digital investigations in a timely and compliant manner. This begins with a forensic-readiness plan that outlines:

What types of data should be collected (e.g., login logs, system snapshots, user access records)

How to preserve the integrity of that data

Who is responsible for evidence collection

How evidence should be documented, stored, and used legally

In the tourism sector, where most organizations depend on third-party vendors for cloud services or payment processing, forensic readiness should extend to contractual obligations, ensuring that vendors comply with evidence-handling standards and provide access to relevant data when needed (Casey, 2011).

A forensic-ready environment also requires the installation of centralized logging systems, maintaining chain-of-custody records, and ensuring timestamp synchronization across platforms. These elements are critical when preparing for legal proceedings or insurance claims following a breach.

Building Capacity for Post-Breach Investigations

The ability to respond to and analyze cyber incidents after they occur is just as important as preventing them. Post-breach investigations help organizations understand how the attack happened, what vulnerabilities were exploited, and how to prevent similar events in the future. However, most tourism organizations lack internal forensic expertise and rely heavily on external consultants—often delaying recovery and increasing cost (Zhang, 2025).

Tourism enterprises should develop in-house or hybrid forensic capacity, which may include:

Training IT staff in forensic tools and techniques

Partnering with cybersecurity firms for 24/7 incident response support

Documenting procedures for evidence preservation, analysis, and reporting

Regularly simulating breach scenarios to test forensic workflows

Organizations must also ensure that their forensic teams are aware of jurisdictional laws, particularly when handling cross-border data or customer records subject to international regulations. A well-documented forensic process not only improves breach response but also demonstrates due diligence to regulators and stakeholders.

5.3 Organizational Strategies

1. Employee Cybersecurity Training

Technology alone cannot secure tourism platforms; human behavior remains the weakest link in cybersecurity. Phishing emails, weak passwords, improper device use, and lack of awareness around social engineering are common entry points for attackers. Regular and role-specific cybersecurity training is therefore essential. Training programs should address- Recognizing phishing attempts and fraudulent websites, roper use of VPNs, password managers, and encrypted communication tools. Safe handling of customer data and regulatory compliance (e.g., GDPR), Incident reporting protocols and escalation procedures, Gamified e-learning, phishing simulation exercises, and scenario-based learning have proven effective in improving staff retention and response (Buhalis & Sinarta, 2019). Importantly, cybersecurity should not be positioned solely as an IT issue but rather as a shared organizational responsibility—emphasized from senior management to frontline employees.

2. Crisis Management and Incident Response Protocols

Every tourism organization should have a well-structured incident response (IR) plan that clearly outlines how to respond to cybersecurity breaches. The plan should include:

Defined roles and responsibilities (e.g., who leads the response, who communicates with customers)

Steps for containment, eradication, and recovery

Legal and regulatory notification timelines

Internal and external communication templates

Integration with business continuity and disaster recovery plans

In addition to creating the plan, organizations should conduct tabletop exercises and live breach simulations to test the effectiveness of their response. These drills expose weaknesses in procedures and help staff become familiar with high-pressure decision-making.

Post-incident reviews should be conducted to assess:

What went well and what failed

How long the detection and response took

Whether forensic evidence was adequately collected and used

Whether communication to customers and regulators was timely and effective

By investing in both preparation and post-event learning, organizations can transform breaches from business disruptions into opportunities for system improvement and trust-building (Tandon et al., 2022).

6. THE FUTURE OF SECURE SMART TOURISM

As the tourism sector continues to embrace digital transformation, the integration of emerging technologies such as the Internet of Things (IoT), Artificial Intelligence (AI), and blockchain is reshaping how tourism services are developed, delivered, and experienced. However, this transformation brings a dual challenge: leveraging innovation for competitive advantage while maintaining the integrity, privacy, and security of digital systems. This section explores the technological, ethical, and regulatory trajectories of smart tourism and outlines a roadmap for future-ready, trustworthy, and secure tourism systems.

6.1 Emerging Technologies: IoT, AI, Blockchain

The Internet of Things (IoT) is a foundational element of smart tourism destinations, enabling real-time data collection and responsiveness through interconnected devices such as smart kiosks, wearable devices, mobile sensors, and connected infrastructure (Gretzel et al., 2015). These technologies support personalized services, real-time crowd management, environmental monitoring, and predictive maintenance of tourism assets. However, their interconnectedness also introduces new cybersecurity vulnerabilities—including unsecured endpoints, poorly encrypted communications, and difficulties in patching or updating legacy systems (Zhang, 2025).

Artificial Intelligence (AI) further enhances tourism through smart recommendations, dynamic pricing, sentiment analysis, and autonomous customer service. While AI improves efficiency and personalization, it also raises concerns related to data privacy, algorithmic bias, and explainability (Ma & Somrak, 2025). If not properly governed, AI systems may process personal data without consent, make opaque decisions, or amplify inequalities in service access.

Blockchain technology offers promising applications in secure transactions, digital identity verification, supply chain transparency (e.g., in sustainable tourism), and immutable travel records (Tapscott & Tapscott, 2017). In cybersecurity terms, blockchain enhances integrity and tamper-proof record keeping, making it a valuable tool for enhancing transparency and accountability in booking, loyalty programs, and even COVID-19 vaccination passports. However, scalability, energy consumption, and regulatory uncertainty remain barriers to its widespread adoption.

6.2 Balancing Innovation with Digital Safety

The adoption of emerging technologies must be accompanied by a cybersecurity-by-design approach. Often, innovation in tourism is driven by market speed and user experience, while cybersecurity is treated as an afterthought. This imbalance creates environments where systems are deployed without adequate threat modeling, secure coding practices, or compliance checks.

- To balance innovation with safety, tourism enterprises must:
- Conduct risk assessments during the design phase of new tech implementations
- Integrate security audits and penetration testing into product development lifecycles
- Prioritize privacy-preserving technologies, such as differential privacy and anonymization

Maintain human oversight of automated systems to prevent misuse or unintended consequences (Srinivas & Deepa, 2020). Smart tourism strategies must recognize that security is a continuous process, not a one-time investment. As cyber threats evolve, so must the systems meant to defend against them.

6.3 Regulatory Considerations and Ethical Implications

Tourism enterprises operate across jurisdictions, making regulatory compliance a complex task. Frameworks such as the General Data Protection Regulation (GDPR) in Europe, California Consumer Privacy Act (CCPA) in the United States, and emerging data protection laws in Asia and Africa define clear standards for consent, transparency, data minimization, and breach notification. Tourism platforms must ensure cross-border compliance and keep up with changing laws to avoid penalties and reputational damage (Tandon et al., 2022).

Moreover, ethical considerations go beyond compliance. Key issues include:

a) Informed consent for data collection in smart environments
b) Digital inclusion, ensuring that vulnerable populations (e.g., elderly, low-income, or digitally illiterate tourists) are not excluded from services
c) Surveillance concerns, especially in destinations using facial recognition, geofencing, or behavioural analytics

Ethical smart tourism requires transparent governance, public engagement, and the embedding of ethical AI principles—such as fairness, accountability, and non-discrimination—into system design (Lee & Song, **2021).**

6.4 Roadmap for Building Trust and Resilience in Future Tourism Systems

To ensure the sustainable and secure development of smart tourism, a forward-looking roadmap must be adopted. This roadmap includes:

a) Cybersecurity Governance Integration.
b) Embed cybersecurity policies into all levels of tourism planning and operations.
c) Establish cross-sectoral partnerships between tourism boards, IT providers, and government cybersecurity agencies.
d) Technology Alignment with Standards.
e) Adopt global security standards such as ISO/IEC 27001 for information security and ISO/IEC 27701 for data privacy.
f) Develop and follow sector-specific security protocols for airlines, hotels, travel aggregators, and transport systems.
g) Digital Literacy and Stakeholder Training.
h) Regular training for staff, management, and even tourists on digital safety practices.
i) Public campaigns promoting cybersecurity awareness in travel apps and tourism websites.
j) Investment in Forensic and Incident Response Capacity.
k) Build internal capacity to investigate incidents quickly and mitigate future risks.
l) Simulate breaches and conduct drills across departments and vendors.
m) Transparent Communication and Consumer Engagement.
n) Inform customers about data collection and protection measures.
o) Enable opt-in features and customizable privacy settings for travelers.
p) Adaptive Risk Management.
q) Use predictive analytics to assess emerging risks (e.g., cyberterrorism, data nationalism, misinformation).
r) Maintain flexibility to upgrade and reconfigure systems as threats evolve

Ultimately, trust will be the currency of smart tourism. Tourists will prefer platforms and destinations that demonstrate a commitment to security, transparency, and ethical digital practice. By embedding these principles into the design and delivery of services, the tourism industry can navigate the complex landscape of innovation and digital safety.

7. IMPLICATIONS OF THE STUDY

7.1. Theoretical Implications

This study contributes to tourism and hospitality literature by extending destination trust theory into the digital domain. Traditionally, trust in tourism has been examined through service quality, safety, destination image, and satisfaction. This research reframes trust as a techno-institutional construct, showing that cybersecurity preparedness and digital forensic capability are critical antecedents of trust in smart and digitally mediated tourism systems. It also bridges tourism studies with cybersecurity and digital forensics theory, offering an interdisciplinary perspective that has been largely absent in existing tourism research.

7.2. Managerial Implications

For tourism and hospitality managers, the findings highlight cybersecurity not merely as an IT issue but as a strategic trust management tool. Secure booking systems, protected payment gateways, and transparent handling of cyber incidents directly influence tourist confidence and repeat visitation (Tong L, Kwan M. 2022). Digital forensics enables organisations to investigate breaches, identify accountability, and demonstrate transparency to stakeholders. Managers who proactively invest in cybersecurity infrastructure and forensic readiness can mitigate reputational damage, maintain operational continuity, and strengthen brand credibility in competitive tourism markets.

7.3. Policy and Governance Implications

At the destination and national level, the study underscores the need for destination-wide cybersecurity governance frameworks. Tourism boards, destination management organisations (DMOs), and regulators must integrate cybersecurity standards into tourism policies, licensing requirements, and smart destination initiatives. Digital forensics capacity building within tourism ecosystems—through collaboration with law enforcement and cyber agencies—can enhance legal compliance, evidence preservation, and dispute resolution. Such coordinated governance improves destination resilience and reinforces public trust in digital tourism platforms.

7.4. Technological Implications

The study implies that emerging technologies such as AI, IoT, cloud computing, and big data, while enhancing tourist experience, also increase system vulnerability. Cybersecurity tools like intrusion detection systems, encryption, and real-time monitoring must be complemented by forensic-by-design architectures, ensuring logs, audit trails, and evidence are preserved during cyber incidents. This technological integration enables faster recovery, accurate incident attribution, and improved system reliability—key factors in sustaining trust.

7.5. Consumer and Trust Implications

From the tourist perspective, secure digital environments reduce perceived risk associated with online bookings, mobile applications, and data sharing. The presence of visible cybersecurity assurances and effective forensic responses enhances perceived safety, transparency, and fairness, which are essential determinants of trust. As tourists become more digitally aware, destinations that demonstrate strong cyber resilience are more likely to attract tech-savvy and international travelers.

7.6. Practical Implications for Destination Competitiveness

The study suggests that cybersecurity and digital forensics can function as competitive differentiators for modern destinations. Secure destinations are better positioned to host international events, attract global travelers, and partner with multinational travel platforms. By reducing cyber disruptions and fraud, destinations can protect economic value chains, enhance visitor satisfaction, and sustain long-term tourism growth.

8. CONCLUSION

8.1 Summary of Key Insights

The importance of cybersecurity and digital forensics in determining the security, robustness, and credibility of contemporary tourism systems in a time of swift digital change has been discussed in this chapter. The results of a mixed-methods study that included semi-structured interviews, case study analysis, and a systematic literature review show that the tourism sector is becoming more and more reliant on technology, which improves customer experience but also exposes digital systems to rising cyberthreats.

Key insights include:

i) Significant gaps in cybersecurity infrastructure exist across tourism enterprises, especially in real-time threat detection, secure authentication, and post-breach forensic capabilities (Tandon et al., 2022; Zhang, 2025).
ii) Despite the increasing frequency and impact of cyber incidents, digital forensics remains underutilized as a tool for breach analysis and system recovery (Casey, 2011).
iii) The presence of visible and user-centric security measures—such as multi-factor authentication and transparent data handling policies—positively influences customer trust, which is vital for digital service adoption and brand loyalty (Buhalis & Sinarta, 2019; Lee & Song, 2021).
iv) Organizational constraints such as limited budgets, lack of staff training, and vendor fragmentation impede the adoption of cybersecurity best practices, particularly in small and medium-sized tourism businesses (Ma & Somrak, 2025).

Furthermore, the chapter identified the strategic importance of emerging technologies—AI, IoT, and blockchain—in transforming tourism operations, while also emphasizing the urgent need for cybersecurity-by-design frameworks and regulatory alignment to prevent misuse, data breaches, and ethical violations.

8.2 Contribution to Theory and Practice

From a theoretical perspective, this chapter extends existing work on smart tourism and digital transformation by explicitly integrating cybersecurity and digital forensics as foundational components of sustainable digital tourism ecosystems. While prior research has predominantly focused on personalization, connectivity, and experience optimization (Gretzel et al., 2015; Buhalis & Amaranggana, 2015), this study argues that these benefits are only sustainable when underpinned by robust security mechanisms. The chapter contributes to the growing discourse in tourism studies, information systems, and cyber governance by positioning cybersecurity readiness as an enabler of customer trust and business continuity in smart destinations & demonstrating the operational and strategic relevance of digital forensics, not just as a reactive measure, but as a tool for long-term system improvement and regulatory compliance. Offering a multi-level framework—combining technical, organizational, and policy perspectives—for understanding and addressing the cybersecurity challenges in tourism systems. From a practical standpoint, the chapter provides actionable recommendations for tourism stakeholders, including destination managers, IT providers, and policymakers. These recommendations include:

a) Investing in AI-powered monitoring systems and encryption tools to secure customer interactions.
b) Building forensic-readiness plans to ensure post-breach accountability and continuous learning.
c) Implementing employee training, incident response drills, and cross-sectoral coordination to enhance organizational preparedness.
d) Promoting ethical AI and privacy-by-design approaches to build digital systems that are not only efficient but also trustworthy and inclusive (Srinivas & Deepa, 2020; Zhang, 2025).

These strategies are designed to address both existing vulnerabilities and future threats, making them applicable to a broad spectrum of tourism businesses regardless of size or geography.

8.3 Final Reflections on Securing Digital Tourism for Sustainable Growth

Alright, let's cut through the corporate mumbo jumbo for a second. Cybersecurity in travel isn't just some boring IT checkbox anymore—it's practically make-or-break for anyone hoping to survive in this wild, hyper-connected tourism jungle. Travelers these days? They're tossing their personal details left, right, and centre, every time they book a flight, rent a scooter, or snap a selfie for loyalty points. Companies are gobbling up that data, and honestly, if they screw up, the damage isn't just a slap on the wrist. It's more like "goodbye, brand reputation" and "see you, customer trust."

Ignoring cybersecurity? Yeah, that's like leaving your suitcase open in the middle of Times Square and hoping nobody peeks inside. On the other hand, if a brand puts in the work—makes their systems tight, transparent, and, you know, not evil—they'll stand out big time. Especially since everyone's fighting for attention in this overcrowded market.

Here's the real deal:

i) If travel companies keep treating cybersecurity as some last-minute fix, they're toast. It's got to be baked into every new gadget and app from the get-go.
ii) They also need to play nice with international rules. No one wants their data lost in some legal Bermuda Triangle.
iii) Tech should help people, not turn them into faceless data points. Let's keep things human, yeah?

iv) And maybe, just maybe, the whole sector should cooperate for once. Travelers, businesses, governments—everyone's got to pitch in or risk getting burned.

Bottom line? Building safe, trustworthy digital tourism isn't a one-and-done deal. It's a marathon, not a sprint, and you can't fake your way through it. Cybersecurity and digital forensics need to be part of the travel world's DNA. Otherwise, this whole "smart tourism" dream is just a security nightmare waiting to happen.

REFERENCES

Buhalis, D., & Amaranggana, A. (2015). Smart tourism destinations: Enhancing tourism experience through personalization of services. Information and Communication Technologies in Tourism, 377–389

Buhalis, D., & Sinarta, Y. (2019). Real-time co-creation and nowness service: Lessons from tourism and hospitality. *Journal of Travel & Tourism Marketing*, *36*(5), 563–582. DOI: 10.1080/10548408.2019.1592059

Casey, E. (2011). Digital Evidence and Computer Crime: Forensic Science, Computers, and the Internet (3rd ed.). Academic Press. Gretzel, U., Sigala, M., Xiang, Z., & Koo, C. (2015). Smart tourism: Foundations and developments. Electronic Markets, 25(3), 179–188.

Florido-Benítez, L. (2025). The role of cybersecurity as a preventive measure in digital tourism and travel: A systematic literature review. *Discov Computing*, *28*(1), 28. DOI: 10.1007/s10791-025-09523-3

Gretzel, U., Sigala, M., Xiang, Z., & Koo, C. (2015). Smart tourism: Foundations and developments. *Electronic Markets*, *25*(3), 179–188. DOI: 10.1007/s12525-015-0196-8

Kaur, R., Gabrijelčič, D., & Klobučar, T. (2023). Artificial intelligence for cybersecurity: Literature review and future research directions. *Information Fusion*, *97*, 101804. DOI: 10.1016/j.inffus.2023.101804

Lee, S., & Song, H. (2021). Impact of perceived cybersecurity on customer trust in digital tourism platforms. *Tourism Management Perspectives*, *39*, 100861.

Ma, C., & Somrak, T. (2025). Digital Infrastructure and Security in the Global Tourism Industry. *Journal of Smart Tourism Systems*, *3*(1), 1–18.

Ma, C., Somrak, T., Manajit, S., & Gao, C. (2025). Exploring the Potential Synergy Between Disruptive Technology and Historical/Cultural Heritage in Thailand's Tourism Industry for Achieving Sustainable Development in the Future. *International Journal of Tourism Research*.

Madnick, B., Huang, K., & Madnick, S. (2021). The Evolution of Cyber Security Norm Development in The Digital Age. In *2021 IEEE International Symposium on Technologies for Homeland Security (HST)*, IEEE.;1–5. DOI: 10.1109/HST53381.2021.9619798

Morrison, A. M., & Buhalis, D. (2024). *Routledge handbook of trends and issues in tourism sustainability, planning and development, management, and technology*. Routledge.

Scott, N., Laws, E., & Prideaux, B. (2010). *Safety and security in tourism: recovery marketing after crises*. Routledge.

Shah, I. A., Jhanjhi, N. Z., & Brohi, S. (2024). *Cybersecurity issues and challenges in civil aviation security*. Cyber Tra., DOI: 10.1002/9781394204472.ch1

Sharma, K., Tandon, A., & Gupta, A. (2021). Emerging cyber threats in tourism and hospitality: Risk awareness and resilience. *International Journal of Hospitality Information Technology, 12*(2), 47–61.

Srinivas, R., & Deepa, R. (2020). Integrating cybersecurity and digital forensics for business resilience. *Cybersecurity Trends Journal, 8*(4), 45–59.

Tandon, A., Kaur, P., Bhatt, Y., & Dhir, A. (2022). Cybersecurity and digital resilience in the tourism industry: A systematic review. *Information Systems Frontiers, 24*(2), 465–488. DOI: 10.1007/s10796-021-10131-z

Tapscott, D., & Tapscott, A. (2017). *Blockchain Revolution: How the Technology Behind Bitcoin Is Changing Money, Business, and the World*. Penguin.

Tong, L., & Kwan, M. (2022). Ensuring cybersecurity in airlines to prevent data breach. *Co Sci Re J., 3*(3), 66–73. DOI: 10.51594/csitrj.v3i3.426

UNWTO. (2021). Digital transformation and tourism. Retrieved from https://www.unwto.org/digital-transformation

Zhang, J. (2025). Patterns of Innovation-Driven Tourism Competitiveness: Insights From 270 Chinese Cities. *Tourism Management, 107*, 105063. DOI: 10.1016/j.tourman.2024.105063

Zhang, J. (2025). Digital Forensics and Cybersecurity Practices in Smart Tourism Environments. *Cybersecurity in Hospitality and Tourism, 5*(1), 21–39.

Compilation of References

Abd El-Maksoud, R. (2024). Exploring the role of cybersecurity in enhancing digital trust of Egyptian travel agencies. *Journal of Association of Arab Universities for Tourism and Hospitality*, *26*(1), 185–204. DOI: 10.21608/jaauth.2024.269299.1553

Abdel-Fattah, F., Fayyad, S., Heyari, A. M., & Al-Zoubi, H. (2023). A Survey of Internet of Things (IoT). *Forensics Frameworks and Challenges*, *373–377*, 373–377. Advance online publication. DOI: 10.1109/ICIT58056.2023.10226103

Abdelhamed, M. (2023). *Electronic signature and its role in securing transactions in the tourism sector. Journal of Tourism, Hotels and Heritage*. Print., DOI: 10.21608/sis.2023.220851.1148

Abdelkader, G., Elgazzar, K., & Khamis, A. (2021). Connected Vehicles: Technology Review, State of the Art, Challenges and Opportunities. *Sensors (Basel)*, *21*(22), 7712. DOI: 10.3390/s21227712 PMID: 34833782

Abeyratne, R. (2020). *Aviation and Cybersecurity in the Digital World*. Springer., DOI: 10.1007/978-3-030-48218-3

Abhishta, A., van Heeswijk, W., Junger, M., Nieuwenhuis, L. J. M., & Joosten, R. (2020). Why would we get attacked? An analysis of attacker's aims behind DDoS attacks. *Journal of Wireless Mobile Networks, Ubiquitous Computing and Dependable Applications*, *11*(2), 3–22. DOI: 10.22667/JOWUA.2020.06.30.003

Abomhara, M., & Køien, G. M. (2015). Cyber security and the internet of things: Vulnerabilities, threats, intruders and attacks. *Journal of Cyber Security and Mobility*, *4*(1), 65–88. DOI: 10.13052/jcsm2245-1439.414

Abrahams, T. O., Ewuga, S. K., Dawodu, S. O., Adegbite, A. O., & Hassan, A. O. (2024). A review of cybersecurity strategies in modern organizations: Examining the evolution and effectiveness of cybersecurity measures for data protection. *Computer Science & IT Research Journal*, *5*(1), 1–25. DOI: 10.51594/csitrj.v5i1.699

Abu-Bonsra, N. A. (2023). Summary Report of the International Institute of Air and SpaceLaw's (IIASL) International Air Law Conference on Aviation Cybersecurity, Leiden, Netherlands on 11 th of May 2023. *Air and Space Law*. DOI: 10.54648/AILA2023057

Accenture. (2021). *Digital transformation in hospitality: Unlocking growth opportunities.* Accenture. https://www.accenture.com

Accor. (2019). *Accor digital innovation and chatbot integration.* Accor Group. https://group.accor.com

Achuthan, K., Ramanathan, S., Srinivas, S., & Raman, R. (2024). Advancing cybersecurity and privacy with artificial intelligence: Current trends and future research directions. *Frontiers in Big Data, 7*, 1497535. DOI: 10.3389/fdata.2024.1497535 PMID: 39703783

Adams, T. (2024). Trends, challenges and opportunities of engaging digital forensics for cybercrime investigations. *Advances in Multidisciplinary and Scientific Research Journal, 15*(1), 1–12. DOI: 10.22624/AIMS/CISDI/V15N1P1

Adel, A. (2020). *Developing a Digital Forensic Capability for Critical Infrastructures: An Investigation Framework.* Auckland University of Technology.

Afolabi, O. O., Ozturen, A., & İlkan, M. (2021). Effects of privacy concern, risk, and information control in a smart tourism destination. Journal of Tourism. *Ekonomska Istraživanja, 34*(1), 3119–3138. DOI: 10.1080/1331677X.2020.1867215

Ahmed, A. A., Farhan, K., Jabbar, W. A., Al-Othmani, A., & Abdulrahman, A. G. (2024). IoT forensics: Current perspectives and future directions. *Sensors (Basel), 24*(16), 5210. DOI: 10.3390/s24165210 PMID: 39204906

Ahmed, M., Kambam, H. R., Liu, Y., Jaidka, S., & Petrova, K. (2024). Impact and Significance of Human Factors in Digital Information Security. *International Journal of Information Science and Technology*, 1-17 Pages. DOI: 10.57675/IMIST.PRSM/IJIST-V7I2.213

Ahmed, W., Bhatti, N. A., Rehman, M. U., Alharbi, A. A. K., & Alotaibi, S. (2024). *Advancements in ADS-B Security: A Comprehensive Survey of Vulnerabilities, Mitigation Strategies, System Requirements, and Emerging Research Trends.* DOI: 10.20944/preprints202405.0586.v2

Aivazpour, Z., Valecha, R., & Chakraborty, R. (2022). Data breaches: An empirical study of the effect of monitoring services. *The Data Base for Advances in Information Systems, 53*(4), 65–82. DOI: 10.1145/3571823.3571829

Ajala, O. A., Arinze, C. A., Ofodile, O. C., Okoye, C. C., & Daraojimba, A. I.Olakunle Abayomi AjalaChuka Anthony ArinzeOnyeka Chrisanctus OfodileChinwe Chinazo OkoyeAndrew Ifesinachi Daraojimba. (2024). Exploring and reviewing the potential of quantum computing in enhancing cybersecurity encryption methods. *Magna Scientia Advanced Research and Reviews*, *10*(01), 321–329. DOI: 10.30574/msarr.2024.10.1.0038

Akella, S., Vydula, D. L., Özer, M., Köse, Y., Bastug, M., Onat, I., Elsayed, N., ElSayed, Z., & Koseli, M. (2023). *Understanding Cyber Threats: Patterns*. ISP Characteristics, Industry Targets, and Geographic Correlations., DOI: 10.1109/CSCI62032.2023.00137

Aksoy, L., Choi, S., Doğru, T., Keiningham, T. L., Lorenz, M. P., Rubin, D., & Tracey, J. B. (2022). Global trends in hospitality. *Journal of Business Research*, *142*, 957–973. DOI: 10.1016/j.jbusres.2021.12.068 PMID: 36540755

Alabdulsalam, S., Schaefer, K., Kechadi, T., & Le-Khac, N.-A. (2018). Internet of things forensics – challenges and a case study. In *Advances in Digital Forensics XIV* (pp. 35–48). Springer International Publishing., DOI: 10.1007/978-3-319-99277-8_3

Alam, T. (2021). Cloud-based IoT applications and their roles in smart cities. *Smart Cities*, *4*(3), 1196–1219. DOI: 10.3390/smartcities4030064

Alavi, R., Islam, S., & Mouratidis, H. (2014). A conceptual framework to analyze human factors of information security management system (ISMS) in organizations. In *Lecture Notes in Computer Science* (pp. 297–305). Springer. DOI: 10.1007/978-3-319-07620-1_26

Alazab, A., Khraisat, A., & Singh, S. (2025). A review on the Internet of Things (IoT) forensics: Challenges, techniques, and evaluation of digital forensic tools. In *The Role of Cybersecurity in the Industry 5.0 Era*. IntechOpen., DOI: 10.5772/intechopen.109840

Al-E'mari, S., Sanjalawe, Y., Makhadmeh, S. N., & Alqudah, H. (2024). Digital forensics meets blockchain: Enhancing evidence authenticity and traceability. *International Conference on Cybersecurity Research*, 1–6. DOI: 10.1109/ICCR61006.2024.10532961

Alghamdi, A. (2025). Quantum Cryptography: Implications for Digital Evidence in Criminal Investigations.

Ali, A. H., & Leblanc, S. (2024). Vulnerabilities of Automatic Dependent Surveillance-Broadcast on Aircraft. *Survey (London, England)*, *1–5*, 1–5. Advance online publication. DOI: 10.1109/ICCIMS61672.2024.10690823

Ali, A., Omar, R., & Bakar, A. A. (2021). Cybersecurity awareness in the hospitality industry: An exploratory study. *Journal of Hospitality and Tourism Technology*, *12*(4), 675–690. DOI: 10.1108/JHTT-10-2020-0274

Ali, S. (2024). Unraveling cyber threats: The role of forensic investigation in cyber security. International Journal of Multidisciplinary Research in Science. *Engineering and Technology*, *7*(05), 10258–10260. DOI: 10.15680/IJMRSET.2024.0705108

Ali, S. M., Kim, D. J., & Kim, Y. G. (2020). The impact of cyber security breach on customer loyalty: Mediating role of consumer emotions. *Journal of Retailing and Consumer Services*, *57*, 102238. DOI: 10.1016/j.jretconser.2020.102238

Al-Khateeb, H., Epiphaniou, G., & Daly, H. (2019). Blockchain for Modern Digital Forensics: The Chain-of-Custody as a distributed ledger. In *Advanced sciences and technologies for security applications* (pp. 149–168). DOI: 10.1007/978-3-030-11289-9_7

Al-Khouri, A. M. (2012). Data protection issues in a cloud computing environment. *European Journal of Law and Technology*, *3*(2), 1–15.

Alnajim, A. M., Habib, S., Islam, M., AlRawashdeh, H. S., & Wasim, M. (2023). Exploring cybersecurity education and training techniques: A comprehensive review of traditional, virtual reality, and augmented reality approaches. *Symmetry*, *15*(12), 2175. DOI: 10.3390/sym15122175

Al-Qarni, E. A. (2023). Cybersecurity in healthcare: A review of recent attacks and mitigation strategies. *International Journal of Advanced Computer Science and Applications*, *14*(5), 135–140. DOI: 10.14569/IJACSA.2023.0140513

Alshammari, K., Beach, T., & Rezgui, Y. (2021). Cybersecurity for digital twins in the built environment: Current research and future directions. *Journal of Information Technology in Construction*, *26*, 159–173. DOI: 10.36680/j.itcon.2021.010

Alt, R. (2021). Digital transformation in the restaurant industry: Current developments and implications. *Journal of Smart Tourism*, *1*(1), 69–74. DOI: 10.52255/smarttourism.2021.1.1.9

Alzahrani, N. M., & Alfouzan, F. A. (2022). Augmented Reality (AR) and Cyber-Security for Smart Cities—A Systematic Literature Review. *Sensors (Basel)*, *22*(7), 2792. DOI: 10.3390/s22072792 PMID: 35408406

Amaro, S., & Duarte, P. (2015). An integrative model of consumers' intentions to purchase travel online. *Tourism Management*, *46*, 64–79. DOI: 10.1016/j.tourman.2014.06.006

Amato, F., Castiglione, A., Cozzolino, G., & Narducci, F. (2020). A semantic-based methodology for digital forensics analysis. *Journal of Parallel and Distributed Computing, 138*, 172–177. DOI: 10.1016/j.jpdc.2019.12.017

Ammar, M., & Khan, I. A. (2024). *Cyber Attacks on Maritime Assets and their Impacts on Health and Safety Aboard: A Holistic View* (Version 1). arXiv. DOI: 10.48550/ARXIV.2407.08406

Amoo, O. O., Atadoga, A., Osasona, F., Abrahams, T. O., Ayinla, B. S., & Farayola, O. A. (2024). GDPR's impact on cybersecurity: A review focusing on USA and European practices. *International Journal of Science and Research Archive, 11*(1), 1338–1347. DOI: 10.30574/ijsra.2024.11.1.0220

Anastasiadou, C. (2006). Tourism and the European Union. In *Tourism in the new Europe: the challenges and opportunities of EU enlargement* (pp. 20–31). CABI. DOI: 10.1079/9781845931179.0020

Ande, R., Adebisi, B., Hammoudeh, M., & Saleem, J. (2020). Internet of Things: Evolution and technologies from a security perspective. *Sustainable Cities and Society, 54*, 101728. DOI: 10.1016/j.scs.2019.101728

Anil, V. K. S., & Babatope, A. B. (2024). Data privacy, security, and governance: A global comparative analysis of regulatory compliance and technological innovation. *Global Journal of Engineering and Technology Advances, 21*(3), 190–202. DOI: 10.30574/gjeta.2024.21.3.0246

Ansar, K., Ahmed, M., Helfert, M., & Kim, J. (2024). Blockchain-Based Data Breach Detection: Approaches, Challenges, and Future Directions. *Mathematics, 12*(1), 107. DOI: 10.3390/math12010107

Anwar, F. A., Deliana, D., & Suyamto, S. (2024). Digital transformation in the hospitality industry: Improving efficiency and guest experience. *International Journal of Management Science and Information Technology, 4*(2), 428–437. DOI: 10.35870/ijmsit.v4i2.3201

Arora, S., & Thota, S. R. (2024). Using Artificial Intelligence with Big Data Analytics for Targeted Marketing Campaigns. *International Journal of Advanced Research in Science Communication and Technology, 4*(3), 593–602. DOI: 10.48175/IJARSCT-18967

Asbaş, C., & Tuzlukaya, Ş. E. (2024). *Aviation Cybersecurity*. CRC Press., DOI: 10.4018/979-8-3693-0732-8.ch003

Ashqar, R. I., Ashqar, H. I., & Ramos, C. M. Q. (2024). *Identity and access management in tourism and hospitality*. In Springer International Publishing., DOI: 10.1007/978-3-031-44131-8_32

Asim, N., Osamor, J., Olajide, F., Iwendi, C., & Okeke, N. (2025, February). Detecting and Mitigating Anti-Forensic Techniques: A Comprehensive Framework for Digital Investigators. In *2025 AI-Driven Smart Healthcare for Society 5.0* (pp. 66-72). IEEE. DOI: 10.1109/IEEECONF64992.2025.10963229

Asimily Blog. (2025). *3 cyberattacks that devastated hospitality in 2023 and 2024*. Asimily. https://asimily.com/blog/3-cyberattacks-hospitality-2023-2024/

Aslam, M., Khan Abbasi, M. A., Khalid, T., Shan, R. U., Ullah, S., Ahmad, T., Saeed, S., Alabbad, D. A., & Ahmad, R. (2022). Getting Smarter about Smart Cities: Improving Data Security and Privacy through Compliance. *Sensors (Basel)*, *22*(23), 9338. DOI: 10.3390/s22239338 PMID: 36502039

Aslan, Ö., Aktuğ, S. S., Ozkan-Okay, M., Yilmaz, A. A., & Akin, E. (2023). A Comprehensive Review of Cyber Security Vulnerabilities, Threats, Attacks, and Solutions. *Electronics (Basel)*, *12*(6), 1333. DOI: 10.3390/electronics12061333

Babikian, J. (2023). Navigating legal frontiers: Exploring emerging issues in cyber law. *Revista Española de Documentación Científica*, *17*(2), 95–109.

Baho, S. A., & Abawajy, J. H. (2023). Analysis of Consumer IoT Device Vulnerability Quantification Frameworks. *Electronics (Basel)*, *12*(5), 1176. DOI: 10.3390/electronics12051176

Baig, Z. A., Szewczyk, P., Valli, C., Rabadia, P., Hannay, P., Chernyshev, M., Johnstone, M., Kerai, P., Ibrahim, A., Sansurooah, K., Syed, N., & Peacock, M. (2017). Future challenges for smart cities: Cyber-security and digital forensics. *Digital Investigation*, *22*, 3–13. DOI: 10.1016/j.diin.2017.06.015

Baisley, T., & Cherrat, Y. (2023). Cyber Threats and Engagements in 2022.

Bakalis, A., Halkiopoulos, C., & Antonopoulou, H. (2024). The Digital Transformation of tourism. Case study of Greek tourism. In *Springer proceedings in business and economics* (pp. 121–157). DOI: 10.1007/978-3-031-54338-8_9

Bakhtiar, H. S. (2023). The role and nature of evidence: Forensic insight. *Jurnal Yuridis*, *10*(2), 10–22. DOI: 10.35586/jyur.v10i2.7072

Bamanga, M. A., Babando, A. K., & Mayer, J. (2024). *Recent advances in steganography*. IntechOpen.

Baroto, W. A. (2024). Advancing digital forensic through machine learning: An integrated framework for fraud investigation. *Asia Pacific Fraud Journal*, *9*(1), 1–16. DOI: 10.21532/apfjournal.v9i1.346

Barykin, S. E., De La Poza, E., Khalid, B., Kapustina, I. V., Kalinina, O. V., & Iqbal, K. M. J. (2021). Tourism industry. In *Advances in educational technologies and instructional design book series* (pp. 414–434). DOI: 10.4018/978-1-7998-8327-2.ch025

BBC News. (2019). British Airways faces record £183m fine for data breach. https://www.bbc.com/news/business-48905907 (accessed on 04-09-2025)

BBC News. The Guardian, & Symantec. (2020). The British Airways cyber-attack. BBC News. https://usercontent.one/wp/www.compliancepartners.com/wp-content/uploads/2024/11/Case-Study-British-Airways.pdf?media=1738570254 (accessed on 03-09-2025)

Bekele, H., & Raj, S. (2024). Digitalization and digital transformation in the tourism industry: A bibliometric review and research agenda. *Tourism Review*. Advance online publication. DOI: 10.1108/TR-07-2023-0509

Belciu, A.-C., & Preda, M. (2024). Cyber Resilience Under the EU Framework: Insights from an Applied Case Study on Critical Sectors. *International Journal of Information Security and Cybercrime*, *13*(2), 18–32. DOI: 10.19107/IJISC.2024.02.02

Berezina, K., Cobanoglu, C., Miller, B. L., & Kwansa, F. A. (2016). Cybersecurity in the hospitality industry: Past, present, and future. *Cornell Hospitality Quarterly*, *57*(4), 370–380. DOI: 10.1177/1938965515624013

Bhardwaj, S., Sharma, I., & Kaur, G. Rohini, & Sharma, S. (2025). Personalization in tourism marketing based on leveraging user-generated content with AI recommender systems. In M. Valeri, S. Shah, & B. Al-Ghazali (Eds.), Redefining Tourism With AI and the Metaverse (pp. 317–346). IGI Global Scientific Publishing. DOI: 10.4018/978-8-3693-8482-4.ch010

Bhardwaj, S., Sharma, I., Mahendru, S., Kaur, R., & Sharma, S. (2025). Exploring the role of AIoT in data privacy and security. In Tariq, M. (Ed.), *Merging Artificial Intelligence With the Internet of Things* (pp. 75–102). IGI Global Scientific Publishing., DOI: 10.4018/979-8-3693-8547-0.ch003

Bhavsar, K. A., Patel, A. M., & Parikh, S. M. (2022). Approaches to digital forensics in the age of big data. In *International Conference on Computing for Sustainable Global Development* (pp. 449–453). DOI: 10.23919/INDIACom54597.2022.9763231

Bilgili, B., & Koc, E. (2021). Digital transformation in tourism. In *Routledge eBooks* (pp. 53–65). DOI: 10.4324/9781003105930-5

Biswal, S. P., & Kulkarni, M. S. (2021). Implications of GDPR on emerging technologies. *Revista Gestão Inovação e Tecnologias, 11*(4), 4898–4912. https://pdfs.semanticscholar.org/787c/1102d0a3150388ca36cab851a37f9446f6c8.pdf

Borkova, E. A., Temnova, N., & Plotnikov, V. (2021). Transition of businesses to online in the Covid-19 pandemic. *The European Proceedings of Social & Behavioural Sciences,* 65-72. DOI: 10.15405/epsbs.2021.12.03.9

Boström, P. (2021). Building and Evaluating a Full Disk Encrypted Secure Multi-user Operating Platform in Linux.

Botwright, R. (2023). *Malware Analysis: Digital Forensics, Cybersecurity, And Incident Response.* Rob Botwright.

Boyd, D. (2014). *It's complicated: The social lives of networked teens.* Yale University Press.

Bradač Hojnik, B., & Huđek, I. (2023). Small and Medium-Sized Enterprises in the Digital Age: Understanding Characteristics and Essential Demands. *Information (Basel), 14*(11), 606. DOI: 10.3390/info14110606

Bratić, M., Marić Stanković, A., Pavlović, D., Pivac, T., Kovačić, S., Surla, T., Čerović, S., & Zlatanov, S. (2025). New Era of Tourism: Innovative Transformation Through Industry 4.0 and Sustainability. *Sustainability (Basel), 17*(9), 3841. DOI: 10.3390/su17093841

Broadhurst, R. (2006). Developments in the global law enforcement of cyber-crime. *Policing, 29*(3), 408–433. DOI: 10.1108/13639510610684674

Buçaj, E., & Idrizaj, K. (2024). The need for cybercrime regulation on a global scale by the international law and cyber convention. *Multidisciplinary Reviews, 8*(1), 2025024. DOI: 10.31893/multirev.2025024

Buchanan, B. (2020). *The hacker and the state: Cyber attacks and the new normal of geopolitics.* Harvard University Press.

Buhalis, D., & Amaranggana, A. (2015). Smart tourism destinations: Enhancing tourism experience through personalization of services. Information and Communication Technologies in Tourism, 377–389

Buhalis, D. (1998). Strategic use of information technologies in the tourism industry. *Tourism Management, 19*(5), 409–421. DOI: 10.1016/S0261-5177(98)00038-7

Buhalis, D., & Amaranggana, A. (2015). Smart tourism destinations: Enhancing tourism experience through personalization of services. In Tussyadiah, I., & Inversini, A. (Eds.), *Information and communication technologies in tourism 2015* (pp. 377–389). Springer., DOI: 10.1007/978-3-319-14343-9_28

Buhalis, D., Harwood, T., Bogicevic, V., Viglia, G., Beldona, S., & Hofacker, C. (2019). Technological disruptions in services: Lessons from tourism and hospitality. *Journal of Service Management, 30*(4), 484–506. DOI: 10.1108/JOSM-12-2018-0398

Buhalis, D., & Law, R. (2008). Progress in information technology and tourism management: 20 years on and 10 years after the Internet. *Tourism Management, 29*(4), 609–623. DOI: 10.1016/j.tourman.2008.01.005

Buhalis, D., & Leung, R. (2018). Smart hospitality—Interconnectivity and interoperability towards an ecosystem. *International Journal of Hospitality Management, 71*, 41–50. DOI: 10.1016/j.ijhm.2017.11.011

Buhalis, D., & Sinarta, Y. (2019). Real-time co-creation and nowness service: Lessons from tourism and hospitality. *Journal of Travel & Tourism Marketing, 36*(5), 563–582. DOI: 10.1080/10548408.2019.1592059

Bulsara, H. P., & Pandya, E. A. (2019). Influence of demographic factors on security and privacy concerns in mobile payments. *International Journal of Innovative Technology and Exploring Engineering, 9*(2), 5135–5138. DOI: 10.35940/ijitee.B8125.129219

Burton, S. L. (2025). Digital Saboteurs: Unmasking Insider Cybersecurity Threats in Aviation and Aerospace. *Law. Economics and Society, 1*(2), 1. DOI: 10.30560/les.v1n2p1

Busra, M. M. (2024). An Economic Downfall: Fragile Data Management Systems a Major Security Threat for Sustainable Tourism.

Cantelli-Forti, A., Longo, G., Oveis, A. H., & Russo, E. (2024). *Insights from Field Experience: Digital Forensics of Event and Voyage Data Recorders in Transportation Systems Accident Investigation*. DOI: 10.21203/rs.3.rs-5418837/v1

Casey, E. (2011). Digital Evidence and Computer Crime: Forensic Science, Computers, and the Internet (3rd ed.). Academic Press. Gretzel, U., Sigala, M., Xiang, Z., & Koo, C. (2015). Smart tourism: Foundations and developments. Electronic Markets, 25(3), 179–188.

Casino, F., Dasaklis, T. K., Spathoulas, G. P., Anagnostopoulos, M., Ghosal, A., Borocz, I., Solanas, A., Conti, M., & Patsakis, C. (2022). Research trends, challenges, and emerging topics in digital forensics: A review of reviews. *IEEE Access : Practical Innovations, Open Solutions*, *10*, 25464–25493. DOI: 10.1109/ACCESS.2022.3154059

Casino, F., Pina, C., López-Aguilar, P., Batista, E., Solanas, A., & Patsakis, C. (2022). SoK: Cross-border criminal investigations and digital evidence. *Journal of Cybersecurity*, *8*(1), tyac014. Advance online publication. DOI: 10.1093/cybsec/tyac014

Cassidy, A. A. T. J., Fuad, A., & As Shofy, M. U. A. (2024). Emerging trends and challenges in digital crime: A study of cyber criminal tactics and countermeasures. *TechComp Innovations*, *1*(1), 38–45. DOI: 10.70063/techcompinnovations.v1i1.25

Castelo Gómez, J. M., Carrillo-Mondejar, J., Roldán-Gómez, J., & Martínez-Martínez, J. M. (2023). A Concept Forensic Methodology For The Investigation Of IoT Cyberincidents. *The Computer Journal*. Advance online publication. DOI: 10.1093/comjnl/bxad062

Cavoukian, A. (2011). Privacy by design: The 7 foundational principles, *Information and Privacy Commissioner of Ontario*. Retrieved from https://www.ipc.on.ca (accessed on 03-09-2025)

Chalupa, S., & Petricek, M. (2020). The application of business process management in the hospitality industry: A case study. *IBIMA Business Review*, *2020*, 1–11. DOI: 10.5171/2020.301930

Chandra, S., Srivastava, S. C., & Theng, Y. (2010). Evaluating the Role of Trust in Consumer Adoption of Mobile Payment Systems: An Empirical Analysis. *Communications of the Association for Information Systems*, *27*, 561–588. DOI: 10.17705/1CAIS.02729

Chang, H.-C., Lund, B. D., Beuerlein, E., & Mote, C. (2025). Investigating the symbiotic relationship between artificial intelligence and blockchain to promote zero-trust cybersecurity in an evolving information ecosystem. *Information Discovery and Delivery*. Advance online publication. DOI: 10.1108/IDD-11-2024-0185

Cheng, M., & Kapoor, B. (2022). Digital transformation and cybersecurity challenges in the tourism and hospitality sector. *Tourism Management Perspectives*, *41*, 100947. DOI: 10.1016/j.tmp.2021.100947

Cheng, X., Xue, T., Yang, B., & Ma, B. (2023). A digital transformation approach in hospitality and tourism research. *International Journal of Contemporary Hospitality Management*, *35*(8), 2944–2967. DOI: 10.1108/IJCHM-06-2022-0679

Chen, H. S., & Fiscus, J. (2018). The inhospitable vulnerability: A need for cybersecurity risk assessment in the hospitality industry. *Journal of Hospitality and Tourism Technology*, *9*(2), 223–234. DOI: 10.1108/JHTT-07-2017-0044

Cheung, C., & To, W. M. (2017). The influence of perceived trust on e-tourism adoption: An empirical study. *Journal of Information Technology & Tourism*, *17*(3), 329–348.

Choi, S., Yeon, J., Song, H. J., & Hu, J. (2022). Information technology as a buffer against COVID-19. *Annals of Tourism Research*, *98*, 103527. DOI: 10.1016/j.annals.2022.103527 PMID: 36575669

Chorna, N., Korzh, N., Kiziun, A., Onyshchuk, N., & Antoniuk, K. (2024). The role of digital technologies in the transformation of the tourism business: Prospects for development and impact on the country's economy. *Journal of Interdisciplinary Research*, *14*(1), 136–140. DOI: 10.33543/140139136140

Chowdhury, N., Gkioulos, V., Olsen, R., & Petersen, S. A. (2020). Phishing attacks: Scenarios and defense mechanisms. *Computers & Security*, *97*, 101947. DOI: 10.1016/j.cose.2020.101947

Chowdhury, R. H., & Mostafa, A. (2024). Digital forensics and business management: The role of digital forensics in investigating cybercrimes affecting digital businesses. *World Journal of Advanced Research and Reviews*, *23*(2), 1060–1069. DOI: 10.30574/wjarr.2024.23.2.2438

Chung, N., & Koo, C. (2015). The use of social media in travel information search. *Telematics and Informatics*, *32*(2), 215–229. DOI: 10.1016/j.tele.2014.08.005

Cinar, K. (2020). The Digital Revolution: Impact on Tourism Education. *Journal of Tourism and Gastronomy Studies*, *8*(4), 2417–2443. DOI: 10.21325/jotags.2020.719

Cloud security for smart sensor network. (2025). In S. Divadari, *Sensor Networks for Smart Hospitals* (pp. 477–503). Elsevier. DOI: 10.1016/B978-0-443-36370-2.00023-2

Conduah, A. K., Ofoe, S., & Siaw-Marfo, D. (2025). Data privacy in healthcare: Global challenges and solutions. *Digital Health*, *11*, 20552076251343959. DOI: 10.1177/20552076251343959

Coombs, W. T. (2015). *Ongoing crisis communication: Planning, managing, and responding* (4th ed.). SAGE Publications.

Coombs, W. T., & Holladay, S. J. (2012). *The handbook of crisis communication*. Wiley-Blackwell.

Costa, M. (2025). Exploring Hacktivism: The Role and Impact of Social Media. *ARIS2 : Advanced Research on Information Systems Security*, *5*(1), 99–111. DOI: 10.56394/aris2.v5i1.56

Crothers, D. J. (2021). The Wrong Road Taken: Social Media Content, Self-Authentication and Misapplication of the Business Records Rule. *North Dakota Law Review*, *96*, 133.

Crotty, J., & Daniel, L. (2021). *Lessons from practice: insights on cybersecurity strategy for business leaders, from SMEs to global enterprises*. Open University.

Culot, G., Nassimbeni, G., Podrecca, M., & Sartor, M. (2021). The ISO/IEC 27001 information security management standard: Literature review and theory-based research agenda. *The TQM Journal*, *33*(7), 76–105. DOI: 10.1108/TQM-09-2020-0202

Cybersecurity in Travel and Tourism. A Risk-Based Approach. (2020). In A. Paraskevas, *Handbook of e-Tourism* (pp. 1–24). Springer International Publishing. DOI: 10.1007/978-3-030-05324-6_100-1

Czuryk, M. (2023). *Cybersecurity and Protection of Critical Infrastructure*. Studia IuridicaLublinensia., DOI: 10.17951/sil.2023.32.5.43-52

Dalal, M., & Juneja, M. (2020). Steganography and Steganalysis (in digital forensics): A Cybersecurity guide. *Multimedia Tools and Applications*, *80*(4), 5723–5771. DOI: 10.1007/s11042-020-09929-9

Daniel, S. A., & Victor, S. S.Sontan Adewale DanielSamuel Segun Victor. (2024). Emerging trends in cybersecurity for Critical Infrastructure protection: A comprehensive review. *Computer Science & IT Research Journal*, *5*(3), 576–593. DOI: 10.51594/csitrj.v5i3.872

Daraojimba, R. E., Farayola, O. A., Olatoye, F. M. O., Mhlongo, N., & Oke, T. T. L. (2023). Forensic accounting in the digital age: a US perspective: scrutinizing methods and challenges in digital financial fraud prevention. *Finance & Accounting Research Journal*, *5*(11), 342–360. DOI: 10.51594/farj.v5i11.614

Das, G., Ali, Y. A., Singh, B., & Nag, K. (2025). Digital Forensics in E-Commerce: Investigating Online Payment Fraud and Data Breaches. *International Journal of Innovations in Science, Engineering And Management*, 262-268.

Das, P., & Sarkar, P. (2022). The Importance of Digital Forensics in the Admissibility of Digital Evidence. *NUJS J. Regul. Stud.*, *7*, 60.

de Magalhaes, M. (2021). Data protection regulation: A comparative law approach. *International Journal of Digital Law*, *2*(2), 33–53. DOI: 10.47975/IJDL.magalhaes.v.2.n.2

Debruyne, C., Pandit, H. J., Lewis, D., & O'Sullivan, D. (2020). "Just-in-time" generation of datasets by considering structured representations of given consent for GDPR compliance. *Knowledge and Information Systems*, *62*(9), 3615–3640. DOI: 10.1007/s10115-020-01468-x PMID: 32647404

Demirer, M., Hernández, D. J., Li, D., & Peng, S. (2024). Data, privacy laws and firm production: Evidence from the GDPR. *SSRN. NBER Working Paper No. w32146*. DOI: 10.2139/ssrn.4731055

Desamsetti, H., & Mandapuram, M. (2017). A Review of Meta-Model Designed for the Model-Based Testing Technique. *Engineering International*, *5*(2), 107–110. DOI: 10.18034/ei.v5i2.661

Dewangan, K. K., Panda, V., Ojha, S., Shahapure, A., & Jahagirdar, S. R. (2024). Cyber Threats and Its Mitigation to Intelligent Transportation System. *SAE Technical Paper Series*. DOI: 10.4271/2024-26-0184

Dhande, K. R. (2024). Fourth Industrial Revolution and the role of cyber security. In *Advances in hospitality, tourism and the services industry (AHTSI) book series* (pp. 241–257). DOI: 10.4018/979-8-3693-2715-9.ch013

Dhande, K. R. (2024). Fourth Industrial Revolution and the Role of Cyber Security: Technologies on the Travel and Tourism Industry and More Specifically Cyber Security in Travel Tourism. In *Corporate Cybersecurity in the Aviation, Tourism, and Hospitality Sector* (pp. 241-257). IGI Global.

Diamantopoulou, V., Tsohou, A., & Karyda, M. (2020). From ISO/IEC27001:2013 and ISO/IEC27002:2013 to GDPR compliance controls. *Information and Computer Security*, *28*(4), 645–662. DOI: 10.1108/ICS-01-2020-0004

Dimakopoulou, A., & Rantos, K. (2024). Comprehensive Analysis of Maritime Cybersecurity Landscape Based on the NIST CSF v2.0. *Journal of Marine Science and Engineering*, *12*(6), 919. DOI: 10.3390/jmse12060919

Dinesha, H. A., & Jayanthila, D. (2023). Forensics: Cybercrime investigation analysis in social networks. *Journal of Digital Security*, *1*(2), 20. DOI: 10.26634/jds.1.2.20377

Disterer, G. (2013). ISO/IEC 27000, 27001 and 27002 for information security management. *Journal of Information Security*, *4*(2), 92–99. DOI: 10.4236/jis.2013.42011

Dodds, R., & Joppe, M. (2005). *CSR in the tourism industry?: The status of and potential for certification, codes of conduct and guidelines*. IFC.

Drake, R., & Ridder, E. (2022). *Healthcare cybersecurity vulnerabilities.*, DOI: 10.19107/CYBERCON.2022.06

Ebuzor, J. (2024). Understanding Customer Perception of Cyber Attacks: Impact on Trust and Security. In *Corporate Cybersecurity in the Aviation, Tourism, and Hospitality Sector* (pp. 83-111). IGI Global.

Efthimiou, S. G. (2024). The adaptation of tourism industry and COVID-19. *Theoretical Economics Letters*, *14*(6), 2081–2094. DOI: 10.4236/tel.2024.146103

El Khoury, P., Kassar, A., & Tohme, M. (2021). Ransomware in hospitality: Threats, challenges, and solutions. *Journal of Information Security and Applications*, *60*, 102887. DOI: 10.1016/j.jisa.2021.102887

El-Bably, A. Y. (2021). Overview of the impact of human error on cybersecurity based on ISO/IEC 27001 information security management. *Journal of Information Security and Cybercrimes Research*, *4*(1), 95–102. DOI: 10.26735/WLPW6121

Eleimat, M., & Őszi, A. (2025). *Cybersecurity in Aviation: Exploring the Significance, Applications, and Challenges of Cybersecurity in the Aviation Sector*. PeriodicaPolytechnica Transportation Engineering., DOI: 10.3311/PPtr.37153

Elmarady, A. A., & Rahouma, K. H. (2021). Studying Cybersecurity in Civil Aviation, Including Developing and Applying Aviation Cybersecurity Risk Assessment. *IEEE Access : Practical Innovations, Open Solutions*, *9*, 143997–144016. DOI: 10.1109/ACCESS.2021.3121230

Elphick, D. (2025, July 23). Hotel guide to Global Distribution System (GDS). SiteMinder. https://www.siteminder.com/r/global-distribution-system/ (accessed on 04-09-2025)

Erbas, M., Khalil, S. M., & Tsiopoulos, L. (2024). Systematic literature review of threat modeling and risk assessment in ship cybersecurity. *Ocean Engineering*, *306*, 118059. DOI: 10.1016/j.oceaneng.2024.118059

Erdem, A., & Şeker, F. (2021). Tourist experience and digital transformation. In *Advances in hospitality, tourism and the services industry (AHTSI) book series* (pp. 103–120). DOI: 10.4018/978-1-7998-8528-3.ch006

Eren, H., Karaduman, Ö., & Gençoğlu, M. T. (2025). Security and Privacy in the Internet of Everything (IoE): A Review on Blockchain, Edge Computing, AI, and Quantum-Resilient Solutions. *Applied Sciences (Basel, Switzerland), 15*(15), 8704. DOI: 10.3390/app15158704

Erol, I., Neuhofer, I. O., Dogru, T., Oztel, A., Searcy, C., & Yorulmaz, A. C. (2022). Improving sustainability in the tourism industry through blockchain technology: Challenges and opportunities. *Tourism Management, 93*, 104628. DOI: 10.1016/j.tourman.2022.104628

European Commission. (2018). *General Data Protection Regulation (GDPR).* Official Journal of the European Union. https://gdpr-info.eu

European Commission. (n.d.). *Data protection.* https://commission.europa.eu/law/law-topic/data-protection_en

European Union. (2016). *General Data Protection Regulation (GDPR): Regulation (EU) 2016/679.* Official Journal of the European Union. https://eur-lex.europa.eu/eli/reg/2016/679/oj

Fakir, F. Z., & Baydeniz, E. (2024). *The Future of Blockchain in Tourism and Hospitality: Global Insights.* Taylor & Francis. DOI: 10.4324/9781003521617

Fan, Z., Wu, F., & Cao, Z. (2022). Blockchain-based secure data sharing for online booking platforms. *Information Systems Frontiers, 24*(2), 361–377.

Faqir, R. S. (2023). Digital criminal investigations in the era of artificial intelligence: A comprehensive overview. *International Journal of Cyber Criminology, 17*(2), 77–94.

Farhad, M. A. (2024). Consumer data protection laws and their impact on business models in the tech industry. *Telecommunications Policy, 48*(9), 102836. DOI: 10.1016/j.telpol.2024.102836

Fatorachian, H., & Kazemi, H. (2024). AI-enhanced fault-tolerant control and security in transportation and logistics systems: Addressing physical and cyber threats. *Complex Engineering Systems, 4*(3). Advance online publication. DOI: 10.20517/ces.2024.35

Fauzi, R., & Lubis, M. (2021). Assessment framework for defining the maturity of information technology within enterprise risk management (ERM). *International Journal of Advanced Computer Science and Applications, 12*(10), 680–689. DOI: 10.14569/IJACSA.2021.0121075

Faye, S., Abdulrahman, J., Talb, R. A., & Martin, R. (2024). Cybersecurity in Aviation: A Case-Based Approach to Preparedness. *International Journal of Information Security and Cybercrime, 13*(2), 33–45. DOI: 10.19107/IJISC.2024.02.03

Ferreira, D. B., & Gromova, E. A. (2024). Digital Evidence: The Admissibility of Leaked and Hacked Evidence in Arbitration Proceedings. *International Journal for the Semiotics of Law-Revue internationale de Sémiotique juridique, 37*(3), 903-922.

Fertik, M., & Thompson, D. (2010). *Wild West 2.0: How to protect and restore your online reputation on the untamed social frontier*. AMACOM.

Fianyi, I. (2016). Curbing cyber-crime and enhancing e-commerce security with digital forensics. arXiv: Cryptography and Security. https://www.arxiv.org/abs/1610.08369

Fjäder, C. (2014). The nation-state, national security and resilience in the age of globalisation. *Resilience, 2*(2), 114–129. DOI: 10.1080/21693293.2014.914771

Florido-Benítez, L. (2024a). The Cybersecurity Applied by Online Travel Agencies and Hotels to Protect Users' Private Data in Smart Cities. *Smart Cities, 7*(1), 475–495. DOI: 10.3390/smartcities7010019

Florido-Benítez, L. (2024b). The types of hackers and cyberattacks in the aviation industry. *Journal of Transportation Security, 17*(1), 13. Advance online publication. DOI: 10.1007/s12198-024-00281-9

Florido-Benítez, L. (2025). The role of cybersecurity as a preventive measure in digital tourism and travel: A systematic literature review. *Deleted Journal, 28*(1), 28. Advance online publication. DOI: 10.1007/s10791-025-09523-3

Frank, M. D. (2023). *Analysis of Malicious Intruder Threats to Data Integrity.*, DOI: 10.1007/978-3-031-33743-7_29

Gadhi, A., Gondu, R. M., Chaudhary, H., & Abiona, O. (2024). Cyber resilience through real-time threat analysis in information security. *International Journal of Communications, Network and Systems Sciences, 17*(4), 51–67. DOI: 10.4236/ijcns.2024.174004

Gajjar, T., Parikh, S., & Shekokar, K. (2025). Integrating Blockchain Technology with AI to Enhance Security Measure. *Indian Scientific Journal Of Research In Engineering And Management, 09*(01), 1–9. DOI: 10.55041/IJSREM40423

Gander, P., Hartley, L., Powell, D., Cabon, P., Hitchcock, E., Mills, A., & Popkin, S. (2011). Fatigue risk management: Organizational factors at the regulatory and industry/company level. *Accident; Analysis and Prevention*, *43*(2), 573–590. DOI: 10.1016/j.aap.2009.11.007 PMID: 21130218

Garach, J., Singh, S. K., N, R. R., Reddy, A. P. C., & Khan, H. (2024). A comprehensive review on artificial intelligence in digital forensics with taxonomies, issues, and solutions. *Advances in Web Technologies and Engineering Book Series*, 1–28. DOI: 10.4018/979-8-3693-6557-1.ch001

Garcia Avila, R. D., F. Miller, J., & S. Iyengar, S. (2024). Current challenges in IoT security and forensics: Strategies for a secure connected future. In Key Issues in Network Protocols and Security. IntechOpen. DOI: 10.5772/intechopen.1007766

George, A. S., Sagayarajan, S., Baskar, T., & Pandey, D. (2023). From paperwork to biometrics: Assessing the digitization of air travel in India through Digi Yatra. *Partners Universal International Innovation Journal*, *1*(4), 110–125.

Ghaderi, Z., Béal, L., Hall, C. M., Zaman, M., Rather, R. A., & Som, A. P. M. (2024). Cybersecurity and smart tourist destinations resilience. *Tourism Recreation Research*, •••, 1–17. DOI: 10.1080/02508281.2024.2434791

Ghaderi, Z., Beal, L., & Houanti, L. (2024). Cybersecurity threats in tourism and hospitality: Perspectives from tourists engaging with sharing economy services. *Current Issues in Tourism*, •••, 1–16. DOI: 10.1080/13683500.2024.2353327

Ghosh, D. (2025, April 15). *2 crore fraud case against fake travel agent*. Times of India. https://timesofindia.indiatimes.com/articleshow/120289096.cms

Giannoukou, I. (2024). Revolutionizing hospitality: Strategic integration of innovation management embracing technological innovation for enhanced customer experiences. *Technium Business and Management*, *7*, 24–39. DOI: 10.47577/business.v7i.10585

Gillespie, T. (2018). *Custodians of the Internet: Platforms, content moderation, and the hidden decisions that shape social media*. Yale University Press.

Gnewuch, U., Morana, S., & Maedche, A. (2018). Towards designing cooperative and social conversational agents for customer service. *Information Systems and e-Business Management*, *16*(3), 491–511. DOI: 10.1007/s10257-017-0364-4

Gong, Y., & Schroeder, A. (2022). A systematic literature review of data privacy and security research on smart tourism. *Tourism Management Perspectives*, *44*, 101019. DOI: 10.1016/j.tmp.2022.101019

González Arias, R., Bermejo Higuera, J., Rainer Granados, J. J., Bermejo Higuera, J. R., & Sicilia Montalvo, J. A. (2024). Systematic review: Anti-forensic computer techniques. *Applied Sciences (Basel, Switzerland)*, *14*(12), 5302. DOI: 10.3390/app14125302

Goodman, M. (2018, November 30). Marriott discloses massive data breach affecting 500 million guests. *The New York Times.*https://www.nytimes.com

Gordon, G. A., & Young, R. R. (2024). *Cyber threats and risks*. Elsevier BV., DOI: 10.1016/B978-0-323-95409-9.00006-9

Gössling, S., & Reinhold, S. (2024). Accelerating small and medium sized tourism enterprises' engagement with climate change. *Journal of Sustainable Tourism*, *33*(5), 840–857. DOI: 10.1080/09669582.2024.2350659

Götzfried, J., & Müller, T. (2014). Analysing Android's Full Disk Encryption Feature. *Journal of Wireless Mobile Networks, Ubiquitous Computing and Dependable Applications*, *5*(1), 84–100.

Grabosky, P. (2007). Requirements of prosecution services to deal with cyber crime. *Crime, Law, and Social Change*, *47*(4–5), 201–223. DOI: 10.1007/s10611-007-9069-1

Granata, D., Mastroianni, M., Rak, M., Cantiello, P., & Salzillo, G. (2024). GDPR compliance through standard security controls: An automated approach. *Journal of High Speed Networks*, *30*(2), 147–174. DOI: 10.3233/JHS-230080

Grechyn, V., & McShane, I. (2021). "Seriously, Australia, why are you so stingy with Wi-Fi?": Customer satisfaction with Wi-Fi speed in Australian hotels and lessons for public Wi-Fi provision. *Journal of Hospitality and Tourism Technology*, *12*(4), 730–744. DOI: 10.1108/JHTT-01-2020-0025

Gretzel, U., Fuchs, M., Baggio, R., Hoepken, W., Law, R., Neidhardt, J., Pesonen, J., Zanker, M., & Xiang, Z. (2020). e-Tourism beyond COVID-19: A call for transformative research. *Information Technology & Tourism*, *22*(2), 187–203. DOI: 10.1007/s40558-020-00181-3

Gretzel, U., Sigala, M., Xiang, Z., & Koo, C. (2015). Smart tourism: Foundations and developments. *Electronic Markets*, *25*(3), 179–188. DOI: 10.1007/s12525-015-0196-8

Grimm, P. W., Grossman, M. R., & Cormack, G. V. (2021). Artificial intelligence as evidence. *Nw. J. Tech. & Intell. Prop.*, *19*, 9.

Grobler, C. P., & Louwrens, C. P. (2007). Digital forensic readiness as a component of information security best practice. In New Approaches for Security, Privacy and Trust in Complex Environments (pp. 13–24). Springer US. DOI: 10.1007/978-0-387-72367-9_2

Gruber, J., Voigt, L., Benenson, Z., & Freiling, F. C. (2022). Foundations of cybercriminalistics: From general process models to case-specific concretizations in cybercrime investigations. *Forensic Science International Digital Investigation*, *43*, 301438. DOI: 10.1016/j.fsidi.2022.301438

Gundu, T. (2024). A cybersecurity collaborative model: Best practices sharing among South African tourism and hospitality businesses. *International Conference on Tourism Research*, 7(1), 222–231. DOI: 10.34190/ictr.7.1.2159

Gurgu, E., Zorzoliu, R. I., Pistol, L., Gurgu, I., Ungureanu, C., & Nae, G. (2021). The relationship between big datadriven technologies and performance management strategies applied to companies in the hospitality, tourism & travel industry. *Annals of Spiru Haret University. Economic Series*, *21*(4), 97–136.

Gursoy, D., & Chi, C. G. (2020). Effects of COVID-19 pandemic on hospitality industry: Review of the current situations and a research agenda. *Journal of Hospitality Marketing & Management*, *29*(5), 527–529. DOI: 10.1080/19368623.2020.1788231

Gursoy, D., Chi, C. G., Lu, L., & Nunkoo, R. (2019). Consumers acceptance of artificially intelligent (AI) device use in service delivery. *International Journal of Information Management*, *49*, 157–169. DOI: 10.1016/j.ijinfomgt.2019.03.008

Guttman, B., White, D. R., Walraven, T., & (U.S.), N. I. of S. and T. (2022). Digital evidence preservation : DOI: 10.6028/NIST.IR.8387

Hamarat, H., Sahin, H., Koç Apuhan, A., & İnan, R. (2024). The dark side of artificial intelligence: Threats to tourism workers. *Worldwide Hospitality and Tourism Themes*, *16*(2), 127–137. DOI: 10.1108/WHATT-03-2024-0061

Harchandani, R., Bansal, P., Jain, S., Sondhi, J. K., & Jacob, L. (2024). Big Data Paradigm in Cybercrime Investigation. In *Artificial Intelligence for Cyber Defense and Smart Policing* (pp. 91–109). Chapman and Hall/CRC. DOI: 10.1201/9781003251781-7

Harison, E., & Zaidenberg, N. J. (2018). *Survey of cyber threats in air traffic control and aircraft communications systems* (Vol. 2018). Springer., DOI: 10.1007/978-3-319-75307-2_12

Hayes, D., & Kyobe, M. (2020). The adoption of automation in cyber forensics. IEEE International Conference on ICT and Automation for Sustainability, 1–6. DOI: 10.1109/ICTAS47918.2020.233977

Helgadottir, D. (2019). The interaction between Directive 2015/2366 (EU) on payment services (PSD2) and Regulation (EU) 2016/679 on general data protection (GDPR) concerning third party players. SSRN *Electronic Journal*. DOI: 10.2139/ssrn.3455428

Herke, C., Tóth, D., & Perkumienė, D. (2025). The role of artificial intelligence in cybercrime in the tourism sector. In *World sustainability series* (pp. 415–433). DOI: 10.1007/978-3-031-81485-3_17

Hernández-White, C., Rodríguez-Díaz, B., & Expósito-García, A. (2024). Tourism intelligence, key to reviving the sector. In Tourism and ICTs: Advances in Data Science, Artificial Intelligence and Sustainability (pp. 123–136). Springer Nature Switzerland. DOI: 10.1007/978-3-031-52607-7_12

Heskett, J. L., Jones, T. O., Loveman, G. W., Sasser, W. E.Jr, & Schlesinger, L. A. (1994). Putting the service-profit chain to work. *Harvard Business Review*, *72*(2), 164–174.

Hilton Worldwide. (2016). *Hilton introduces "Connie" the robot concierge powered by IBM Watson.* Hilton Newsroom. https://newsroom.hilton.com

Hinduja, S., & Patchin, J. W. (2014). *Cyberbullying: Identification, prevention, and response*. Cyberbullying Research Center.

Ho, F. N., Ho-Dac, N., & Huang, J. S. (2023). The Effects of Privacy and Data Breaches on Consumers' Online Self-Disclosure, Protection Behavior, and Message Valence. *SAGE Open*, *13*(3), 21582440231181395. DOI: 10.1177/21582440231181395

Holloway, J. (2012). Crisis communication in the digital age: Social media's role in crisis communication. *Journal of Business Continuity & Emergency Planning*, *6*(1), 84–92. PMID: 22948108

Holt, T. J., Bossler, A. M., & Seigfried-Spellar, K. C. (2022). *Cybercrime and digital forensics*. DOI: 10.4324/9780429343223

Hua, N., Li, B., & Zhang, T. (2020). Crime research in hospitality and tourism. *International Journal of Contemporary Hospitality Management*, *32*(3), 1299–1323. DOI: 10.1108/IJCHM-09-2019-0750

Huang, H. Y., Ku, E. C., & Chen, C. D. (2022). Cloud infrastructure enhancing product competitive advantage of tourism SMEs on online consumption values of tourists. *Business Process Management Journal*, *28*(4), 1146–1163. DOI: 10.1108/BPMJ-05-2022-0246

Hundal, G. S., Rhodes, D. H., & Laux, C. (2025). Digital transformation of healthcare enterprises in the era of disruptions—A structured literature review. *Sustainability (Basel)*, *17*(13), 5690. DOI: 10.3390/su17135690

Hurst, W., & Shone, N. (2024). *Critical infrastructure security: Cyber-threats, legacy systems and weakening segmentation*. Elsevier BV., DOI: 10.1016/B978-0-323-99330-2.00010-6

Hussein, H. S., Albadry, O. M., Mathew, V., Al-Romeedy, B. S., Alsetoohy, O., Kamar, M. A., & Khairy, H. A. (2024). Digital leadership and sustainable competitive advantage: Leveraging green absorptive capability and eco-innovation in tourism and hospitality businesses. *Sustainability (Basel)*, *16*(13), 5371. DOI: 10.3390/su16135371

Hutchings, A. (2021). Flying in cyberspace: Policing global travel fraud. *Policing: A Journal of* Ibrahim, F. M., Alawsi, H., & Mohammed, M. N. (2025). The Evolution of Cybercrime: Challenges and Advancements in Digital Forensics. In *Tech Fusion in Business and Society: Harnessing Big Data, IoT, and Sustainability in Business* (Vol. 2, pp. 455–464). Springer Nature Switzerland.

Illiashenko, O., Kharchenko, V., Babeshko, I., Fesenko, H., & Di Giandomenico, F. (2023). Security-Informed Safety Analysis of Autonomous Transport Systems Considering AI-Powered Cyberattacks and Protection. *Entropy (Basel, Switzerland)*, *25*(8), 1123. DOI: 10.3390/e25081123 PMID: 37628153

Information Commissioner's Office. (2020). *Marriott International fined for data breach*. ICO. https://ico.org.uk

Institute", N. T. U. of U. "Igor S. K. P., Pronin, Y., Zubok, V., & Ukraine, G. E. P. I. for M. in E. E. N. A. of S. of. (2025). Methods and models for ensuring information security during the collection of digital evidence. Elektronnoe Modelirovanie, 47(3), 104–111. DOI: 10.15407/emodel.47.03.104

International Aviation and Megatrends. (2020). In R. Abeyratne, *Aviation in the Digital Age* (pp. 13–42). Springer International Publishing. DOI: 10.1007/978-3-030-48218-3_2

Isaak, J., & Hanna, M. J. (2018). User data privacy: Facebook, Cambridge Analytica, and privacy protection. *Computer*, *51*(8), 56–59. DOI: 10.1109/MC.2018.3191268

ISO. (2013). *ISO/IEC 27001: Information technology — Security techniques — Information security management systems — Requirements.* International Organization for Standardization. https://www.iso.org/isoiec-27001-information-security.html

ISO. (2022). *ISO/IEC 27001:2022 Information security, cybersecurity and privacy protection — Information security management systems — Requirements.* https://www.iso.org/standard/27001

Ivanov, S., & Webster, C. (2019). Adoption of robots, artificial intelligence and service automation by travel, tourism and hospitality companies – A cost-benefit analysis. *International Journal of Contemporary Hospitality Management, 31*(7), 2510–2528. DOI: 10.1108/IJCHM-05-2018-0370

Ivanov, S., Webster, C., & Berezina, K. (2017). Adoption of robots and service automation by tourism and hospitality companies. *Revista Turismo & Desenvolvimento (Aveiro), 27/28*, 1501–1517.

Ivanov, S., Webster, C., & Garenko, A. (2018). Young Russian adults' attitudes towards the potential use of robots in hotels. *Technology in Society, 55*, 24–32. DOI: 10.1016/j.techsoc.2018.06.004

Iyelolu, T. V., Agu, E. E., Idemudia, C., & Ijomah, T. I. (2024). Leveraging Artificial Intelligence for Personalised Marketing Campaigns to Improve Conversion Rates. *International Journal of Engineering Research and Development, 20*(8), 253–270.

Iyengar, S. S., Nabavirazavi, S., & Hariprasad, Y. HB, P., & Mohan, C. K. (2025). Digital Forensics: Tools, Techniques, and Methodologies. In *Artificial Intelligence in Practice: Theory and Application for Cyber Security and Forensics* (pp. 89-137). Cham: Springer Nature Switzerland.

Jamal, T., Kircher, J., & Donaldson, J. P. (2021). Re-visiting design thinking for learning and practice: Critical pedagogy, conative empathy. *Sustainability (Basel), 13*(2), 964. DOI: 10.3390/su13020964

Jayabalan, J., & Jeyanthi, N. (2022). Scalable blockchain model using off-chain IPFS storage for healthcare data security and privacy. *Journal of Parallel and Distributed Computing, 164*, 152–167. DOI: 10.1016/j.jpdc.2022.03.009

Jha, A. K., Agi, M. A. N., & Ngai, E. W. T. (2020). A note on big data analytics capability development in supply chain. *Decision Support Systems, 138*, 113382. DOI: 10.1016/j.dss.2020.113382

Jimmy, F. (2021). Emerging threats: The latest cybersecurity risks and the role of artificial intelligence in enhancing cybersecurity defenses. *Valley International Journal Digital Library, 1*(2), 564–574. DOI: 10.18535/ijsrm/v9i2.ec01

Johnson, M. S., Kang, M. J., Lawson, T., & Singh, A. J. (2018). The impact of data breaches on hotel and restaurant firm stock returns. *The Journal of Hospitality Financial Management*, *26*(2), 75–86. https://core.ac.uk/reader/220129940

Jones, P., & Comfort, D. (2021). Corporate digital responsibility in the hospitality industry. *Athens Journal of Tourism*, *8*(1), 9–18. DOI: 10.30958/ajt.8-1-1

Judijanto, L., Endrianto, E., & Vandika, A. Y. (2024). Mapping the Cybersecurity Research through Bibliometric Analysis. *West Science Information System and Technology*, *2*(03), 374–382. DOI: 10.58812/wsist.v2i03.1534

Kalinaki, K. (2024). Ransomware threat mitigation strategies for protecting critical infrastructure assets. In *Ransomware Evolution* (pp. 120–143). CRC Press. DOI: 10.1201/9781003469506-10

Kamal, R., Hemdan, E. E.-D., & El-Fishway, N. (2022). Forensics chain for evidence preservation system: An evidence preservation forensics framework for internet of things-based smart city security using blockchain. *Concurrency and Computation*, *34*(21), e7062. Advance online publication. DOI: 10.1002/cpe.7062

Kande, S. K. (2024). Comparative Study of CTEM Frameworks: NIST, MITRE, and Beyond. *Journal of Engineering and Applied Sciences Technology*, *1–2*. Advance online publication. DOI: 10.47363/JEAST/2025(7)283

Kansakar, P., Munir, A., & Shabani, N. (2019). Technology in hospitality industry: Prospects and challenges. *IEEE Consumer Electronics Magazine*, *8*(3), 60–65. DOI: 10.1109/MCE.2019.2892245

Kapse, I. (2022). Digital Evidence: Admission, Tampering and Its Prevention. *Issue 1 Indian JL & Legal Rsch.*, *4*, 1.

Karadayi-Usta, S. (2024). Cybersecurity Risks Analysis in the Hospitality Industry: A Stakeholder Perspective on Sustainable Service Systems. *Systems*, *12*(10), 397. DOI: 10.3390/systems12100397

Karagiannis, C., & Vergidis, K. (2021). Digital evidence and cloud forensics: Contemporary legal challenges and the power of disposal. *Information (Basel)*, *12*(5), 181. DOI: 10.3390/info12050181

Karchefsky, S., & Rao, H. R. (2017). *Toward a Safer Tomorrow: Cybersecurity and Critical Infrastructure*. Palgrave Macmillan., DOI: 10.1057/978-1-137-60228-2_15

Karthikeyan, P., Nachimuthu, P., Vadivelu, V., & Priyadharshini, S. (2026). Transforming Tourism: Exploring the Potential of Blockchain Technology. *Blockchain Technology for the Engineering and Service Sectors*, 307-343.

Kasper, A., & Laurits, E. (2016). Challenges in collecting Digital Evidence: A Legal perspective. In *Springer eBooks* (pp. 195–233). DOI: 10.1007/978-3-319-26896-5_10

Kaur, R., Gabrijelčič, D., & Klobučar, T. (2023). Artificial intelligence for cybersecurity: Literature review and future research directions. *Information Fusion, 97*, 101804. DOI: 10.1016/j.inffus.2023.101804

Kazaure, A. A., Jantan, A., & Yusoff, M. N. (2023). Digital forensics investigation approaches in mitigating cybercrimes: A review. *Journal of Information Science Theory and Practice, 11*(4), 14–39. DOI: 10.1633/JISTaP.2023.11.4.2

Khadka, K. (2025). Cybersecurity Challenges and Solutions in the Digital Transformation of Hospitality. *Available at SSRN* 5219742. DOI: 10.2139/ssrn.5219742

Khaleefah, A. D., & Al-Mashhadi, H. M. (2024). Methodologies, Requirements, and Challenges of Cybersecurity Frameworks: A Review. *Iraqi Journal of Science*, 468–486. Advance online publication. DOI: 10.24996/ijs.2024.65.1.38

Khan, W. A. (2023). Innovating with AI-Driven Threat Detection and Blockchain-Based Data Protection: Exploring the Benefits and Challenges of Implementing Emerging Technologies in Cybersecurity. *Design of Single Chip Microcomputer Control System for Stepping Motor*, 1–15. DOI: 10.47363/JAICC/2023(2)E171

Khan, A. A., Shaikh, A. A., Laghari, A. A., Dootio, M. A., Rind, M. M., & Awan, S. A. (2022). Digital forensics and cyber forensics investigation: Security challenges, limitations, open issues, and future direction. *International Journal of Electronic Security and Digital Forensics, 14*(2), 124. DOI: 10.1504/IJESDF.2022.121174

Khan, S., Nicholson, B., & Tsoukas, H. (2021). Vulnerabilities in global value chains: A case study of the tourism sector. *Journal of Business Research, 124*, 240–252.

Kietzmann, J. H., Hermkens, K., McCarthy, I. P., & Silvestre, B. S. (2011). Social media? Get serious! Understanding the functional building blocks of social media. *Business Horizons, 54*(3), 241–251. DOI: 10.1016/j.bushor.2011.01.005

Kim, J., Kim, S., & Nam, C. (2019). Data privacy concerns and the adoption of mobile tourism applications. *Sustainability, 11*(19), 5209.

Kitsios, F., Chatzidimitriou, E., & Kamariotou, M. (2022). Developing a risk analysis strategy framework for impact assessment in information security management systems: A case study in IT consulting industry. *Sustainability (Basel), 14*(3), 1269. DOI: 10.3390/su14031269

Kiyimba, N., Lester, J. N., & O'Reilly, M. (2018). Utilising media and text-based sources. *Using naturally occurring data in qualitative health research: A practical guide*, 159–178. DOI: 10.1007/978-3-319 94839-3_7

Kizildag, M., Dogru, T., Zhang, T., Mody, M. A., Altin, M., & Ozturk, A. B. (2019). Blockchain and smart contracts: Applications in travel, tourism, and hospitality. *Journal of Hospitality and Tourism Technology*, *10*(3), 410–422. DOI: 10.1108/JHTT-02-2019-0026

Klasén, L., Fock, N., & Forchheimer, R. (2024). The invisible evidence: Digital forensics as key to solving crimes in the digital age. *Forensic Science International*, *362*, 112133. DOI: 10.1016/j.forsciint.2024.112133 PMID: 39089208

Koepsel, K. M. (2016). *Commercial Aviation and Cyber Security: A Critical Intersection*. SAE International., DOI: 10.4271/T-132

Krabokoukis, T. (2023). Technology tools in hospitality: Mapping the landscape through bibliometric analysis and presentation of a new software solution. *Digital*, *3*(1), 81–96. DOI: 10.3390/digital3010006

Krombholz, K., Hobel, H., Huber, M., & Weippl, E. (2015). Advanced social engineering attacks. *Journal of Information Security and Applications*, *22*, 113–122. DOI: 10.1016/j.jisa.2014.09.005

Krügel, C., Toth, T., & Kerer, C. (2001, December). Decentralized event correlation for intrusion detection. In *International Conference on Information Security and Cryptology* (pp. 114-131). Berlin, Heidelberg: Springer Berlin Heidelberg.

Krzan, B. (2021). Admissibility of evidence and international criminal justice. *Rev. Brasileira de Direito Processual Penal*, *7*(1), 161. DOI: 10.22197/rbdpp.v7i1.492

Kshetri, N. (2017). The emerging role of big data in key development issues: Opportunities, challenges, and concerns. *Big Data & Society*, *4*(2), 1–20. DOI: 10.1177/2053951717726557

Kumar, A., & Raina, A. (2025). The crucial role of cybersecurity in protecting service infrastructure. In Advances in Hospitality, Tourism, and the Services Industry (pp. 93–102). IGI Global. DOI: 10.4018/979-8-3693-7447-4.ch006

Kumar, M. (2024). A comprehensive framework for preventing digital arrest scams: Integrating predictive crime script models, cognitive resilience, advanced forensics, and public awareness. International Journal of Advanced Research in Science. *Tongxin Jishu*, •••, 736–745. DOI: 10.48175/IJARSCT-18796

Kumar, M. V. S., Khekare, G., & Sankriti, A. (2025). Enhancing knowledge management integrity through fake news detection: A hybrid LSTM-XGBoost approach for cybersecurity. In *Cybersecurity in Knowledge Management* (pp. 131–150). CRC Press., DOI: 10.1201/9781003498094-9

Kumar, S., Kumar, V., Bhatt, I. K., Kumar, S., & Attri, K. (2023). Digital transformation in tourism sector: Trends and future perspectives from a bibliometric-content analysis. *Journal of Hospitality and Tourism Insights*, *7*(3), 1553–1576. DOI: 10.1108/JHTI-10-2022-0472

Kumar, V., Ashraf, A. R., & Nadeem, W. (2024). AI-powered marketing: What, Where, and how? *International Journal of Information Management*, *77*, 102783. DOI: 10.1016/j.ijinfomgt.2024.102783

Kumar, V., Asthana, A., & Tripathi, G. (2025). Enhancing data security in IOT-based UAV networks through blockchain integration. *Engineering Technology & Applied Science Research*, *15*(2), 21800–21804. DOI: 10.48084/etasr.9922

Labadie, C., & Legner, C. (2023). Building data management capabilities to address data protection regulations: Learnings from EU-GDPR. *Journal of Information Technology*, *38*(1), 16–44. DOI: 10.1177/02683962221141456

Lam, C. Y. T., & Law, R. (2018). Readiness of upscale and luxury-branded hotels for digital transformation. *International Journal of Hospitality Management*, *79*, 60–69. DOI: 10.1016/j.ijhm.2018.12.015

Lanjewar, U., Khekare, G., & Wahi, A. (2024, December). *An in-depth review of machine learning, blockchain, and deep learning models for intelligent security and resilience enhancement in smart cities* [Conference session]. 2024 International Conference on Artificial Intelligence and Quantum Computation-Based Sensor Application (ICAIQSA), Nagpur, India. DOI: 10.1109/ICAIQSA64000.2024.10882264

Lee, S. K., & Min, S. R. (2021). Effects of information quality of online travel agencies on trust and continuous usage intention: An application of the SOR model. *The Journal of Asian Finance, Economics and Business*, *8*(4), 971–982.

Lee, S., & Song, H. (2021). Impact of perceived cybersecurity on customer trust in digital tourism platforms. *Tourism Management Perspectives*, *39*, 100861.

Lehto, M. (2020). *Cyber Security in Aviation, Maritime and Automotive*. Springer., DOI: 10.1007/978-3-030-37752-6_2

Li, M., Bonn, M. A., & Ye, B. H. (2021). Hotel digitalization and customer engagement: The role of artificial intelligence technologies. *International Journal of Hospitality Management*, *94*, 102876. DOI: 10.1016/j.ijhm.2020.102876

Li, M., Fang, Y., & Lim, K. H. (2018). Institutional antecedents and consequences of information reuse: A cross-country investigation. *Journal of Management Information Systems, 34*(4), 1098–1133.

Lin, K.-C., Matthews, W., & Olsen, S. (2024). Middle spacepowers' integration with the global supply chain for the space industry: Taiwan and Thailand. *Business and Politics*, •••, 1–27. DOI: 10.1017/bap.2024.18

Lin, X., Huang, X., Liu, S., Li, Y., Luo, H., & Yu, S. (2022). Competitive Price-Quality Strategy of Platforms under User Privacy Concerns. *Journal of Theoretical and Applied Electronic Commerce Research, 17*(2), 571–589. DOI: 10.3390/jtaer17020030

Lirosi, M. (2024). *Cybersecurity: Hackers don't go on holiday, cyber attacks in tourism are growing*. First Online. https://www.firstonline.info/en/cybersecurity-hackers-don't-go-on-holiday-cyber-attacks-in-tourism-are-increasing/

Li, Y., & Liu, Q. (2021). A comprehensive review study of cyber-attacks and cyber security; Emerging trends and recent developments. *Energy Reports, 7*, 8176–8186. DOI: 10.1016/j.egyr.2021.08.126

Li, Z., Wang, D., Abbas, J., Hassan, S., & Mubeen, R. (2022). Tourists' health risk threats amid COVID-19 era: Role of technology innovation, Transformation, and recovery implications for sustainable tourism. *Frontiers in Psychology, 12*, 769175. DOI: 10.3389/fpsyg.2021.769175 PMID: 35465147

Lopes, I., Guarda, T., & Oliveira, P. (2019). Implementation of ISO 27001 standards as GDPR compliance facilitator. *Journal of Information Systems Engineering & Management, 4*(2), 1–8. DOI: 10.29333/jisem/5888

Louati, A., Louati, H., Alharbi, M., Kariri, E., Khawaji, T., Almubaddil, Y., & Aldwsary, S. (2024). Machine Learning and Artificial Intelligence for a Sustainable Tourism: A Case Study on Saudi Arabia. *Information (Basel), 15*(9), 516. DOI: 10.3390/info15090516

Lovell, D., Vella, K., Muñoz, D., McKague, M., Brereton, M., & Ellis, P. (2022). Exploring technologies to better link physical evidence and digital information for disaster victim identification. *Forensic Sciences Research, 7*(3), 467–483. DOI: 10.1080/20961790.2021.2023418 PMID: 36353313

Lu, L., Cai, R., & Gursoy, D. (2019). Developing and validating a service robot integration willingness scale. *International Journal of Hospitality Management, 80*, 36–51. DOI: 10.1016/j.ijhm.2019.01.005

Luo, X., & Homburg, C. (2007). Neglected outcomes of customer satisfaction. *Journal of Marketing*, *71*(2), 133–149. DOI: 10.1509/jmkg.71.2.133

Lykou, G., Iakovakis, G., & Gritzalis, D. (2019). *Aviation Cybersecurity and Cyber-Resilience: Assessing Risk in Air Traffic Management*. Springer., DOI: 10.1007/978-3-030-00024-0_13

Lykou, G., Moustakas, D., & Gritzalis, D. (2020). Defending Airports from UAS: A Survey on Cyber-Attacks and Counter-Drone Sensing Technologies. *Sensors (Basel)*, *20*(12), 3537. DOI: 10.3390/s20123537 PMID: 32580402

Lyu, J., Khan, A. A. F., Bibi, S., Chan, J. H., & Qi, X. (2022). Big data in action: An overview of big data studies in tourism and hospitality literature. *Journal of Hospitality and Tourism Management*, *51*, 346–360. DOI: 10.1016/j.jhtm.2022.03.014

Ma, C., & Somrak, T. (2025). Digital Infrastructure and Security in the Global Tourism Industry. *Journal of Smart Tourism Systems*, *3*(1), 1–18.

Ma, C., Somrak, T., Manajit, S., & Gao, C. (2025). Exploring the Potential Synergy Between Disruptive Technology and Historical/Cultural Heritage in Thailand's Tourism Industry for Achieving Sustainable Development in the Future. *International Journal of Tourism Research*.

Madnick, B., Huang, K., & Madnick, S. (2021). The Evolution of Cyber Security Norm Development in The Digital Age. In *2021 IEEE International Symposium on Technologies for Homeland Security (HST)*, IEEE.;1–5. DOI: 10.1109/HST53381.2021.9619798

Magoutas, A. I., Manolopoulos, D., Manouka, M., & Dimitropoulou, M. (2024). Digitalization of the alternative tourism marketspace: Evidence from an EU peripheral economy. *Tourism and Hospitality*, *5*(4), 1151–1166. DOI: 10.3390/tourhosp5040064

Mahmood, H., Arshad, M., Ahmed, I., Fatima, S., & Rehman, H. ur. (2024). *Comparative study of IoT forensic frameworks*. DOI: 10.1016/j.fsidi.2024.301748

Malik, A. W., Bhatti, D. S., Park, T. J., Ishtiaq, H. U., Ryou, J. C., & Kim, K. I. (2024). Cloud digital forensics: Beyond tools, techniques, and challenges. *Sensors (Basel)*, *24*(2), 433. DOI: 10.3390/s24020433 PMID: 38257526

Malik, P., Dawar, H., Patel, P., Ahuja, D., & Jain, A. (2024). Enhancing Forensic Analysis of Digital Evidence Using Machine Learning: Techniques, Applications, and Challenges. *International Journal of Innovative Research in Engineering & Multidisciplinary Physical Sciences*, *12*(5), 230988. Advance online publication. DOI: 10.37082/IJIRMPS.v12.i5.230988

Manca, S., & Ranieri, M. (2016). Facebook and the others: Potentials and obstacles of social media for teaching in higher education. *Computers & Education*, *95*, 216–230. DOI: 10.1016/j.compedu.2016.01.012

Mandayam, R. (2024). The intersection of Criminal Justice and Cybersecurity: Legal implications. *INTERANTIONAL JOURNAL OF SCIENTIFIC RESEARCH IN ENGINEERING AND MANAGEMENT*, *09*(02), 1–7. DOI: 10.55041/IJSREM41544

Mandayam, R. (2025). The impact of artificial intelligence on digital forensics. *International Journal of Innovative Research in Engineering & Multidisciplinary Physical Sciences*, *13*(1), 231816. Advance online publication. DOI: 10.37082/IJIRMPS.v13.i1.231816

Mangini, V., & Tal, I., & Moldovan, A.-N. (2020). An empirical study on the impact of GDPR and right to be forgotten – organisations and users perspective. *Proceedings of the 17th International Conference on Availability, Reliability and Security*, 1–9. DOI: 10.1145/3407023.3407080

Marhad, S. S., Goni, S. Z. A., & Sani, M. K. J. A. (2024). Implementation of information security management systems for data protection in organizations: A systematic literature review. *Environment-Behaviour Proceedings Journal*, *9*(SI18), 197–203. DOI: 10.21834/e-bpj.v9iSI18.5483

Mariani, M. M., & Borghi, M. (2021). Customers' evaluation of AI-enabled services in tourism: The role of anthropomorphism, intelligibility, and transparency. *Annals of Tourism Research*, *91*, 103313. DOI: 10.1016/j.annals.2021.103313

Mariani, M., & Baggio, R. (2022). Big data and analytics in hospitality and tourism: A systematic literature review. *International Journal of Contemporary Hospitality Management*, *34*(1), 231–278. DOI: 10.1108/IJCHM-03-2021-0301

Markovic, S. (2025). *Cyberattacks are draining millions from the hospitality industry*. Help Net Security. https://www.helpnetsecurity.com/2025/07/03/hospitality-industry-cybersecurity-challenges/

Marriott International. (2017). *Marriott's ChatBotlr makes service easier.* Marriott News Center. https://news.marriott.com

Marwick, A. E., & Boyd, D. (2011). To see and be seen: Celebrity practice on Twitter. *Convergence (London)*, *17*(2), 139–158. DOI: 10.1177/1354856510394539

Mazhar, M. S., Saleem, Y., Almogren, A., Arshad, J., Jaffery, M. H., Rehman, A. U., Shafiq, M., & Hamam, H. (2022). Forensic analysis on internet of things (IoT) device using machine-to-machine (M2M) framework. *Electronics (Basel)*, *11*(7), 1126. DOI: 10.3390/electronics11071126

Md Ramli, A., Asby, P. N. K., Mohd Noor, H., & Afrizal, T. (2022). Challenges of SME in The Tourism Industry: A review. *Environment-Behaviour Proceedings Journal, 7*(21), 249–256. DOI: 10.21834/ebpj.v7i21.3721

Mhara, M. A. A., Abdulrahman, A. A., & Baroud, A. A. (2024). Cyber attacks and threats: Study of the types of cyber attacks: Hacking, viruses, targeted attacks, and electronic espionage. *Int. J. Electr. Eng. and Sustain.*, 38-47.

Milano, S., Taddeo, M., & Floridi, L. (2021). Recommender systems and their ethical challenges. *AI & Society, 36*(1), 105–113.

Mishra, A., Alzoubi, Y. I., Gill, A. Q., & Anwar, M. J. (2022). Cybersecurity Enterprises Policies: A Comparative Study. *Sensors (Basel), 22*(2), 538. DOI: 10.3390/s22020538

Modern Weapons. Possibilities and Limitations. (2020). In A. Belous & V. Saladukha, *Viruses, Hardware and Software Trojans* (pp. 731–820). Springer International Publishing. DOI: 10.1007/978-3-030-47218-4_8

Mohamed, N., Al-Jaroodi, J., & Jawhar, I. (2020). Cyber–Physical Systems Forensics: Today and tomorrow. *Journal of Sensor and Actuator Networks, 9*(3), 37. DOI: 10.3390/jsan9030037

Mohan, J., Wasserman, M. F., & Chidambaram, V. (2019). *Analyzing GDPR compliance through the lens of privacy policy*. arXiv. /arXiv.1906.12038DOI: 10.1007/978-3-030-33752-0_6

Morrison, A. M., & Buhalis, D. (2024). *Routledge handbook of trends and issues in tourism sustainability, planning and development, management, and technology*. Routledge.

Mulyana, R., Rusu, L., & Perjons, E. (2024). Key ambidextrous IT governance mechanisms for successful digital transformation: A case study of Bank Rakyat Indonesia (BRI). *Digital Business, 4*(2), 100083. DOI: 10.1016/j.digbus.2024.100083

Musa, N., Mirza, N. M., & Ali, A. (2023). Navigating the complex landscape of IoT forensics: Challenges and emerging solutions. *The International Arab Journal of Information Technology, 20*(3A), 492–504. DOI: 10.34028/iajit/20/3A/7

Nagaraj, G. (2024). *Framework Analysis and Zero Trust Security Issues in Contemporary Network Systems*. 1–6. DOI: 10.1109/CSITSS64042.2024.10816783

Nagy, J. (2023). *Maintenance check flight accidents (a new approach to air safety investigations)*. DOI: 10.26192/Z58X7

Naldi, S., Maulina, E., Herawaty, T., & Irawati, R. (2022). Hospitality and tourism innovation: A systematic literature review. [Bisnis Dan Manajemen]. *BISMA, 14*(2), 94–109. DOI: 10.26740/bisma.v14n2.p94-109

Naseem, S., & Yong, T. (2025). Blockchain-based risk management in cross-border data supply chains: A comparative analysis of Alibaba and Infosys. *Sustainability (Basel), 17*(17), 7704. DOI: 10.3390/su17177704

Nasir, R., & Iqbal, W. (2025, May). Digital Forensics Showdown: Encase and FTK Head-to-Head. In *2025 5th International Conference on Innovative Research in Applied Science, Engineering and Technology (IRASET)* (pp. 1-6). IEEE.

Navigating the Regulatory Landscape. (2024). In S. K. Shandilya, A. Datta, Y. Kartik, & A. Nagar, *EAI/Springer Innovations in Communication and Computing* (pp. 127–240). Springer Nature Switzerland. DOI: 10.1007/978-3-031-53290-0_3

Neisse, R., Steri, G., & Fovino, I. N. (2018). Blockchain-based identity management and data usage control (extended abstract). In: Hansen, M., Kosta, E., Nai-Fovino, I., Fischer-Hübner, S. (eds) *Privacy and Identity Management. The Smart Revolution. Privacy and Identity 2017.* IFIP Advances in Information and Communication Technology, vol 526. Springer, Cham. DOI: 10.1007/978-3-319-92925-5_15

Neo, H. F., & Teo, C. C. (2022). Biometrics in tourism: Issues and challenges. *Handbook of e-Tourism*, 1835-1849.

Nessa, J. J., Kleczkowska, A., & Hasar, S. (2024). Digest of state practice: 1 July – 31 December 2023. *Journal on the Use of Force and International Law, 11*(1–2), 297–372. DOI: 10.1080/20531702.2024.2413800

Niescieruk, A., Księżopolski, B., Nielek, R., & Wierzbicki, A. (2017). How to train people to increase their security awareness in IT. In *Lecture Notes in Electrical Engineering* (pp. 12–17). Springer., DOI: 10.1007/978-981-10-5041-1_3

Nifakos, S., Chandramouli, K., Nikolaou, C. K., Papachristou, P., Koch, S., Panaousis, E., & Bonacina, S. (2021). Influence of Human Factors on Cyber Security within Healthcare Organisations: A Systematic Review. *Sensors (Basel), 21*(15), 5119. DOI: 10.3390/s21155119 PMID: 34372354

Nikkel, B. J. (2020). Fintech forensics: Criminal investigation and digital evidence in financial technologies. *Forensic Science International Digital Investigation, 33*, 200908. DOI: 10.1016/j.fsidi.2020.200908

NIST, G. M. (2024). *The NIST Cybersecurity Framework (CSF) 2.0 (French translation)*. DOI: 10.6028/NIST.CSWP.29.fre

Nithyasree, N., Kumaraguru, V., Hariharan, T., Balaji, S., Harris, M., & Selvam, A. V. (2025). Unified Digital Forensic Toolkit (UDFT): Streamlining Digital investigation. In *Algorithms for intelligent systems* (pp. 367–385). DOI: 10.1007/978-981-96-5265-5_28

Nobles, C. (2017). *Cyber Threats in Civil Aviation*. IGI Global., DOI: 10.4018/978-1-5225-0741-3.ch011

Nosál, J. (2023). Crime in the Digital Age: A New Frontier. In *The Implications of Emerging Technologies in the Euro-Atlantic Space: Views from the Younger Generation Leaders Network* (pp. 177–193). Springer International Publishing. DOI: 10.1007/978-3-031-24673-9_11

Oginni, O. S. (2017). Towards black box forensic cybercrime investigation model (BBFCIM): Beyond the rule of thumb. In Global, I. G. I. (Ed.), (pp. 168–187)., DOI: 10.4018/978-1-5225-1031-4.ch010

Okoye, C. C., Nwankwo, E. E., Usman, F. O., Mhlongo, N. Z., Odeyemi, O., & Ike, C. U. (2024). Securing financial data storage: A review of cybersecurity challenges and solutions. *International Journal of Science and Research Archive, 11*(1), 1968–1983. DOI: 10.30574/ijsra.2024.11.1.0267

Ombu, A. (2023). Role of digital forensics in combating financial crimes in the computer era. *Journal of Forensic Accounting Profession*, *3*(1), 57–75. DOI: 10.2478/jfap-2023-0003

Özçağdavul, M. (2024). General Data Protection Regulation compliance and privacy protection in wearable health devices: Challenges and solutions. *Artuklu Health*, *10*(10), 29–37. DOI: 10.58252/artukluhealth.1566573

Panda, S., & Alexander, A. (2019). Implementation of information security management system (ISMS) aligned with ISO 27001. *International Journal for Research in Applied Science and Engineering Technology*, *7*(5), 218–227. DOI: 10.22214/ijraset.2019.5034

Pandey, P., & Kapoor, A. (2025). Cybercrime In The Digital Era: Impacts, Awareness, And Strategic Solutions For A Secure Future. *Sachetas*, *4*(1), 32–37. DOI: 10.55955/410004

Paraskevas, A. (2020). *Cybersecurity in travel and tourism: A risk-based approach.* Springer Nature., DOI: 10.1007/978-3-030-05324-6

Park, E., & Kim, K. J. (2021). Can an AI chatbot be a customer's friend? *Service Business*, *15*(4), 529–548. DOI: 10.1007/s11628-021-00451-0

Park, J., Shin, W., Kim, B., & Kim, M. (2025). Spillover effects of data breach on consumer perceptions: Evidence from the e-commerce industry. *Internet Research, 35*(1), 1–24. https://www.emerald.com/intr/article/35/1/1/1241722/Spillover-effects-of-data-breach-on-consumer. DOI: 10.1108/INTR-11-2022-0898

Park, S., Kim, Y., Park, G., Na, O., & Chang, H. (2018). Research on digital forensic readiness design in a cloud computing-based smart work environment. *Sustainability (Basel), 10*(4), 1203. DOI: 10.3390/su10041203

Parmar, M., & Miles, A. (2024). *Cyber Security Frameworks (CSFs): An Assessment Between the NIST CSF v2.0 and EU Standards*. DOI: 10.23919/3S60530.2024.10592293

Pasupuleti, M. K. (2024). *Digital Forensics Uncovering Cyber Evidence*. 41–49. DOI: 10.62311/nesx/97422614

Patsakis, C., Arroyo, D., & Casino, F. (2024). The malware as a service ecosystem. In *Malware: Handbook of Prevention and Detection* (pp. 371–394). Springer Nature Switzerland.

PCI Security Standards Council. (2022). *Payment Card Industry Data Security Standard: Requirements and testing procedures (Version 4.0)*. https://www.pcisecuritystandards.org

PCI Security Standards Council. (2022). *PCI DSS: Payment Card Industry Data Security Standard*.https://www.pcisecuritystandards.org

Pencarelli, T. (2020). The digital revolution in the travel and tourism industry. *Information Technology & Tourism, 22*(3), 455–476. DOI: 10.1007/s40558-019-00160-3

Petersons, E. (2024). *Cybersecurity challenges in the era of digitalization. SSRN*. DOI: 10.2139/ssrn.4723047

Phillips, A., Ojalade, I., Taiwo, E., Obunadike, C., & Oloyede, K. (2023). Cybersecurity tactics in mitigating cyber-crimes: A review and proposal. *Int. J. Cryptogr. Inf. Secur. IJCIS, 13*.

Poornima, B. (2022). Cyber Threats and Nuclear Security in India. *Journal of Asian Security and International Affairs, 9*(2), 183–206. DOI: 10.1177/23477970221099748

Poulaki, I., Koufodontis, N. I., & Papadimitriou, S. (2025). Airline revenue management, distribution and passengers: Market trends in a technology driven triangle. *Worldwide Hospitality and Tourism Themes, 17*(1), 35–47. DOI: 10.1108/WHATT-12-2024-0304

Pring, E. T., Malietzis, G., Kendall, S. W. H., Jenkins, J. T., & Athanasiou, T. (2021). Crisis management for surgical teams and their leaders, lessons from the COVID-19 pandemic; A structured approach to developing resilience or natural organisational responses. *International Journal of Surgery, 91*, 105987. DOI: 10.1016/j.ijsu.2021.105987 PMID: 34091086

Pumaleque, A. P., Fernandez, I. R., Perez, D. D. I., & Bedriñana, M. A. (2021). *Digital transformation model for the development of tourism companies.* Dialnet. https://dialnet.unirioja.es/servlet/articulo?codigo=7701789

PwC. (2020). *Global digital trust insights survey 2020.* PwC. https://www.pwc.com

Quader, F., & Janeja, V. P. (2021). Insights into organizational security readiness: Lessons learned from cyber-attack case studies. *Journal of Cybersecurity and Privacy, 1*(4), 638–659. DOI: 10.3390/jcp1040032

Raissouni, K., Errabih, Z., Charroud, S., Raissouni, R., Raissouni, M. R., & Bourekkadi, S. (2023). Cybersecurity in the context of Moroccan energy companies. *E3S Web of Conferences, 412*, 01038. DOI: 10.1051/e3sconf/202341201038

Rajamäki, J., Ofem, P., Kallio, A., & Vakkuri, M. (2025a). The critical role of cybersecurity education in health tourism. *International Conference on Tourism Research*, 8(1), 234–242. DOI: 10.34190/ictr.8.1.3455

Rakhra, M., Singh, A., & Singh, D. (2024, March). Digital Signature Verification In Cloud Computing. In *2024 11th International Conference on Reliability, Infocom Technologies and Optimization (Trends and Future Directions)(ICRITO)* (pp. 1-6). IEEE. DOI: 10.1109/ICRITO61523.2024.10522372

Raki, A., Nayer, D., Nazifi, A., Alexander, M., & Seyfi, S. (2021). Tourism recovery strategies during major crises: The role of proactivity. *Annals of Tourism Research, 90*, 103144. DOI: 10.1016/j.annals.2021.103144 PMID: 36540883

Ramya, S., Smera, C., & Sandeep, J. (2025). Navigating Network Security: A Study on Contemporary Anomaly Detection Technologies. *Quantum Computing Models for Cybersecurity and Wireless Communications*, 183-199.

Rashideh, W. (2020). Blockchain technology framework: Current and future perspectives for the tourism industry. *Tourism Management, 80*, 104125. DOI: 10.1016/j.tourman.2020.104125

Reddy, K., & Venter, H. S. (2013). The architecture of a digital forensic readiness management system. *Computers & Security, 32*, 73–89. DOI: 10.1016/j.cose.2012.09.008

Rehman, S., & Rassias, M. (2024). Security Challenges in the 21st Century: Addressing Cybersecurity Threats in International Diplomacy.

Riadi, I., Yudhana, A., Pramuja, G., & Fanani, I. (2023). Mobile forensic tools for digital crime investigation: Comparison and evaluation. *International Journal of Safety and Security Engineering*, *13*(1), 11–19. DOI: 10.18280/ijsse.130102

Riasat, I., Shah, M., & Gönül, M. S. (2025). Strengthening cybersecurity resilience: An investigation of customers' adoption of emerging security tools in mobile banking apps. *Computers*, *14*(4), 129. DOI: 10.3390/computers14040129

Ribble, M. (2012). *Digital citizenship in schools: Nine elements all students should know* (3rd ed.). ISTE.

Rizal, R., & Selamat, S. R., & Masâ€TMud, M. Z. (2023). An overview diversity framework for internet of things (IoT) forensic investigation. *JOIV: International Journal on Informatics Visualization*, *7*(2), 569. DOI: 10.30630/joiv.7.2.1520

Roberts, S. S. (2023). *International Investments in Luxury Real Estate: An Evaluation of International Real Estate Investors and Developers Entering a Cross-Continental Market* (Doctoral dissertation, Massachusetts Institute of Technology).

Robinson, T. (2016, January 15). *Hyatt discovers malware at 250 hotels*. SC Media. https://www.scmagazine.com/news/hyatt-discovers-malware-at-250-hotels

Roman, R., Zhou, J., & Lopez, J. (2013). On the features and challenges of security and privacy in distributed internet of things. *Computer Networks*, *57*(10), 2266–2279. DOI: 10.1016/j.comnet.2012.12.018

Rose, S., Borchert, O., Mitchell, S., & Connelly, S. (2020). *NIST special publication 800-207: Zero trust architecture*. National Institute of Standards and Technology., DOI: 10.6028/NIST.SP.800-207

Rupeika-Apoga, R., Petrovska, K., & Буле, Л. (2022). The effect of digital orientation and digital capability on digital transformation of SMEs during the COVID-19 pandemic. *Journal of Theoretical and Applied Electronic Commerce Research*, *17*(2), 669–685. DOI: 10.3390/jtaer17020035

Ruzimatjon, Y. (2024). Digital technologies: How they are transforming our lives. *Web of Scientists and Scholars: Journal of Multidisciplinary Research*, *2*(6), 73–79.

Rystov, G., Loxley, Q., Blackwood, R., Loxley, K., & Kingsley, S. (2024). *A Framework for Real-Time Ransomware Detection Using Convergent Behavioural Signal Mapping*. DOI: 10.31219/osf.io/vd2ew

Saber, A. F., Helmy, S. H., & Abdel Gaber, M. H. (2025). The Role of Internet of Things in Improving Hotel Operations in Hospitality and Tourism Services and Its Impact on Customers Loyalty. *Journal of Tourism. Hotels and Heritage*, *10*(1), 102–126. DOI: 10.21608/sis.2025.383006.1193

Sabourin, V. (2021). *Strategic management for the hospitality and tourism industry*. CRC Press., DOI: 10.1201/9781003105831

Safitra, M. F., Lubis, M., & Fakhrurroja, H. (2023). Counterattacking Cyber Threats: A Framework for the Future of Cybersecurity. *Sustainability (Basel)*, *15*(18), 13369. DOI: 10.3390/su151813369

Salem, Y., Owda, M., &Owda, A. Y. (2023). *A Comprehensive Review of Digital Forensics Frameworks for Internet of Things (IoT) Devices*. 89–96. DOI: 10.1109/ICIT58056.2023.10226145

Santarsiero, F., Carlucci, D., Lerro, A., & Schiuma, G. (2024). Navigating digital transformation and business model innovation in the tourism sector: Challenges opportunities, and leadership styles. *Measuring Business Excellence*, *28*(3/4), 426–438. Advance online publication. DOI: 10.1108/MBE-09-2023-0137

Sarfraz, M., Khawaja, K. F., Han, H., Ariza-Montes, A., & Arjona-Fuentes, J. M. (2023). Sustainable supply chain, digital transformation, and blockchain technology adoption in the tourism sector. *Humanities & Social Sciences Communications*, *10*(1), 557. Advance online publication. DOI: 10.1057/s41599-023-02051-9

Schapel, H. (2013). The new approach to the new approach: The juridification of harmonized standards in EU law. *Maastricht Journal of European and Comparative Law*, *20*(4), 521–533. DOI: 10.1177/1023263X1302000404

Schindler, S., Dembska, M., Bonnarel, F., Lacy, M., Johnson, M., & Desai, V. (2024). Data Documentation Beyond Provenance: Metadata, Research Data Management, FAIR Principles. In *Data-Intensive Radio Astronomy: Bringing Astrophysics to the Exabyte Era* (pp. 397–418). Springer International Publishing. DOI: 10.1007/978-3-031-58468-8_14

Scott, N., Laws, E., & Prideaux, B. (2010). *Safety and security in tourism: recovery marketing after crises*. Routledge.

Senecal, D. (2024). *The Reign of Botnets: Defending Against Abuses, Bots and Fraud on the Internet*. John Wiley & Sons.

Sethi, S., Patil, R., Rani, S., Anjum, M., & Chaudhary, A. (2024, February). Decrypting Secrets: Deep Learning for Unmasking Malicious Traffic. In *2024 11th International Conference on Computing for Sustainable Global Development (INDIACom)* (pp. 1249-1254). IEEE.

Shah, I. A., Jhanjhi, N. Z., &Brohi, S. N. (2024). *Cybersecurity Issues and Challenges in Civil Aviation Security*. 1–23. DOI: 10.1002/9781394204472.ch1

Shandilya, S. K., Datta, A., Kartik, Y., & Nagar, A. (2024). A Study in Attack and Breaches. *Digital Resilience: Navigating Disruption and Safeguarding Data Privacy*, 279-309.

Shanti, R., Siregar, H., Zulbainarni, N., & Tony, T. (2023). Role of digital transformation on digital business model banks. *Sustainability (Basel)*, *15*(23), 16293. DOI: 10.3390/su152316293

Sharma, K., Tandon, A., & Gupta, A. (2021). Emerging cyber threats in tourism and hospitality: Risk awareness and resilience. *International Journal of Hospitality Information Technology*, *12*(2), 47–61.

Sharma, P., & Verma, R. (2019). Digital literacy and ethical practices among university students: A study of online behaviour and institutional reputation. *Journal of Media and Communication Studies*, *11*(4), 35–45. DOI: 10.5897/JMCS2019.0641

Sharma, R., & Verma, S. (2019). Digital literacy and online behavior: A pedagogical approach for ethics in the digital age. *Journal of Education and Learning*, *8*(4), 100–109.

Shenare, N., & Moon, S. (2025). Emerging trends, analytical tools, challenges and opportunities in cyber security: A steganography and digital forensics approach. *International Journal of Environmental Sciences*, •••, 1114–1125. DOI: 10.64252/tt797t90

Shevchuk, R., Martsenyuk, V., Adamyk, B., Benson, V., & Melnyk, A. (2025). Anomaly Detection in Blockchain: A Systematic Review of Trends, Challenges, and Future Directions. *Applied Sciences (Basel, Switzerland)*, *15*(15), 8330. DOI: 10.3390/app15158330

Shin, D.-H., Han, S.-J., Kim, Y.-B., & Euom, I.-C. (2024). Research on digital forensics analyzing heterogeneous Internet of Things incident investigations. *Applied Sciences (Basel, Switzerland)*, *14*(3), 1128. DOI: 10.3390/app14031128

Shin, Y., Kim, K., Lee, J. J., & Lee, K. (2022). Focusing on the weakest link: A similarity analysis on phishing campaigns based on the att&ck matrix. *Security and Communication Networks*, *2022*(1), 1699657. DOI: 10.1155/2022/1699657

Shutenko, V., & Solovei, A. (2025). *Cybersecurity in the hospitality industry: 6 threats and solutions*. Techmagic. https://www.techmagic.co/blog/hospitality-cybersecurity

Sibe, R. T., & Kaunert, C. (2024). Digital Evidence, Digital Forensics, and Digital Forensic Readiness. In *Cybercrime, Digital Forensic Readiness, and Financial Crime Investigation in Nigeria* (pp. 57–83). Springer Nature Switzerland. DOI: 10.1007/978-3-031-54089-9_3

Sigala, M. (2018). Social media and customer engagement in the hotel industry. *International Journal of Hospitality Management*, *77*, 183–185. DOI: 10.1016/j.ijhm.2018.07.009

Simkin, L. (2021). Cybersecurity risks in hospitality: Balancing digital innovation and guest trust. *Journal of Business Research*, *136*, 242–250. DOI: 10.1016/j.jbusres.2021.07.045

Singh, A., & Raj, A. (2024). Convergence of Digital Forensics and Intelligent Data in Cyberspace. *Studies in Autonomic, Data-Driven and Industrial Computing*, 111–119. DOI: 10.1007/978-981-97-5862-3_9

Singh, N., Khan, M. Z., Kaur, B., & Mishra, A. (2025). Revolutionizing Crime Investigation: The Role of Deep Learning in Forensic Intelligence. In *Forensic Intelligence and Deep Learning Solutions in Crime Investigation* (pp. 281-300). IGI Global Scientific Publishing.

Singh, G., & Chopra, M. R. (2025). Security Challenges & Techniques to Prevent Cyber Crime Threats in Tourism Industry. *Management*, *5*(3), 35–40.

Singh, R., Gehlot, A., Akram, S. V., Thakur, A. K., Gupta, L. R., Priyadarshi, N., & Twala, B. (2024). Integration of advanced digital technologies in the hospitality industry: A technological approach towards sustainability. *Sustainable Engineering and Innovation*, *6*(1), 37–55. DOI: 10.37868/sei.v6i1.id208

Sinno, N. (2019). The effect of digital transformation on innovation and entrepreneurship in the tourism sector: the case of Lebanese tourism services providers. In *Lecture notes in business information processing* (pp. 29–39). DOI: 10.1007/978-3-030-30874-2_3

Sirigina, P. V. (2023). Digital payment security: A developer framework. *International Journal of Scientific Research in Computer Science Engineering and Information Technology*, *9*(4), 664–675. DOI: 10.32628/CSEIT23564520

Solanke, A. A. (2022). Digital forensics AI: On practicality, optimality, and interpretability of digital evidence mining techniques.

Sonkar, N. (2025). *Scaling an ISO compliance practice: Strategic insights from building a $1m+ cybersecurity certification line.* arXiv. DOI: 10.48550/ARX-IV.2505.11583

Sonone, S. S., Gawade, R. K., Hake, D. M., & Rathod, N. V. (2024). Admissibility of Electronic Record under Section 65B of The Indian Evidence Act Vis-à-vis Judicial Interpretation. *Int J Sci Res Sci & Technol. Jan-Feb, 11*(16), 36-41.

Spagnuelo, D., Bartolini, C., & Lenzini, G. (2020). Qualifying and measuring transparency: A medical data system case study. *Computers & Security, 91*, 101717. DOI: 10.1016/j.cose.2020.101717

Srinivas, R., & Deepa, R. (2020). Integrating cybersecurity and digital forensics for business resilience. *Cybersecurity Trends Journal, 8*(4), 45–59.

Stalmirska, A. M., & Camprubí, R. (2022). Conducting a systematic qualitative content analysis in hospitality and tourism research. In *Contemporary Research Methods in Hospitality and Tourism* (pp. 127–141). Emerald Publishing Limited. DOI: 10.1108/978-1-80117-546-320221009

Stati, A., & Udin, U. (2025). The Impact of Digital Transformation on the Development of the Tourism Industry: Bibliometric Analysis. *International Research Journal of Multidisciplinary Scope, 6*(1), 603–616. DOI: 10.47857/irjms.2025.v06i01.02510

Statista. (2022). *Mobile check-in and digital key adoption in hotels worldwide.* Statista. https://www.statista.com

Stoyanova, M., Nikoloudakis, Y., Panagiotakis, S., Pallis, E., & Markakis, E. K. (2020). A survey on the internet of things (IoT) forensics: Challenges, approaches, and open issues. *IEEE Communications Surveys and Tutorials, 22*(2), 1191–1221. DOI: 10.1109/COMST.2019.2962586

Stoykova, R. (2023). The right to a fair trial as a conceptual framework for digital evidence rules in criminal investigations. *Computer Law & Security Review, 49*, 105801. DOI: 10.1016/j.clsr.2023.105801

Sudheer, S. A. (2024). Ransomware Attacks and Their Evolving Strategies: A Systematic Review of Recent Incidents. *Journal of Technology and Systems, 6*(7), 32–59. DOI: 10.47941/jts.2399

Suryal, A., Vishwakarma, P., & Malik, A. (2024). Impact of artificial intelligence in digital forensics: A review study. Social Science Research Network. DOI: 10.2139/ssrn.4492420

Sweeney, J. C., & Soutar, G. N. (2001). Consumer perceived value: The development of a multiple item scale. *Journal of Retailing*, *77*(2), 203–220. DOI: 10.1016/S0022-4359(01)00041-0

Symantec. (2021). *Internet security threat report 2021*. Symantec. https://www.broadcom.com

Tahir, S., Shahbaz, M. A., Tahir, H., Awais, M., Khan, F., Tahir, R., Saeed, S., & Almuhaideb, A. M. (2022). A Novel Approach to Reduce Breaches of Aircraft Communication Data. *Electronics (Basel)*, *12*(1), 172. DOI: 10.3390/electronics12010172

Tahmasebi, M. (2024). Cyberattack ramifications, the hidden cost of a security breach. *Journal of Information Security*, *15*(2), 87–105. DOI: 10.4236/jis.2024.152007

Talukder, M. B., Hoque, M., & Kumar, S. (2024). Impact of cybersecurity in the aviation, tourism, and hospitality industries. In Advances in Hospitality, Tourism, and the Services Industry (pp. 200–215). IGI Global. DOI: 10.4018/979-8-3693-2715-9.ch011

Talukder, M. B., Hoque, M., & Kumar, S. (2024). Impact of Cybersecurity in the Aviation, Tourism, and Hospitality Industries. In *Corporate Cybersecurity in the Aviation, Tourism, and Hospitality Sector* (pp. 200-215). IGI Global.

Talwar, S., Dhir, A., Kaur, P., & Mantymaki, M. (2020). Why do people purchase from online travel agencies (OTAs)? A consumption values perspective. *International Journal of Hospitality Management*, *88*, 102534. DOI: 10.1016/j.ijhm.2020.102534

Tandon, A., Kaur, P., Bhatt, Y., & Dhir, A. (2022). Cybersecurity and digital resilience in the tourism industry: A systematic review. *Information Systems Frontiers*, *24*(2), 465–488. DOI: 10.1007/s10796-021-10131-z

Tapscott, D., & Tapscott, A. (2017). *Blockchain Revolution: How the Technology Behind Bitcoin Is Changing Money, Business, and the World*. Penguin.

Tariq, M. U. (2024). Cybersecurity risk assessment models and theories in the travel and tourism industry. In *Advances in hospitality, tourism and the services industry (AHTSI) book series* (pp. 1–17). DOI: 10.4018/979-8-3693-2715-9.ch001

Tariq, M. U. (2024). Data breach incidents and prevention in the hospitality industry. In *Corporate cybersecurity in the aviation, tourism, and hospitality sector* (pp. 181–199). IGI Global. DOI: 10.4018/979-8-3693-2715-9.ch010

Tariq, U., Ahmed, I., Bashir, A. K., & Shaukat, K. (2023). A critical cybersecurity analysis and future research directions for the Internet of Things: A comprehensive review. *Sensors (Basel), 23*(8), 4117. Advance online publication. DOI: 10.3390/s23084117 PMID: 37112457

Testón Franco, N., & Muñoz Ibáñez, C. A. (2025). The Cybersecurity: An emerging topic for tourism professional training. *The Journal of American Science, 7*(13), 12–15. DOI: 10.29057/jas.v7i13.14268

Tevdoradze, S., Mushkudiani, Z., Tevdoradze, N., & Tevdoradze, N. (2024). The effect of criminal activity on tourism. *Axali Ekonomisti, 19*(01), 25–31. DOI: 10.36962/NEC19012024-04

Thapaliya, S., & Gurung, M. B. (2025). Mitigating Insider Threats and Data Breaches. *Enhancing Data Loss Prevention Systems with Behavioral Analytics And NLP., 02*(01). Advance online publication. DOI: 10.58806/ijmir.2025.v2i1n03

Thayananthan, V., Qasem, M., Qureshi, M. S., & Qureshi, M. B. (2024). Security management of autonomous transportation services in the tourism industry. In *Lecture notes in networks and systems* (pp. 53–67). DOI: 10.1007/978-981-97-3973-8_4

The World of Companies Pro Social No Frills. (2020). In G. Grefe, *Shapes of Tourism Employment* (1st ed., pp. 187–207). Wiley. DOI: 10.1002/9781119751342.ch12

Thomas, O. D., Salek, M. S., Tine, J.-M., Rahman, M., Hockstad, T., & Chowdhury, M. (2025). *Cybersecurity in Transportation Systems: Policies and Technology Directions.* /arxiv.2501.05356DOI: 10.48550

Tian, F. (2016). An agri-food supply chain traceability system for China based on RFID & blockchain technology. *13th International Conference on Service Systems and Service Management (ICSSSM),* 1–6. DOI: 10.1109/ICSSSM.2016.7538424

Tikanmaki, I., Savolainen, J., & Ruoslahti, H. (2024). The role of standards in enhancing cybersecurity and business continuity management for organizations. *Information & Security: An International Journal, 55*(1), 63–82. DOI: 10.11610/isij.5523

Tikkinen-Piri, C., Rohunen, A., & Markkula, J. (2017). EU general data protection regulation: Changes and implications for personal data collecting companies. *Computer Law & Security Review, 34*(1), 134–153. DOI: 10.1016/j.clsr.2017.05.015

Tok, Y. C., & Chattopadhyay, S. (2022). Identifying threats, cybercrime and digital forensic opportunities in smart city infrastructure via threat modeling. *Forensic Science International Digital Investigation, 45*, 301540. DOI: 10.1016/j.fsidi.2023.301540

Tong, L., & Kwan, M. (2022). Ensuring cybersecurity in airlines to prevent data breach. *Co Sci Re J., 3*(3), 66–73. DOI: 10.51594/csitrj.v3i3.426

Torregosa, J. T., Orong, M. Y., Ricalde, G. T., Amin, W. D., Lonzon, H. A., & Alcontin, R. B. (2021). Assessing the conformity level of information security management system of the higher education institutions: Basis for the development of policies and guidelines. *Mediterranean Journal of Basic and Applied Sciences, 5*(1), 57–71. *SSRN*. DOI: 10.2478/picbe-2021-0050

Torres, Á., Molina, J. P., García, A. S., & González, P. (2024). Prototyping of Augmented Reality interfaces for air traffic alert and their evaluation using a Virtual Reality aircraft-proximity simulator. *2024 IEEE Conference Virtual Reality and 3D User Interfaces (VR)*, 817–826. DOI: 10.1109/VR58804.2024.00101

Trustwave. (2020). *2020 Global security report.* Trustwave. https://www.trustwave.com

Tsohou, A., Magkos, E., Mouratidis, H., Chrysoloras, G., Piras, L., Pavlidis, M., Debussche, J., Rotoloni, M., & Crespo, B. G. N. (2020). Privacy, security, legal and technology acceptance elicited and consolidated requirements for a GDPR compliance platform. *Information and Computer Security, 28*(4), 531–553. DOI: 10.1108/ICS-01-2020-0002

Tung, V. W. S., & Law, R. (2020). The potential for tourism and hospitality experience research in human–robot interactions. *International Journal of Contemporary Hospitality Management, 32*(11), 3509–3523. DOI: 10.1108/IJCHM-09-2019-0792

Turluev, R., & Mutsurova, Z. M. (2021). Digital technologies: Problems and trends. *SHS Web of Conferences, 101*, 2006. DOI: 10.1051/shsconf/202110102006

Turukmane, A. V., Khekare, G., Shelke, N., Sakarkar, G., & Buchade, S. (2024, December). *Evasion techniques in cybersecurity: An in-depth analysis* [Conference session]. 2024 International Conference on Artificial Intelligence and Quantum Computation-Based Sensor Application (ICAIQSA), Nagpur, India. DOI: 10.1109/ICAIQSA64000.2024.10882284

Turukmane, A. V., & Khekare, G. (2023). Cyber quantum computing (security) using rectified probabilistic packet mark for big data. In *Quantum computing in cybersecurity* (pp. 1–15). Wiley Scrivener Publishing LLC., DOI: 10.1002/9781394167401.ch1

Tussyadiah, I. P. (2020). A review of research into automation in tourism: Launching the annals of tourism research curated collection on artificial intelligence and robotics in tourism. *Annals of Tourism Research, 81*, 102883. DOI: 10.1016/j.annals.2020.102883

Tussyadiah, I. P., & Park, S. (2018). Consumer evaluation of hotel service robots. In Stangl, B., & Pesonen, J. (Eds.), *Information and communication technologies in tourism 2018* (pp. 308–320). Springer., DOI: 10.1007/978-3-319-72923 7_24

Tussyadiah, I., & Miller, G. (2019). Perceived impacts of artificial intelligence and responses to positive behavior change intervention. *Computers in Human Behavior, 92*, 13–24.

Tzolov, T. V. (2019). ISO 27552 as a model for establishment personal information management systems. *Proceedings of the 2019 International Conference on Information Technology*, 1–4. DOI: 10.1109/InfoTech.2019.8860898

Ukwandu, E., Ben Farah, M. A., Hindy, H., Bures, M., Atkinson, R., Tachtatzis, C., & Bellekens, X. (2021). Cyber-Security Challenges in Aviation Industry: A Review of Current and Future Trends. *arXiv: Cryptography and Security.* https://dblp.uni-trier.de/db/journals/corr/corr2107.html#abs-2107-04910

Ukwandu, E., Ben-Farah, M. A., Hindy, H., Bures, M., Atkinson, R., Tachtatzis, C., Andonovic, I., & Bellekens, X. (2022a). Cyber-Security Challenges in Aviation Industry: A Review of Current and Future Trends. *Information (Basel), 13*(3), 146. DOI: 10.3390/info13030146

UNWTO. (2021). Digital transformation and tourism. Retrieved from https://www.unwto.org/digital-transformation

Urosevic, U., & Čubrović, M. (2023). Security in Cyber-Physical and IoT Systems. *Tehnika, 78*(1), 45–51. DOI: 10.5937/tehnika2301045U

Vaghela, R., Gowda, V. D., Taj, M., Arudra, A., & Chopra, M. (2024). Digital evidence collection and preservation in computer network forensics. In *Handbook of Research on Innovative Approaches to Information Technology in Library and Information Science* (pp. 42–62). IGI Global Scientific Publishing. DOI: 10.4018/979-8-3693-0807-3.ch003

Vala, J. B., & Vekariya, V. M. (2024). The Role and Importance of Digital Forensics and Digital Evidence in Cyber Crime Detection. *International Journal of Life Sciences Biotechnology and Pharma Research, 13*(6), 413–420. DOI: 10.69605/ijlbpr_13.6.2024.80

van Niekerk, B. (2017). *Analysis of Cyber-Attacks against the Transportation Sector.* IGI Global., DOI: 10.4018/978-1-5225-1938-6.ch004

van Niekerk, B. (2018). Analysis of cyber-attacks against the transportation sector. In *Cyber Security and Threats* (pp. 1384–1402). IGI Global., DOI: 10.4018/978-1-5225-5634-3.ch069

Vardakis, G., Hatzivasilis, G., Koutsaki, E., & Papadakis, N. (2024). Review of smart-home security using the internet of things. *Electronics (Basel)*, *13*(16), 3343. DOI: 10.3390/electronics13163343

Vasuki, & Department of Master of Computer Application India., S. M. V. E. C. P.-605 107. (2024). Shielding healthcare data strategies for preventing breaches. INTERANTIONAL JOURNAL OF SCIENTIFIC RESEARCH IN ENGINEERING AND MANAGEMENT, 08(05), 1–5. DOI: 10.55041/IJSREM33345

Veletsianos, G. (2020). *Learning online: The student experience*. Johns Hopkins University Press. DOI: 10.1353/book.73824

Veletsianos, G., & Kimmons, R. (2013). Scholars and faculty members' lived experiences in online social networks. *The Internet and Higher Education*, *16*, 43–50. DOI: 10.1016/j.iheduc.2012.01.004

Verizon Business. (2024). *Data breach investigations report*. https://www.verizon.com/business/resources/reports/dbir/

Verma, A., & Shri, C. (2022). Cyber security: A review of cyber crimes, security challenges and measures to control. *Vision (Basel)*, •••, 09722629221074760.

Vinod, B. (2022). Introduction to Hotel Revenue Management. In *Revenue Management in the Lodging Industry: Origins to the Last Frontier* (pp. 1–50). Springer International Publishing. DOI: 10.1007/978-3-031-14302-1_1

Vlastos, E., & Patel, A. (2007). An open source forensic tool to visualize digital evidence. *Computer Standards & Interfaces*, *30*(1–2), 8–19. DOI: 10.1016/j.csi.2007.03.003

Voigt, P., & Von dem Bussche, A. (2017). *The EU General Data Protection Regulation (GDPR): A practical guide*. Springer. DOI: 10.1007/978-3-319-57959-7

Voronova, O., Khareva, V., & Khnykina, T. (2020). Modern information technologies in the hotel business: Development trends and implementation issues. *E3S Web of Conferences, 164*, 09017. DOI: 10.1051/e3sconf/202016409017

Wang, D., Xiang, Z., & Fesenmaier, D. R. (2016). Smartphone use in everyday life and travel. *Journal of Travel Research*, *55*(1), 52–63. DOI: 10.1177/0047287514535847

Wang, Y., & Kandampully, J. (2020). Building service brand equity through social media in tourism and hospitality: The role of digital engagement. *Journal of Services Marketing*, *34*(4), 463–472. DOI: 10.1108/JOSM-11-2019-0342

Warren, K. (2010). Weighing the option of biometrics in the hospitality industry. *Worldwide Hospitality and Tourism Themes*, *2*(1), 100–109. DOI: 10.1108/17554211011012630

Wasserman, L., & Wasserman, Y. (2022). Hospital cybersecurity risks and gaps: Review (for the non-cyber professional). *Frontiers in Digital Health*, *4*, 862221. Advance online publication. DOI: 10.3389/fdgth.2022.862221 PMID: 36033634

Watkins, S. G. (2022). *ISO/IEC 27001:2022*. IT Governance Publishing. DOI: 10.2307/j.ctv30qq13d

Wider, W., Gao, Y., Chan, C. K., Lin, J., Li, J., Tanucan, J. C. M., & Fauzi, M. A. (2023). Unveiling trends in digital tourism research: A bibliometric analysis of co-citation and co-word analysis. *Environmental and Sustainability Indicators*, *20*, 100308. DOI: 10.1016/j.indic.2023.100308

Wiedmer, T. (2011). The role of social media in shaping public perception of institutions. *Journal of Educational Administration*, *49*(4), 386–410. DOI: 10.1108/09578231111146416

Wiedmer, T. (2011). The world of cyber reputation: Avoiding the pitfalls. *Delta Kappa Gamma Bulletin*, *77*(3), 24–27.

Wilson, G., Johnson, O., & Brown, W. L. (2024). *Exploring the impact of digital transformation on marketing strategies in the retail sector*. *Preprints*.Org. DOI: 10.20944/preprints202407.2371.v1

Wyatt, B. (2023). 50 dark destinations: Crime and contemporary tourism. *Journal of Heritage Tourism*, *1–2*(5), 730–731. Advance online publication. DOI: 10.1080/1743873X.2023.2210431

Wynn, M., & Lam, C. Y. T. (2023). Digitalisation and IT strategy in the hospitality industry. *Systems*, *11*(10), 501. DOI: 10.3390/systems11100501

Xiang, Z., Du, Q., Ma, Y., & Fan, W. (2015). Characteristics of online reviews: Evidence from the hospitality industry. *International Journal of Hospitality Management*, *43*, 77–83.

Xie, Y., Gardi, A., &Sabbatini, R. (2023). *Cybersecurity Risks and Threats in Avionics and Autonomous Systems*. 0814–0819. DOI: 10.1109/DASC/PiCom/CBDCom/Cy59711.2023.10361328

Yap, J. S., Teo, Y. C., & Raslan, M. A. H. bin M., Subramaniam, M. R., Lim, Y. X., Say, J. K., Moh, S. L., &Sindiramutty, S. R. (2024). *In-Depth Analysis and Countermeasures for Ransomware Attacks: Case Studies and Recommendations.* DOI: 10.20944/preprints202408.2261.v1

Yoon, J., Shin, Y., & Kim, J. (2018). A study on the information security management index through analysis of EU-GDPR (European Union-General Data Protection Regulation). *Asia-Pacific Journal of Law Politics and Administration*, *2*(2), 13–32. DOI: 10.21742/ajlpa.2018.2.2.03

Yu, H., Meng, Q., Fang, Z., & Liu, M. (2023). Literature review on maritime cybersecurity: State-of-the-art. *Journal of Navigation*, *76*(4-5), 1–14. DOI: 10.1017/S0373463323000164

Yun, J. J., Zhao, X., Jung, K., & Yigitcanlar, T. (2020). The culture for open innovation dynamics. *Sustainability*, *12*(1), 1–21. DOI: 10.3390/su12010290

Zaman, R., & Hassani, M. (2020). On enabling GDPR compliance in business processes through data-driven solutions. *SN Computer Science*, *1*(4), 210. DOI: 10.1007/s42979-020-00215-x

Zan, T. T., & Min, S. T. T. K. (2025). Cybercrimes and the illicit financial flows in Myanmar. *Journal of Academics Stand Against Poverty*, *6*(1), 43–69.

Zeng, Z., Chen, X., & Lew, A. A. (2021). Managing big data in the hospitality and tourism industry: Potential applications and challenges. *Tourism Management*, *83*, 104247. DOI: 10.1016/j.tourman.2020.104247

Zeqiri, A., Ben Youssef, A., & Maherzi Zahar, T. (2025). The Role of digital tourism platforms in advancing sustainable development goals in the Industry 4.0 era. *Sustainability (Basel)*, *17*(8), 3482. DOI: 10.3390/su17083482

Zhang, H., & Gong, X. (2023). The research on an electronic evidence forensic system for cross-border cybercrime. *The International Journal of Evidence & Proof*, *28*(1), 21–44. DOI: 10.1177/13657127231187059

Zhang, J. (2025). Digital Forensics and Cybersecurity Practices in Smart Tourism Environments. *Cybersecurity in Hospitality and Tourism*, *5*(1), 21–39.

Zhang, J. (2025). Patterns of Innovation-Driven Tourism Competitiveness: Insights From 270 Chinese Cities. *Tourism Management*, *107*, 105063. DOI: 10.1016/j.tourman.2024.105063

Zhang, Y. (2023). Analysis of the digital transformation development path for travel enterprises. *Open Journal of Applied Sciences, 13*(8), 1370–1385. DOI: 10.4236/ojapps.2023.138109

Zorz, Ž. (2015, November 23). *PoS malware hit 54 Starwood luxury hotels.* Help Net Security. https://www.helpnetsecurity.com/2015/11/23/pos-malware-hit-54-starwood-luxury-hotels

About the Contributors

Mohammad Badruddoza Talukder is a distinguished academic, researcher, and industry professional, currently serving as Associate Professor and Chair of the College of Tourism and Hospitality Management (CTHM) at the International University of Business Agriculture and Technology (IUBAT), Dhaka, Bangladesh. With a strong academic foundation and extensive professional experience, he has established himself as a prominent voice in tourism, hospitality, and technology-driven innovation. He earned his Ph.D. in Hotel Management from Lovely Professional University, India, where his research focused on the transformative role of emerging technologies in reshaping the global tourism and hospitality landscape. Since beginning his academic career in 2008, Dr. Talukder has remained deeply committed to teaching excellence, research advancement, and academic leadership. Recognised among the top 2% of Scientists in the World, Dr. Talukder's scholarly contributions have gained significant international visibility and impact. His research primarily explores the integration of Artificial Intelligence (AI), the Internet of Things (IoT), Blockchain, and other emerging digital technologies within tourism, hospitality, and aviation. He is particularly interested in how these technologies can enhance operational efficiency, improve service quality, optimise guest experiences, and support the development of smart tourism ecosystems. His work also addresses sustainability challenges by examining how digital innovations can support environmentally responsible, resource-efficient hospitality practices. By bridging theoretical innovation with practical application, his research remains highly relevant to both academia and industry. He has developed an impressive research portfolio, including a large number of publications indexed in leading international databases in Scopus. His scholarly output spans peer-reviewed journal articles, book chapters, conference papers, and edited volumes. He has authored and edited numerous influential books with globally recognised publishers, including IGI Global, Cambridge Scholars Publishing, Emerald, CABI, Bentham Science, Springer Nature, and many more. His publications address a wide range of contemporary themes, such as AI-driven hospitality operations, smart tourism systems, digital transformation strategies, aviation innovation, sustainable tourism development, and emerging business models such as cloud kitchens. Several of his ongoing editorial projects with major publishers further demonstrate his continued commitment to advancing knowledge and innovation in these areas. In addition to his research achievements, Dr. Talukder plays an active and influential role in the global academic community. He regularly serves as a keynote speaker, distinguished speaker, session chair, and resource person at international conferences, seminars, and faculty development programs. His participation in academic events across Asia and beyond reflects his growing international reputation as a thought leader in tourism and hospitality innovation. He has also served as a technical committee member at international conferences, supporting the development of high-quality research and scholarly discourse. His academic career is strongly complemented by extensive industry experience in the hospitality sector. Prior to fully transitioning into academia, he held several managerial positions in reputed business-class hotels in Bangladesh, particularly in food and beverage management. This practical background provides him with valuable insights into real-world hospitality operations and challenges. It also enables him to integrate industry perspectives into his teaching, research, and training activities. His ability to connect academic knowledge with practical application is widely appreciated by students, industry professionals, and research collaborators. Beyond his roles in teaching and research, Dr. Talukder has made significant contributions to professional training and capacity development within the tourism and hospitality sector. As a certified trainer, he has been actively involved in delivering training programs, workshops, and skill development initiatives to enhance workforce capabilities. His engagement in training and development reflects his commitment to building a competent, innovative, and future-ready workforce capable of adapting to technological advancements and evolving industry demands. He is also actively involved in academic service and scholarly publishing. He serves as a reviewer for several reputable international journals, including those published by Springer Nature, Inderscience, and other academic platforms. His expertise is further recognised through his membership on the editorial boards of international journals, where he contributes to maintaining research quality and advancing scholarly standards. His involvement in peer review and editorial responsibilities highlights his dedication to academic integrity and the continuous improvement of research in tourism and hospitality studies. His research interests are broad yet strategically focused on the intersection of technology and hospitality. These include Artificial Intelligence applications in tourism and hospitality, IoT-enabled smart hotel systems, Blockchain for secure and transparent travel operations, digital transformation strategies, sustainable tourism development, aviation safety and innovation, and emerging trends such as cloud kitchens and technology-driven service models. His interdisciplinary approach enables him to address complex industry challenges and deliver innovative, practical solutions that benefit both academic research and industry practice. As an academic leader, Dr. Talukder continues to play a vital role in curriculum development, research initiatives, and institutional growth at IUBAT. He is dedicated to fostering a culture of innovation, critical thinking, and global engagement among students and faculty members. His vision emphasises integrating advanced technologies, sustainability principles, and industry collaboration into tourism and hospitality education, ensuring that graduates are well-prepared to meet the demands of a rapidly evolving global industry. His research, teaching, publications, and professional engagements, Dr. Mohammad Badruddoza Talukder has made substantial contributions to the advancement of tourism and hospitality studies. His work not only enriches academic knowledge but also supports the transformation of the global hospitality industry into a more intelligent, sustainable, and technology-driven sector. His continued dedication to innovation, collaboration, and excellence positions him as a key contributor to the future of tourism and hospitality worldwide.

***

Shelley Duggal is an accomplished hospitality academician with over 18 years of teaching and research experience. She currently serves as Assistant Professor III at Amity School of Hospitality, Amity University, Noida. A Ph.D. in Hotel and Tourism Management, her research explores digital hospitality, website evaluation, consumer behavior, and sustainable tourism. Dr. Duggal is a prolific researcher with multiple Scopus and Web of Science-indexed publications and has co-authored books on Indian regional cuisine and food tourism. She has played a pioneering role in shaping hospitality education, having been a founding faculty member at the Central University of Haryana. Her e-content development for ePG Pathshala by MHRD highlights her expertise in instructional design. She has actively coordinated numerous academic events and served as a resource person in national and international forums. A French language trainer for over a decade, she brings intercultural competency to her teaching. Dr. Duggal is a life member of the Professional Housekeepers' Association, Assistant editor of Scopus indexed journal "International Journal of Hospitality and Tourism Systems", and editorial member of "Palash- A Journal of Hospitality and Tourism Service Management", and Executive Member of the Indian Hospitality Congress. She has received accolades such as the "Aspiring Researcher Award" and "Emerald Literati Award 2022." Her academic influence extends through editorship roles and as a mentor for doctoral research.

Md. Afzal Hossain is currently serving as an Assistant Professor at the College of Business Administration at IUBAT-International University of Business Agriculture and Technology, Dhaka, Bangladesh. He was awarded a Ph.D. in Business Administration from the Beijing Institute of Technology(BIT), China in 2023. He was awarded the China Government Counsel Scholarship (CSC) in 2018. Before that, Dr. Afzal obtained MBA and BBA degrees from the Department of Accounting & Information Systems, University of Dhaka (DU). His areas of teaching include Financial Accounting, Management Accounting, Cost Accounting, Advanced Financial Accounting, Auditing, and International accounting standards. Dr. Md. Afzal Hossain has published several research articles on the Web of Science and Scopus. He has carried out his research in the fields of accounting, environmental economics, corporate social responsibility, energy, and marketing. Dr. Afzal is an active reviewer for the journal Environmental Science and Pollution Research (ESPR), which is a SCI and Scopus-indexed journal. Dr. Afzal has attended several national and international conferences as a paper presenter, participant, and guest. Previously, Dr. Afzal Worked as an Assistant Professor at Shanto-Mariam University of Creative Technology and Green University of Bangladesh in the Department of Business Administration. He also worked as an Adjunct Faculty of the Independent University, Atish Dipankar University of Science & Technology" and International Islamic University Chittagong.

Firoj Kabir is a researcher, Lecturer of the Department of "Tourism and Hospitality Management" at the Daffodil International University, Dhaka, Bangladesh, with a solid academic background in BBA and MBA majoring in Tourism and Hospitality Management from the University of Dhaka. His passion lies in exploring the intersection of travel and culture. His diverse areas of interest include archaeological tourism, sustainable tourism, and the unique characteristics of Generation Z travelers. Through extensive research and insightful writing, he sheds light on the intricate connections between historical sites, responsible tourism, and the evolving preferences of the next generation of travelers. His work not only enriches the field of tourism but also inspires readers to engage with the world around them in meaningful and responsible ways.

Mayank Kapila is an Assistant Professor (Senior Scale) in the Department of Law at M.S. College, Motihari, under Babasaheb Bhimrao Ambedkar Bihar University, Muzaffarpur, Bihar, India, and can be reached at kapilalegal.brabu@gmail.com; he is registered as a researcher with the ORCID identifier 0009-0001-4874-8283, reflecting his engagement in academic and scholarly activities in the field of law.

Ganesh Khekare is currently working as an Associate Professor in the department of Computer Science & Engineering at Vellore Institute of Technology, Vellore, India. He has done Ph.D. from Bhagwant University India. He pursued a Master of Engineering from G H Raisoni College of Engineering, Nagpur in the year 2013, and a Bachelor of Engineering from Priyadarshini College of Engineering, Nagpur in 2010. He has been a member of ACM since 2014, and a lifetime member of the ISTE and IEEE Senior Member, IAENG, IFERP, and IERD member since 2018. He has published more than 70 research articles in reputed highly indexed international journals and conferences including Thomson Reuters, IGI Global, Inderscience, Springer, IEEE, Taylor & Francis, etc. He has published four patents and four copyrights. His main research work focuses on Data Science, the Internet of Everything, Machine Learning, Computer Networks, Artificial Intelligence, Intelligent Transportation Systems, etc. He has more than 15 years of teaching and research experience.

Sanjeev Kumar Is a Professor in Lovely Professional University Punjab India. He received Undergraduate in Hotel Management from Osmania University, Postgraduate in Tourism Management from Madurai Kamaraj University. He completed Doctor of Philosophy in Hospitality Management in 2019 from Amity University Jaipur India. His research areas lies in food Service Industry, his research focuses on Alcoholic beverages, Event management and Sustainable Management Practices, Metaverse, AI Machine Learning and Artificial Intelligence. He published more than 80 research papers, articles and chapters in Scopus Indexed, UGC Approved and peer reviewed Journals and books. Dr. Sanjeev Kumar participated and acted as resource person in various National and International conferences, seminars, session chair, research workshops and industry talks and his work has been widely cited. Dr. Sanjeev also edited more than 20 books with various International Publishers such as IGI Global, Cambridge Scholars, Emerald, CABI, Bentham Science, Taylor & Francis. Dr Sanjeev is an active researcher and has published numerous research articles in prestigious National and International journals and books.

Urvashi Kumari is presently working as Associate Professor in the School of Engineering and Technology, Sushant University, Gurgaon, India. She has been awarded a PhD from the School of Computer Management, Pune University, Pune, Maharashtra, India. Dr. Urvashi has over 20 years of academic experience teaching in Indian engineering colleges. She has published papers in peer-reviewed international journals of nature, UGC CARE, ABDC, SCOPUS, IGI PUBLISHING, and EMERALD PUBLICATION. Dr. Urvashi is guiding three PhD students in the interdisciplinary field of information technology, hospitality, and Tourism.

Zokir Mamadiyarov is a Professor in the Department of Finance and Tourism at Termez University of Economics and Service, Termez, Uzbekistan. With academic expertise spanning finance, economics, and tourism studies, he contributes to advancing research and education in sustainable tourism development and financial management. His work emphasizes bridging theoretical knowledge with practical applications to support regional economic growth and the global tourism sector.

Vijaishree Dubey Pandey, a distinguished academician and legal professional, serves as the President of the Artificial Intelligence for Women's Empowerment and Representation Council, spearheading initiatives at the intersection of law, technology, and gender equality. Experienced and accomplished academician with a demonstrated history of working in the legal services industry and a passion for research and publication. Her expertise in Human Rights and IPRs and had undergone trainings related to Artificial Intelligence. She has worked in collaboration with jails, orphanages, schools, and RWAs, aiming to provide legal aid and basic legal rights. Her leadership skills, coupled with her dedication to professional ethics and academic excellence, have earned her the respect of her peers and students alike. Her dedication to social causes is evident through her involvement in legal aid programs, advocacy efforts, and community outreach initiatives. Beyond academia, Dr. Pandey is a sought-after resource person and guest speaker, lending her expertise to various institutions and organizations. Her expertise spans across various domains, coupled with her leadership acumen and commitment to women's empowerment. As the President of the Artificial Intelligence for Women's Empowerment and Representation Council, Dr. Pandey spearheads initiatives aimed at bridging the gender gap in AI and fostering inclusivity. Her research prowess is evidenced by a prolific publication record, comprising numerous papers, chapters, and books on diverse legal topics. She has also been an active participant in conferences, seminars, and webinars, contributing to the advancement of legal scholarship and continuously expanding her knowledge and professional network. With an extensive portfolio including multiple paper publications in reputed national and international journals, workshops, book chapters in edited books, and conference presentations, she has established a strong presence in the academic community. Experienced Legal Professional with a strong background in Web 4.0 and Artificial Intelligence. She is skilled in analysing complex legal cases and providing innovative solutions. Proficient in applying cutting-edge technology to the legal field, effectively utilizing AI tools to streamline processes and enhance efficiency. She has developed a deep understanding of the intersection between technology and law, with a focus on leveraging AI advancements to improve access to justice. Looking ahead, her goal is to continue making significant contributions to the legal field and to establish myself as a leading expert and thought leader in the field of law while also mentoring and inspiring the next generation of scholars. She is driven, meticulous, and committed to fostering academic excellence.

Jyoti Prakash is a highly experienced professional, who has a Master's degree in Hotel Management. His academic journey, spanning over 8 years, reflects a strong commitment to both the hospitality industry and academia. Currently, he is pursuing PhD in Hospitality from GD Goenka University in Sohna, Haryana, India. Prakash's career is characterized by an unwavering dedication to education and the development of future hospitality professionals. He has published more than 13 research papers and a few book chapters in reputed journals. His core expertise revolves around various domains and promoting culinary education in the realm of Hospitality Academics, where he is deeply committed to fostering the growth and excellence of the next generation of professionals in the field. He is enthusiastic about embracing learning opportunities and staying updated with industry trends and academic advancements. His research interests include Culinary Promotion, Food Safety and Security, Destination Marketing, and Odisha Cuisine Promotion. Prakash is known for his proficient hold in analytical and problem-solving skills, and provides freelance research assistance utilizing tools for data analysis

Ravikumar R. Natarajan is an experienced academician with over 12+ years of teaching and research expertise across institutions in India, the UAE, and the Maldives. He currently serves as an Assistant Professor at Marwadi University, Rajkot, specializing in Machine Learning, Recommender Systems, and AI-driven applications in healthcare and security. He holds a Ph.D. in Machine Learning and Recommender Systems from Amity University, Jaipur, a Master of Engineering in CSE from VMRF University, Salem, and a Bachelor of Engineering in CSE from Anna University. He also has a MiniMBA from the Swiss eLearning Institute. Dr. Ravikumar has authored more than 8+ multiple SCIE/Scopus-indexed journal articles, 25+ IEEE/Springer conference papers, and co-authored a book on Artificial Intelligence. He has also published 9 patents and contributed 10+ book chapters in emerging domains such as Federated Learning, Blockchain, and Digital Twins for IGI Global, Wiley and Springer publisher. He actively mentors students through initiatives like the Research Activities Club (RAC) and Student Research Internship Training (SRIT), promoting innovation and research culture.

Arif Rana A highly motivated educator and senior professional executive having Ph.D. in Artificial Intelligence and Talent Management) from Innovative Knowledge Institute - Paris Graduate School (IKI-PGS), Paris, France and MBA (Management Science) from Institute of Business Administration-Dhaka University (IBA-DU), Dhaka Bangladesh. and with achievements that have clearly demonstrated the ability to deliver truly business-focus and client/user need based solutions. Effective team player as a trainer with well-developed relationship skills, supported by an open style of management. He has developed the ability and the experience to lead and manage a number of diverse business functions of an organization, Information Systems and related activities with a forward thinking acquiring of enhanced teaching and added managerial skills. He has 18 plus years teaching experience in various private universities in Bangladesh starting from Senior Lecturer to Associate Professor both in Undergraduate (BBA) and in post graduate level (MBA). As an Associate Professor, he was the Dean, Department of Business Studies, University of Information Technology & Sciences (UITS) having a teaching experience from 2004 to 2019. Also, as an Associate Professor (Adjunct Faculty), Independent University, Bangladesh (IUB) from 2014-2018. Areas of Involvement (in teaching) is Management Information Systems (MIS), Accounting Information Systems (AIS), E-Commerce, Data Communication and Networking (DCN), Computer Applications in Business (CAB), Human Resource Information Systems, (HRIS), Entrepreneurship Development, Web Technology, Database Management Principles of Accounting. At present he is the Director of Academic, PENSTON Academy of International Studies (PAIS), Dhaka, Bangladesh from 2019. He believes in empathetic and forwarded teaching which is learning by doing, learners' preparation for sustainable career. ORCID : 0000-0002-0602-1182

Aarthi S is a dedicated Assistant Professor in Computer Science with over six years of teaching experience. She is currently pursuing her Ph.D. at Marwadi University, Gujarat, and holds an M.Phil. and MCA from Bharathiar University, Tamil Nadu. Throughout her academic career, Aarthi has specialized in programming languages such as C++, Java, and C, and contributed to research in recommender systems and AI-related data privacy. She has published journal articles, contributed to book chapters, and actively participated in technical workshops. Known for her student mentorship and engagement in academic events, Aarthi remains committed to fostering innovation and excellence in computer science education.

Kalpna Sharma is an Assistant Professor at Law Centre-II, Faculty of Law, University of Delhi, India. She holds a Ph.D. in Law and a Post Graduate Diploma in Personnel Management & Labour Welfare (PGDPM & LW) from Himachal Pradesh University, Shimla. Her areas of interest and specialization include Human Rights and Humanitarian Law, Refugee Law, Information Technology Law, Women & Children Law, and Criminal Law. She is registered with ORCID under the ID 0000-0002-4511-7988 and can be contacted at dr.kalpanasharma8@gmail.com

Swati Sharma, Ph.D. is currently working as an Associate Professor with Amity University, India. She holds 18 years of teaching and industry experience. She is Vice- President of Women's Indian Chamber of Commerce and Industry. She is First Indian to receive the Certified Tourism Educator award from Asia Pacific Institute of Events Management. She is the reviewer of Consumer Behavior in Tourism & Hospitality & Inderscience Journals & IGI Global . She has authored & Edited 15 books & published research papers in National & International journals of repute. (IGI Global, Taylor & Francis, Springer, Apple Academy Press, CABI, Edward & Elgar).

Akanksha Singh Assistant Professor of Law CHRIST (Deemed to be University) I am a dedicated legal academician with over eight years of teaching experience in the field of law, with a specialised focus on Cyber Law and Cyber Security Law. My academic journey is currently complemented by my ongoing doctoral research in the same domain, reflecting my deep commitment to advancing in emerging areas of legal studies. I am passionate about classroom teaching and strive to create an engaging, student-centric learning environment that encourages critical thinking and practical understanding of complex legal issues. My teaching philosophy is rooted in bridging theoretical concepts with real-world applications, particularly in the rapidly evolving digital landscape. Alongside teaching, I actively contribute to legal research and academic writing, with a keen interest in issues surrounding data protection, cyber crimes, digital governance, and technology-driven regulatory frameworks. I remain committed to continuous learning and contributing meaningfully to both academia and the broader legal community.

Kuldeep Singh currently serves as an Assistant Professor in Amity School of Hospitality, Amity University, Haryana, India. He completed his Ph.D. in tourism from Maharshi Dayanand University (Rohtak) India in 2021. He is also a UGC (Net- JRF qualified). Dr. Singh has also served the tourism industry for a couple of years and more than three years in academics. Dr. Singh has so far published more than 70 research articles in both international and national referred journals as well as in edited books in the field of Tourism. Currently, He is serving as an editor of book series in various reputed publications (Emerald,CABI,Bentham ,IGI Global and IIP series). Dr. Singh is passionate about the academic areas of Service Quality Management, Rural tourism, Ecotourism, and Sustainable tourism. He also won an aspiring researchers welcome award from Indian Hospitality Congress. His credentials may be verified on various research platforms like Google Scholar, SSRN, LinkedIn, Academia, and Research Gate.

Sheetal Singh is a seasoned legal academic with over 15 years of experience in teaching, research, and academic administration. Currently serving as Assistant Professor at the School of Law, CHRIST (Deemed to be University), Delhi NCR Campus, she previously held senior faculty roles at Amity Law School, Noida, where she also founded the Amity Legal Aid Cell. She holds a Ph.D. in Law from Amity University and is UGC-NET qualified, with expertise spanning Family Law, Criminal Law, Constitutional Law, Property Law, and Human Rights. Dr. Singh has guided more than 150 LLB and LLM dissertations and supervises Ph.D. research on gender justice and victimology. Her scholarly contributions include chapters in edited volumes published by Thomson Reuters, CRC Press, Springer, and Cambridge Scholars Publishing, covering topics such as media law, reproductive rights, cybersecurity, and comparative constitutional analysis. She has presented papers at national and international conferences, delivered guest lectures, and organized seminars and workshops on legal education, gender sensitization, and human rights. Her administrative roles include serving as Head of Department, Program Coordinator, and member of various university committees such as IQAC, Moot Court, and Placement. Widely recognized for her commitment to legal education and interdisciplinary research, Dr. Singh continues to contribute meaningfully to academia and social justice initiatives.

Vipin Singh is a distinguished expert in the field of Tourism and Hospitality Management, known for his in-depth knowledge and extensive experience.r. With over a decade of diversified experience, Dr. Vipin Singh has made significant contributions both in the hotel industry and academia. His expertise spans a wide range of areas, making him a valuable asset in the field. In his illustrious career, Dr. Vipin Singh has had the privilege of working with renowned establishments like Taj Hotel and Domino's Pizza. During his time in the hotel industry, he has successfully managed operations, ensuring the seamless functioning of the establishments under his care. His hands-on approach and leadership skills have proven instrumental in enhancing efficiency and guest satisfaction.

Shashank Solanki is a B.B.A. LL.B (Hons.) student at CHRIST (Deemed to be University), Delhi NCR. With a strong academic foundation and a keen interest in Arbitration, Securities, In Corporate Law, Banking & Finance, Shashank has actively contributed to legal scholarship. His research works have been accepted for publication in esteemed Scopus-indexed platforms. addressing critical areas such as medical big data, digital healthcare ethics, and the Metaverse. Beyond academics, he has demonstrated excellence through multiple internships, gaining hands-on experience in dispute resolution, corporate law, and judicial research.

Shashank's dedication to academic pursuits and practical legal applications reflect his commitment to contributing meaningfully to the legal domain.

Bruno Miguel Barbosa de Sousa is a distinguished academic with a Ph.D. in Marketing and Strategy. He graduated in Business Management in 2006 and has since held various academic positions. Currently, he serves as a Professor Coordenador at the Polytechnic University of Cávado and Ave (IPCA), Portugal and has previously lectured at the University of Minho (Portugal). Bruno Sousa is a researcher at the Applied Management Research Unit (UNIAG) and the Center for Research, Development and Innovation in Tourism (CiTUR), both in Portugal. Bruno Sousa's research focuses on diverse areas including marketing and strategy, sustainable development, tourism behavior, organizational performance and niche marketing. He has authored several books and numerous book chapters, along with contributing to prestigious journals such as Current Issues in Tourism; EuroMed Journal of Business; Annals of Leisure Research; Journal of Cultural Heritage Management and Sustainable Development; Tourism Management Perspectives; Wine Economics and Policy; Journal of Hospitality and Tourism Insights; Journal of Tourism, Heritage & Services Marketing; Journal of Organizational Change Management, among others.

Akshita Tiwari is currently working as an Assistant Professor at Amity School of Hospitality, Amity University, Noida, Uttar Pradesh, where she teaches Front Office Operations and Management to Bachelor's in Hotel Management students and Master's in Hospitality students. She has also authored multiple Scopus publications and presented papers at international conferences. With a keen interest in teaching and research, she looks forward to contributing to the field of hospitality and continue to strive for excellence in her work.

Index

A

B

C

D

E

F

G

H

I

www.ingramcontent.com/pod-product-compliance
Lightning Source LLC
LaVergne TN
LVHW062323300926
849161LV00007B/1548
* 9 7 9 8 3 3 7 3 5 8 2 6 0 *